PROGRESSIVE WINEMAKING

By

PETER DUNCAN and BRYAN ACTON

A textbook covering fully the theory and practice of winemaking, and a guide to the production of superior wines of popular types

Published by

"Amateur Winemaker" Publications Ltd., Andover. Hants.

Cover design and illustrations by George Hodgson

FIRST IMPRESSION 1967
SECOND IMPRESSION 1968
THIRD IMPRESSION 1970
FOURTH IMPRESSION 1970
FIFTH IMPRESSION 1971
SIXTH IMPRESSION 1971
SEVENTH IMPRESSION 1972
EIGHTH IMPRESSION 1972
NINTH IMPRESSION 1973
TENTH IMPRESSION 1975
ELEVENTH IMPRESSION 1976
TWELFTH IMPRESSION 1977
THIRTEENTH IMPRESSION 1978
FOURTEENTH IMPRESSION 1978
FIFTEENTH IMPRESSION 1979
SIXTEENTH IMPRESSION 1980
SEVENTEENTH IMPRESSION 1981

SBN 0 900841 05 2

Printed in Great Britain by:
Standard Press (Andover) Ltd., South Street,
Andover, Hants. Tel. 2413

CONTENTS

Part I. Theory and Practice

Chapter		*Page*
	Introduction to Part I	5
I	Equipment	9
II	Sterilisation and Sulphite	41
III	The Hydrometer and its Uses	53
IV	Sugar	71
V	Acidity	83
VI	The Meaning of pH	105
VII	Tannin	113
VIII	Water	117
IX	Yeast	123
X	Yeast Nutrients	139
XI	Preparation of the Must	143
XII	Fermentation	161
XIII	Racking and Clarification	177
XIV	A Continuous Wine Filter	199
XV	Maturing	203
XVI	Blending for Quality	213
XVII	Alcohol and Fortification	239
XVIII	Wine Disorders and their Treatment	253
XIX	A Selection of Recipes	263
XX	Rack and Cloth Press	273
XXI	Cleaning and Conditioning Oak Casks	281

Part II. Commercial Wines and their Simulation

Chapter		*Page*
	Introduction to Part II	285
XXII	White Table Wines	289
XXIII	Dry Red Table Wines	317
XXIV	Sauternes-Type Wines	341
XXV	Sparkling Wines	353
XXVI	Sherry-Type Wines	377
XXVII	Port-Type Wines	399
XXVIII	Madeira-Type Wines	413

INTRODUCTION TO PART I

WINE of some description has been made in Britain for a great many centuries. Fruit, grain, honey and similar ingredients have undoubtedly been used for winemaking purposes for countless generations, but the history of grape wine seems to be particularly well preserved, possibly because it has often been associated with or even the cause of many wars and invasions. Records show that vines were planted here at the time of the Roman conquest some 2 millennia ago, and there are numerous references in historical documents to productive vineyards located in climatically favourable areas of the country. Unfortunately few if any of these vineyards are now in commercial operation and most have just disappeared without trace. Even before the Roman era, however, it has been fairly well established that the Ancient Britons knew how to make alcoholic beverages and mead in particular. Indeed, archaeologists have discovered evidence to support the belief that mead was in vogue as long as 10,000 years ago at the time when the last Pleistocene ice sheet began to retreat and allowed immigrants from other parts of Europe to settle the land.

More recently, at least in the period following the Middle Ages, it was customary for most homes to make a quota of wine each year to satisfy the needs of the household for a pleasant and stimulating beverage. These wines were produced from whatever ingredients happened to be available according to traditional methods and recipes handed down through the generations, and they continued to enjoy wide popularity until about the middle of the 19th century. Thereafter, the consumption of wine began to decline in favour of tea whose price came within reach of all but the poorest classes with the advent of the tea clippers. Since tea was cheap, easy to prepare and provided a refreshing drink, it is not difficult to understand why wines and beers, whose production made no little demand on the time and attention of the householder, were gradually displaced by tea as the standard beverage of the working classes. As a result, winemaking in Britain eventually became a lost art. Fortunately, it did not die out altogether, for a few stalwarts in farms and villages throughout the country still continued to make their own wines and their knowledge provided the foundation on which the present revival of interest in amateur winemaking was built.

The renaissance in amateur winemaking can be traced to the period following the last war. Once sugar was taken off the ration, there was little to hinder its development and the idea of making wine at home slowly gathered impetus. Tourism in Europe whereby people from this country were introduced to, and enjoyed, wine for the first time also undoubtedly contributed significantly to the growing interest in the subject. Finally, in 1954, the first clubs for amateur winemakers were founded and since that time things have never looked back. A magazine called "The Amateur Winemaker," devoted solely to the making of wines at home, was brought out in December 1957, and has subsequently served to consolidate the position even further. Nowadays, of course, there are over 1000 clubs scattered all over Britain and the Commonwealth as well as numerous suppliers offering a wide range of equipment and other winemaking accessories.

The budding winemaker of some 25 years ago had many problems to face. Equipment was difficult to obtain as there were few suppliers to cater for a demand of this nature. Wine yeasts were virtually unknown and cultures could only be purchased from certain research institutes which charged a considerable sum of money for this service. In short, most winemaking supplies which are now cheap and commonplace were then expensive and scarce and the winemaker simply had to make do with what little was available.

There was also a dearth of published information on the subject of amateur winemaking. One or two recipe books could be obtained, but most of these were based upon traditional methods and devoted very little space to anything other than recipes. A few paragraphs covered yeast, fermentation, racking and so on very briefly, but little else could be expected. No attempt was made to explain the basic principles of winemaking upon which the quality of a wine depends. Such recent developments as the use of the hydrometer, sulphite and wine yeasts, unheard of when most recipes were compiled, simply had no place in traditional books of this type. Indeed, some authors even went so far as to militate violently (and often incorrectly) against the introduction of any modern innovations. Although it hardly need be said that this attitude is outmoded and prejudiced, traditional ideas do die hard and still, unfortunately, have many adherents who are content to follow recipes and old practices blindly without giving any thought to what they are doing. How consistently high quality wines can be expected under these circumstances is a matter for conjecture !

Within the past few years, a certain number of more enlightened authors have begun to put recipes into their proper perspective. Recipes are no longer intended to be sets of instructions which are followed mechanically, but rather should be regarded as guides which the winemaker can consult when formulating other recipes for producing similar wines from other ingredients. Thus, while books which are basically just collections of recipes will continue to be popular for some years to come, a different style of presentation in which far less space is devoted to recipes is now coming to the fore. In these publications, fundamental winemaking techniques and the main factors influencing wine quality are discussed in a sensible and logical manner so that the winemaker receives sound practical advice and at the same time gains some understanding of the basic principles involved. This trend can only be welcomed since it marks the beginning of a more positive and progressive approach to amateur winemaking.

This book may be regarded as an extension of these ideas. The number of recipes has been cut to a minimum and those which do appear have been carefully designed to illustrate the concepts more fully discussed in the text. As the title implies, special emphasis is placed upon modern techniques and developments but all aspects of winemaking have received close attention since we intend this work to act as a standard reference book dealing with both the theory and practice of amateur winemaking. Beginners may find that it covers rather too much ground for their immediate needs, but on the other hand it is not meant to appeal solely to the advanced winemaker. Its purpose is rather to provide the average winemaker with a comprehensive source of information and reference which can be consulted when guidance is required or some problem arises. We can only hope that we have succeeded in achieving this objective and filled the gap which we feel existed between the simpler books of this nature and speciality publications dealing specifically with one particular subject.

P. M. DUNCAN.

G. W. B. ACTON.

Chapter I

EQUIPMENT

IT has often been said that wines can be successfully made at home with little or no more equipment beyond that normally found in the kitchen. In actual fact, this idea only holds true when the amount of wine produced is limited to a few gallons, and even then sundry items of equipment such as gallon jars, fermentation locks and the like must usually be bought from a supplier. If the winemaker contemplates making larger amounts of wine than an occasional gallon, however, the purchase of more refined equipment capable of handling these quantities of wine (and their ingredients) becomes almost essential, otherwise the labour involved is likely to prove somewhat arduous. In general, then, the best policy is to begin in a small way with as much equipment as can reasonably be afforded and gradually increase the scale of operations over the ensuing months and years, at the same time acquiring additional items of equipment when their need becomes apparent. This approach not only avoids a heavy initial capital expenditure but also allows the winemaker to gain experience and build up equipment simultaneously so that each new article is obtained with some definite purpose in mind. It also does seem advisable to mention that the rising popularity of amateur winemaking has resulted in numerous inventions and labour-saving devices being put on the market. Some such equipment is extremely useful, but a great deal is simply not worth buying so that the gradual acquisition of items as the need arises helps to minimise the chances of purchasing an apparently attractive but actually quite useless article about which exaggerated claims are being made.

Before launching into a detailed discussion on winemaking equipment, it is perhaps advisable at this point to issue a word of warning about the materials from which this equipment is constructed. As a general rule, metal articles should never be allowed to come into contact with acid fruit juices, fermenting musts or maturing wines even for short periods of time. The reason is that the acids found in fruit juices and wines readily dissolve small amounts of most common metals whose presence in a wine in concentrations as low as a few parts per million can cause objectionable hazes and/or peculiar metallic off-flavours. Indeed, some metals such as lead can render a wine poisonous. In particular, copper, zinc, brass, iron, lead, tin and galvanised or soldered ware should be avoided at all costs since these articles are rapidly attacked and minute amounts can irreparably spoil a wine. Stainless steel, monel metal, aluminium and undamaged enamel vessels are more resistant and can thus be employed when the period of contact is short, but they should still not be used for fermentation or storage Prolonged exposure to any metal is in fact highly undesirable because even the most resistant types will be attacked to some.

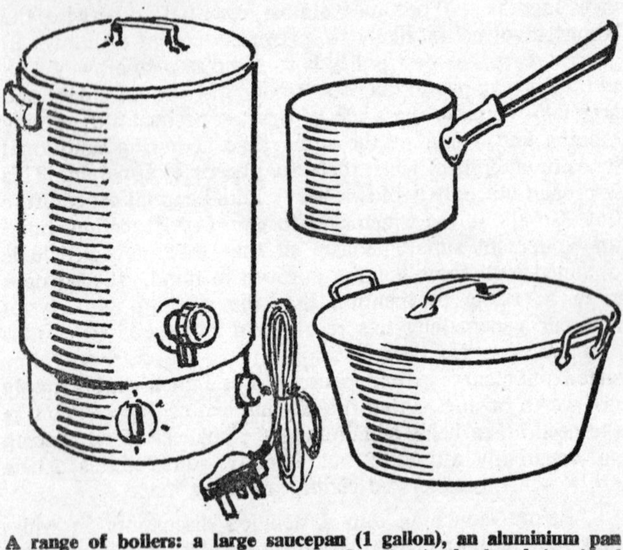

A range of boilers: a large saucepan (1 gallon), an aluminium pan (3-5 gallons) and an electric boiler (5 gallons), the last being ideal for winemaking or brewing.

extent given enough time, and the quality of the wine will consequently suffer as a result of metal contamination. Hence, it is best to avoid all metal equipment entirely except possibly when the ingredients must be boiled in water. Enamel saucepans free from cracks and chips or stainless steel containers are thus preferable although aluminium is also permissible when dealing with mildly acid ingredients such as vegetables or bananas.

Plastic equipment is now becoming popular among amateur winemakers and rightly so, but care should be taken to ensure that it has been produced from a grade approved for food packaging. Polyethylene, polypropylene, PVC, nylon and terylene are all suitable provided no plasticiser has been incorporated during manufacture, but articles made from plasticised PVC and the like should be avoided in case the wine becomes contaminated with plasticiser extracted by the alcohol during fermentation and/or storage. Wood (oak), glass and salt-glazed earthenware are also ideally suited for winemaking purposes so that there is a wide range of acceptable materials from which to choose.

The only other point to note is that secondhand articles, notably containers, should be checked carefully prior to purchase or use to ascertain that their previous contents have not left any permanent contamination. For example, plastic containers which once held hair oil, or old vinegar barrels are absolutely useless because nothing can be done to remove the smell and taste of hair oil or vinegar. Free gifts of this nature may therefore turn out to be expensive if their potential is not properly assessed from the outset!

The following list covers the most important items of equipment which the winemaker is likely to encounter. It is by no means exhaustive, of course, for a whole book could be devoted to this subject alone were it discussed in any detail. Nothing of importance has been omitted, however, so that the complete list will give a good indication of what is available for different purposes. Few winemakers will possess everything which is mentioned here nor really is there any need to do so, but the less experienced winemaker will at least be able to assess the relative merits of various alternative types of equipment from the information provided in this chapter. Actual prices have deliberately not been quoted since fluctuations inevitably occur from time to time, but wherever possible it is stated whether a particular article is cheap or expensive.

CONTAINERS

Winemakers require a considerable number of different types of containers for fermentation and storage. Both wide and narrow-necked vessels have their place here. The former, particularly when equipped with a well-fitting lid, are preferable for pulp fermentations where ease of access during the fermentation, easy removal of pulp and easy cleaning are important. Narrow-necked containers are better suited for juice fermentations and storage because they are more readily sealed from the air by means of a fermentation lock, rubber bung or cork, although plastic closures with a small central aperture can be used very successfully with wide-necked containers to reduce the size of the opening. Wood,

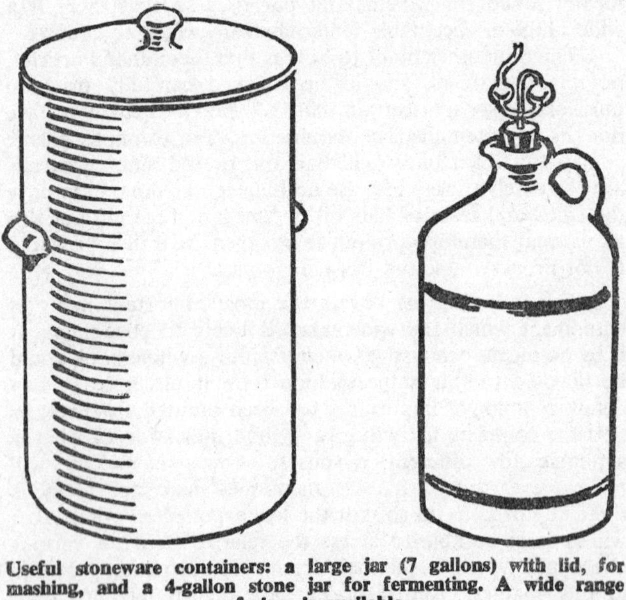

Useful stoneware containers: a large jar (7 gallons) with lid, for mashing, and a 4-gallon stone jar for fermenting. A wide range of sizes is available.

glass, plastic and earthenware vessels of both types are all now readily available, and each has certain advantages.

The use of earthenware is traditional but nowadays such containers are becoming less popular, partly because they tend to be somewhat expensive. Their opacity prevents the winemaker from seeing what is taking place during fermentation and also in storage, although it does have the advantage of keeping the wine in the dark and thus avoids the risk of photochemical deterioration. Red wines in particular should not be exposed to the light or their colour will fade. Earthenware is heavy and breaks easily so that it needs careful handling, but its smooth surface does permit easy cleaning. The glaze is extremely important, however, for modern earthenware is salt-glazed whereas lead compounds were formerly employed for this purpose. Salt glazes are perfectly safe, but the acids in wines will leach out lead from a lead glaze and render the wine highly poisonous. Salt and lead glazes are easily distinguished since the former are thin, clear and produce a sharp ring when tapped while the latter are thick, opaque and honey-coloured and give a dull ring. If there is any doubt at all about the glaze on an earthenware vessel, it is safest not to use it as lead poisoning could occur, possibly with fatal results. Old Oriental crocks should certainly be avoided for this reason. Both wide and narrow-necked earthenware containers with or without tap holes and with a capacity ranging from one gallon upwards can be purchased from most suppliers, but on the whole such vessels are not a worthwhile investment (unless obtained gratis!) because other equally as good if not better materials are considerably cheaper.

Glass containers are favoured by many winemakers and 5 or 10 gallon glass carboys are now available at moderate prices. The 4 to 5 gallon size is probably the optimum for most winemakers because it can still be handled when full of wine without too much effort, whereas larger vessels must be emptied before being moved. The 1 gallon "eared" jar is extremely popular, but its size makes it more suitable for the production of experimental wines or as a bulk storage container unless the winemaker is content to make only a gallon or so of wine at a time. The half-gallon jar of the same type is best reserved solely for storage purposes as it

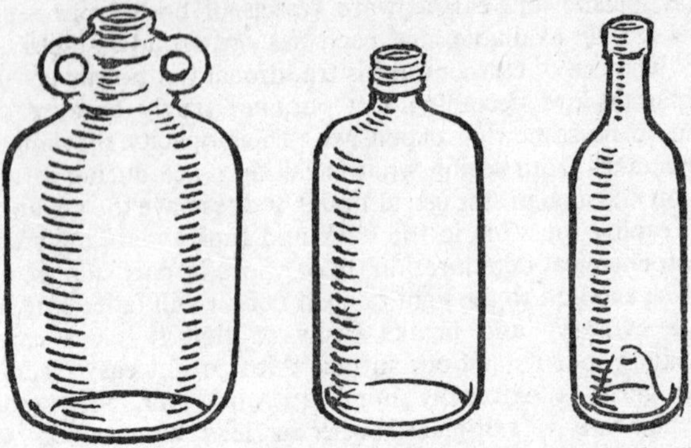

Glassware: 1 gallon jar with ear handles, Winchester (half-gallon) and standard wine bottle (26⅔oz.)

s really too small to serve as a fermentation vessel. In actual fact, if a 5-gallon jar is too large, the next best size is about 2½ gallons since any smaller quantity of must will tend to ferment too rapidly and may fail to attain its full latent quality. Glass bottles are useful for storing wines, but only genuine wine bottles with a punt in the base should be selected as there is then less risk of breakage should refer-mentations subsequently occur in the bottle. Flat-bottomed spirit bottles, sauce bottles and the like should never be employed for reasons of safety and because they are aesthetically unsuitable. Wine served in a sauce bottle definitely loses some of its appeal!

The main advantages of glass vessels are their cheapness transparency and ready availability. Gallon jars can often be obtained for little or nothing while even large carboys are now none too expensive. The main drawback of glassware is its fragility, so that large containers are best kept protected in a wire or wickerwork cage to avoid unfortunate accidents. The transparency of glass enables the winemaker to inspect a wine visually at any time, but unless coloured glass vessels (deep amber or green) are employed, red wines must be shielded from the light to prevent their colour from fading. Cleaning is easily carried out provided no deposit has been allowed to dry on the surface and, like glazed earthenware, a wine leaves no permanent colour, smell or taste to contaminate its successor. The only other point to note is that most glass containers have relatively narrow necks which restricts their use mainly to juice fermentations and storage purposes, but apart from this limitation they are of inestimable value to the winemaker.

Polythene ware: 11 gallon dustbin for mashing or soaking (one can also obtain a 5 gallon size) and a polythene bucket (1½ or 2 gallons). With its bottom pierced, a bucket makes an excellent strainer for large quantities.

Plastic fermentation and storage vessels have recently begun to make their presence felt among amateur winemakers, and it seems likely that their reception will continue to be favourable. Such containers combine the advantages of being light in weight, translucent and unbreakable and may be rigid, semi-rigid or collapsible. The latter must, of course, be supported in a cardboard or wooden box when full but conveniently fold up for storage in a small space when empty. Polyethylene, polypropylene and unplasticised PVC are the commonest materials encountered in this connection, and all are excellent for winemaking purposes provided they are of a grade which has been approved for use in the food industry. Secondhand semi-rigid or collapsible plastic bags formerly employed for transporting fruit juices are cheap, readily available and ideal for fermentation and storage. So too are many rigid containers such as those in which distilled water is shipped. Indeed, there is a very broad range of plastic containers from which to choose and prices vary accordingly. Both wide and narrow-necked types can be obtained in sizes from one gallon upwards. Plastic buckets and garbage cans with or without lids are on sale in most hardware stores and make excellent pulp fermentation vessels if care is taken to select a bucket with a well-fitting lid. Most buckets are also graduated in both litres and gallons which makes the measurement of large volumes relatively simple. The winemaker is therefore well-advised to consider plastics very carefully when purchasing containers of any description.

Wooden vessels are also traditional in winemaking, and long experience has shown that oak is the only really suitable wood for the construction of casks and barrels. Unfortunately, the high price of good oak together with the high labour charges of coopering contrive to make casks and the like extremely expensive items of equipment. Reconditioned

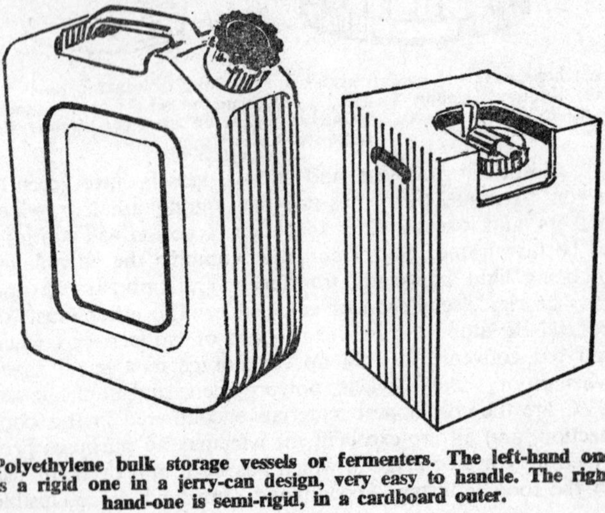

Polyethylene bulk storage vessels or fermenters. The left-hand one is a rigid one in a jerry-can design, very easy to handle. The right hand-one is semi-rigid, in a cardboard outer.

casks are certainly much cheaper and equally as satisfactory as new casks provided they are constructed from oak which was originally part of a wine (or beer) cask, but even then their cost is still high in comparison with other competitive materials. This situation is doubly unfortunate because there is no real substitute for oak casks or barrels for maturing wines. The latter aspect is more fully discussed in a later chapter, but it is worth mentioning here that every wine-maker should aim to possess at least one or two casks in which to mature superior wines.

A half cask and fruit pulper made from hardwood.

Open oak half-casks, which are often made simply by sawing a large barrel transversely in half and adding an extra hoop at the top for reinforcement and to prevent the staves from parting, were formerly widely used as pulp fermentation vessels. Such tubs are expensive and difficult to keep clean and sterile, however, and in addition the staves tend to dry out and come apart on standing so that a preliminary soaking in water is necessary to tighten up the staves prior to use. Other disadvantages could also be mentioned, but sufficient has already been said to show that plastic buckets and garbage cans are far superior to oak half-casks for pulp fermentation purposes. The latter are in fact more trouble than they are worth and are consequently best left severely alone.

By way of contrast, oak casks and barrels are extremely valuable winemaking accessories. Although their cost may be high, the improvement in quality which can be achieved by maturing a wine in wood amply repays any such investment. Various sizes of cask ranging from 3 gallons to over 50 gallons in capacity can be obtained either new, reconditioned or secondhand. Some of the commoner sizes of casks include the pin (4½ gallons), the six (6 gallons), the firkin (9 gallons), the kilderkin (18 gallons), the barrel (36 gallons) and the hogshead (54 gallons). The optimum capacity for the amateur is probably around 9 to 18 gallons, but in most instances the 4½ to 6-gallon sizes will be considered much more convenient for ease of handling and so on. The ratio of surface area to volume begins to become rather large for casks containing less than about 9 gallons, so that prolonged maturing in such casks can result in too much oxygen reaching the wine by diffusion through the pores of the wood. Red wines are usually quite safe even in 4½-gallon casks, but only the most robust white wines can withstand more than a few months in anything smaller than a 9-gallon cask without becoming over-oxidised. No wine except perhaps for a sherry should be stored in a 3-gallon cask for any length of time as it is really too small for this purpose.

Casks should always be inspected very carefully before being purchased to ascertain that their condition is sound. Musty or vinegary casks should never be accepted as it is extremely difficult if not impossible to eradicate the mould or vinegar bacteria which have penetrated into and between the staves and would therefore contaminate any wine subsequently stored therein. Both new and reconditioned or secondhand casks require thorough cleaning and conditioning prior to being used for the fermentation or storage of wine to ensure absolute cleanliness, sterility and freedom from objectionable wood constituents which would coarsen the wine. An excellent and highly recommended procedure for treating newly-acquired casks will be found in a later chapter and could advantageously be adopted as a standard technique. Although this treatment is lengthy and fairly arduous, it need only be carried out once provided the cask is subsequently kept filled with wine and never allowed to stand empty for more than an hour or two at the outside. Once the cask has been cleaned and conditioned in this manner, it should preferably be employed initially as a fermentation rather than a storage vessel (juice, not pulp, fermentation, of course) because the wood can then come into equilibrium with the wine without significantly influencing its character. It is a well-established fact that a new cask will be less likely to abstract tannin, body and so on from a finished wine if it has first served as a fermentation vessel.

The correct way of supporting a cask.

The manner in which casks are set up in the wine cellar is extremely important. Not only is it incorrect but it is also detrimental to stand a cask on end, for then the exposed end piece will dry out and leakage will almost certainly be observed within a relatively short time. A cask should always be positioned horizontally with the bunghole uppermost and kept full to the brim at all times so that every part of the interior remains moist and drying out cannot occur. It must also be supported at both ends in a shaped wooden cradle or on two pieces of wood on which it is held in place by means of wedges. Whatever else, a cask must never be allowed to rest directly upon the ground permanently or it will eventually spring a stave at the point of contact and thereafter will leak progressively more seriously. Casks will last almost indefinitely provided they are looked after carefully, e.g. by painting the hoops to prevent rusting and by setting up each cask properly, but they will become leaky and otherwise faulty if no such precautions are taken.

A final point regarding casks concerns taps and tapholes. If a tap is used, it should never be inserted until the wine is due for racking or bottling as wooden taps will dry out within a few weeks or months and the wine will then begin to seep out around it. Considerable amounts of wine can be lost in this way which is an annoying enough occurrence in itself, but to make matters worse the spilt wine is very likely to become contaminated with spoilage organisms whose depredations will not be confined to the original site of infection. A tap should always be inserted confidently and boldly, preferably with one powerful blow from a mallet, to avoid losing any wine as it is driven into place. Any careless or hasty move at this stage can be disastrous and may result in a great deal of wine ending up on the floor, much to the dismay and chagrin of the winemaker. In actual fact, it is far better not to utilise the taphole at all or even buy casks only with a bung-hole and remove the wine by siphoning, as is usually the case with other containers. This procedure is probably simpler and certainly less risky than inserting a tap through which to withdraw the wine and also avoids the need to plug the taphole with a new cork after the cask has been emptied. If this procedure is adopted, a piece of solid oak can be used to plug the taphole permanently so that the danger of leakage due to the deterioration of a cork left therein for years is averted.

MEASURES

The winemaker frequently has to weigh out ingredients or measure a volume of water, must or wine with reasonable accuracy so that some equipment for this purpose is essential. Ordinary kitchen scales which will weigh out ten pounds or more at a time to within an ounce or two are quite cheap and will normally prove perfectly adequate for most occasions. More refined equipment capable of weighing to within about one gram is required for weighing small amounts of acids or tannin. Since a suitable balance would be costly, however, the stock solution procedure suggested in the chapters on acid and tannin is infinitely preferable to avoid undue expense.

It is much easier to measure volumes accurately. Large volumes can be conveniently measured in plastic buckets which are usually graduated in both gallons and litres. Glass or plastic measuring jugs calibrated in pints and fluid ounces are useful for adding small quantities of sugar syrup and the like. Still smaller cups showing portions of a fluid ounce can be used with stock acid and tannin solutions to obtain the requisite accuracy. Measuring cylinders with metric graduations are also worthwhile investments. A 250 mls cylinder will serve as a hydrometer trial jar as well as for measuring purposes. The 100 mls size is excellent for preparing trial blends since any quantity from 10 mls to 100 mls can be added to the blend. A 10 mls or 25 mls cylinder is ideal for introducing small amounts of stock sulphite solution to a wine since 5 mls of this solution per gallon gives a sulphite dose of 50 p.p.m.

STRAINERS

Pulp fermentations are a very common feature of amateur winemaking, possibly to a greater extent than is really necessary. Whatever its merits, there comes a time in every pulp fermentation when the juice and pulp must be separated, the latter subsequently being pressed and the spent residue discarded. Straining off the pulp at this stage can be a messy business, but with proper equipment this operation can be considerably simplified.

In the first place, a large plastic colander with relatively large holes is excellent for removing the bulk of the coarse pulp fragments. It rarely becomes plugged up with pulp, is easily emptied when full and is both rapid and efficient. In addition, its plastic construction makes for easy cleaning and sterilisation. Finer pulp particles which are small enough to pass through the holes in the colander still remain in the must, however, and it is preferable if not essential to effect their removal also in case off-flavours due to pulp decomposition develop later in the fermentation. A fine-meshed nylon sieve is ideal for this purpose, but it must be as large as possible—at least six inches in diameter—to do its job properly. Nylon is tough, flexible, resistant to attack by wines and easy to clean and sterilise, so that such sieves have many attractive features and can be highly recommended. Several passes through a nylon sieve will remove all but the finest pulp particles, and, unless the pulp has disintegrated very badly, fermentation can then be allowed to proceed in the normal manner.

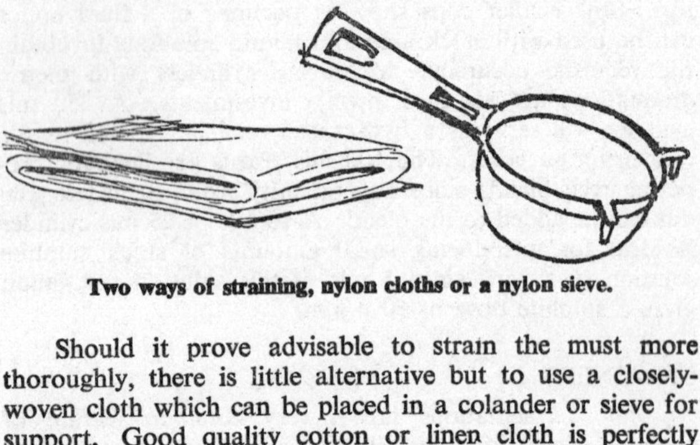

Two ways of straining, nylon cloths or a nylon sieve.

Should it prove advisable to strain the must more thoroughly, there is little alternative but to use a closely-woven cloth which can be placed in a colander or sieve for support. Good quality cotton or linen cloth is perfectly satisfactory as are jelly bags, but nylon or terylene cloth is even better because the fibres are extremely tough and are not wetted by the wine, thereby allowing easy, rapid and efficient cleaning and sterilisation.

FUNNELS AND FILTERS

Large plastic funnels are almost indispensable items of equipment because they serve so many useful functions. Wine can be poured or racked from one container to another very easily with the aid of a funnel with very little danger of spillage. Asbestos pulp filtrations also call for a large funnel —the larger the better—and nowadays such an article with a capacity of one gallon can be obtained from most suppliers. The half-gallon size is also extremely versatile. Indeed, it is quite a good idea to amass a range of sizes of funnel from the very large to the very small. Most cost only a few pence, and the time will always come when a certain size of funnel is required for a particular job so that several should be available in anticipation of future needs.

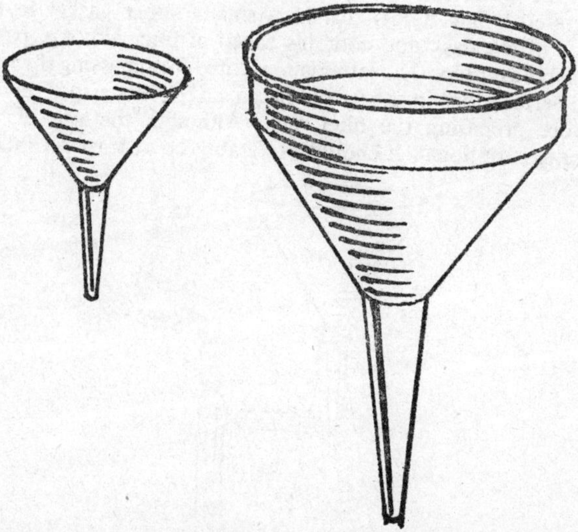

Funnels can be obtained in glass or polyethylene. A really large one to assist in handling large quantities and for filtration is a boon.

Various types of filtration equipment can be purchased. The continuous filter described in Chapter XIV can be highly recommended for its simplicity, ease of operation, reliability and efficiency. Vacuum filter systems are also quite popular but suffer from the disadvantage of being comparatively expensive. In the first place, a filter pump which operates from the cold water tap is needed to draw the vacuum. These water pumps may be constructed from glass, metal or plastic, but the latter are preferable for reasons of cheapness and durability. The receiver for the filtered wine is a thick-walled glass filter flask designed specifically for vacuum filtration. It is fitted with a side arm to which is attached a rubber tube (thick-walled so as not to flatten under vacuum) leading to a similar arm on the water pump. This receiving flask should be as large as possible, but most winemakers will settle for the one-litre size which strikes a reasonable balance between cost and capacity. Finally, a special perforated porcelain filter funnel called a Buchner funnel is required. This funnel fits on a small rubber gasket in the neck of the flask and contains a bed of filter aid, e.g. paper or asbestos pulp. The latter is prevented from passing through the perforations in the funnel by placing a filter paper therein before preparing the filter bed. Although the size of the funnel is optional, it should preferably be at least six inches

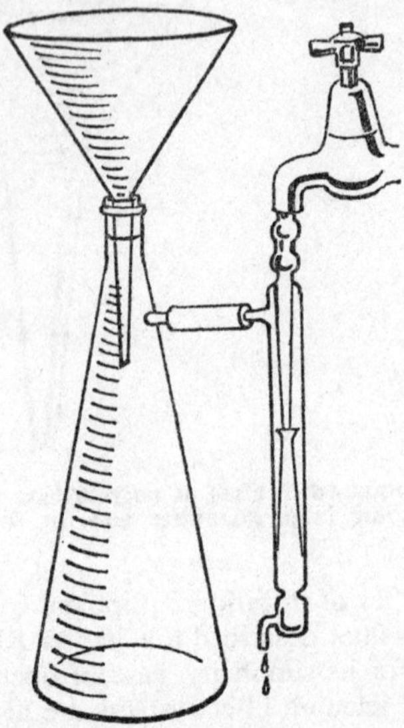

A vacuum pump assembly like this, coupled to a domestic water tap, will speed the filtration of wine in the funnel.

in diameter in order to offer a reasonably large surface area, otherwise the rate of filtration may become somewhat slow. Such an arrangement works quite well, but the filter bed may occasionally become plugged if a very cloudy wine is being filtered. There is then no alternative but to prepare a new bed.

Vacuum filters are rather expensive to set up if all the equipment must be purchased at one time. The winemaker should therefore carefully assess its potential worth to ascertain that the expenditure is really justified before deciding definitely to make the purchase. In many cases, the continuous filter described in Chapter XIV will perform equally as well (if not better) provided its slower operation is acceptable. Moreover, several passes through a vacuum filter may sometimes be necessary to match what the continuous filter achieves in a single pass because poorer clarification is generally observed at faster rates of filtration.

FERMENTATION LOCKS

One of the first items of equipment which the beginner usually acquires right at the outset is a fermentation or air lock of some kind. It is common to hear or read that these locks are essential winemaking adjuncts, but in actual fact this whole idea is a popular misconception. Fermentation locks are by no means indispensable, but they are extremely useful and serve a number of worthwhile functions. In short, however, their use is more a matter of convenience than necessity.

Air locks are basically traps partly filled with water designed to seal the mouth of a container during fermentation. The water seal allows the pressure inside and outside the container to remain virtually equal at all times so that the gas generated during fermentation can escape freely to the atmosphere. The rate at which gas bubbles through the lock is indicative of the rate of fermentation, thus enabling the winemaker to judge at a glance how it is proceeding. Locks also provide an effective seal which bars the ingress of insects, mould spores, airborne bacteria and the like to the fermenting must, but, contrary to popular opinion, are of no particular value in preventing air from reaching the must. The carbon

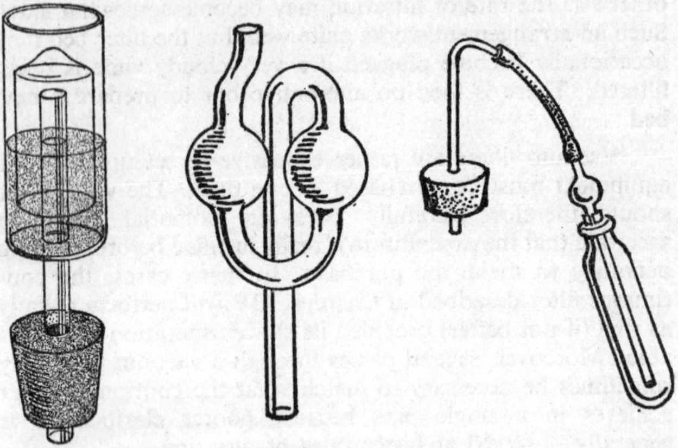

Three types of fermentation lock; the left-hand one is in plastic, the other two in glass.

dioxide continuously liberated by the action of the yeast on the sugar sweeps out any air initially present in the container, and thereafter the gas evolved during a fermentation maintains a blanket of carbon dioxide above the surface of the must. A continuous stream of gas thus emerges from the air lock and obviously no air can enter against this outward flow of carbon dioxide. Since the same would apply whether or not the container was sealed with a fermentation lock—a cotton wool plug would be equally as effective—it is quite incorrect to state that locks cut off the air supply to the fermenting must. In addition, air locks can work in both directions, for if the pressure inside the container for any reason becomes less than that outside, air will bubble through the lock in the reverse direction, i.e. into the vessel.

There are nowadays many different types of fermentation locks. Glass locks of various designs consisting essentially of a glass U-tube with bubbles blown in each upright and a vertcal arm which fits into a bored cork or rubber bung are available but still tend to be rather expensive, although many circles and a few suppliers have managed to reduce their prices considerably. The main disadvantage of glass locks is their fragility, but many of the supposedly unbreakable plastic locks currently on the market are not much better in this respect. Plastic locks are certainly not smashed to pieces so readily as glass locks, but they do crack easily and subsequently fail to do their job properly. Such cracks also harbour bacteria and fungi so that a cracked lock may act as a source of infection unless it is thoroughly sterilised frequently.

In view of the large number of different fermentation lock designs, it would not be practical to discuss each in detail. All have their own unique advantages and disadvantages, and often it is purely a matter of personal preference as to which type is employed. Cost, durability and reliability are probably the main factors which decide the superiority of one lock over another, and in these respects no one design or material of construction is vastly better than any other. Hence, the winemaker should study the fermentation locks offered by different suppliers and select whichever types seem to combine the most attractive features. Experience will also help to show which lock design best suits the individual winemaker.

PRESSES, JUICE EXTRACTORS AND CRUSHERS

It is fairly safe to say that most winemakers aspire to own a press or juice extractor of some description. In the first place, such an item of equipment saves a great deal of labour and is considerably more efficient than pressing by hand. Even more important is the contribution a press makes to wine quality. Many fruits, e.g. apples, pears, peaches, cherries and the like, which are often pulp fermented because the winemaker has no equipment for extracting their juice, can be dealt with very successfully by juice fermentation techniques when a press is available. Since this procedure usually gives rather more delicate and refined wines, its adoption is preferable in table wine production, especially where white wines are concerned.

A number of presses are now being offered by the various equipment suppliers. The majority of these operate

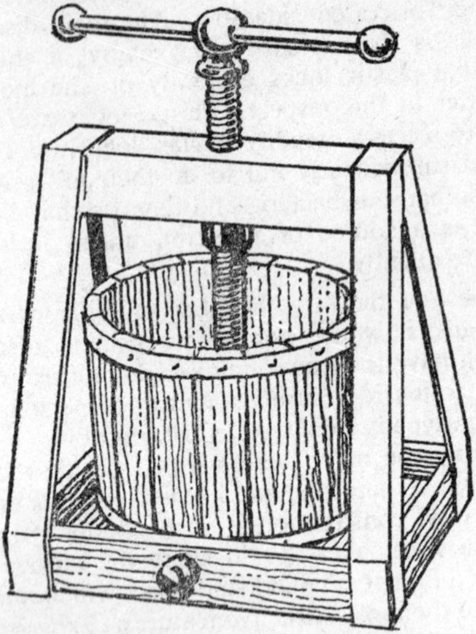

A popular small fruit press, ideal for amateur home use.

on the screw principle whereby a low pitch screw is employed to drive a thick, closely fitting wooden block into a reinforced basket containing the pulp. The latter is thus submitted to a steady, powerful compression which forces out the juice, the screw being tightened up gradually to maintain the pressure until no more juice can be expressed. This brief description is, of course, vastly over-simplified, but at least it does give some indication how a screw press operates. Other presses are based on the rack and cloth design. Here, cloth envelopes or "cheeses" filled with pulp are built up in alternate layers with thin wooden lattice-work racks to which pressure is applied by means of a screw or hydraulic jack. Such presses are extremely efficient and can be highly recommended for their excellent performance.

Unfortunately, many winemakers are deterred from acquiring a press for financial reasons. Even the cheapest type costs some £4–£5 and most range from around £15 to over £50 which is well beyond the pocket of the average winemaker. Wine circles are in a much better position in this respect, for club funds could be put to good use to purchase a press for collective operation by the members. Alternatively, a circle or group of winemakers could easily build a press as a joint project and detailed instructions how to construct a rack and cloth press have therefore been included in Chapter XX for this reason. It may be added that this press is both cheaper and performs better than most of the types currently on the market, so that wine circles are well advised to undertake its construction.

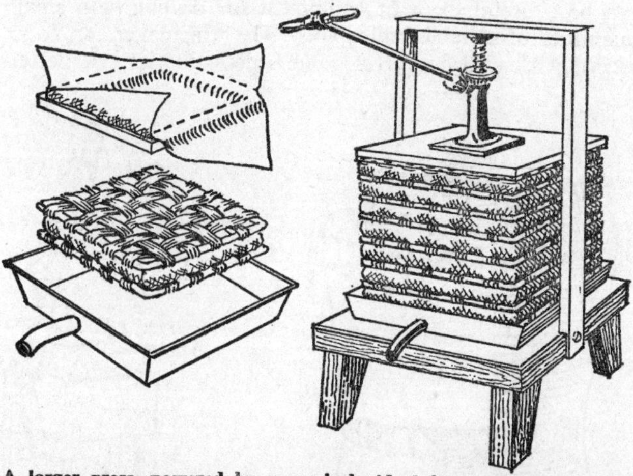

A larger press, powered by a car jack, ideal for a winemaker with large quantities of fruit to process, or for construction by a Wine Circle. Plans for such a press are given on Page 273. The fruit is made up into "cheeses" and pressed between laths, as shown on the left.

A variety of juice extractors can also be obtained. A typical example is the "Jumbo" juicer which is manually operated and resembles an ordinary mincer in many respects. The motivating power is supplied by a tapered screw which drives the pulp along the barrel of the juicer. The pulp is thus compressed during its passage through the juicer and the spent residue emerges at the back. The juice released by the pressure drops through a perforated plate below the screw and then runs down a trough to the front. This type of juicer works very well with such fruits as elderberries and oranges, but more pulpy ingredients tend to be reduced to a sludge of crushed pulp and juice which can only be separated by straining. Apples, for example, cannot be satisfactorily pressed with a Jumbo juicer.

Another disadvantage is that there is a distinct tendency for it to crush any seeds or stones in the fruit so that undesirable oils are released into the juice. Provided these limitations are recognised, however, the "Jumbo" juicer can be a useful piece of equipment for dealing with small quantities of suitable ingredients. The winemaker can soon ascertain by trial and error what fruits come into the latter

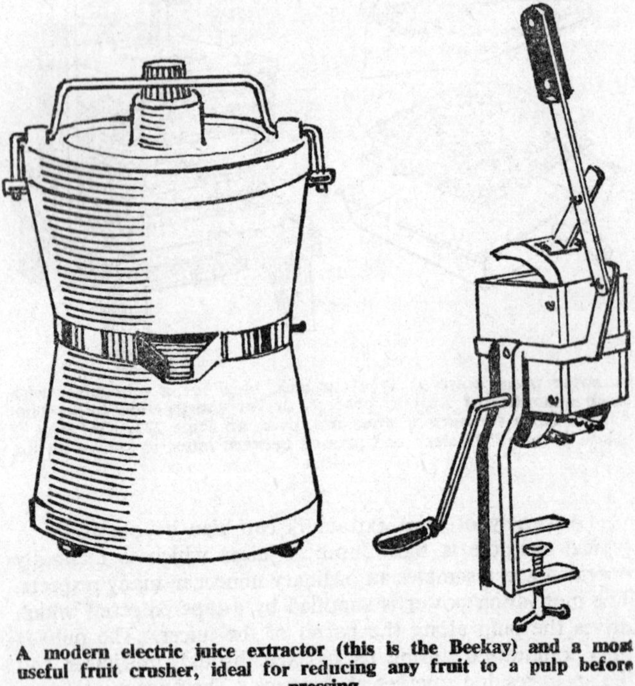

A modern electric juice extractor (this is the Beekay) and a most useful fruit crusher, ideal for reducing any fruit to a pulp before pressing.

category, but it may be noted that elderberries, rhubarb, citrus fruits and seedless grapes can be handled very well.

Electric juice extractors are more refined items of equipment than their manually operated counterparts, but by the same token they are considerably more expensive. Several types are currently on sale, most of which work on the pattern of a centrifuge. Fruit is fed in through an opening in the top and is forced against a rotating, horizontal, circular, stainless steel plate on which series of teeth are arranged in radial rows. These teeth shred the fruit finely and the speed of rotation then throws the resultant mixture of pulp and juice against the walls of an aluminium basket (which also rotates) perforated with small holes through which the juice escapes. The latter flows along a juice trough into the receiving vessel while the spent pulp is retained in the basket.

Once the basket is full, the pulp must, of course, be removed but this task only occupies a few minutes. More modern juice extractors are even easier to operate since both juice and spent pulp are ejected automatically at separate points, a big advantage, since less cleaning is required. As much as 1 cwt. of fruit can thus be pressed before any cleaning is required. These types of juice extractors work extremely well with firm-fleshed fruit, notably apples, elderberries, oranges and the like, but soft pulpy fruits such as peaches tend to yield a sludge of pulp and juice. There is also a danger of breaking seeds or stones in the fruit and releasing unpleasant oils into the juice. Electric juice extractors are very efficient with suitable ingredients, however, for 56 lbs. of apples can be processed in 1 to 2 hours to give 3 to 4 gallons of juice, but a conventional press is probably more versatile and is therefore a better investment.

Fruit crushers are very useful adjuncts to presses. The operation of the latter can often be rendered more rapid and efficient if the ingredients are crushed or milled finely before pressing commences. For example, apples yield more juice if the fruit is first milled to a fine pulp, while grapes and cherries press more readily if the individual berries are crushed and the skins broken before the press is loaded. In addition, colour extraction during pulp fermentation proceeds more rapidly when the fruit is crushed prior to adding the yeast. Small fruit crushers are relatively cheap and will deal with a surprising amount of fruit for their size, but larger versions suitable for use in conjunction with a big press cost rather more. Unfortunately, no good designs for the construction of a fruit crusher have as yet appeared, although it has been suggested that the rolls of an old mangle or wringer may be spirally studded so that it can serve in this capacity. This arrangement is in fact said to give quite good results. Apart from this solution, the only alternative is for the individual winemaker to buy a small crusher or for a wine circle to obtain a larger type for the collective use of its members.

HYDROMETERS AND VINOMETERS

The hydrometer is undoubtedly one of the most valuable aids to quality which amateur winemakers have at their disposal. Indeed, its importance is such that it cannot be adequately discussed in a few paragraphs. For this reason, a separate chapter has been devoted solely to the hydrometer and its uses and should be consulted for further details on this subject.

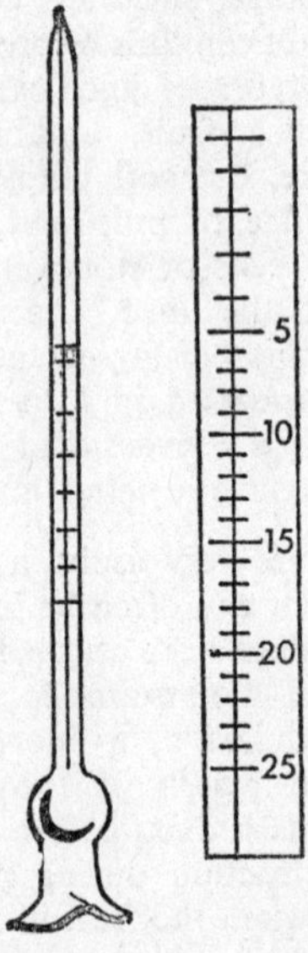

A vinometer

The vinometer is an instrument commonly advocated for determining the alcoholic strength of wines. It consists of a narrow glass capillary tube graduated from 0 to 25 to which is attached a thistle shaped funnel. A few drops of wine are introduced into the funnel until a droplet appears at the base of the capillary tube. The instrument is then inverted (funnel downwards) on a flat surface when the wine in the capillary will run back to a certain point on the scale. The scale reading obtained in this manner gives the percentage alcohol by volume in the wine.

Although this procedure is very simple and rapid, the results obtained with the aid of the vinometer are of doubtful value. It works upon the principle of surface tension which varies according to alcoholic strength, but unfortunately other substances in the wine besides alcohol also have some effect on its surface tension. Sugar in particular has quite a marked influence on this property of the wine. Hence, while the vinometer may be moderately accurate for dry wines, it is absolutely useless for measuring the alcoholic strength of sweet wines whose sugar content interferes with the determination. In such cases, the vinometer will indicate the wine contains far more alcohol than it actually does, so that no reliance whatsoever can be placed on any results obtained under these circumstances. On the whole, then, there is little point in buying a vinometer, especially as a considerably better estimation of alcoholic strength can be made from hydrometer data.

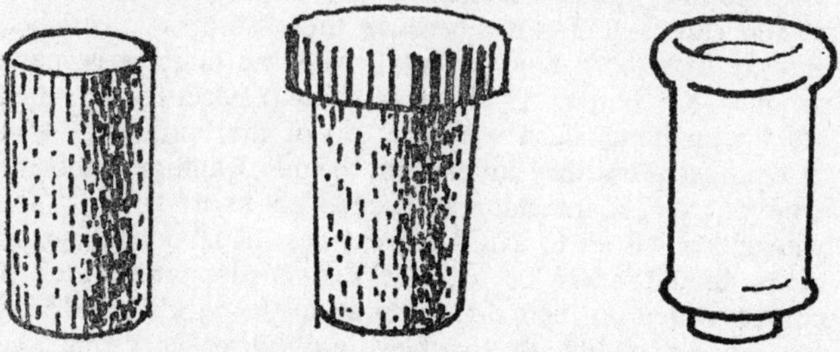

An ordinary cylindrical wine cork, a stopper cork as used for wine competitions, and a polyethylene stopper.

CORKS, BUNGS AND ALLIED ITEMS

A good supply of corks and rubber or plastic bungs is essential in any wine cellar. Whatever sizes of containers are used for fermentation and storage, they must be sealed in some way to keep the wines sound and free from contamination. Bottles and bulk storage vessels should be fitted with tight closures, while fermentation locks are inserted in bored corks or bungs which in turn fit tightly in the mouth of a fermentation vessel. Since bottles, gallon jars, carboys, casks and so on all have necks of different diameters, it is clear that a variety of corks and bungs are required to seal this range of containers.

Rubber bungs are probably the best closures to use for fermentation and bulk storage vessels. They are relatively impermeable to air, their flexibility makes for a tight fit and they will last for years without deterioration. Sterilisation also presents no problems since rubber can be boiled in water or washed in a sulphite solution quite safely. On the debit side, rubber bungs cost several times as much as corks and cannot be left in contact with wine for any length of time otherwise it may acquire a distinct and unpleasant rubbery flavour. It nevertheless is cheaper in the long run to build up a stock of rubber bungs for use with fermentation and bulk storage containers for which a new cork would be required each time the contents are replaced.

There is little choice but to use corks when wine is stored in bottles. Cork stoppers fitted with a cap or flange for ease of removal are cheap and perform very well, but a plastic cap is preferable because those stoppers fashioned entirely from cork tend to break when an attempt is made to open the bottle. Cylindrical straight-sided corks which are driven home flush with the top of the bottle may also be employed, but they suffer from the disadvantage that some type of corking machine is needed to insert them if the winemaker wishes to avoid a great deal of labour. Tapered corks should never be used to seal bottles which are, of course, stored on their sides to prevent the cork from drying out, since it is difficult to achieve a good seal, but this type of cork is best for fermentation and bulk storage vessels which are kept upright at all times. Plastic stoppers may also be employed to seal bottles although it has been observed that some leakage tends to occur with this type of closure. Some authorities also maintain the wine acquires an off-flavour from plastic stoppers, but convincing proof of this assertion still seems wanting. Casks are, of course, sealed with oak, cork or rubber bungs according to the personal preference of the winemaker.

If the winemaker does intend to bottle wines rather than store them in ½–1 gallon bulk containers, the corks should be sterilised by washing in weak sulphite solution and then softened by soaking them in cold water containing a little glycerine for 24 hours prior to use. Corks should never be immersed in boiling water which will damage their cellular structure and result in their disintegrating a few months later.

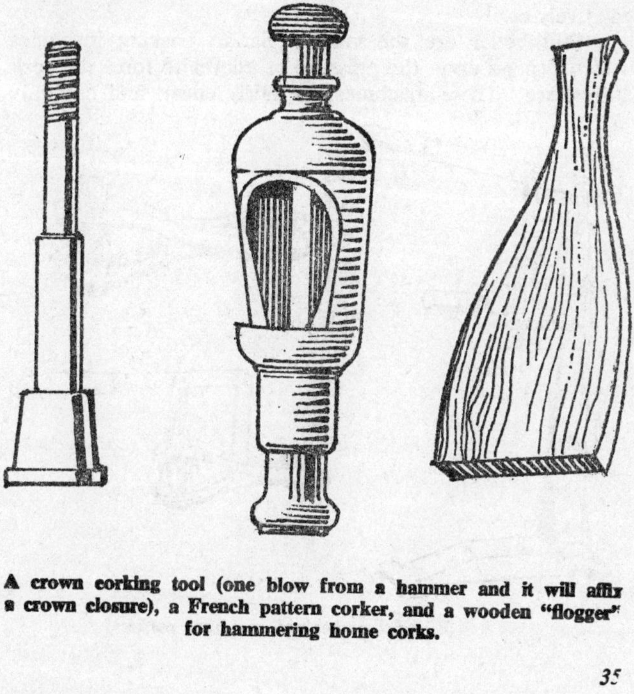

A crown corking tool (one blow from a hammer and it will affix a crown closure), a French pattern corker, and a wooden "flogger" for hammering home corks.

The actual job of inserting the corks into the bottles can be accomplished in several ways. The simplest method is to drive the cork home with the heel of the hand or with the aid of a wooden mallet or cork flogger (merely a shaped piece of wood). A short piece of plastic-covered wire should be slipped between the cork and the neck of the bottle during this operation so that the air compressed as the cork is inserted can escape when the wire is withdrawn once the cork is in place.

A slightly more refined piece of equipment for this purpose is known as the French corker and consists of a shaped, hollow, wooden cylinder through which a wooden plunger passes. The cork is placed in the cylinder (which has an opening in the side for doing so) and is driven into the bottle by hitting the plunger with a mallet or cork flogger. The cylinder is so shaped that the cork is compressed as it passes down through it and consequently slips into the bottle relatively easily.

Still better are the various Sanbri corking machines which depend upon the pressure of a lever to force the cork into place. These machines are fairly cheap and certainly

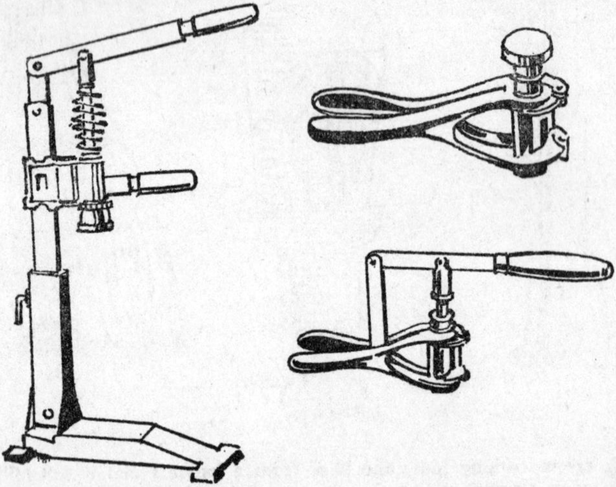

A bench model corker and two hand corkers.

save a great deal of labour, although the hand model does tend to be rather slow. When a considerable amount of bottling is envisaged, however, the Sanbri bench model corking machine can be highly recommended for both speed and efficiency. Its price is also quite reasonable.

Bottles can be given an attractive finish by applying foil or plastic capsules over the corks. Foil capsules are simply crimped into place round the neck of the bottle and are mainly decorative. Plastic capsules, on the other hand, help to provide a better seal as well as enhancing the appearance of the bottle. These capsules are supplied in a bath of liquid in which they must be stored at all times because they dry and harden on exposure to air. To apply this type of capsule, one is removed from the liquid, placed over the cork (and projecting an eighth of an inch beyond it if the capsule is of the "ring" type), and finally left to dry and harden. The dry capsule will tighten and adhere firmly to the bottle and cork and must be cut away when the time comes to open the bottle.

Both foil and plastic capsules can be obtained in a variety of colours and can, if desired, be made to serve as a colour code identification for specific types of wine in addition to being merely decorative. For example, red capsules could be used to denote red table wines, white capsules for white table wines and so on.

It is perhaps advisable at this point to mention the subject of boring corks and bungs, since bored closures are required for fermentation locks and the like. Cork borers, which consist of a hollow metal tube (of various diameters) sharpened at one end and fitted with a metal T-piece at the other, should always be used for this purpose since an ordinary twist drill makes an untidy, jagged hole in a cork. The size of borer to choose naturally depends upon the diameter of the tube which will be inserted into the hole, but most suppliers offer a size which is suitable for boring holes to take a standard fermentation lock. Otherwise, the borer should be one size smaller than the one which just slips over the tube the winemaker intends to insert in the cork. The procedure is to hold the cork firmly in one hand and bore the hole with a twisting motion until it is about halfway through the cork. The borer should then be removed and the hole completed from the other end of the cork. Although a little practice may be needed to bore a straight hole, this is the only correct way to bore a hole because it does avoid making a jagged exit hole which boring all the way through in one direction almost invariably causes. Rubber bungs can, however, be bored directly from one end to the other quite safely. Alternatively, of course, bored corks and bungs of various types can be purchased from most suppliers comparatively cheaply.

How to wire corks.

Wire ties are accessories of interest in sparkling wine production where it is essential to have some means of holding the cork in place so that the pressure inside the bottle cannot force it out. They are also useful means of ensuring that bottles binned on their sides cannot blow their corks and spill precious wine maturing therein. The wire is placed over the cork, wrapping it tightly beneath the neck ring of the bottle and finally twisting the two ends of the tie together so that it cannot be pulled off the bottle. Screw top bottles should never be used for sparkling wines unless the winemaker is content to leave the sediment in the bottle because it will be wellnigh impossible to carry out the process of dégorgement under these circumstances. It may be worth noting that crown capping is a perfectly satisfactory method of sealing bottles of sparkling wine. Indeed, now that equipment for applying crown caps can be purchased fairly cheaply, this type of closure will probably become more popular in both sparkling wine and beer production.

LABELS

Labels are virtually indispensable in the wine cellar. Failure to label containers of wine clearly can cause a great deal of confusion because, even with a good memory, it is rarely possible to remember exactly what every bottle and jar contains. Casks and large containers of wine can be identified very effectively by means of tie-on luggage labels, whilst small white gummed labels will suffice for smaller fermentation and storage vessels which will not appear on the table. When the wine is likely to be served directly from the bottle, however, it is preferable to use a larger and more decorative label which will enhance the appearance of the bottle considerably. Several very attractive labels of this type can now be bought quite cheaply from most suppliers and can be highly recommended. Many clubs also print their own labels so that the winemaker usually has a selection of designs from which to choose. Since some of these labels are supplied without gum on the back, it is advisable to have a bottle of paste or gum at hand for sticking them in place.

MISCELLANEOUS ITEMS

There are many useful items of equipment which cannot logically be included under any of the preceding headings. For example, a bottle brush enables the winemaker to remove stubborn deposits which have dried on the inside walls of bottles and jars, a task which otherwise proves both awkward and tedious. A thermometer graduated from 0°C. to 100°C. (32° F. to 212° F.) can also be put to good use for checking if a must has cooled sufficiently to permit the introduction of the yeast and to determine what temperature corrections should be applied to a gravity reading. In addition, it will also serve to check the temperature of the wine cellar and will show how widely its temperature fluctuates over a given period of time or from season to season. A maximum/minimum thermometer is even more revealing in this connection.

A selection of rubber, plastic and glass tubing is required for racking and transferring wines from one container to another. A good grade of rubber or flexible plastic tubing should be chosen for this purpose and care should be taken

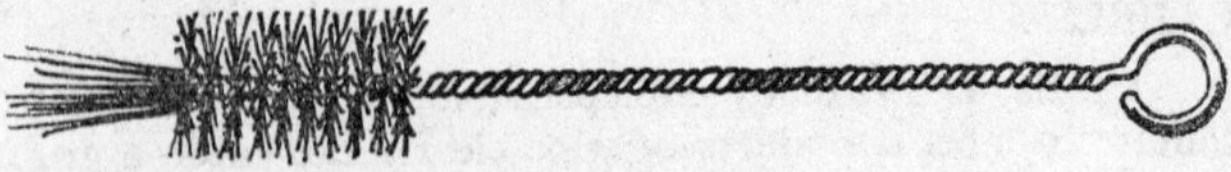

A useful bottle brush.

to ensure that its internal diameter is at least 3/8ths inches, otherwise the flow of wine through the tube will be rather too slow. Indeed, it is preferable to use tubing with a ½-inch or greater internal diameter for racking large containers holding more than about five gallons of wine. A piece of glass tubing turned up slightly at one end will also allow more efficient racking since less sediment will then be sucked up from the bottom of the jar by the outward flow of wine. More details concerning this piece of equipment will be found in the chapter on racking and clarification.

Wine matured in bottles must normally be stored in such a way that the corks are always kept moist and do not dry out or leakage and spoilage will almost certainly occur. Hence, bottles of wine must always be stored on their sides. The winemaker who is contemplating maturing wine in bottles is therefore well advised to consider obtaining storage bins or bottle racks of some description to hold the bottles. A number of different types of bottle storage bins are now available. Some are complete and ready for use as received, others must be assembled and many are designed so that extension racks can be added to the existing installation. Unfortunately, most such bins are fairly expensive, but often it is convenient to build up a stock of wine and bottle storage racks simultaneously so that the cost can be spread over a comparatively long period. Alternatively, of course, the winemaker can design and build storage bins directly in the cellar.

In conclusion, it may be said that this impressive list covers all the important pieces of equipment the winemaker is likely to encounter. Such sundry items as wooden spoons, saucepans and so on have not been mentioned since their uses need no explanation. Indeed, many common kitchen utensils of this nature can be pressed into service when the occasion arises, but there would be little point in discussing these minor winemaking accessories in any detail. It is well known that most winemakers can be counted on to take full advantage of whatever suitable articles the kitchen has to offer!

Chapter II

STERILISATION AND SULPHITE

FEW people nowadays would dispute that the terrible diseases and plagues which were so common in this country during the Middle Ages have more or less been completely eradicated mainly as a result of improved sanitation and an increased awareness of the importance of personal and communal hygiene. The modern approach to the problem devolves around the adage " prevention is better than cure." Since germs thrive in dirty, insanitary surroundings, it follows that cleanliness is the key to good health.

Since wine at all stages in its production provides a very rich medium capable of supporting the growth of numerous bacteria and fungi injurious to its continued well-being, it too must be protected from the ravages of inimical micro-organisms. For this reason, cleanliness is as important in winemaking as it is in the field of medical science. Indeed, wine cannot be stored for long periods of time unless strict precautions are taken to prevent the development of spoilage organisms. Thus, in the past, before the existence of these microscopic predators was even suspected, wine was almost invariably consumed within a few months of the vintage because spoilage by acetification or some other equally ruinous infection usually occurred if lengthier maturing was attempted.

Wine will normally remain bacteriologically sound even if it is matured for many years provided that the winemaker always observes scrupulous cleanliness and permits the development of no other organism than the yeast used to conduct the fermentation either in the wine itself or in its immediate surroundings. This aim can obviously be achieved only if every likely source of infection is neutralised before it can contaminate the wine. For this purpose, the winemaker requires some simple, safe but effective method of sterilisation which can be used whenever the occasion arises. In winemaking, sterilisation can be effected either by heat treatment or by means of sulphur dioxide (the gas given off by burning sulphur). The two methods are really complementary.

Dirty equipment is probably the most obvious source of infection. Apart from providing sites upon which airborne bacteria and fungi may alight and proliferate, it will also attract insects, particularly the fruit fly Drosophila Melanogaster. Although these fruit flies (the so-called vinegar flies) are harmless in themselves, they frequently act as carriers of disease and can therefore spread infection from one place to another with amazing rapidity. Fermenting musts left exposed to the air, lees left in uncorked bottles or jars, splashes of wine from racking operations and equipment of any description which has been put to one side still wet with wine will all attract fruit flies like a magnet attracts iron filings, with the result that in a few days literally thousands of colonies of spoilage organisms may have developed from these small beginnings. Cleaning-up should therefore never be neglected even though it is undoubtedly the most tedious chore in winemaking, otherwise much good wine may be lost by its becoming infected by bacteria or fungi originating from these sources. Moreover, little effort is usually needed to clean and sterilise equipment soon after it has been used, whereas a day or two later a great deal of extra work will almost certainly be required e.g. yeast allowed to dry on the inside of a glass jar is notoriously difficult to remove. The prevention of infection and ease of cleaning are therefore two excellent reasons why dirty equipment should never be allowed to accumulate.

It is seldom realised that the actual ingredients used to make the wine can be equally as potent a source of infection as dirty equipment. Thus, fruits are invariably covered with a bloom which in this country consists of diverse species of wild yeasts, moulds and bacteria whose unrestricted growth in the must or wine could rapidly cause spoilage. Over-ripe or damaged fruit is particularly likely to be heavily contaminated with injurious micro-organisms since mould growth or fermentation by wild yeasts may have commenced around those parts of the fruit where the skin has been broken or bruising has occurred. In many instances, fruit showing signs of fermentation will also be infected by acetifying bacteria, raspberries being a notable example, and many cases of acetification can be traced back to the use of infected fruit which has not been properly sterilised. Similar remarks apply to grain, flowers, vegetables and so on which possess their own characteristic flora of micro-organisms. Honey is basically a concentrated sugar syrup prepared from the nectar of flowers and may therefore contain spoilage organisms which were originally present in the nectar e.g. wild yeasts, acetifying bacteria. As it is obviously impossible to prevent contamination of the must by spoilage organisms derived from the ingredients, sterilisation of the must prior to fermentation is essential to keep the wine free from infection.

It has already been mentioned that both equipment and ingredients can be sterilised either by heat treatment or by the use of sulphur dioxide, and that both methods are of value to amateur winemakers. Heat treatment includes such techniques as boiling in water, scalding with boiling water, baking in the oven and so on. These procedures do have the advantage of ensuring almost complete sterility when properly applied, but their effects are only of a temporary nature and have no lasting bactericidal action since re-infection can occur on cooling. Small articles of equipment e.g rubber bungs, wooden spoons and taps, siphon tubing, glass fermentation locks and the like can be conveniently and thoroughly sterilised by boiling in water for about 10 minutes, and with the exception of glassware may be dropped directly into a saucepan of boiling water. Glass utensils should never be treated in this way in case the sudden change of temperature causes breakage through thermal shock, but instead should be placed in a pan of cold water which is then brought to the boil. Larger items of equipment including bottles, gallon jars, carboys and so on obviously cannot be sterilised in this manner and are best treated with sulphur dioxide solution as described below. Under no circumstances should glassware be baked in the oven since this rather drastic procedure often causes breakage, not to mention burned fingers. Wooden casks require special treatment before they can be used for winemaking, but this procedure has been described in detail in another chapter.

The sterilisation of ingredients either by boiling in water or by scalding with boiling water is usually best avoided for a number of reasons. In the first place, a great many ingredients contain pectins, complex substances discussed more fully later, which can retard or even prevent clarification by stabilising hazes. These pectins are more soluble in hot than in cold water so that a higher proportion of pectins is found in musts prepared with the aid of boiling water.

As a result, the subsequent clarification of these wines often proves rather more difficult than is normally the case. Moreover, the natural pectin destroying enzymes found in the ingredients are inactivated by the heat and cannot therefore catalyse the breakdown of the pectins in the must during fermentation as usually happens. The addition of an artificial preparation containing these enzymes, e.g. pectozyme, pectinol, to the must is consequently essential to ensure clarification of the wine under these circumstances.

Again, delicate flavours and aromas may be dissipated in the steam if boiling water is used, a common occurrence when flowers are an important ingredient. The wine produced from certain ingredients may also acquire a " cooked " flavour if heating has been practised.

At times, the use of heat during the preparation of the must has certain advantages. For example, some fruits which contain little or no pectin e.g. bananas, are most conveniently and efficiently extracted by cutting into slices and boiling in water, thus avoiding a pulp fermentation. It may also be added that few fruits are amenable to this treatment either because of their pectin content or because of the danger of introducing a cooked flavour into the wine.

Most vegetables must be boiled in water, however, both to extract the maximum flavour and to remove certain volatile constituents which would otherwise coarsen the flavour of the wine. An open vessel should therefore be used for boiling vegetables to allow these undesirable substances to become dissipated in the steam. The addition of pectinol or pectozyme to the must prior to fermentation is then usually necessary to destroy any pectin extracted from these ingredients during boiling, especially in the case of parsnips. Finally, ingredients which require a pulp fermentation are often best treated by scalding with boiling water to avoid heavy sulphiting if the fruit is damaged. This preliminary heat treatment permits the use of less sulphur dioxide in such cases.

The sterilising action of sulphur dioxide has long been known to commercial wine producers. In the past, casks were commonly sterilised by inserting a sulphur match or a ladle of burning sulphur through the bung-hole and allowing the fumes to fill the barrel. Although this procedure rarely failed to sterilise the cask, it did suffer from certain drawbacks. Thus, particles of sulphur falling inside could be reduced during fermentation to substances injurious to the flavour of the wine. Also, because it was impossible to add an accurate, predetermined dose of sulphur dioxide each time, too much or too little could easily be introduced and the quality of the wine could consequently suffer. Nowadays, the burning of elemental sulphur for sterilising purposes has been superseded by the introduction of either liquid sulphur dioxide or aqueous solutions of the solid salts sodium or potassium metabisulphite ($Na_2S_2O_5$ or $K_2S_2O_5$), usually known simply as sulphite, which constitute sources of readily available sulphur dioxide and enable strictly controlled amounts of the gas to be used as required.

Since few amateur winemakers could obtain liquid sulphur dioxide, much less handle it properly, it follows that aqueous solutions of sulphite must be employed. Sulphite can be purchased in the form of Campden tablets which are actually fruit preserving tablets each containing 7 grains (0.44 gms.) of sulphite. On the other hand, it is considerably cheaper and more convenient to buy solid sodium metabisulphite from a chemist and prepare a stock sulphite solution for general use. A 10% stock sulphite solution can easily be prepared by dissolving ¼ lb. sodium metabisulphite in one pint of hot water and diluting this solution to a final volume of one quart with cold water once all the crystals have been dissolved. Such a solution is usually assumed to contain 5% by weight of available sulphur dioxide and will keep for months with little deterioration in a well stoppered container. It is nevertheless advisable to prepare a fresh solution every 4–6 months according to how often it is used.

Several authors have suggested that a 1% instead of a 10% sulphite solution is preferable for certain purposes, notably for sterilising equipment. Admittedly, a 1% solution does possess a much less pungent odour and is consequently more pleasant to handle, but in other respects it is inferior to a 10% solution. The latter not only contains sufficient sulphur dioxide to effect rapid and efficient sterilisation but will also retain its bactericidal activity for several months under suitable storage conditions. While a freshly prepared 1% solution is quite an effective sterilising agent, it does deteriorate rather quickly with use or even during storage and should therefore not be re-used more than a few times nor stored longer than a few weeks. In comparison, a 10% solution may be used over and over again for several months before losing its potency.

The addition of a little citric or tartaric acid is sometimes recommended as a means of increasing the potency of sulphite solutions. Although acid will certainly succeed in achieving this object, it does so only at the expense of reducing the stability and hence the keeping powers of the solution which then cannot be stored for more than a few days. This procedure is therefore best avoided whenever possible even with 1% solutions and is certainly of no benefit to 10% solutions which need no such promotion because their bactericidal activity is already ample for winemaking purposes.

These facts indicate that it is much better to employ the stock 10% sulphite solution directly for any task which repuires the use of sulphite. As far as adding sulphite to musts and wines is concerned, however, a small amount of the stock solution should be set aside solely for this purpose whenever a fresh batch is prepared so that it remains clean and retains its potency longer than the remainder which will be used for a multiplicity of tasks. A freshly prepared 1% solution may still be used occasionally at the discretion of the winemaker, of course, but its use should only really be considered when the strong unpleasant odour of the 10% solution would cause inconvenience e.g. in a small enclosed area. The techniques described in this book have thus been based on the assumption that the 10% solution will be used at all times.

Glass or plastic containers are very easily sterilised by means of sulphite, but it must always be remembered that sterilisation is the final phase of cleaning operations. The container must first be washed thoroughly in hot soapy water to remove any sediment or deposit. A bottle brush is an indispensable item for this purpose. Sterilisation is then effected by pouring a little of the stock solution of sulphite into the container through a funnel and swirling it around so that the sulphite reaches every part of the container. After a few minutes, the sulphite solution may be poured out, but it should be returned to the bulk of the solution and not discarded since it can be re-used many times before losing its potency. The container is then ready for immediate use and need not even be rinsed unless an actively fermenting must is going to be introduced.

Large containers are obviously most simply and conveniently sterilised in this way, and little difficulty will be experienced even with 10 gallon glass carboys which otherwise prove almost impossible to deal with. Empty containers can be kept sweet by storing them firmly stoppered with about an inch of sulphite solution in the bottom, while awkward or unwieldly items of equipment such as fruit presses can readily be sterilised by washing with a cloth dipped in sulphite. A cloth soaked in sulphite solution can be used to wipe over the exteriors of fermentation vessels, especially when the must has frothed out during a vigorous primary fermentation, and to mop up splashes of wine spilled during straining or racking operations. Any such potential source of infection can thus be simultaneously cleaned up and sterilised. Many other examples of this nature could also be quoted, but from remarks already made it is clear that sulphite is an extremely useful and versatile, if not indispensable, sterilising agent which no winemaker should really be without. Sulphite should therefore be used liberally to keep equipment and its surroundings free from infection.

Musts can also be treated with sulphite to prevent spoilage by micro-organisms introduced from its ingredients, but here rather a different principle operates since only a small fraction of the amount of sulphite required to effect complete sterilisation is added. The object in this case is to kill sulphite-sensitive micro-organisms, which include the highly undesirable acetifying bacteria and many of the equally undesirable lactic acid bacteria, and to inhibit temporarily the growth of the more sulphite-resistant organisms for a long enough period to allow the selected wine yeast later added to the must to become firmly established without having to face severe competition from other wild yeasts or bacteria during the initial critical stages of its growth. Once a healthy thriving yeast colony has been built up, it will then, of course, tend to swamp any competitors by sheer weight of numbers. The anaerobic conditions and alcohol produced during the fermentation will further discourage the growth of other micro-organisms. Sulphiting the must will also promote the formation of glycerol, a normal fermentation by-product which in small amounts helps to improve the quality of a wine by giving added body and smoothness of flavour

The addition of sufficient sulphite solution to produce a sulphur dioxide concentration of about 50 parts per million (ppm) is usually adequate for this purpose. This concentration can be achieved by adding 5 mls. stock sulphite solution (or 1 Campden tablet) per gallon of must.

Where a pulp fermentation is conducted, a slightly higher sulphur dioxide concentration is advisable and 100 p.p.m. should then be employed (10 mls. stock solution or 2 Campden tablets per gallon). Musts prepared from overripe or damaged fruit which are likely to be more heavily contaminated than normal also require heavier sulphiting and at least 100 p.p.m. but more often 150 p.p.m. will then frequently be necessary. The use of boiling water i.e. scalding and sulphite in conjunction, is often worth considering under these circumstances to cut down the amount of sulphite required, for then no more than about 100 p.p.m. should be needed. It should also be noted that sulphite becomes more effective as the acidity of the must increases so that less than the above amounts of sulphite may very well suffice when dealing with the more acid musts.

Many winemakers fail to understand why sulphite should kill or inhibit the growth of undesirable micro-organisms in the must yet allow the selected wine yeast to proliferate seemingly without hindrance. Most wine yeasts are tolerant of moderate amounts of sulphur dioxide and certain strains in fact grow better if a low concentration of sulphite is present in the must. Secondly, sulphite only retains its bactericidal and bacteriostatic properties for a comparatively short period of time and much of its potency is lost within 24 hours. The yeast is therefore never added to a newly sulphited must but instead is introduced one day later, when the action of the sulphite has abated considerably. The other micro-organisms in the must which were exposed to the full power of the sulphite will not have recovered by this time, so that the yeast is free to grow with little or no competition from these spoilage organisms. Moreover, if an actively fermenting starter was added, the yeast will very rapidly establish a healthy thriving colony because it was already in an active state of growth and reproduction prior to its introduction into the must. Under these conditions, the yeast will be virtually unaffected by the now weakened sulphite and only the less resistant cells are likely to be killed or inhibited, a factor which favours the continued well-being of the colony in any case by weeding out its weakest individuals.

The bactericidal action of sulphite also makes it an effective agent for treating wines which have become infected by spoilage organisms, for the majority of bacteria and fungi responsible for wine spoilage are readily killed by quite low concentrations of sulphur dioxide (50 p.p.m. or 100 p.p.m.). Indeed, sulphite is virtually the only agent which can safely be employed for this purpose, but its uses in this field are more fully discussed in another chapter and may therefore be omitted here.

In view of the fact that prevention is much better than cure, winemakers are well advised to add a small amount of sulphite to the must prior to its inoculation with the yeast starter as already recommended and as a further precaution to add another 50 p.p.m. sulphur dioxide immediately after the first few rackings (except a preliminary first racking).

Apart from helping to keep a wine free from spoilage, sulphite added after racking also performs several other useful functions. Thus, it aids the stabilisation and clarification of a wine by discouraging the growth of a new yeast colony (the conditions here are already rather unfavourable for further yeast growth and the presence of fresh sulphite merely aggravates matters). By neutralising the electrical charges on suspended colloidal particles, sulphite promotes their coagulation and settling and consequently assists clarification. Moreover, sulphite has anti-oxidant properties so that a proportion of the oxygen absorbed by wines during racking will preferentially combine with the sulphite rather than with certain constituents of the wine itself, and over-oxidation due to excessive aeration during racking should therefore be largely prevented. Certain wines, notably those prepared from over-ripe fruits, are also susceptible to oxidative browning which is caused by the presence of unduly large amounts of certain enzymes (o-polyphenyloxidases) catalysing the oxidation of complex substances in the wine to brown oxidation products. Sulphite will also prevent this enzymic browning, known as oxidative casse, by acting as an anti-oxidant and combining with any dissolved oxygen before it can be utilised by these enzymes.

In passing, it should also be noted that some bleaching of red musts and wines may be observed immediately after sulphite has been added, but this effect is only temporary and the must or wine will regain its colour in the space of a few days.

A final use of sulphite which is worth mentioning is in connection with fermentation locks, the U-bends of which are better filled with stock sulphite solution than with water. Fruit flies are often attracted to the open ends of these locks and not uncommonly commit suicide in the water they contain. The latter may therefore become contaminated with spoilage organisms which can subsequently spoil the wine. Sulphite instead of water in the lock is a sure way of avoiding this danger, but the sulphite solution should be changed every few weeks as it soon loses its potency when carbon dioxide is continuously bubbling through the lock. The open end of a fermentation lock may, of course, be sealed with a plug of cotton wool as an added precaution.

Recently, other sterilising agents e.g. BHC 318 have been introduced but these substances are sterilising detergents and therefore only have a limited application in winemaking. They are ideal for equipment since they permit simultaneous cleaning and sterilising, but thorough rinsing is necessary as no more than a trace of detergent should be incorporated into a wine for obvious reasons despite the fact that BHC 318 is claimed to be both odourless and tasteless. These preparations cannot be added directly to musts or wines, however, so that sulphite is unlikely to be ousted from its present position as one of the most useful and versatile reagents at the disposal of the winemaker, at least for some years to come. Nevertheless, it is worthwhile having a supply of BHC 318 on hand since it is an excellent detergent which will enable the winemaker to clean and sterilise equipment rapidly, a very desirable object if a large number of bottles, jars and so on are awaiting attention after an evening of very hard work in the wine cellar.

CHAPTER III

THE HYDROMETER AND ITS USES

THE hydrometer is a simple scientific instrument, used to measure the specific gravity or density of liquids, which has a number of valuable applications in amateur winemaking. Indeed, the hydrometer is considered by many winemakers to be such an important, if not indispensable, item of equipment that its uses can only be adequately discussed by devoting a complete chapter to this subject. For example, some of its more notable functions include checking the progress of a fermentation, measuring the natural sugar content of a must and providing data from which the approximate alcoholic strength of a wine can be calculated. Information of this nature is, of course, invaluable to winemakers seeking to improve the quality of their wines. The hydrometer may therefore rightly be regarded as one of the keys to successful winemaking.

From the accompanying diagram, the hydrometer can be seen to consist of a hollow glass bulb or cylinder weighted at the base with lead shot or mercury (the float) to which is attached a long, slender, hollow glass tube (the stem) containing a graduated scale printed on paper. As already mentioned, the purpose of the hydrometer is to measure the specific gravity of liquids, and to accomplish this object the instrument is allowed to float freely in a jar of the liquid under examination. The depth to which the hydrometer sinks is determined by the specific gravity of the liquid, which can be read directly off the printed scale in the stem at the point where the latter is cut by the surface of the liquid.

In detail, the technique for using the hydrometer is as follows. A trial jar an inch or so wider and taller than the hydrometer itself is first filled to within about an inch of the top with the must or wine under examination. The hydrometer is then gently lowered into the jar, pushed carefully

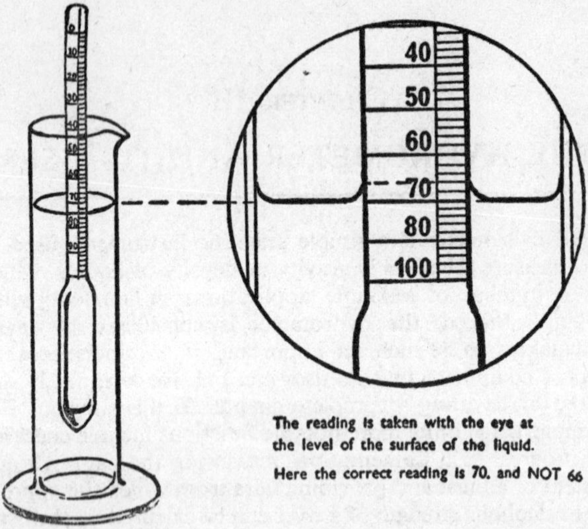

The reading is taken with the eye at the level of the surface of the liquid.
Here the correct reading is 70. and NOT 66

below the surface once or twice to wet the stem thoroughly and finally given a gentle spin to dislodge any gas bubbles which would increase its buoyancy and alter the reading.

Once the hydrometer has come to rest, the point at which the main liquid surface should cut the stem is observed with the eye at the level of the surface. The scale reading is then noted. Care must be taken not to read the scale at the top of the meniscus which is caused by the surface tension effect, otherwise a slightly low specific gravity will be recorded. A rather exaggerated illustration of this feature is shown in the diagram.

This procedure obviously permits the winemaker to measure the specific gravities of musts and wines with ease and rapidity, but what in fact is specific gravity and what is its significance in winemaking ? The specific gravity of a liquid is defined as the weight of a given volume of that liquid compared with the weight of an equal volume of water under identical conditions. Since specific gravity is by definition a ratio of weights, it obviously cannot be expressed in units of measurement such as degrees. It is merely a number denoting how much a given liquid is lighter or heavier than water. Water has been chosen as the reference liquid mainly for reasons of convenience and has arbitrarily been assigned a specific gravity of 1.000. Other liquids usually have a higher or lower specific gravity e.g. the value for (ethyl) alcohol is 0.794.

The specific gravity of a pure liquid is constant provided it is always measured under the same conditions, but should the latter be altered in any way some corresponding change in the specific gravity will also be observed. Temperature has an important effect in this respect so that all hydrometers are calibrated for use at a specified temperature, commonly 60°F (15.5°C). If the temperature of the liquid is above or below this figure, its specific gravity will differ to some extent from the true value as a result of expansion or contraction. For this reason, it is advisable to take the temperature of the must or wine when measuring its specific gravity. The full significance of this temperature effect can be seen in these temperature correction tables:

TEMPERATURE CORRECTION FACTORS

Temperature °C	Temperature °F	Specific Gravity correction	Gravity correction
10°	50°	—0.001	—1
15°	59°	None	None
20°	68°	+0.001	+1
25°	77°	+0.002	+2
30°	86°	+0.003	+3
35°	95°	+0.005	+5
40°	104°	+0.007	+7

The specific gravity of a liquid is also affected by the presence of dissolved solids and other liquids. Thus, a solution of sugar in water has a specific gravity different from that of pure water, and similarly a mixture of water and alcohol has a specific gravity different from that of either pure water or pure alcohol. The important point is that the specific gravity of solutions of this type depends mainly upon the amount of sugar or alcohol present in the water.

Dissolved solids usually increase the specific gravity of water by an amount depending upon the weight of solid present per unit volume of solution, while the specific gravity of a mixture of alcohol and water is mainly determined by the respective specific gravities of the pure liquids and the proportions in which each is present. In other words, the specific gravity of a solution of sugar or alcohol in water is a function of the concentration of the solute i.e. it depends upon the amount of sugar or alcohol in solution.

These facts are clearly of great interest and value to the winemaker. If tables showing the relation between the specific gravity of a sugar solution and the weight of sugar it contains are readily available, then it is a simple matter to determine the amount of sugar present in a must merely by measuring its specific gravity and referring to the appropriate tables. Specific gravity/sugar tables suitable for winemaking purposes have therefore been included in this chapter for reference.

It is worth noting that in these tables the amount of sugar corresponding to a given specific gravity is expressed as that weight of sugar present in one gallon of the sugar solution i.e. the total volume of sugar and water together is one gallon. A rather lower specific gravity would be recorded if the above weight of sugar were added to one gallon of water. More than one gallon of sugar solution would then be obtained because sugar occupies a finite volume (2 lbs. sugar in fact occupy the equivalent of one pint of water). In addition to the columns headed " specific gravity " and " weight of sugar," the headings " Balling or Brix," " Twaddell " and "Baumé" will also be observed in this table. These names denote alternative scales of measurement to specific gravity which the winemaker may encounter occasionally. Conversion from one of these other scales to specific gravity can therefore be accomplished should the need arise e.g. American books on wine technology usually employ the Balling scale.

Winemakers may also be confused by reference to gravity rather than specific gravity, but the two terms are actually very closely related. The gravity of a solution is its specific gravity minus unity, the position of the decimal point then being disregarded. For example, the specific gravities 1.001

and 1.105 correspond to gravities of 1 and 105 respectively, while the specific gravity 0.993 corresponds to the gravity −7.

Gravity Tables

Specific Gravity	Gravity	Balling or Brix	Twaddell	Baumé	Weight of Sugar ozs/gal.	Weight of Sugar gms/1	Potential Alcohol (% by vol)
1.000	0	0.0	0	0.0	½	4	0
1.005	5	1.7	1	0.7	2¾	17	0.8
1.010	10	3.0	2	1.4	4¾	30	1.7
1.015	15	4.3	3	2.1	7	44	2.5
1.020	20	5.5	4	2.8	9	57	3.3
1.025	25	6.8	5	3.5	11	70	4.1
1.030	30	8.0	6	4.2	13¼	83	4.9
1.035	35	9.2	7	4.9	15½	97	5.8
1.040	40	10.4	8	5.6	17½	110	6.5
1.045	45	11.6	9	6.2	19½	123	7.3
1.050	50	12.8	10	6.9	21½	136	8.0
1.055	55	14.0	11	7.5	23¾	149	8.8
1.060	60	15.2	12	8.2	25¾	163	9.6
1.065	65	16.4	13	8.8	28	176	10.4
1.070	70	17.6	14	9.4	30	189	11.2
1.075	75	18.7	15	10.1	32	202	12.0
1.080	80	19.8	16	10.7	34¼	215	12.8
1.085	85	20.9	17	11.3	36½	228	13.6
1.090	90	22.0	18	11.9	38½	242	14.4
1.095	95	23.1	19	12.5	40½	255	15.2
1.100	100	24.2	20	13.1	42¾	268	16.0
1.105	105	25.3	21	13.7	45	282	16.8
1.110	110	26.4	22	14.3	47	295	17.5
1.115	115	27.5	23	14.9	49	308	18.3
1.120	120	28.5	24	15.5	51¼	321	19.1
1.125	125	29.6	25	16.0	53¼	335	19.9
1.130	130	30.6	26	16.6	55½	348	20.7
1.135	135	31.6	27	17.1	57½	361	21.5
1.140	140	32.7	28	17.7	59¾	374	22.2
1.145	145	33.7	29	18.3	62	387	23.0
1.150	150	34.7	30	18.8	64	401	23.8
1.155	155	35.8	31	19.4	66	414	24.6
1.160	160	36.8	32	19.9	68¼	427	25.5

The reasons for employing gravity instead of specific gravity in winemaking become apparent when considering the effects of dilution. The gravity decrease, but not the specific gravity decrease, observed when a must is diluted with water is approximately inversely proportional to the increase in volume. For example, the addition of an equal volume of water to a must of gravity 100 doubles the volume but almost halves the gravity to 50, the corresponding specific gravities being, of course, 1.100 and 1.050 respectively. Although this relationship is not strictly true because, amongst other things, a slight contraction in volume occurs when sugar is dissolved in water, the errors involved are so small that they may be ignored for most practical purposes.

From the accompanying tables, it is clear that the winemaker is mainly interested in the specific gravity range 1.000 to 1.200 so that at first sight a single hydrometer covering the whole of this range would seem to be the most obvious choice. Since a hydrometer spanning this comparatively wide range is less accurate than an instrument of the same size which covers a narrower range cf. the better definition of a 1in. scale map compared to a ½in. map of the same area, two hydrometers measuring between the specific gravity limits 1.000-1.100 and 1.100-1.200 would really be more useful and considerably more accurate. Furthermore, most winemakers will find that the 1.100-1.200 hydrometer is not strictly essential as few musts with an initial gravity greater than 100 are normally encountered. This instrument therefore need not be purchased as a basic item of equipment. Indeed, as will be seen shortly, a hydrometer covering the range 0.990-1.000 would probably be more valuable since most dry wines have a specific gravity below 1.000 and it is often helpful to record their exact final gravity.

The amount of sugar derived from the ingredients of the must is an extremely important factor which has to be taken into account when calculating the amount of sugar required to produce a wine containing a specified amount of alcohol. The determination of the natural sugar content of a must is but one of the problems which can very easily be solved with the aid of the hydrometer. On the other hand, it must be remembered that all fruit juices and musts contain a small proportion of suspended matter and dissolved solids other than sugar e.g. organic acids, salts, pectins, etc., all of which increase the specific gravity. Hence, because the tables in this book are only valid for pure sugar solutions, it is essential to subtract from the recorded gravity an arbitrary figure between 5 and 10, say 7 for an average must, to allow for the effects of these substances before consulting the tables to determine the weight of natural sugar present. For example, a must whose recorded gravity was 32 before any sugar was added would have a true gravity due to its natural sugar of about 25 so that it would contain approximately 11 ozs. natural sugar per gallon. In the case of pulp fermentations, it is impossible to determine the natural sugar content of the must with any real degree of accuracy. An approximate indication of its natural sugar content can be obtained by taking a small but representative sample of the must (juice and pulp) and pressing the pulp. The gravity of this extract (juice and pulp pressings) may then be determined in the usual manner after carefully straining out any residual pulp particles through muslin.

Probably the most valuable purpose for which the hydrometer can be employed is to provide trustworthy information regarding the progress of a fermentation. Every winemaker is naturally anxious to ensure that all goes well during this critical phase in the production of a wine. Unless a hydrometer is available, however, the only means of assessing how a fermentation is progressing involves tasting the wine at intervals to gain some idea of its sugar content and observing the rate at which bubbles of carbon dioxide pass through the air-lock. Unfortunately, these rather empirical tests can all too easily give misleading results, especially if the winemaker is relatively inexperienced. It therefore seems logical to replace this somewhat outmoded combination of guesswork and experience by the more concrete and altogether more reliable evidence supplied by the hydrometer.

Throughout the period of fermentation the yeast is steadily converting sugar into alcohol and carbon dioxide. It is because this transformation of the sugar is accompanied by changes in the gravity of the must that the hydrometer can be used for checking the progress of a fermentation. Since the gravity of a must depends principally upon its sugar content, a steady gravity decrease is observed as more and more sugar is metabolised by the yeast and the concentration of sugar in the must diminishes.

Although the magnitude of the gravity drop experienced in a given interval of time is mainly governed by the weight of sugar which has been utilised by the yeast during that period, other factors also play a minor but significant part. Thus, the alcohol produced during fermentation is lighter than water and its effect is therefore to depress the gravity of the must below the value which would be recorded if the solution only contained sugar and water.

Also, the volume of the must gradually decreases as fermentation proceeds due to the loss of carbon dioxide (which, of course, occupies a finite volume prior to its release by fermentation) and to the fact that a small contraction occurs when alcohol is mixed with water. These volume changes are more apparent when dealing with large quantities of wine, say five gallons or more, for then a contraction of several pints may be noticed. Obviously, some corresponding change in the gravity of the must will accompany these volume changes.

It is clear from these remarks that the hydrometer cannot be used to determine the sugar content of a must with any degree of accuracy once fermentation has started. The recorded gravity then depends upon the proportion of alcohol in the must and to a much lesser extent upon the contraction in volume which has occurred as well upon the weight of sugar present. Nevertheless, a gravity reading recorded during fermentation is of some value in this respect since the must will always contain rather more sugar than the weight corresponding in the tables to that particular gravity, due mainly to the effects of alcohol present. The winemaker can therefore be sure that the must does not contain less than that weight of sugar. The significance of this information will become obvious later when the technique of feeding the yeast with sugar is discussed.

Fortunately, the absolute weight of sugar remaining in the must does not need to be known accurately for the purpose of checking the progress of a fermentation. The gravity drop, or rather the rate at which the gravity decreases, is in fact the principal guide since this quantity is a measure of the rate and vigour of fermentation. For example, a rapid gravity drop is a sure sign that the yeast is extremely active and that fermentation is proceeding vigorously. On the other hand, a slow decrease in gravity indicates that the yeast is becoming sluggish and fermentation is nearing completion.

Feeding the yeast at intervals with small doses of sugar, or preferably sugar syrup, is a very common practice amongst more experienced winemakers. Under these conditions, the yeast seems better able to cope with the sugar than if the latter had all been added at the outset. Since yeast in its natural habitat is used to living in fairly dilute sugar solutions, such as fruit juices, it often finds difficulty in fermenting musts containing high initial concentrations of sugar. Fermentation is thus likely to proceed rather slowly and may even stick should too much sugar be present initially. If the sugar is added gradually in small controlled doses, however, at no time is the yeast forced to live undercon ditions not entirely to its liking. Hence, feeding with sugar in this way enables the yeast to deal with a greater weight of sugar than would otherwise be possible and therefore leads to higher yields of alcohol. In other words, feeding effectively raises the maximum alcohol tolerance of the yeast and promotes a sounder fermentation.

Although feeding is generally unnecessary for the production of table wines which on the whole contain less than 14% alcohol by volume at the most, this technique should always be adopted when aiming for wines after the style of the commercial fortified wines such as port, sherry and madeira. In this latter case, as much alcohol as possible must be produced by natural fermentation in order to avoid or at least cut down the cost of fortification. It follows that the progress of the fermentation must be checked at frequent intervals if feeding is to be carried out with any degree of success. The information provided by the hydrometer is, of course, indispensable for this purpose.

Since most yeasts can produce at least 10% alcohol with ease, the first stage in feeding is to augment the natural sugar content of the must with cane sugar so that a total of approximately 1½–2½ lbs. sugar per gallon is present. The initial gravity should thus lie between 60 and 100 or thereabouts, and certainly should not be higher than 100. After the yeast starter has been added, and active fermentation commences, the gravity of the must should be checked every few days because a very rapid gravity drop will normally be observed in the early stages of fermentation. A drop of 40 or more may very well be experienced in the first day or two because the yeast colony is very active and fermentation is extremely vigorous.

When the gravity of the must has decreased to between 0 and 5, a further 4 ozs. dose of sugar per gallon (as sugar syrup) may be added. This quantity of sugar will increase the gravity of the must by about 9. This procedure should then be repeated whenever the gravity drops below 5. As fermentation continues, the rate at which the gravity decreases will become slower and slower until eventually a drop of even a few points may take several weeks. It is then immediately apparent that the yeast is approaching its maximum alcohol tolerance and will not therefore be able to cope with much more sugar.

Once this stage is reached, the winemaker can allow the fermentation to proceed to completion without adding any more sugar when a sweet or medium-sweet or possibly a dry wine will be obtained according to its final sugar content. Alternatively, a final dose of 4 ozs. or less of sugar per gallon may be added so that a sweet wine is produced. In this way, it is possible to produce a sweet or medium-sweet wine with a high alcohol content but without the danger of fermentation sticking and leaving a sickly oversweet wine. Even if the addition of the final dose of sugar is misjudged and fermentation ceases without any of that sugar being used up by the yeast, the final gravity of the wine will only be about 14 which is not an excessively high figure i.e. the wine would not be oversweet.

A strong dry wine can be produced by refraining from adding further doses of sugar when a gravity drop of 1–2 per day is still being experienced. In most cases, all the residual sugar in the must will then be converted into alcohol to give a dry wine.

An even safer technique once the rate of fermentation oegins to slow down is to allow the gravity to fall below –5 and then add only 2 oz. sugar per gallon so that the gravity is always kept below 0 at this stage. If these sugar additions are again finally terminated when the gravity is still dropping at the rate of 1–2 per day, fermentation will almost invariably continue until no sugar remains in the wine. This latter procedure will very rarely fail to give a strong but completely dry wine.

Mention has been made earlier of sticking or stuck fermentations, and this phenomenon, which is due to the onset of conditions inimical to the continued growth and reproduction of the yeast in the must, can readily be detected by means of the hydrometer. The identifying feature of a stuck fermentation is that the yeast has ceased its activity while a considerable amount of unfermented sugar still remains in the must. The causes of a stuck fermentation are fully discussed in the chapter on fermentation, but it is worth noting at this juncture that should a stuck fermentation be suspected this condition can be confirmed simply by measuring the gravity of the must. If a gravity greater than about 25 is recorded but no gravity drop can be detected at the end of a week or ten days, then fermentation has undoubtedly stuck.

Yeast ferments sugar into approximately equal weights of alcohol and carbon dioxide according to the simple chemical equation given below.

$$\underset{\text{Glucose or Fructose}}{C_6H_{12}O_6} = \underset{\text{Alcohol}}{2CH_3CH_2OH} + \underset{\text{Carbon Dioxide}}{2CO_2}$$

In practice, the yield of alcohol is slightly below the theoretical figure predicted by this equation for reasons more fully discussed in the chapter on fermentation. Nevertheless, it has been found that yeast will produce a fairly constant amount of alcohol from a given weight of sugar under normal conditions of fermentation. This yield is usually expressed as the potential alcohol by volume corresponding to a particular weight of sugar in the must. The significance of the final column in the sugar/gravity tables at once becomes clear, for it merely shows the amount of alcohol which would be obtained by the complete fermentation of the corresponding weight of sugar e.g. 32 ozs. per gallon would yield about 12.0% alcohol by volume on complete fermentation. These potential alcohol figures are, of course, statistical values and are therefore subject to small variations, particularly towards the upper and lower ends of the table where it is less easy to predict what losses of sugar and alcohol will be sustained during fermentation. It is unlikely that an error much greater than about ± 0.5% alcohol by volume will arise, however, and this degree of accuracy is quite sufficient for most winemaking purposes. Furthermore, the most accurate values are grouped together in the centre of the table and cover the alcohol range 10%—14% by volume which is of greatest interest to the winemaker.

This information clearly enables the winemaker to produce wines with a predetermined alcohol content, for from the potential alcohol column it can be seen at a glance how much sugar is required to produce the desired yield of alcohol.

Once the natural sugar content of the must has been determined, it is a simple matter to calculate the amount of cane sugar which should be added to give a wine of the chosen strength. For example, a must was found to have a gravity of 47 so that, on subtracting 7 to allow for non-sugar solutes, its true gravity due to sugar is 40 which corresponds to 17½ ozs. natural sugar per gallon. Hence, a further 14½ ozs. sugar per gallon would be required to produce a dry wine containing about 12% alcohol by volume. In actual fact, however, the alcohol content in this case will only be about 11.2% by volume since no correction has been applied for the increase in volume of about ½ pint per gallon of must caused by the addition of 14½ ozs. sugar to each gallon of must.

This dilution effect obviously cannot be ignored, but complications of this nature can be avoided if the must is diluted to a predetermined volume after adding the sugar. Thus, it was decided to use 4 gallons of the must described in the preceding example to make 5 gallons of wine containing about 12% alcohol. Since the must already contains

17½ ozs. natural sugar per gallon, the total weight present in the 4 gallons is about 70 ozs. To achieve a final alcoholic strength of 12% by volume, however, the must should contain 32 ozs. sugar per gallon so that a total weight of 160 ozs. will be needed for 5 gallons. It follows that 90 ozs. sugar should be added to the 4 gallons of must and the volume then adjusted to 5 gallons with water.

One point warrants careful attention when calculating the sugar requirements of a must. Since the potential alcohol figures quoted here are based on the surmise that all the sugar in the must has been completely utilised by the yeast, it is clear that the above procedure can only be applied to dry wines whose residual sugar content is no higher than about 1% as measured by the Clinitest method described elsewhere. An analogous calculation cannot be performed for sweet wines because it is impossible to predict or decide in advance the gravity at which fermentation will cease when all the sugar is not metabolised by the yeast.

The hydrometer may also be used to calculate the approximate alcohol content of any wine provided a record has been kept of its initial and final gravities. The difference between these two values gives the total gravity drop experienced during fermentation. The approximate percentage of alcohol can then be evaluated simply by dividing this figure by 7.4. No corrections for non-sugar solutes need be applied here since their influence on both the initial and final gravity readings will be the same and their difference will not be affected. For example, a must was found to have an initial uncorrected gravity of 75 (corrected gravity of about 70) and a final gravity of 0 so that the total drop was 75. On dividing this figure by 7.4, the alcoholic strength of the wine can at once be seen to be just over 10% by volume. Had all the sugar in the must been utilised by the yeast, a final gravity of about –10 (specific gravity 0.990) would have been recorded and the total drop would then have been about 85. Dividing the latter by 7.4 gives an alcohol content of 11.5% which compares quite favourably with the 11.2% predicted in the potential alcohol tables for the complete fermentation of a must with an initial corrected gravity of 70.

The preceding estimation can still be carried out even if the sugar has been added in stages during the fermentation.

Many authors recommend summing all the incremental gravity drops recorded as fermentation proceeds, but this method will give a completely meaningless result unless corrections are applied throughout for the volume changes which each addition of sugar or sugar syrup causes. A far superior procedure is to note the total weight of sugar, including natural sugar, which has been added per gallon of must during fermentation. The gravity corresponding to this weight of sugar per gallon is then easily evaluated by reference to the sugar/gravity tables. If the wine is dry (if it contains 1% or less residual sugar by Clinitest), its alcoholic strength will, of course, be given directly by the figure in the potential alcohol column of the table. Otherwise, its alcohol content must be calculated as before by dividing the total gravity drop by 7.4. In this case, the initial gravity uncorrected for non-sugar solutes is required so that 7 must be added to the initial gravity obtained in the above manner from the sugar/gravity tables since the latter only give corrected figures. Alternatively, 7 may be subtracted from the final measured gravity to achieve the same result. The point is that both the initial and the final gravity figures must either be corrected or uncorrected for non-sugar solutes to evaluate the true gravity drop.

The following example will perhaps help to clarify these remarks. Three gallons of must were found to have a measured gravity of 57. The corrected gravity is thus 50 which corresponds to 21½ ozs. natural sugar per gallon. The total weight of natural sugar supplied by the ingredients is therefore about 4 lbs. A total of 11 lbs. sugar was subsequently added to the must during fermentation and the final volume of wine produced was 5 gallons. Hence, 15 lbs. sugar were added in 5 gallons of wine giving a sugar content of 3 lbs. per gallon. From the tables this weight of sugar per gallon can be seen to correspond to a corrected gravity of 115.

If the wine finishes dry, then its alcoholic strength is given directly by the potential alcohol column of the table as 18.3% by volume. Should some unfermented sugar remain, however, the alcohol content of the wine must be calculated from the total gravity drop. The initial corrected gravity of the must is 115 so that its uncorrected gravity will be about

122 (115 + 7). Its final gravity was found to be 12, thereby giving a total gravity drop of 110. On dividing the latter by 7.4, the alcoholic strength of the wine is discovered to be 14.9% by volume. Had the final gravity been -5 (specific gravity 0.995), the total drop would have been 127 which corresponds to an alcohol content of 17.2% by volume.

Several authorities on winemaking have correctly pointed out that the use of a single factor such as 7.4 for the preceding type of calculation is not entirely satisfactory. The figure of 7.4 should really be applied only over a limited range of gravity drops and initial gravities if it is to provide even a reasonably reliable indication of the alcoholic strength of a wine. Outside this range the accuracy of the results obtained with a single factor becomes progressively poorer. Indeed, strictly speaking, a different factor should be employed according to the initial gravity of the must if the winemaker wishes to reduce errors to a minimum.

Fortunately, a relatively simple formula has been derived to allow the winemaker to calculate the factor F which should be applied to a must whose initial corrected gravity is G in order to evaluate the alcoholic strength of the finished wine from the magnitude of the gravity drop experienced during fermentation. The requisite factor F is first determined from the equation given below, then the gravity drop is divided by F to obtain the alcoholic content of the wine. For convenience, the values of F corresponding to a given initial corrected gravity have been tabulated and will be found in the accompanying table for quick reference.

$$F = 7.75 - \frac{3G}{800}$$

The procedure to follow is perhaps best illustrated by an example. Thus, a must with an initial corrected gravity of 110 finished with a final uncorrected gravity of 2, thereby giving a total gravity drop of 115 (7 is added to the difference between the initial and final gravities above since one is corrected for non-sugar solutes and the other is not). From the table, the factor F corresponding to an initial gravity of 110 can be seen to be 7.34. Hence, the alcohol content of the wine is 115 divided by 7.34, or about 15.7% by volume.

The hydrometer does not permit an entirely accurate determination of the alcoholic strength of a wine because the perturbing effects of non-sugar solutes, alcohol and so on do not permit exact measurement of the initial and final sugar contents of the wine.

INITIAL GRAVITY/ALCOHOL FACTOR TABLES

Initial Corrected Gravity G	Factor F	Initial Corrected Gravity G	Factor F
5	7.73	85	7.43
10	7.71	90	7.41
15	7.69	95	7.39
20	7.67	100	7.37
25	7.66	105	7.35
30	7.64	110	7.34
35	7.62	115	7.32
40	7.60	120	7.30
45	7.58	125	7.28
50	7.56	130	7.26
55	7.54	135	7.24
60	7.52	140	7.22
65	7.50	145	7.20
70	7.49	150	7.19
75	7.47	155	7.17
80	7.45	160	7.15

It must nevertheless be admitted that the results obtained in this way compare surprisingly favourably with those obtained using much more elaborate and costly equipment such as the ebullioscope. Indeed, the agreement is often so close that the figures are within ± 0.5% of each other, especially when the alcoholic strength lies around 10%—14% by volume which is the range encountered in table wine production. The winemaker can therefore be reasonably sure that alcohol contents determined with the aid of the hydrometer will be fairly close to the true value (probably within 0.5%), and this degree of precision and accuracy will certainly be adequate for all practical purposes.

As a final application, it is worth noting that the hydrometer is sometimes used as a rough guide in the classification of wines. Many shows have a regulation stating that a dry wine should have a gravity of 0 or less, a medium sweet wine a gravity in the range of 1–14 inclusive and a sweet wine a gravity of 15 or more. These ranges do no more than provide a very approximate indication of the nature of the wine, however, for it has already been mentioned that the final gravity of a wine is a very unreliable index of its sugar content. For example, a wine low in alcohol may contain sufficient sugar to give a final gravity of 2, yet it may be drier than a much stronger wine whose gravity is −2 (specific gravity 0.998). The alcoholic strength of a wine cannot be ignored in this connection. Hence, it is far better to define a dry wine as a wine dry to the taste and containing 1% or less sugar as determined with a "Clinitest" sugar testing kit. The introduction of table wine classes will also help to resolve this difficulty since a table wine need not be completely dry but may equally well be medium dry as are many of the white wines from the Graves region of Bordeaux. Sweet wines would then be entered in dessert or after dinner wine classes.

CHAPTER IV

SUGAR

SUGAR is an essential basic constituent of all wine musts, its importance being due, of course, to the fact that it is fermented by yeast into alcohol and carbon dioxide. In the commercial field, ample natural sugar to produce a wine containing at least 10% alcohol by volume is usually present in the grape juice, so that professional winemakers rarely need to augment the natural sugar content of their musts. Amateur winemakers are less fortunate, however, for the great majority of their ingredients are deficient in sugar. Moreover, fruit juices and the like commonly require dilution with water prior to fermentation for one reason or another, e.g. to reduce their acidity, with the result that the natural sugar content of the must, which is already low, is decreased still further in this way. It is therefore extremely common to find that the bulk of the sugar in amateur musts does not come from the ingredients but instead is added by the winemaker.

Since amateur winemaking depends upon the fermentation of added sugar to provide much of the alcohol in the wines, it is clearly not only useful but also advisable to have at least some basic information on this subject. Such vexed questions as the relative merits of cane-sugar and invert sugar may then be sensibly discussed and evaluated.

The unqualified word sugar is generally taken to refer to household canoe-sugar, otherwise known as sucrose. It may therefore come as a surprise to some winemakers to learn that sugar is really a generic term used to describe a very large number of chemically closely related substances. Most sugars are composed of only the three elements carbon, hydrogen and oxygen whose chemical symbols are C, H and O respectively. In addition, the composition of many sugars corresponds to the empirical formula $(C.H_2O)_n$. Early workers in this field concluded from this data that the sugars were hydrates of carbon and hence called them carbohydrates. Although this latter description was later proved to be erroneous (sugars are not hydrates of carbon!), by that time the term had become so firmly entrenched that it was allowed to stand. Thus, even today, carbohydrate chemistry means the study of sugars.

It has already been mentioned that many different sugars have been discovered. While their chemistry is complex, their classification is relatively straightforward. For example, simple sugars are collectively known as monosaccharides and are further sub-divided according to the number of carbon atoms in the molecule. Hexoses (6), pentoses (5) and tetroses (4) are three such sub-classes of monosaccharides, the figures in parentheses indicating the number of carbon atoms per molecule of sugar. More complex sugars are formed by the combination of two or more monosaccharides (which may be the same or different) and are called polysaccharides. The prefix "poly" actually means "many" and it may be replaced by the more definite prefixes "di-," "tri-," "tetra-" and so on according to the number of monosaccharide residues the carbohydrate contains. Other indefinite names such as oligosaccharides—"oligo" meaning "a few"—may also be encountered.

This terminology may be better illustrated by its application to some of the sugars important in winemaking. Thus, glucose and fructose are both hexose monosaccharides represented by the formula $C_6H_{12}O_6$. Sucrose is a disaccharide formed when one molecule each of glucose and fructose combine. Its chemical formula is $C_{12}H_{22}O_{11}$, however, because a molecule of water (H_2O) is eliminated during its formation from the two parent hexoses. Maltose is another disaccharide, important in beer production, with the same formula as sucrose but obtained by linking two glucose units together. The only other carbohydrate worth mentioning here is starch which is a polysaccharide formed by the condensation of a large number of glucose residues. Its formula may conveniently be written as $C_{6n}H_{10n+2}O_{5n+1}$ where *n* is a large number. Dextrins are partly degraded starch molecules in which the value of *n* is smaller than for starch itself, and are obtained together with maltose (for which

$n=2$) when the diastase in malt acts on the starch therein during the preparation of beer worts.

The observant reader will doubtless have already noticed that the same chemical formula has been used to represent more than one sugar. This apparently anomalous situation arises because carbohydrates have very large complicated molecules whose properties depend much more upon their structure than upon their chemical formula. Each sugar possesses its own unique structure and thus differs in its behaviour from any other sugar whose chemical formula happens to be identical. This latter similarity is only of secondary importance. Indeed, compounds with the same formula but different structures are by no means encountered solely among the carbohydrates but are very common throughout organic chemistry. Such substances are said to be isomers and the phenomenon itself is called isomerism.

The winemaker is perhaps fortunate in some respects that the yeasts employed for winemaking purposes can only ferment a few specific carbohydrates. It does at least restrict the choice of sugar to use to a limited number and minimises arguments as to which of these is the best! The three monosaccharide hexoses glucose, fructose and mannose are fermented with great ease and another hexose, galactose, is metabolised with some difficulty. The allied disaccharides sucrose and maltose are also readily accepted because the enzyme system possessed by yeast cells can split or hydrolyse these sugars into their fermentable monosaccharide components. Certain oligosaccharides, notably rhamnose, can be partly or even completely utilised by the yeast for the same reason, but higher polysaccharides such as starch cannot be metabolised because the cells have no enzymes capable of effecting their degradation to more amenable simpler sugars.

This inability of yeast to ferment all types of sugars can at times be turned to good account. It is often desirable to sweeten a wine or beer slightly yet at the same time avoid the danger of an inconvenient refermentation which is quite likely to occur if a sugar such as sucrose is added. This problem can be neatly solved by using a little lactose as the sweetening agent since this sugar is not utilised by yeast and can be purchased without difficulty. Its only disadvantage is that its sweetening power is rather inferior to sucrose. Arabinose, a pentose, may also be used for this purpose with advantage, but unfortunately it is not usually readily available.

The attitudes of commercial and amateur winemakers differ very radically insofar as the subject of adding sugar to a must is concerned. The reason is, of course, that the professional rarely needs to do so whereas exactly the opposite is normally true for the amateur. Indeed, in commercial wine production, the addition of sugar to a must, or chaptalisation as it is often called, is regarded very much as a last resort to be practised only when the grapes have failed to ripen fully and their juice contains too little natural sugar to permit its direct conversion into wine. Even then, however, the amount of sugar which may be added is strictly limited by law to prevent abuses, and the fact that chaptalisation has proved necessary must also usually be disclosed. It follows that such sugared wines are mainly encountered in the cooler northern regions of Europe, especially Germany, following a cold wet summer.

Sucrose is almost certainly the most widely used sugar for both amateur and commercial wine production, probably because it combines the virtues of being cheap, readily available and easily utilised by the yeast. It is extracted from either sugar-cane or sugar-beet. Although the extraction processes and impurities removed during refining differ according to which raw material is used, the final product is identical in both cases. Formerly, the sugar obtained from cane was much preferable to that produced from beet because the latter was blue in colour and less pure due to the presence of persistent contaminants. Nowadays, howe er, improved refining techniques have overcome this obstacle so that no differences can be detected between cane and beet sugar. Indeed, much of the sucrose now on the market is a mixture of the two types. The container may say "pure cane-sugar," but chemically cane-sugar is synonymous with sucrose so that its contents may come from any source as long as they are in fact pure sucrose. Demerara, brown and other such sugars are also sucrose, but their purity is lower than that of white household sugar.

It can be stated quite categorically at this point that sucrose may be supplied as the sole source of sugar for any of the musts and yeasts used in winemaking. The ordinary white household sugar (granulated) is usually preferable because it has no significant effect on the colour and flavour of the wine, and, of course, because it is cheap. Demerara sugar may also be employed, but it should then be remembered that this grade of sucrose will modify the flavour of the wine to some extent and deepen its colour to a golden yellow.

Wines whose principal ingredients are vegetables or which are intended to resemble madeiras often benefit if part or even all the sugar added to the must is Demerara. Otherwise, its higher cost and influence on the character of the wine do not favour its general use. Brown sugar, molasses and the like (and to a lesser extent golden syrup) are on the whole unsuitable for winemaking since their flavour tends to come out too strongly in the wine, which consequently lacks delicacy and finesse. Any recipes which recommend these grades of sugar are either best avoided entirely or an equal weight of household sugar employed instead.

The winemaker will occasionally come across references to candy, loaf, lump, preserving and similarly qualified white sugars. For example, many old recipes specify the use of candy sugar which is nowadays stocked almost exclusively by amateur winemaking suppliers because it is in very small demand for any other purpose. The reason these recipes call for candy sugar is that at the time they were devised this form of sugar was the purest form available. Today, of course, the picture is entirely different because modern refining techniques produce a grade of ordinary granulated household sugar whose purity is extremely high. Hence, since candy, loaf and other similar types of white sugar are essentially only different, though often more expensive, types of household sugar, their replacement by the latter is usually both more convenient and cheaper and will certainly not have any noticeable effect on the quality of the wine.

Household sugar and for that matter any other grade of sucrose, invert sugar and honey should preferably be employed in the form of syrup rather than being added directly to the must. The reason is simply that any sugar must be dissolved and mixed thoroughly with the bulk of the must, especially when it is added during fermentation, to prevent some from settling to the bottom of the container and there forming a layer of solid sugar and/or saturated sugar solution. Such an occurrence can often prove quite detrimental because the high concentration of sugar in the must immediately surrounding the yeast deposit can seriously impair its activity and may even cause fermentation to stick.

The use of sugar syrup instead of solid sugar helps to eliminate this risk since the sugar is already in solution and need only be blended with the rest of the must by vigorous stirring. A syrup of gravity 300 is ideal for this purpose and can be prepared very easily by adding 2 lbs. granulated sugar to 1 pint water, bringing the mixture to the boil and boiling it for a few moments until the solution becomes quite clear. The syrup, should, of course, be allowed to cool before being used. Since 2 lbs. sugar occupies the same volume as 1 pint water, each pint of the syrup contains 1 lb. sugar which makes it easy to calculate how much sugar syrup must be added to supply a given weight of sugar.

It has already been mentioned that sucrose can be utilised by yeast because its enzyme system can split or hydrolyse this disaccharide into its two monosaccharide components glucose and fructose. The enzyme responsible for this hydrolysis is called invertase. Since yeast happens to be particularly well endowed with invertase, remarks made by certain speakers at wine circle meetings to the effect that it cannot readily ferment sucrose are obviously complete fiction. Maltose is similarly degraded into glucose by invertase which explains why beer worts are fermentable. Here, of course, the maltose is obtained during mashing when the diastase produced by malting acts on the starch in the barley grains.

The true situation is actually rather more complex than the above ideas suggest because aqueous solutions of sucrose slowly hydrolyse into glucose and fructose of their own accord. Invertase enormously increases the rate of this spontaneous reaction, but so too do both acids and bases, through the agency of their hydrogen ions H^+ or hydroxyl ions OH^-. Since all wine musts contain a small amount of acid, it follows that this acid-catalysed hydrolysis will supplement the action of the invertase to an extent depending upon the acidity, or more correctly, upon the pH of the must. The lower is its pH, the greater will become the rate of hydrolysis induced in this way. Although the bulk of the sucrose in a must will generally be degraded by the more rapidly acting invertase, the activity of this enzyme may be somewhat reduced at low pH values. A significant proportion of the sucrose may then be converted into glucose and fructose by acid catalysis. The point is that sucrose can be utilised by the yeast under any normal conditions encountered in a wine must, even if its pH is sufficiently low to inhibit the activity of invertase to some degree. Moreover, the hydrolysis of the sucrose is generally complete long before the glucose and fructose formed in this way can be fermented into alcohol. The use of sucrose does not therefore result in slower fermentations as is sometimes claimed.

$$\underset{\text{Sucrose}}{C_{12}H_{22}O_{11}} + \underset{\text{Water}}{H_2O} \xrightarrow[\text{and/or } H^+ \text{ions}]{\text{Invertase}} \underset{\text{Glucose}}{C_6H_{12}O_6} + \underset{\text{Fructose}}{C_6H_{12}O_6}$$

The hydrolysis of sucrose to glucose and fructose illustrated in the preceding equation is often referred to as the inversion of cane-sugar. Since the origin of this term puzzles many winemakers and is closely related to the subject of invert sugar which will be discussed next, the explanation may be conveniently dealt with at this juncture.

The key to the problem lies in the optical properties of carbohydrate solutions, all of which possess the peculiar ability of rotating the plane of a beam of plane-polarised light either to the right or to the left. For example, an aqueous solution of sucrose does so strongly to the right and is thus said to be a dextrorotatory or a d-sugar solution. Glucose is also a d-sugar in aqueous solution, but it is less powerfully dextrorotatory than sucrose. Fructose solutions, on the other hand, are very strongly laevorotatory and rotate the plane of plane-polarised light far to the left. In other words, fructose forms an l-sugar solution. The names dextrose and laevulose, by which glucose and fructose respectively were formerly known, originated as a direct result of their optical properties.

The reasons for calling the hydrolysis of sucrose its inversion now begin to become clear. The initial sucrose solution is dextrorotatory, but as more and more sucrose is converted into glucose and fructose the very powerful laevorotatory properties of the latter exert a progressively more noticeable influence on the optical rotation of the solution. The combined dextrorotatory effects of the glucose and the residual sucrose are insufficient to compensate for that of the powerfully laevorotatory fructose so that the solution gradually becomes less strongly dextrorotatory as hydrolysis proceeds, and its inversion point is reached when no optical rotation at all is observed. Thereafter, the solution becomes progressively more laevorotatory until hydrolysis is complete. This reaction is therefore called the inversion of sucrose simply because the direction of the optical rotation of the solution becomes inverted during the hydrolysis.

It follows from this explanation that invert sugar is merely a mixture comprising equal weights of glucose and fructose. Indeed, a great deal of the invert sugar on the commercial market is produced by hydrolysing sucrose with acid, removing the acid once the reaction is complete and finally concentrating the solution by evaporation. Since the complete removal of the water in this final stage is a matter of great practical difficulty, invert sugar prepared in this way usually contains about 20% water of crystallisation. It is still a solid, of course, but 1 lb. of the material only contains 0.8 lb. of glucose and fructose, the rest being water. Allowance must therefore be made for this fact when purchased invert sugar is used for winemaking purposes.

A great deal of nonsense has been spoken and written about invert sugar. Several prominent winemakers have asserted it is preferable to sucrose because it is completely fermentable, which is a meaningless statement since the same applies to sucrose. A few winemakers have said that sucrose is converted into harmful by-products as well as alcohol during fermentation. This idea is also too ridiculous for words. The truth of the matter is that the yeast immediately proceeds to invert any sucrose added to the must and thereafter fermentation continues exactly as it would were inverted sugar introduced in the first instance.

Experiments have shown that invert sugar offers no advantage over sucrose regarding either the rate of fermentation, the degree of attenuation or the quality of the finished wine. In one case, a must was divided into two parts which were subsequently treated identically except that invert sugar was added to one part and sucrose to the other. No difference in bouquet, flavour, clarity and so on could be detected between the two wines even after a long period of maturing. It may therefore be concluded that nothing will be gained by using invert sugar instead of sucrose since the two are to all intents and purposes equivalent for winemaking purposes.

Despite these remarks, some winemakers will doubtless continue to prefer adding invert sugar to their musts and those who wish to do so can certainly rest assured that no detrimental effects on quality will thereby result. Nor, on the other hand, will any advantage be gained! Invert sugar may be purchased directly, but if this is the case the 20% water content must not be overlooked when calculating how much should be added to a must. Alternatively, a solution of sucrose may be prepared and inverted by boiling it with a little tartaric acid for a short time. In this instance, of course, every pound of sucrose added will give an equivalent weight of invert sugar which will simplify matters when estimating the sugar requirements of a must.

It may be of interest to note here that exponents of invert sugar commonly argue that yeast in its natural habitat lives in fruit juices which are complex solutions of invert sugar. Although it is true that all or most of the sugar in many fruit juices is invert sugar, there are also many fruits in which this is not the case. For example, plums contain roughly equal amounts of invert sugar and sucrose while peaches contain almost entirely sucrose. Nevertheless, some of the more important sources of natural sugar commonly employed in winemaking, e.g. grape concentrate and raisins do contain mainly invert sugar.

Honey is another source of invert sugar which does have a real advantage over sucrose or other forms of invert sugar. Its superiority is not due to the fact that it is a solution of invert sugar, but to its containing small amounts of beneficial substances other than sugars. Pollen grains, trace elements, floral esters and the like all have some influence on the bouquet and flavour and help to create a smoother, richer and altogether more harmonious wine. Honey can often replace part and sometimes, at the discretion of the winemaker, even all of the sugar which would normally be added to a must. The inclusion of some honey will almost invariably prove beneficial and many outstanding wines owe their greatness at least partly to the judicious use of this ingredient. There is consequently a great deal to be said for advocating a much wider use of honey by amateur winemakers than is now the case, despite its relatively high cost in comparison to sugar.

The question then arises as to which type of honey is best, and here some general advice can be offered. Very few honeys are unsuitable for winemaking, but one which should be avoided at all costs is Australian eucalyptus honey. Many Australian honeys are satisfactory for winemaking, but some is produced from eucalyptus flowers whose flavour is not especially apparent in the honey where it is effectively masked by the sugar, but it is immediately and unpleasantly obvious even in a sweet wine. As a result, Australian eucalyptus honey can ruin a wine completely by introducing a strong unconcealable eucalyptus flavour. British honeys are excellent but expensive for winemaking purposes, although heather honey must be used with caution due to its strong flavour. Canadian clover and other imported honeys, notably acacia blossom honey, now on sale in this country are also excellent and many are much cheaper than the domestic article, a feature which commends their use.

The important point to bear in mind when employing honey is to choose a honey whose character is in keeping with that of the wine. Thus, only light delicately flavoured honeys such as clover should be used for producing light white wines. Darker, full-flavoured honeys should be reserved for heavier sweeter wines, especially red wines of this type. A light honey may, of course, be selected for any purpose should this be more convenient, but it is often worth experimenting to find out which type will best suit a particular wine. As far as the amount to add is concerned, it is generally accepted that 5 lbs. honey are equivalent to 4 lbs. sucrose, and it makes no difference whether the honey is liquid or crystalline.

There is one final feature of honey to which more attention should always be paid. Because honey is prepared by insects from the nectar and pollen of flowers, it cannot logically be expected to be free from undesirable micro-organisms unless it has been pasteurised prior to packing. Indeed, unpasteurised honeys can readily be shown to contain many different species of yeasts, bacteria and the like, notably wild yeasts and acetifying bacteria. It is usually recommended to boil in water for at least ten minutes any honey not definitely known to be pasteurised already to kill any spoilage organisms which may be present. Equal quantities of honey and water should be used for this purpose as higher concentrations of honey tend to froth badly on boiling. A larger ratio of water to honey will further reduce this risk, but often it is preferable to keep the volume of honey syrup to a minimum. The syrup should, of course, be allowed to cool to room temperature before being added to an actively fermenting must. The use of sulphite to kill undesirable micro-organisms in honey is definitely preferable to boiling, however as the wine then has a far better bouquet and flavour.

The ingredients used to prepare a must can at times be an important source of sugar which should never be overlooked. The amount of sugar supplied by the ingredients can usually be ascertained by means of the hydrometer, but it is as well to know in advance how much sugar can be expected from certain very widely used ingredients. Grape concentrate and raisins or sultanas are perhaps the most notable examples in this category. The winemaker should therefore endeavour to remember that 1 pint of grape concentrate is roughly equivalent to 1 lb. sugar and 5 lbs. raisins or sultanas to about 3 lbs. sugar. It is also worth noting that 50%–70% of the weight of most dried fruits is sugar, e.g. the figure for raisins is 60% although for sugary raisins it may be as high as 70%.

A final word may be said about determining small amounts of sugar in a wine, a task which the hydrometer is unable to perform for reasons fully discussed in the chapter devoted to this instrument. All reducing sugars such as glucose, fructose and maltose, but not sucrose, react quantitatively with a reagent called Fehling's solution which is consequently widely used to determine these carbohydrates whenever the need arises. Although the normal analytical procedure is fairly simple, it requires equipment well beyond the means of most amateur winemakers. Fortunately, a pocket kit based upon this method and called the "Clinitest" has now been developed and is available from "Boots" for 50p. Admittedly, it was specifically designed for diabetics, but it can serve the purposes of amateur winemakers equally well!

Since the "Clinitest" enables winemakers to measure how much sugar there is in a wine up to a maximum of 2% sugar, it is clearly a useful complement to the hydrometer. Actually, of course, the "Clinitest" can be employed to determine sugar contents above 2% if the sample is first suitably diluted with water. Most wines, even the driest, will normally give a slightly positive result (about 0.25%) due to the presence of unfermentable pentoses and the like, but if the "Clinitest" indicates more than about 0.25% sugar it is reasonably certain some residual unfermented sugar remains.

In conclusion, it may also be noted that the "Clinitest" offers an ideal solution to the vexed problem of what constitutes a dry wine. The latter may now be specifically and correctly defined as a wine dry to the palate which contains 1% or less sugar by "Clinitest."

CHAPTER V

ACIDITY

IT is only in comparatively recent years that amateur winemakers have begun to realise how prominent a part the acid content of a must or wine plays in determining wine quality. There can now be little doubt that the relatively low quality of many wines exhibited at some National and other shows is at least partly due to inadequate acidity control. A wine simply cannot attain top quality unless it has a good acid balance, although the latter is, of course, insufficient in itself to guarantee a superior wine. Even more important, however, is the fact that acidity adjustments should always be made at the time the must is prepared or as soon as possible thereafter since any attempts to do so once fermentation has ceased may very well fail to promote any real improvement. In particular, fermentation should never be allowed to proceed when the must contains little or no acid, otherwise strange and persistent off-flavours, which no subsequent efforts to balance the acidity of the wine will succeed in eliminating, are likely to develop during fermentation. A thorough understanding of acidity and its implications is therefore an essential prerequisite if the winemaker wishes to achieve a consistently high average standard of quality.

Many of the problems encountered in connection with acidity can be traced to the use of recipes which were largely designed at a time when little was known about the significance of the acids found in musts and wines. Admittedly, recipes often do make some attempt to provide a wine with a reasonably well-balanced acid content by adding citrus fruits to the must and/or by diluting it with water, but even at best these procedures can hardly be expected to permit an effective degree of control in this direction. Few recipes are sufficiently flexible to take into account the wide variations to which the amount of acid in many common ingredients, especially fruits, is subject. Hence, even winemakers who are content to rely entirely upon recipes cannot afford to neglect the subject of acidity and still hope to produce a high proportion of superior wines every year.

All musts and wines are mildly acid in character because the ingredients used for their production contain small quantities of certain organic acids collectively known as the plant acids. The latter are considered to be weak acids because they ionise only incompletely and reversibly in aqueous solutions, and consequently differ radically from such strong and fully ionised mineral acids as sulphuric acid. As their name implies, the plant acids are found in all types of green vegetation where one of their most important functions concerns their participation in the Krebs cycle upon which the basic processes of plant respiration depend. The distribution of these acids throughout a plant nevertheless shows quite pronounced variations. Thus, fruits seems to concentrate plant acids to an extent rarely encountered elsewhere. Roots, stems, leaves, seeds and so on all possess their own quota of plant acids, but in comparison with fruits the amounts found in these parts of the plant are negligibly small. It follows that amateur winemakers need only be concerned with fruits when considering the acid supplied to the must by its ingredients, for root vegetables, flowers, grain and the like contain so little acid that their contribution in this direction may be quite safely ignored.

Although a very large number of plant acids have been isolated, the winemaker is really interested only in citric, malic and tartaric acids which are the three members of this group most extensively found in fruits. To simplify matters even further, the majority of fruits usually contain significant amounts of only one or sometimes two of these acids, and the following table lists the principal acid occurring in some common fruits.

Thus, the main acid in lemons and citrus fruits generally is citric acid, in apples it is malic acid and in ripe grapes it is tartaric acid. Rhubarb, strictly a leaf petiole but popularly regarded as a fruit, is exceptional in that its major acid

Principal Acid Present in Some Common Fruits

Principal Acid	Name of Fruit
CITRIC ACID	Bananas, Black, Red and White Currants, Elderberries, Grapefruit, Lemons, Limes, Loganberries, Oranges, Pears, Pineapples, Raspberries, Strawberries, Tangerines.
MALIC ACID	Apricots, Apples, Blackberries, Bullaces, Cherries, Damsons, Greengages, Gooseberries, Nectarines, Peaches, Plums, Rhubarb, Rowanberries, Sloes.
TARTARIC ACID	Grapes, Raisins, Sultanas.

NOTES. Many fruits whose principal acid is citric acid also contain significant amounts of malic acid and vice-versa.

Rhubarb contains a small amount of oxalic acid although malic acid predominates.

Grapes are unusual in that tartaric acid is commonly the principal acid, but considerable amounts of malic acid are also usually present and the latter may actually at times predominate, especially in grapes which have not ripened fully.

---

component, malic acid, is accompanied by a very small proportion of the poisonous oxalic acid. Other plant acids which deserve some mention here because they are present in wine as fermentation by-products include succinic acid and lactic acid, but it should be noted that very little of these substances is supplied by the actual ingredients of the must.

There are many sound reasons why acid control should be adopted as a standard practice in amateur winemaking, but the fact that all fruits do not contain the same fixed amount of acid is one of the most important. The acid content of fruits first of all depends upon their type and variety, for it is obvious that such fruits as bananas and oranges or cooking and dessert apples differ radically in this respect. The degree of ripeness is also a prominent factor, and as a general rule the riper a fruit is the more sugar and the less acid it will contain. Hence, most fruits should not be picked or used for winemaking purposes until they are fully ripe and the optimum sugar/acid balance has been reached. Two exceptions to this rule are worth mentioning here. Gooseberries are better employed for table wine production in the unripe green condition when their acid content is high and before a strong gooseberry flavour has developed. Pears have also been found to make a finer flavoured perry or wine if they are picked and pressed before attaining full ripeness but are at the stage commonly termed "firm ripe."

The composition and condition of the soil and related growth factors obviously have a profound effect upon the quality and hence on the acidity of fruits grown therein. Variations in the acid content of different batches of the same fruit coming from several localities can often be attributed to this cause. Weather conditions and climate also contribute greatly in this direction. Indeed, the influence of climatic factors on the acidity of fruits grown in different parts of the country and/or in successive years may be very pronounced. The weather may be much better in one area than in another so that a corresponding difference in quality will be observed in the fruits from the two regions. A poor summer can be disastrous because it means that many fruits then fail to ripen fully and consequently contain considerably more acid and less sugar in that year than is normally the case. In view of the unpredictable nature of the British climate and the wide range of soil profiles found throughout the country, it is easy to see that relatively large local and annual fluctuations in the acidity of indigenous fruits must be expected as a matter of course. Some indication of the extent to which the acid content of fruits may vary can be gleaned from the atble on the opposite page showing the acidity range quoted in the literature for a number of fruits.

It follows from these remarks that the only safe way of ensuring that a wine has a good acid balance is to determine how much acid is present in the fruit juices or must from which it is produced. Any alteration to the acid content of the must which may prove necessary can then be made

Typical Acid and Sugar Content of some Common Fruit Juices		
Fruit Juice	Acid Content p.p.t.	Sugar Content %
Apple (Dessert)	1.0– 6.5	9.0–15.0
Apricot	6.0–15.0	4.0–11.0
Black Cherry (Sweet)	3.5– 7.0	9.0–18.0
Elderberry	6.0–15.0	7.0– 9.0
Grape	2.0–12.0	15.0–25.0
Orange (Bitter)	10.0–35.0	2.0– 7.0
Peach	3.0–10.0	6.0–12.0
Pear (Dessert)	1.0– 3.5	7.0–13.0
Rowanberry	15.0–25.0	2.5– 6.5
Sloe	18.0–25.0	7.0–12.0

Notes: All acidities in this table are expressed as p.p.t. of sulphuric acid. The reader should note that most of these figures have been taken from the literature on the subject and are only typical ranges, so that acid or sugar contents outside the limits quoted above may occasionally be encountered. This table is therefore only meant to serve as a general guide.

prior to or at least early in the fermentation when its maximum benefit will be achieved with the minimum danger of adversely affecting the quality of the wine. Such adjustments should in fact always be carried out at the earliest opportunity for this reason and certainly not delayed until fermentation is nearing completion or the wine is maturing.

Experienced winemakers usually regard checking the acidity of their must as a routine procedure. It is certainly not difficult to do so by chemical analysis; the procedure can be completed in a matter of minutes once the elementary experimental technique has been mastered, a task which very few winemakers should find beyond their capabilities.

This method determines what is usually termed the titratable acidity of the must. Surprisingly enough, it is commonly expressed as parts per thousand (p.p.t.) of sulphuric acid, a substance which is not a normal constituent of wines and which should certainly never be added to a must. In this instance, however, sulphuric acid is simply acting as a convenient reference standard or scale of measurement and has no other significance. One reason for selecting sulphuric acid as the reference standard here was that it is widely used in Europe for this purpose, but several acids may in fact serve in this capacity. For example, acidity is often expressed as parts per thousand tartaric acid in America, while several books on amateur winemaking refer to parts per thousand citric acid. To avoid confusion, it is clear that amateur winemakers should settle definitely upon one acid as their reference standard and then keep to it. All acidities in this book will therefore be quoted as p.p.t. of sulphuric acid unless otherwise stated.

For convenience, however, the table below lists acidities in p.p.t. sulphuric acid together with the corresponding

CORRESPONDING ACIDITIES IN PARTS PER THOUSAND OF VARIOUS ACIDS

Sulphuric Acid	Citric Acid	Malic Acid	Tartaric Acid
0.5	0.72	0.69	0.77
1.0	1.43	1.37	1.53
1.5	2.14	2.03	2.29
2.0	2.86	2.74	3.06
2.5	3.58	3.42	3.83
3.0	4.29	4.10	4.59
3.5	5.01	4.78	5.36
4.0	5.72	5.47	6.12
4.5	6.44	6.15	6.89
5.0	7.15	6.84	7.65
5.5	7.87	7.52	8.42
6.0	8.58	8.21	9.19
6.5	9.30	8.89	9.96
7.0	10.0	9.58	10.7
7.5	10.7	10.3	11.5
8.0	11.4	10.9	12.2
8.5	12.1	11.6	13.0
9.0	12.9	12.3	13.8
9.5	13.6	13.0	14.6
10.0	14.3	13.7	15.3

values in p.p.t. citric, malic and tartaric acids so that the winemaker can convert from one scale to another should the need to do so arise. Thus, it can be seen from this table that 3.5 p.p.t. sulphuric acid is the same as 5.01 p.p.t. citric acid or 4.78 p.p.t. malic acid or 5.36 p.p.t. tartaric acid.

Determining Titratable Acidity

Apparatus
- 1 × 25 mls. burette graduated in 0.1 mls. divisions.
- 1 × 10 mls. pipette
- 2 × 100 mls. conical flasks
- A burette stand is a useful optional extra.

Reagents
- Decinormal (0.1N) sodium hydroxide solution.
- Distilled water.
- 1% solution of phenolphthalein in methylated spirits.
- The sodium hydroxide solution should always be kept in a sealed bottle otherwise it will slowly absorb carbon dioxide from the air and thus decrease in strength.

Procedure: Take a small but representative sample (say 100 mls.) of the must or wine, suck a little into the pipette to rinse it out and discard these washings. Controlling the level of liquid in the pipette by means of the index finger, transfer a 10 mls. sample of must or wine to each of the two conical flasks. This operation may require a little practice to master the technique. Add to each conical flask about 25 mls. distilled water and three drops of the phenolphthalein indicator solution. Double this amount of distilled water should be added to strongly coloured samples e.g. red wines.

Rinse out the burette with the sodium hydroxide solution, discard the washings then fill up the burette and zero it, making sure that the part between the outlet jet and the stopcock is also filled with alkali and not with an air bubble. Titrate the solution in one of the flasks with the sodium hydroxide solution in the burette, adding the latter fairly slowly and swirling the contents of the flask continuously until the first faint but permanent pink colour which marks the end-point is observed. A vivid pink colour indicates that the end-point has been overshot to some extent. Note the volume of sodium hydroxide required in the titration.

Refill the burette and again zero it. Repeat the above procedure with the solution in the second conical flask and note the volume of alkali required for this titration.

Take the average of these two results. The acidity of the must or wine expressed as parts per thousand (p.p.t.) of sulphuric acid is then ONE-HALF of this mean value. For example, two samples of a wine must required 7.9 mls. and 8.1 mls. respectively of sodium hydroxide solution, giving an average titration figure of 8.0 mls. The acidity of this must is therefore 4.0 p.p.t.

NOTES : Although the colour change is most readily seen when the solution in the flask has little or no colour of its own, little added difficulty is normally experienced when analysing more deeply coloured musts or wines. The addition of 50 mls. instead of 25 mls. distilled water prior to titration (as recommended) usually dilutes the colour of the solution in the flask sufficiently to prevent masking the end-point. Red musts and wines pose rather more of a problem even when 50 mls. distilled water has been added. In most cases, however, the solution in the flask will assume a greyish or greenish tint shortly before the end-point is reached. The pink tint subsequently developing at the end-point can then usually be readily detected. Performing the titration in daylight rather than artificial light also helps to sharpen the colour change at the end-point.

Two determinations are always advisable for checking purposes. The two results should not differ by more than 0.5 mls., and with experience the winemaker will find that they will often agree to within 0.1 mls. A larger difference than 0.5 mls. indicates that some error has crept into the analysis. Further determinations should then be carried out until at least two results are within 0.5 mls. of each other. The average of these two figures should then be used to calculate the acidity.

A 5 mls. sample of must or wine can be employed instead of the recommended 10 mls. sample (this requires a 5 mls. pipette). In this case, the acidity is EQUAL to the average titration figure. The procedure here is the same as for a 10 mls. sample, but the accuracy of the determination is slightly less.

It is important to remember that the indicator phenolphthalein is sensitive to carbon dioxide and would not therefore give reliable results with fermenting musts or very young or sparkling wines unless steps are taken to remove the gas dissolved in these samples. Under these conditions, a small but accurately known volume of the must or wine, say 100 mls., should be taken and boiled for a few minutes. On cooling, it should then be readjusted to its original volume of 100 mls., with distilled water, and shaken vigorously to ensure a homogenous solution. The acidity of this de-gassed sample may then be checked in the normal way.

Once the acidity of a must has been determined by chemical analysis, steps can then be taken to adjust it to a level which will ensure a good acid balance unless, of course, it is already satisfactory in this respect. Although no exact correlation has been discovered between the titratable acidity and acid taste of a wine, it is generally recognised that a titratable acidity lying in the range 3.0–4.5 p.p.t. rarely fails to provide a satisfactory acid balance. Wines containing more than about 4.5 p.p.t. acid are not uncommonly found commercially, especially German hocks and moselles, but, as will be explained later, the amateur must take certain precautions to avoid obtaining an unduly acid flavour when attempting to produce such highly acid wines. The exact acidity at which to aim for a particular wine depends mainly upon the character of that wine and can best be judged on the basis of past experience.

As a general rule, however, a lower acidity is usually preferable for dry wines (3.0–4.0 p.p.t.) and a higher acidity for sweet wines (3.5–4.5 p.p.t.) because the sugar content of the latter often demands more acid should be used to achieve the optimum flavour balance, but these suggestions should merely be regarded as a guide and not interpreted too literally. Indeed, a good average acidity suitable for almost any type of wine is 3.5 p.p.t., and less experienced winemakers may initially find it advisable to stay close to these figures.

The acid content of wines which will be drunk young at an age of a few months should also be kept fairly low in the region of 3.0–3.5 p.p.t. since they will then be more palatable in a shorter time than would otherwise be the case.

Although the subject of pH is fully discussed in the next chapter, it is perhaps worth mentioning here that some winemakers advocate using the pH of a must as a means of assessing its acid balance. There can certainly be no question that the pH of a wine, which is a measure of its hydrogen ion concentration, does have some influence on its acid taste. Unfortunately, pH seems to be a much less reliable index in this respect than titratable acidity, possibly because the pH of a must depends markedly upon its composition whereas its titratable acidity does not. In addition, unless the winemaker happens to possess a pH-meter, the accuracy to which pH can be assessed leaves a great deal to be desired. Narrow range indicator papers are far too insensitive to be of any real service since any determination or adjustments made with their aid are at best accurate to about 0.3 pH unit.

It may therefore be concluded from these remarks that pH should never be employed instead of titratable acidity as the criterion on which to base acidity control. Even commercial winemakers, who deal almost exclusively with grape juice, subscribe to this view so that amateur winemakers with their incomparably wider choice of ingredients are well advised to follow this lead. In any case, pH control is often completely unnecessary because a must with a satisfactory titratable acidity quite frequently has a pH in the range 3.0–3.4 which is moderately close to the figure of 3.2 commonly considered to represent the optimum acid balance.

The winemaker will by now have gathered from what has already been said that the acid content of a must can vary very widely according to the type, quality and quantity of the ingredients used for its preparation. It is consequently hardly surprising that many musts possess a poor acid balance which may be due to either a deficiency or an excess of acid. Since neither of these defects is particularly conducive to good quality, the winemaker is frequently obliged to increase or decrease the amount of acid in the must to a more suitable level. The importance of doing so at the time the must is prepared or as soon as possible thereafter has already received attention and need not be discussed here again.

A deficiency of acid is most commonly encountered in musts prepared primarily from such ingredients as root vegetables, grain, flowers and the like which contain little acid of their own. Bananas and a few dried fruits, e.g. dates and figs, also come into this category. Too little acid can here have quite disastrous effects on wine quality. If fermentation is allowed to proceed in a must which lacks acid, curious off-flavours may develop. Indeed, in extreme cases, a peculiar and most unpleasant medicinal bouquet and flavour may predominate so that the final product bears more resemblance to a cough mixture than a wine. Little can be done to remedy matters once this late stage has been reached and there is then no real alternative but to discard the "wine." It may also be noted that a low acidity tends to favour the growth of moulds and bacteria and thus enhances the risk of spoilage occurring during storage.

These problems can very easily be avoided simply by increasing the acid content of the must to a more suitable level. Most books on amateur winemaking advise using citric acid for this purpose and their reasons for doing so apparently stem from the traditional practice of adding to the must the juice of lemons and/or other citrus fruits which are rich in this commodity. It has now been quite definitely established that citric acid alone does not give the best results. This conclusion is not altogether unexpected, however, for malic and tartaric acids would seem to be a much more logical choice for this application since both are important minor constituents of grapes whereas citric acid is not.

Tartaric acid is usually the major acid found in grape wines produced from fully ripe fruit. In small amounts (1–2 p.p.t.), it improves the keeping qualities of a wine, but if too much is present a hard sharp acid flavour will obtrude on the palate. The mono-potassium salt of tartaric acid, better known as cream of tartar, is less soluble in wines than in the unfermented must. Maturing wines containing cream of tartar thus tend to deposit this salt during storage and gradually build up a hard crystalline layer of tartrate on the walls and base of the container. This deposit constitutes the so-called wine stone or argols mentioned in many books on winemaking. Since this process occurs slowly over a long period of time, persistent hazes consisting of tiny crystals of cream of tartar in suspension may be observed in the wine until the excess tartrate has all been precipitated. Refrigeration considerably hastens the rate at which cream of tartar is deposited and is often practised commercially to stabilise the wine in this respect. The wine is simply chilled to a temperature just above its freezing point and held under these conditions for a few days until what is termed tartrate stability is achieved. It is then racked off the deposit of cream of tartar while still cold to prevent the crystals from redissolving. Small amounts of tartaric acid are unlikely to provoke this problem, however, and even if it does arise the excess cream of tartar can always be removed by refrigeration. This risk is worth taking anyway in view of the benefits the presence of a little tartaric acid confers on a wine.

Malic acid is also a common constituent of grape wine. The actual amount in a wine depends significantly upon the ripeness of the grapes from which it was produced since ripe grapes generally contain less malic acid than unripe fruit. This acid is believed to be at least partly responsible for the fresh fruity character of certain wines, particularly those whose acidity is fairly high. It has also been discovered that a wine can tolerate a much higher proportion of malic acid than of either citric or tartaric acid before a strongly acid flavour becomes noticeable, and advantage can be taken of this fact in the production of the more highly acid types of wine. Indeed, the value of malic acid in amateur winemaking is only now becoming apparent, for it has just recently been realised that the type of acid added to or present in a must can have an important bearing on the character and quality of the wine.

Experiments with acid-deficient musts have indicated that neither citric, malic nor tartaric acids on their own provide a perfect acid balance. The best results were in fact achieved with a mixture of these three acids, and for most winemaking purposes "Acid Mixture A" which contains 50% tartaric acid, 30% malic acid and 20% citric acid will prove eminently satisfactory. This mixture should not be employed when an acidity greater than about 4.5 p.p.t. is desired, however, for it is then essential to have a high proportion of malic acid in the wine otherwise too sharp and acid a flavour will almost certainly result. Under these circumstances, " Acid Mixture B " which contains 50% malic acid, 30% tartaric acid and 20% citric acid must be employed. Ideally, of course, allowance should be made for the type as well as the amount of acid contributed by the ingredients of the must and the composition of the acid mixture used to increase its acidity suitably altered to take this factor into account. Should any winemaker decide to adopt the more refined approach, the table in which is listed the principal acids present in a selection of common fruits will undoubtedly prove useful. Most amateurs will probably not consider the effort involved in doing so justified and will find one or other of the two acid mixtures perfectly adequate for this purpose.

The accompanying table shows the weights, in ounces per gallon, of the individual three acids and two acid mixtures required to provide a given acidity. The latter is in all cases expressed in terms of parts per thousand of sulphuric acid. The main purpose of this table is to enable the winemaker to see at a glance exactly how much acid will be needed to increase the acidity of a must to any chosen value. The following example will perhaps help to illustrate how it operates. A must was found to contain 1.1 p.p.t acid by chemical analysis. Since a light dry table wine was desired, it was decided to increase its acidity to 3.2 p.p.t. with acid mixture A. The table immediately shows that an acidity of 1.1 p.p.t. is equivalent to $\frac{1}{4}$ oz. per gallon of this acid mixture and that an acidity of 3.2 p.p.t. is equivalent to $\frac{3}{4}$ oz. per gallon of the same acid mixture. It follows directly that $\frac{1}{2}$ oz. per gallon of Acid Mixture A will be required to increase the acidity of the must from 1.1 p.p.t. to the desired 3.2 p.p.t.

Once the actual amount of acid which must be added has been calculated in this manner, the next step is to weigh it out accurately. Since few winemakers are likely to possess a balance capable of weighing as little as $\frac{1}{8}$ oz. (3.5 gms) acid to any degree of accuracy, it is best to use solutions containing a known weight of acid or acid mixture per unit volume

Weights of Various Acids and Acid Mixtures in Ounces per Gallon Required to Provide a Given Acidity

Weight of Acid ozs/gallon	Citric Acid	Malic Acid	Tartaric Acid	Acid Mixture A	Acid Mixture B
⅛	0.54	0.57	0.51	0.53	0.55
¼	1.09	1.14	1.02	1.07	1.10
⅜	1.63	1.71	1.53	1.60	1.65
½	2.19	2.28	2.04	2.13	2.19
⅝	2.73	2.85	2.55	2.66	2.74
¾	3.29	3.42	3.04	3.20	3.29
⅞	3.83	3.99	3.57	3.73	3.83
1	4.37	4.56	4.07	4.26	4.38
1⅛	4.91	5.13	4.58	4.80	4.93
1¼	5.66	5.70	5.09	5.33	5.48
1⅜	6.00	6.27	5.60	5.86	6.03
1½	6.56	6.84	6.11	6.40	6.57
1⅝	7.10	7.41	6.62	6.92	7.12
1¾	7.66	7.98	7.13	7.46	7.67
1⅞	8.20	8.55	7.64	8.00	8.21
2	8.73	9.12	8.15	8.53	8.76

for this purpose. The correct amount of acid can then be introduced simply by adding the requisite volume of acid solution to the must.

For example, if 2½ ozs. tartaric acid, 1½ ozs. malic acid and 1 oz. citric acid are dissolved in about 1½ pints of cold water and the volume then adjusted to exactly two pints with water, a solution containing ⅛ oz. Acid Mixture A per fluid ounce will be obtained. In the same fashion, a similar solution containing ⅛ oz. Acid Mixture B per fluid ounce can be prepared from 2½ ozs. malic acid, 1½ ozs. tartaric acid and 1 oz. citric acid. The addition of 1 fluid ounce of this solution to each gallon of must would then be equivalent to adding ⅛ oz. of the corresponding acid mixture. It hardly need be said that acid solutions of this nature should be stored in tightly stoppered bottles to reduce evaporation losses and to prevent bacterial or fungal contamination.

Turning now to the problem of over-acid musts, it may first be mentioned that a high acidity does help to prevent spoilage because many organisms commonly responsible for wine spoilage do not grow well, if at all, in strongly acid media. Yeast is much more tolerant of acid so that yeast starters should preferably be kept fairly acid to discourage the development of other unwanted micro-organisms while the yeast colony is expanding. The same ideas unfortunately cannot be applied to musts as it would be pointless to produce a wine which, though sound, proved undrinkable because it contained far too much acid.

An excess of acid is usually encountered in musts prepared from fruits, certain of which are noted for their very high acid content. Members of the currant family, raspberries and related berries, rhubarb and citrus fruits are particularly outstanding in this respect. Too much acid in a wine is undesirable because it confers a very sharp or acid flavour which at times may be so pronounced that the wine becomes undrinkable. Hence, although the fermentation of over-acid musts does not cause the development of ruinous off-flavours as is often the case with under-acid musts, it will result in poorer quality wines and should therefore be avoided for this reason.

The simplest means of reducing the acid content of a fruit juice is by dilution with water and/or sugar syrup, and the majority of recipes seem to favour this procedure, possibly because it is easy to describe and carry out. The actual degree of dilution necessary can be calculated from the titratable acidity of the fruit juice. For example, a pure fruit juice was found to contain 10 p.p.t. acid so that it must be diluted with two volumes of water and sugar syrup to reduce its acidity to about 3.3 p.p.t. which is a suitable level for a light dry table wine.

Although dilution is undoubtedly a simple and convenient means of decreasing acidity, it does have the effect of producing lighter bodied wines whose bouquet and flavour are muted to an extent depending upon the quantity of water added. Sometimes this is an advantage, especially in table wine production, but in certain cases a fruit juice may require so much dilution to reduce its acidity to a palatable level that a very unattractive wine would be obtained. The effect of dilution upon body, bouquet and flavour as well as acidity must therefore be very carefully assessed before making a final decision regarding the amount of water to add to a highly acid fruit juice.

The acidity of a juice or must can also be reduced by means of precipitated chalk which is a pure, finely divided type of calcium carbonate. This substance reacts with the acids in the must to form insoluble calcium salts which are precipitated out of solution and settle in the lees. A proportion of the acid in the must is thus removed entirely by this treatment and is not merely neutralised as would be the case if a reagent such as sodium carbonate were employed for this purpose. Chalk is most useful for making relatively minor reductions in the acid content of a must, particularly when dilution is preferably avoided for one reason or another. The addition of ¼ oz. chalk per gallon will in fact reduce the acidity of a must by about 1.5 p.p.t., but it is advisable not to exceed ½ oz. per gallon otherwise a slight chalky background flavour may be detectable in the wine.

The technique of adding chalk to a must merits a few words of explanation. Since chalk is a carbonate, carbon dioxide is evolved when it reacts with the acids in the must so that a certain amount of foaming often occurs. Consequently, in order to avoid losses if the must does froth badly, plenty of headroom should be left in the container and the chalk should be added slowly in small portions with a spoon or on the point of a knife, each such increment being allowed to react completely before the next is introduced. The size of the portions may, of course, be increased if no problems with foaming are encountered.

The white precipitate of calcium salts resulting from this treatment is so fine that it would require several weeks to settle out unless it was removed by filtration. Fortunately, there is no need to do so since the precipitate will settle out of its own accord with the yeast and other detritus accumulated during fermentation and will then be separated out in the lees left after the first racking. The winemaker may therefore inoculate the must with the yeast starter immediately and allow fermentation to proceed in the usual manner.

When a must contains so much acid that neither dilution with water nor chalk treatment alone are likely to prove effective, a combination of the two methods will often provide a satisfactory solution to the problem. The technique involved is probably best illustrated by an example. Citrus fruit juices commonly contain as much as 24 p.p.t. acid and would therefore require too much dilution or excessive chalk treatment to reduce their acidity to a palatable level. In this case, dilution with three volumes of water would lower the acid content to 6.0 p.p.t. which is, of course, still too high for most types of wine. The addition of ¼ oz. chalk per gallon would then reduce its acidity to about 4.5 p.p.t. which is suitable for a sweet wine. If the amount of chalk is increased to ⅜ oz. per gallon, the must would only contain some 3.7 p.p.t. acid and could then be used to produce a dry wine.

It is perhaps worth digressing at this point for a few minutes to discuss the special case of rhubarb. This ingredient is unusual in that it contains significant amounts of the poisonous oxalic acid in addition to malic acid. Many books on amateur winemaking consequently advise removing all the acid from rhubarb juice by chalk treatment and then replacing this acid with citric acid. Quite apart from the fact than an acid mixture should be employed instead of citric acid for this purpose, a drastic treatment of this nature is not particularly conducive to good quality. It does effectively remove the oxalic acid, but there is some doubt if it is really necessary to do so. The amount of oxalic acid in rhubarb is sufficiently small that the winemaker would need to consume several bottles of wine regularly before any ill-effects would be noticed ! Since few winemakers are likely to face this problem, it follows that rhubarb is best regarded simply as an over-acid ingredient and treated as such.

Certain precautions can nevertheless be taken to minimise the proportion of oxalic acid which rhubarb contributes to the must. Rhubarb should always be pressed directly or extracted with cold water to obtain the juice because these procedures leave much of the oxalic acid in the discarded pulp. The former method is particularly good in this respect. Extraction with hot water or pulp fermentation should never be practised with rhubarb otherwise most of the oxalic acid in the pulp will be retained in the must. In addition, chalk should preferably be employed to decrease the acidity of the juice or extract since oxalic acid will be removed by this treatment before any malic acid reacts. Normally, however, the amount of acid in rhubarb juice is so high that both chalk treatment and dilution with water are necessary to reduce it to a tolerable degree.

Winemakers who do not check and adjust the acidity of their musts quite commonly produce wines with a poor acid balance. An insipid flavour can often be traced to a deficiency of acid and such wines are said to be flabby. On the other hand, a pronounced sharpness or tartness can almost invariably be attributed to the presence of too much acid.

Although the addition of acid to wines lacking this commodity will often effect some improvement if no off-flavours have developed during fermentation, over-acid wines rarely benefit from treatments designed to reduce their acidity. Dilution or the addition of chalk both tend to be detrimental to quality while the use of sugar or glycerol to mask the acid taste is at best a defeatist remedy. Chilling may sometimes be effective when the wine contains an excess of tartaric acid and a little 1% potassium carbonate solution (1 fluid ounce per gallon) may be added to increase the amount of potassium available for the precipitation of cream of tartar should very little of the latter be deposited during the initial period of refrigeration. In most cases, however, blending offers the only real solution to the problem of acid imbalances so that any wines suffering from this defect are best reserved for this purpose and no other remedial action attempted.

Wines containing malic acid occasionally become infected by certain species of micrococci or rod forms of lactic acid bacteria which are able to convert the dibasic malic acid into the monobasic lactic acid and carbon dioxide. This malo-lactic fermentation, as it is called, can therefore effect a considerable reduction in the acidity of a wine and at at the same time may confer a slight sparkle. Such wines are variously described as petillant, spritzig or frizzante and are prickly on the tongue due to the presence of dissolved carbon dioxide, small bubbles of which can usually be seen clinging to the sides of the glass. Many of the more northerly wine regions produce light wines of this type, and certain commercial wines, notably the Matéus Rosé of Portugal, are in fact expected to exhibit this feature as an integral part of their character.

A malo-lactic fermentation will often prove beneficial when it occurs in a slightly over-acid dry wine, but it should be avoided at all costs in a sweet wine because off-flavours will develop under these conditions. The bacteria responsible for its occurrence are very catholic in their tastes and will attack sugar as avidly as malic acid, to form a number of by-products such as mannitol which confer an unpleasant flavour on the wine. Any sweet wine discovered to be undergoing a malo-lactic fermentation should therefore immediately be treated with 100 p.p.m. sulphite to destroy the bacteria and prevent the development of undesirable off-flavours.

Dry wines which contain an excess of malic acid will commonly show a considerable improvement as a result of a malo-lactic fermentation. It is thus rather unfortunate that there is no sure method of inducing it to begin. The species of bacteria which cause the malo-lactic fermentation are very unpredictable and not infrequently fail to develop even under what appear to be ideal conditions. Certain measures can be taken to encourage their growth, however, and then a moderate degree of success can be expected. In the first place, the alcoholic strength of the wine should be kept around 10% by volume since the bacteria prefer such an environment. Sulphite should not be added to the wine at any stage in its production except possibly prior to fermentation. Indeed, sulphiting is one sure way to terminate a malo-lactic fermentation because the bacteria are very sensitive to sulphite and cannot tolerate more than 25–50 p.p.m. at the very most. The addition of a small amount of nutrients may also prove helpful.

It is usually advisable to attempt to induce a malo-lactic fermentation soon after the yeast activity has ceased. The wine should be racked for the first time in the normal manner, but just before the second racking is due the yeast deposit at the bottom of the container should be stirred up vigorously to promote autolysis and thereby provide extra nutrients for bacterial growth. If the wine is then stored in a warm place at about 75°F for a few weeks, there is a strong possibility that a malo-lactic fermentation will develop. The wine should, of course, be racked once the yeast deposit has settled and bacterial activity is observed, but whether or not the latter does occur it should not be left on the yeast deposit for more than about a month beyond the normal time for carrying out the second racking otherwise musty off-flavours due to excessive yeast autolysis may result. It may be added that the introduction of a small quantity of wine already undergoing a malo-lactic fermentation will greatly enhance the chances of success, although even this technique does not always work.

Once a wine has become infected in this way, care should be taken to ensure that too much acid is not lost because the bacteria will continue to convert malic acid into lactic acid until the supply of the former becomes exhausted. The winemaker should therefore check the acidity of the wine about once a month to ascertain how rapid a reduction its acid content is actually experiencing. About 50–100 p.p.m. sulphite should be added to terminate bacterial activity as soon as the desired acid level is reached. The wine can then be matured in cask and/or bottle in the normal manner.

Although the bacteria responsible for the malo-lactic fermentation are very easily killed by sulphite, the potency of the latter diminishes with time until eventually no bactericidal effects remain. It is for this reason that apparently stable wines containing malic acid will occasionally undergo a malo-lactic fermentation after spending several months or years stored in a sealed container. The bacteria penetrate the cork and then begin their work. A pressure of carbon dioxide gradually builds up in the container until ultimately the cork blows out without warning, much to the amazement of the winemaker. Hence, to avoid such unfortunate accidents, the corks of bottles containing dry wines suspected or known to be undergoing a malo-lactic fermentation should be wired down. Insufficient pressure will be generated to break the bottle and a petillant wine will be obtained. Alternatively, the wine may be sulphited to kill the bacteria and this practice should always be adopted with sweet wines for the reasons stated earlier (except when yeast is responsible for a refermentation). In this latter case, a sediment will be observed in the container and the wine should then be allowed to complete its fermentation under an air lock.

In conclusion, a final word may be said on the subject of ion exchange resins which may be roughly described as insoluble synthetic resins with the ability to replace one ion in solution with another from the resin. In other words, ions are exchanged between the solution and the resin. Without going into details, it does appear that certain types of these resins could be used to alter the acidity of musts and wines. Unfortunately, very little work seems to have been done in this particular field although Californian wine technologists are now recognising that ion exchange resins can be of great value to winemakers. At present, however, much experimental work remains to be done, but some experienced amateur may consider it worthwhile to pursue this matter further.

Chapter VI

THE MEANING OF pH

IN recent years there has been a growing tendency towards using the pH of a must or wine as a measure of its acid content, primarily because pH can be determined much more easily and cheaply than titratable acidity. This trend is rather unfortunate since the relation between pH and titratable acidity is at best only vaguely understood by the majority of amateur winemakers. As a result, a number of erroneous ideas regarding the applications of pH in winemaking have now arisen, and one of the objects of this chapter is to correct these misconceptions so that the meaning of pH is brought into its proper perspective.

One of the principal difficulties encountered when attempting to explain the subject of pH is the virtual impossibility of expressing the basic principles in simple language. Technical details just cannot be avoided and the usual result is to render the whole matter incomprehensible to the layman. This chapter should therefore be omitted unless the winemaker is prepared to study it very carefully.

The concept of pH was first introduced by Sorensen in 1909 as a convenient means of expressing the hydrogen ion concentration, denoted by $[H^+]$, of a solution. On this basis, the definition of pH is most easily expressed in terms of the following mathematical relation:—

$$pH = -\text{Log}_{10}\,[H^+]$$

Since the hydrogen ion concentration of a solution depends upon the concentration of acid it contains, it would at first sight appear that pH immediately provides an easy method of determining acidity. Unfortunately, the pH of a solution is also influenced by several other factors amongst which may be mentioned the nature of the acid itself and he presence of other dissolved solids.

If the effects of the latter are ignored for the moment, the rôle played by the acid can be studied. In chemistry, most acids can be classed as either strong or weak acids, and as only the latter are encountered in winemaking strong acids need be given no further consideration. Now, an acid may be defined as a substance which dissociates or ionises in solution to produce hydrogen ions, and the fundamental feature of weak acids is that this ionisation is only partial and reversible. Since the pH of the solution is determined by its hydrogen ion concentration, it is clear that the factors influencing the ionisation of the acid will also affect the pH. The only two factors of importance here are the dissociation constant and the concentration of the acid.

The mathematical relation between the pH of a solution and the concentration of acid it contains (titratable acidity) can best be derived by considering the case of a pure aqueous solution of an imaginary weak acid HA. The chemical equation representing the ionisation of this acid is given below and beneath it the mathematical symbols required in the calculations have been defined:—

$$HA \rightleftharpoons H^+ + A^-$$

$[H^+]$ = Hydrogen ion concentration in gram-ions per litre (gm-ions/l)

K = Dissociation or ionisation constant of the acid HA

M = Molecular weight of the acid HA

c = Concentration of the acid HA in gram-molecules per litre (gm-mols/l)

The hydrogen ion concentration of an acid solution can easily be evaluated from its pH by reference to logarithm tables, e.g. a pH of 3.7 is equal to a hydrogen ion concentration of approximately 2×10^{-4} gm-ions/l. The following approximate relation for weak acids can then be derived from the theory of ionisation:—

$$[H^+] = \sqrt{K.c}$$

$$\therefore [H^+]^2 = K.c$$

$$\therefore c = \frac{[H^+]^2}{K} \text{ gm-mols/l}$$

$$= \frac{M\,[H^+]^2}{K} \text{ gms/l}$$

$$\therefore \text{Titratable acidity} = \frac{M\,[H^+]^2}{K} \text{ p.p.t. of HA}$$

This calculation has been performed on the assumption that the acid HA is monobasic, i.e. it possesses only one acid group in the molecule. In reality, of course, the three main acids present in musts and wines are dibasic (malic and tartaric acids) or tribasic (citric acid) and thus have two or three acid groups per molecule respectively. Since each acid group does make some contribution to the total hydrogen ion concentration, the preceding calculations would be enormously complicated had this factor to be taken into account. Fortunately, only one of these acid groups provides most of the hydrogen ions and a negligible error is therefore introduced by ignoring the contribution made by the other acid groups. The procedure used to calculate the titratable acidity of a solution of the imaginary acid HA from its pH is consequently directly applicable to solutions of citric, malic and tartaric acids provided the appropriate values of K and M are known.

The accompanying table summarises the formula, molecular weight M and dissociation constant K for citric, malic and tartaric acids. This data will enable the winemaker to calculate the titratable acidity of solutions of these acids from their pH and vice-versa. A sample calculation is given below for a pure solution of tartaric acid with a pH of 2.0. This example may be worked backwards to obtain the pH of the solution from its titratable acidity.

Name of Acid	Chemical Formula	Molecular Weight M	Dissociation Constant K
Citric Acid	$C_6H_8O_7.H_2O$	210.2	8.4×10^{-4}
Malic Acid	$C_4H_6O_5$	134.1	4.0×10^{-4}
Tartaric Acid	$C_4H_6O_6$	150.1	1.1×10^{-3}

$$pH = -Log_{10}\,[H^+] = 2.0$$

$$\therefore Log_{10}\,[H^+] = -2.0$$

$$\therefore [H^+] = 10^{-2}\text{ gm-ions/l}$$

$$\text{Titratable acidity} = \frac{M\,[H^+]^2}{K}$$

$$= \frac{150.1 \times 10^{-2} \times 10^{-2}}{1.1 \times 10^{-3}}\text{ gms/l}$$

$$\therefore \text{Titratable acidity} = 13.7\text{ ppt of Tartaric acid}$$

It will doubtless have been noted that this method of calculation expresses the titratable acidity as parts per thousand of the acid concerned and not as p.p.t. sulphuric acid which was the reference standard employed in the previous chapter. Conversion to p.p.t. sulphuric acid can be accomplished by consulting the tables which are included in the previous chapter for this purpose.

For reasons beyond the scope of this book, the pH of an acid solution is always less than 7.0. Moreover, it is important to remember that the lower is the pH the higher is the acidity, e.g. a solution of pH 2.5 is considerably more acid than a solution of pH 4.5. In actual fact, a difference of one pH unit represents a ten-fold difference in hydrogen ion concentration.

The approximate pH of a must or wine can easily and rapidly be measured by means of narrow range indicator papers, a modern development of the older litmus papers which merely showed whether a solution was acid or alkaline.

These papers are supplied as a series of small books measuring about 2½ in. × ½ in. which cover most of the pH range (from 1 to 14) in 0.3 unit divisions although a universal book covering the range 1–11 in 1.0 unit divisions is also available. To determine the approximate pH of a must or wine, a leaf is torn out of the book and dipped into a small sample taken for this purpose. The leaf will then change colour according to the pH of the sample. By comparing the colour of the paper with the colour chart printed on the inside or outside cover of the book, the approximate pH of the must or wine can be evaluated to within 0.3 unit.

Despite the simplicity of this procedure, there are several reasons why it does not give a reliable measure of the titratable acidity. In the first place, the estimation is usually only accurate to about 0.3 pH unit which covers a rather wide range of titratable acidity. Greater accuracy cannot normally be achieved because it is rarely possible to match the colour of the test paper exactly with one particular colour on the printed chart, especially in artificial light. In most cases, the winemaker is forced to conclude that the pH appears to be intermediate between two values, e.g. between pH 3.3 and 3.6. Additional difficulties are encountered when testing red musts or wines due to interference by the red pigments already present in the solution. These problems are inherent in the use of narrow range indicator papers and little can be done to improve matters. The only method of determining pH values accurately requires the use of a special instrument called a pH-meter which is far too expensive for the average winemaker to purchase.

Although these remarks serve to illustrate some of the defects and inaccuracies attending the use of narrow range indicator papers, they are obviously not in themselves valid grounds for stating that the pH of a must or wine does not provide a reliable measure of its titratable acidity. Moreover, this argument could not be applied to pH values determined by means of a pH-meter. The real reason is not in fact concerned with accuracy of the actual pH measurement. Instead, a much more fundamental issue closely linked to the composition of the must or wine is involved.

It will be remembered that one of the factors influencing the pH of a solution was earlier said to be the presence of dissolved solids other than the acid under consideration.

The effects of these other solutes have been conveniently ignored until now, and it is as well to point out at this juncture that the preceding calculations relating pH and titratable acidity are only valid for pure aqueous solutions of the acids concerned and not for musts and wines.

All musts and wines are extremely complex solutions containing weak organic acids and their salts, sugars, proteins, pectins, tannins and so on. In this respect, they are therefore very far removed from the idealised conception of a pure aqueous solution of a weak acid previously considered and, as might be expected, have properties very different from those of such ideal solutions. In actual fact, musts and wines behave as what are called buffer solutions. The latter are defined as solutions which show only abnormally small changes in pH even on the addition of comparatively large amounts of acid or alkali. Their pH consequently differs radically from the value calculated solely on the basis of the concentration of acid in the solution.

The pH of simple buffer solutions can be calculated without too much difficulty, but for this purpose the composition of the solution must be accurately known. Since the composition of musts and wines is extremely complex, it is clear that no satisfactory correlation can possibly be derived between the pH and titratable acidity of a must or wine. The concentration of acid is only one of the many factors which determine the pH under these conditions, so that the pH of a must or wine is merely a measure of its hydrogen ion concentration and no more.

It is therefore patently ridiculous to state that a must or wine whose pH lies within a specified range (commonly 3.0–4.5) has approximately the correct acid content. A high pH is not necessarily an indication of a relatively low acid content and vice-versa. For example, a pure elderberry juice in the 1961 season was found to have a pH of 3.70 (measured on a Pye pH-meter), but its titratable acidity was nevertheless discovered to be 16.5 p.p.t. Even on dilution with three volumes of water the pH only rose to 3.82 despite the fourfold reduction in titratable acidity.

The idea has been advanced that the pH of a wine should be a reliable index of its acid taste since the latter may logically be expected to depend upon the hydrogen ion concentration. Surprisingly enough, experiments have shown that this is not the case and pH is only one of the factors upon which the acid taste of a wine depends. Indeed, titratable acidity has been found a much more reliable guide for this purpose. Although no exact correlation exists between titratable acidity and acid taste, provided the former is within a range quoted in the previous chapter, it is generally true that the wine will possess a balanced acid flavour. The reasons for this are still not fully understood, but it is probably due to the fact that the titratable acidity of a must or wine is an absolute measure of its acid content which is virtually independent of its overall composition whereas the pH is not a constant quantity of this type. It is for this reason that the winemaker should always use the titratable acidity in preference to the pH of a must or wine for the purpose of checking and adjusting its acid content.

The pH of a must or wine nevertheless does have some useful applications in amateur winemaking. For example, important information regarding the susceptibility of a wine to bacterial spoilage can be gleaned from its pH.

Although yeasts and many moulds are not particularly sensitive to the pH of the medium in which they are growing, the same is often not true for bacteria. Many of the latter cannot grow in wines whose pH is below about 3.4 so that a wine with a pH below 3.4 is less likely to be lost through spoilage by bacterial infection. On the other hand, yeast growth and fermentation may be retarded if the pH of the medium is much below 3.0 so that the pH of the must should preferably not be less than 3.0. The pH of a must or wine should thus ideally lie in the range 3.0–3.4. Fortunately, many do meet this requirement automatically, for a well balanced must or wine has a pH around this ideal range.

The winemaker will doubtless have rightly concluded by now that the concept of pH has only limited applications in amateur winemaking. Experienced winemakers may find it useful to record the pH values of their musts and wines for reference purposes, especially when preparing experimental wines, but on the whole no harm will be done if this subject is ignored altogether. It certainly cannot be emphasised too strongly that the pH of a must or wine is best not employed as a measure of its acid content.

Chapter VII

TANNIN

RED and white table wines differ in a number of respects beside colour, and one such contrasting feature of fundamental importance is their tannin content. Red wines contain on the average about 0.2% tannin whereas the corresponding figure for white wines is normally less than 0.05%. The larger proportion of tannin in red wines is due to the fact that tannin as well as colouring matter is extracted from the skins of the fruit during a period of pulp fermentation. Indeed, the bulk of the tannin in most red wines is derived from this source, for the amount in the juice itself is usually relatively small. Only a few fruits, notably elderberries, possess juice which is rich in this commodity. By way of contrast, pulp fermentation is rarely practised in white wine production. Instead, the fruit is pressed, the pulp discarded and the juice alone fermented. The tannin content of white wines thus depends solely upon how much is present in the juice. It is consequently quite low since the amount of tannin in most fruit juices is around 0.05% and considerably less is found in vegetable juices. Apple juice, especially that from cider or crab varieties, is one of the few exceptions in this respect as its tannin content can at times be remarkably high.

Tannin is an extremely important minor constituent of every wine. It assists clarification by combining with and precipitating proteins and allied nitrogenous substances which tend to promote and/or stabilise hazes. This is why red wines which are naturally rich in tannin tend to fall bright and clear more rapidly than white wines. It is also a quality factor of the utmost importance. Despite the fact that very little is present in any wine, tannin has so bitter a flavour that even these tiny amounts are quite sufficient to impart a certain degree of astringency. Indeed, a balanced tannin content is an essential prerequisite of good quality. Too little will result in an insipid wine which lacks depth of character while too much will cause a harsh rough flavour.

It is common to find that red wines produced from such fruits as elderberries, sloes, damsons and the like contain an excess of tannin. Admittedly, this situation is at times difficult to avoid because a fairly lengthy pulp fermentation may be required to achieve an adequate depth of colour, but careful control at this stage will often help matters. The pulp should always be removed immediately a satisfactory depth of colour is achieved to minimise the risk of extracting too much tannin which would coarsen the flavour of the wine. This latter defect is naturally less apparent in sweet than in dry red wines since the sugar content of the former masks some of their astringency, but it merely means that greater care is necessary when attempting to produce dry red wines. Even so, the winemaker still cannot afford to be lax with sweet red wines on this account.

The high tannin content of red wines improves their keeping qualities but at the same time increases the period of maturing needed before the wine reaches its best. At least one and often two or three years in cask followed by several more years in bottle are required before the wine becomes fully mature. During this time, particularly that which the wine spends in cask, its tannin content will decrease slightly due to loss by oxidation, combination with aldehydes and proteins and so on. A harsh red wine will thus gradually mellow with age, especially in wood, and cask maturing is in fact almost essential if a red wine is to develop its full potential. Wines high in tannin require longer maturing than wines better balanced initially, but in many instances eventually turn out to be superior in quality. A slight excess of tannin can thus be beneficial to a red wine since it permits longer, slower and hence more satisfactory maturing, but the wine will take many years to reach its best. A large excess of tannin will, of course, serve no useful purpose since the wine will tend to remain harsh and coarse no matter how long it is matured.

Red wines which are still far too astringent even after spending a year or so in cask can often be improved by fining. Most fining agents are proteins which form insoluble complexes with tannin so that some of the latter is removed by this treatment. An excellent fining agent for this purpose is egg-white, one of which will suffice for 5–10 gallons of wine. The egg-white is simply switched into a few pints of wine and this mixture added to the bulk of the wine. The latter is then racked as soon as the precipitated protein-tannin complex has settled. Harsh elderberry wines usually respond well to this treatment. Other remedies for over-astringency e.g. the addition of sugar or glycerol to mask the harshness, are on the whole best avoided and, if the winemaker does not wish to try fining, the wine should preferably be reserved for blending.

Unlike red wines, many amateur white wines often suffer from the defects associated with a tannin deficiency. This state of affairs is commonly encountered when vegetables, grain or flowers are the principal ingredients of the must, but certain fruits e.g. oranges, bananas also tend to produce wines of this type. Blending ingredients can frequently be practised to help prevent too serious a deficiency of tannin, but in many cases some still must be added. Moreover, because tannin assists clarification, it is advisable to rectify any imbalance prior to or early in the fermentation to achieve the best results.

The question now arises as to which type of tannin should be used for this purpose. Strong cold tea, BP tannic acid and grape tannin (extracted from grape pips and skins) have all been recommended at one time or another. The use of cold tea is certainly inadvisable since it is impossible to add controlled amounts of tannin in this way due to variations both in the tannin content of the tea itself and in the strength of the infusion. On the other hand, there seems to be little to choose between tannic acid and grape tannin provided the former is of BP quality. Their effects on the flavour and general character of a wine seem to be identical so that the winemaker may use either according to personal preference.

Since white wines normally contain less than 0.05% tannin, it is clear that the maximum requirement for any must will not exceed 1/12th oz. grape tannin or tannic acid per gallon. Very little natural tannin will be present in musts whose principal ingredients are vegetables, grain or flowers and in such cases the addition of 1/12th–1/15th oz. per gallon is desirable. Less specific advice can be given for fruit musts since their requirements can vary quite widely. For example, apple juices usually contain sufficient natural tannin whereas orange juice has very little and would benefit by the addition of about 1/15th oz. per gallon. In these instances, the winemaker must rely on previous experience to decide how much tannin, if any, should be added to the must or make the necessary adjustments to the finished wine. The latter procedure is, of course, less satisfactory.

The extremely small amounts of grape tannin or tannic acid required for these purposes obviously pose a serious weighing problem as few amateur winemakers will be able to weigh quantities of 1/15 oz. or less with any degree of accuracy. It is therefore best to use a stock tannin solution prepared by dissolving ½ oz. grape tannin or tannic acid in ¾ pint boiled water. Every fluid ounce of this solution then contains 1/30th oz. tannin so that the addition of two fluid ounces to a gallon of must would be equivalent to adding 1/15 oz. of the solid material. As little as 1/60th oz. tannin can thus be added to the must without difficulty. The stock tannin solution should, of course, be stored in a tightly stoppered bottle, preferably in a refrigerator, and renewed if any such infection as mould growth is noticed.

It will doubtless have been noticed that so far no mention has been made of a method for determining tannin despite its great importance as a quality factor. The reason is simply that tannin estimations are difficult to carry out and call for a high degree of analytical skill. The procedure is considerably more elaborate than for acidity determinations and each analysis takes some time to complete. It is therefore best not to attempt tannin analysis unless some training in volumetric analysis has been received.

In addition, it is currently only possible to determine tannin plus colouring matter. Hence, until a number of determinations have been carried out for a given type of wine, the results must be interpreted with care because the amount of colouring matter in different wines can vary quite widely. Most winemakers will thus find no real advantage in determining the tannin content of their wines except possibly for experimental purposes. Full details of the analytical procedure can then be found in a text book on wine technology e.g. "Table Wines" by Amerine and Joslyn (C.U.P).

CHAPTER VIII

WATER

WATER undoubtedly occupies a very important place in amateur winemaking. In general, fruit juices and the like are diluted with water for one reason or another during the preparation of the must, often to such an extent that water becomes the principal constituent. The question then arises as to how the composition of the water used for this purpose affects the fermentation and/or quality of the wine or if indeed it has any influence at all in this connection.

Since commercial wines are mainly produced from pure grape juice, the amateur unfortunately cannot seek guidance from this quarter regarding the influence of water composition on wine quality. Some information may be gleaned from the fact that the character of a beer is strongly dependent upon the nature of the water used to prepare the wort, but care must obviously be taken in the interpretation of this data. What is true for beer need not necessarily apply to wine.

Pure water is a rare and expensive commodity. Its solvent powers are such that it will dissolve small amounts of almost any substance with which it comes into contact. In many cases, of course, the quantity which actually goes into solution is quite negligible and can often only be detected by very sensitive instruments. The domestic water supply in most homes is thus invariably contaminated to some extent by a variety of dissolved substances of one type or another.

The presence of oxygen, nitrogen and other gases absorbed from the air by tap water can easily be demonstrated by gently warming a small sample. This treatment forces the dissolved gases out of solution and they appear as small bubbles clinging to the walls of the container. The yeast is thus assured of a supply of oxygen during the initial

CONCENTRATION OF CONSTITUENTS

City	Source of Supply	pH	Total Solids	Ammoniacal Nitrogen	Albuminoid Nitrogen	O_2 absorbed from $KMnO_4$ in 4 hrs. at 27° C.	Total hardness as $CaCO_3$
Birmingham	Elan	7.3	43	0.005	0.038	1.10	18
Cardiff	Llandegfedd Reservoir ...	8.4	163	0.010	0.040	0.45	113
	Rhiwbina Reservoir ...	7.5	58	0.003	0.021	0.32	35
Edinburgh	Eastern Areas ...	7.1	67	0.010	0.010	1.78	32
	Western Areas ...	7.1	60	NIL	0.010	1.32	27
	High City Areas ...	7.4	147	NIL	0.10	0.45	112
Glasgow	Loch Katrine ...	6.0	32	0.002	0.025	0.95	9
	Gorbals	7.1	108	0.104	0.105	0.99	56.5
Liverpool	Rivington ...	7.7	89	0.080	0.030	0.50	39
	Vyrnwy	6.8	41	NIL	0.040	1.60	14
	Green Lane Well	7.0	407	NIL	NIL	NIL	277
	Dudlow Lane Well	6.2	232	NIL	NIL	NIL	118
London	Average of Thames Intakes	7.9	—	0.041	0.076	1.10	266
	River Lee ...	8.0	—	0.043	0.096	1.28	320
	New River ...	7.9	—	0.043	0.058	0.58	302
	Kent & Southern Area Wells ...	7.2	—	0.011	0.031	0.10	318
	Eastern Area Wells	7.4	—	0.092	0.034	0.22	308
Plymouth	——	6.7 to 7.2	45 to 80	NIL to 0.140	0.088 to 0.300	0.25 to 0.45	20 to 49

* Fluoridation (1 p.p.m.)

DOMESTIC WATER SUPPLIES

IN PARTS PER MILLION

Calcium Ca	Magnesium Mg	Sodium Na	Silica SiO_2	Chloride Cl	Sulphate SO_4	Nitrate NO_3	Fluoride F	Phosphate PO_4	Carbonate CO_3	Iron Fe
5.1	1.5	4.1	3.5	9.5	6.3	0.44	*0.05	—	5.4	0.23
—	—	—	—	16	—	1.10	—	—	—	—
—	—	—	—	10	—	0.10	—	—	—	—
—	—	—	—	7.7	—	—	—	—	—	—
—	—	—	—	6.4	—	—	—	—	—	—
—	—	—	—	8.5	—	—	—	—	—	—
2.1	0.6	3.9	0.7	5.8	4.2	0.10	0.09	0.0001	—	0.01
18.6	2.9	8.8	2.0	12	17.2	0.45	0.15	0.001	—	0 10
—	—	—	—	15.5	—	Nil	—	—	—	—
—	—	—	—	10.2	—	Nil	—	—	—	—
—	—	—	—	42.6	—	8.8	—	—	—	—
—	—	—	—	33.2	—	9.5	—	—	—	—
—	—	—	10	31	61	4.0	0.25	1.3	—	—
—	—	—	—	45	101	4.6	0.30	1.4	—	—
—	—	—	—	38	63	5.5	0.25	0.7	—	—
—	—	—	—	19	—	5.5	—	—	—	—
—	—	—	—	34	—	0.6	—	—	—	—
—	—	—	—	11 to 24	Nil	Nil	—	Nil	—	Nil

began June 1964

stages of its growth in the must. Since boiling expels this oxygen, it is always desirable to stir vigorously any must prepared from boiled water in order to aerate it and replenish the oxygen lost by boiling.

Even more important are the mineral salts held in solution. Rain water dissolves small amounts of various gases, notably carbon dioxide, from the air as it falls to the ground. Subsequently, it may percolate for miles through soil and rock before reaching a river or reservoir from which a domestic supply is drawn. During its passage from the catchment area, the water may dissolve considerable amounts of mineral salts from the surroundings because carbon dioxide in solution makes the water slightly acid and this greatly enhances its solvent properties. The actual quantity and type of salts found in the water naturally depends upon the nature and chemical composition of the soil and rock through which it percolates. The mineral content of the water supply in different cities throughout the country consequently shows quite pronounced variations as the analyses quoted in the accompanying table clearly illustrate.

Perhaps the most important mineral salts encountered in tap waters are the bicarbonates and sulphates of calcium and magnesium whose presence or absence determines whether the water is hard or soft. The more of these salts the water contains the harder it will be and vice-versa. Rainwater is thus very soft because few mineral impurities are present whereas the large amounts of calcium salts in London water make it extremely hard.

Two types of water hardness are recognised. Temporary hardness is usually caused by calcium bicarbonate and can be eliminated by boiling the water. Heating decomposes this bicarbonate into calcium carbonate and carbon dioxide, and as the former product is almost completely insoluble in water it is deposited as a hard coating or "fur" on the inside of the container. On the other hand, permanent hardness is caused by the presence of calcium and magnesium sulphates and cannot be removed by boiling because these salts are unaffected by this treatment. Both types of hardness can be removed by treating the water with sodium carbonate (washing soda), but this process renders it undrinkable and fit only for industrial applications. Home water softening devices utilising ion-exchange resins are now readily available, however, so that any hard domestic water supply can quite easily be softened by passing the water through a device of this type prior to use.

Little information regarding the effects of water composition on fermentation and wine quality currently seems to be available. The limited number of experiments so far carried out have indicated some differences can be detected in the fermentation of musts prepared from water obtained from various localities. For example, musts prepared from rain water or soft water tended to ferment rather more slowly than those prepared from hard London water. Since the addition of a pinch of magnesium sulphate per gallon rectified matters, it seems likely that the use of soft water may occasionally result in a slight deficiency of magnesium and/or sulphate which are both required in minor amounts by the yeast. The bouquet and flavour of the wines produced from hard and soft waters appeared to be very similar, however, and the small differences which could be detected could have been caused by other factors. At any rate, it may tentatively be concluded that wine quality is not strongly dependent upon the nature of the water used to prepare the must, although it is highly probable that minor variations in the general character of a wine can be attributed to this cause.

CHAPTER IX

YEAST

THE importance of yeast in winemaking can be summarised by the statement that no wine of any description could be produced without the aid of yeast. Even wines made according to the so-called "no-yeast" recipes are not excluded from this definition since their success depends upon a colony of wild yeast becoming firmly established in the must. It is nevertheless quite true to say that, although the yeast actually makes the wine, the winemaker determines its quality by the degree of control exercised over the conditions under which the yeast does its work. The value of the hydrometer and acid estimation in this latter connection has already been discussed.

Yeast is a living organism which is scientifically classified with the fungi because it contains no chlorophyll and cannot therefore manufacture its own food supply from carbon dioxide and water as normal green plants do. The word yeast is a collective term used to describe an enormous number of related fungi, however, for there are hundreds of different types of yeast, many of which have but a very limited ability to induce alcoholic fermentation. Indeed, certain pathogenic varieties of yeast are known, e.g. a species of Candida (*C. albicans*) is responsible for the infection called thrush. As a family, the yeasts have an almost universal distribution and can be found throughout the tropics and temperate zones of the world. Indeed, a few species have even been reported recently in the Antarctic where they exist at temperatures close to or below freezing point. Yeasts are present in the bloom of fruits, in the nectar of flowers and hence in honey, on grain and seeds, and to a lesser extent in the soil and floating in the air. Such is the diversity of the yeasts that several species may exist side by side on the same fruit, yet it is not inconceivable that an adjacent tree or even an adjacent fruit may possess quite a different yeast flora. Often, however, one particular type of yeast will tend to predominate in a given area of the world, because this species is slightly better adapted than any other to living in this environment.

The yeasts are a very simple form of life in that most of them are unicellular species, i.e. each individual cell is complete in itself and usually leads an existence independently of its fellows. It is comparatively rare to find an organised yeast colony in which certain cells have special functions as is the case with some of the algae. Single yeast cells are so small as to be invisible to the naked eye and can only be seen under a microscope, preferably at a magnification of 500 × or more. Some idea of their minute size can be gleaned from the fact that one fluid ounce of an actively fermenting must contains in the region of 6,000 million yeast cells. Although it is often possible to distinguish different species of yeast under the microscope solely upon the basis of their cell shapes which may be elliptical, lemon-shaped, triangular and so on, a study of their behaviour in culture media and of their general fermentation characteristics may also be necessary before a yeast can be identified with certainty, particularly when dealing with closely related species. Indeed, some yeasts are so similar that they can only be distinguished by stimulating spore formation, a technique which normally permits unequivocal identification.

Although certain species of yeast reproduce themselves by simple cell fission or even by the sexual union of what are termed positive and negative strains, the majority of yeasts have rather a novel and peculiar mode of reproduction known as vegetative budding. A mature yeast cell gives rise to a small protuberance known as a bud which gradually increases in size until at maturity this bud is identical in all respects to the parent cell. This daughter cell may then either break away from its parent or remain attached to it, but whichever course of action is pursued both cells have an independent existence. What is more, both cells can now give birth to daughter cells and so the process continues until the original cells become exhausted and die. Since each yeast cell can on the average produce about 30 daughter cells in this way

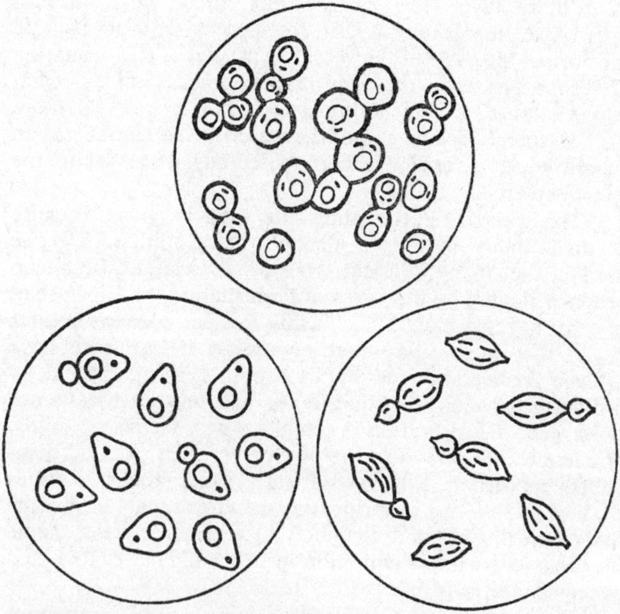

Yeast cells under the microscope: (Top) saccharomyces cerevisiae, (baker's yeast); (left) saccharomyces ellipsoideus (wine yeast); (right) kloeckera apiculata (wild yeast)

before it dies, it is clear that a thriving yeast colony can be built up very rapidly even from a single yeast cell under favourable conditions.

Sometimes conditions unsuited to the continued growth and reproduction of the yeast are established and then the yeast may be forced to hibernate. Many of the cells die, of course, but a certain number of them make preparations to ensure that the colony will re-establish itself once the danger period has passed. For example, the walls of these yeast cells may thicken to form a protective coat within which one or more spores are formed. Because these spores are very resistant to extremes of temperature, desiccation and similar conditions inimical to normal yeast cells, they can survive but remain dormant for long periods until the advent of a more favourable environment stimulates them into activity. A new colony is then founded by these spores and the normal life cycle of the yeast begins anew. The formation of resting spores in this way may sometimes explain what happens when a fermentation sticks, but it gives no more than a general background of the reasons why a fermentation should stick, a topic which is more fully discussed in the next chapter.

The winemaker is mainly interested in yeasts because of their ability to induce alcoholic fermentation. Despite the fact that many different types of bacteria and fungi can produce alcohol by a process of fermentation, certain species of yeast have developed this faculty to a considerably greater degree than most other micro-organisms. These yeasts have evolved fermentation as a means of producing the energy necessary for their growth and reproduction in the absence of oxygen. Fermentation is actually a very inefficient source of energy since one molecule of glucose when oxidised completely to carbon dioxide and water yields about 25 times the energy obtained by fermenting the same weight of glucose to carbon dioxide and alcohol. It nevertheless does enable the yeast to live under conditions which could not be tolerated by higher forms of life.

Alcoholic fermentation will take place both in the presence and in the absence of oxygen, i.e. under aerobic or anaerobic conditions, but the amount of alcohol produced from a given weight of sugar decreases as the oxygen supply increases. If the yeast is given all the oxygen it can utilise, very little alcohol is formed. The reason is that, when plenty of oxygen is available, the yeast can oxidise a considerable proportion of the sugar completely to carbon dioxide and water, and in this way it obtains a great deal more energy than fermentation alone could provide. This additional energy then enables the yeast colony to grow and multiply very rapidly. At the same time, it allows the yeast cells to convert some of the sugar into glycogen, a polysaccharide similar to starch, which is stored in the cell as a food reserve. In actual fact, active growth and reproduction of yeast is only observed under aerobic conditions. In the absence of oxygen, the yeast is forced to rely solely upon fermentation for its metabolic energy. As a result, life in the colony just ticks over while alcohol production reaches its maximum efficiency. It follows that aerobic conditions favour the growth and reproduction of the yeast at the expense of alcohol production whereas under anaerobic conditions the converse is true.

In winemaking, it is desirable that a thriving colony of yeast should be built up in the shortest possible time, but once this stage is reached the supply of oxygen must be cut off so that the maximum amount of alcohol is formed from the sugar in the must. These conditions are almost automatically introduced by normal winemaking procedures. During its preparation, the must is aerated to a greater or lesser extent by stirring or pouring it into the fermentation vessel, and an air space is usually left above the surface of the must. The yeast uses this oxygen for the initial phases of its growth and, by the time the supply is exhausted, the original yeast colony has grown large enough to maintain a satisfactory rate of fermentation until the first racking is due.

Once fermentation starts, the must and any air space above it quickly become saturated with carbon dioxide. Since this gas is heavier than air and is being evolved rapidly and continuously, it effectively blankets the fermenting must and prevents any further access of oxygen, thus ensuring anaerobic conditions during the later stages of fermentation. A cotton wool plug in the outlet of the container is therefore equally as effective as a fermentation lock insofar as restricting the entry of air to the must during fermentation is concerned. The latter merely has the advantage of indicating the rate of fermentation by showing at a glance how rapidly carbon dioxide is being evolved.

Yeast will usually continue to ferment either until it exhausts the sugar present in the must and produces a dry wine or until it is inhibited from further activity by the amount of alcohol which has been formed. In this latter case, the yeast is said to have reached its maximum alcohol tolerance, although many yeasts can be encouraged to exceed their normal maximum alcohol tolerance by regular feeding with small amounts of sugar during fermentation. Different species of yeast show marked variations in their maximum alcohol tolerance, however, and because a wine containing less than about 10% alcohol is unlikely to keep well, the winemaker is obviously very interested in this aspect of yeast behaviour.

Although the main function of yeast in winemaking is to produce alcohol, the overall quality of a wine can also be greatly influenced by the yeast. In view of the hundreds of different types of yeasts, the selection of a particular species for winemaking purposes must be based not only upon its maximum alcohol tolerance but also upon its effect on clarification, bouquet, flavour and so on. Thus, apart from a high alcohol tolerance, a yeast ideally suited for winemaking should preserve or enhance the natural bouquet and flavour of the ingredients, particularly when the latter have little character of their own, yet it should not impart the slightest trace of an off-flavour into the most delicate wines. Fermentation should proceed quietly from the bottom of the must and show no signs of sticking at all temperatures between about 50°F. and 75°F. Yeast cells suspended in the must should settle rapidly towards the end of fermentation to form a firm compact coherent deposit, thus facilitating both clarification and racking. Finally, autolysis of the dead yeast cells should be a slow process so that unpleasant musty off-flavours do not develop in the wine through the release of excessive amounts of decomposition products into the wine. Clearly, very few yeasts can hope to match these high standards, and it is therefore hardly surprising that the choice of yeasts suitable for winemaking is very limited.

In the past, many wines were made simply by allowing the natural or wild yeast present on the fruit to ferment the must, or the must would be left exposed to the air for several days in the hope that fermentation would be started by a strong airborne yeast cell. The so-called no-yeast recipes still encountered occasionally in older books also work on this principle. Sometimes a successful fermentation would begin and quite a good wine would be obtained, but more often either a yeast with a low alcohol tolerance would dominate the fermentation and produce an inferior wine or spoilage bacteria and moulds would gain the upper hand and completely ruin the wine. As a result, very few good wines were produced in this way. Indeed, many turned out to be so poor that they were almost undrinkable, which is probably why country wines made according to traditional recipes of this type fell into disrepute, a prejudice still not altogether dispelled even nowadays.

The commonest wild yeast found in this country is called *Kloeckera Apiculata*, frequently wrongly known as *Saccharomyces Apiculatus*, which can easily be recognised under the microscope by its typical lemon-shaped cells. This yeast is not at all well-suited for winemaking since it shows a very low alcohol tolerance, the short frothy fermentation rarely producing more than about 4% alcohol before the yeast becomes inhibited. Many winemakers also believe that *K. Apiculata* introduces off-flavours into a wine. Although it certainly does not make any notable contribution to either the bouquet or the flavour of a wine, the yeast itself does not seem to be harmful in this respect. Off-flavours are likely to develop if the wine is not racked regularly and frequently, however, for the dead cells of *K. Apiculata* autolyse very rapidly and their decomposition products can very quickly spoil a wine.

There are a number of other species of wild yeast indigenous to this country. While these yeasts are less common than *K. Apiculata*, they are nevertheless encountered quite frequently. The majority of these other wild yeasts resemble *K. Apiculata* very closely in their behaviour and fermentation characteristics and are therefore of little interest to the winemaker, but among the rarer species there are some wild yeasts with a high alcohol tolerance which can give good quality wines. It is for this reason that traditional no-yeast recipes occasionally produce worthwhile wines, but the chances of these yeasts not only entering the must but also dominating the fermentation are so slim that leaving a must to become infected with wild yeasts should never be attempted except perhaps for experimental purposes. For the record, however, Californian wine technologists have isolated and studied a loganberry yeast from Seattle which is capable of producing over 20% alcohol.

Perhaps the most familiar of the yeasts used for winemaking is baker's yeast, *Saccharomyces Cerevisiae*. At one time, this yeast was almost exclusively used by winemakers in this country. Since in former years a great deal of bread was baked in the home, it is hardly surprising that baker's yeast achieved its pre-eminence for winemaking purposes because it was most convenient to use the same yeast for both baking and winemaking. The function of the yeast in baking is simply to produce rapidly sufficient gas to make the dough rise, however, whereas in winemaking its main task is to produce alcohol. Hence, baker's yeast induces a vigorous frothy fermentation that is usually of comparatively short duration, after which the dead and inhibited yeast cells slowly settle to the bottom of the must to form a rather loose and easily disturbed deposit. Clarification is therefore a slow process and racking often proves troublesome due to the loose nature of the sediment. Moreover, because dead cells of baker's yeast autolyse rapidly, frequent racking is necessary to prevent off-flavours developing in this way.

It is clear from these remarks that baker's yeast is quite definitely not the best yeast for winemaking purposes. It nevertheless does offer some advantages to the beginner with little or no experience or knowledge of the subject. Baker's yeast is cheap, readily obtainable and easy to use because it can be added directly to the must. The fermentation is vigorous and thus very reassuring and will continue quite strongly at comparatively low temperatures. The alcohol tolerance of baker's yeast is also acceptably high and about 12% to 14% alcohol can normally be expected. The first few wines produced by beginners are often best made with baker's yeast since the experience gained in this way will prove invaluable when dealing with the more sensitive and delicate wine yeasts described later.

Baker's yeast can be purchased either direct from a bakery or in the form of dried granules, but whereas the former must be fresh and in good condition the latter will keep for months in a sealed tin. Many recipes recommend one ounce of baker's yeast (often spread upon a piece of toast) to start fermentation in a gallon of wine, but a teaspoonful of the dried granules sprinkled over the surface of a must will serve equally well. It is important to note that these quantities of yeast need not be proportionately increased for more than one gallon of must, however, otherwise an excessively violent frothing fermentation is likely to occur and an unduly large yeast deposit will almost certainly be formed. Thus, 2–3 ozs. of fresh baker's yeast or 3–4 teaspoonfuls of the dried form will suffice for up to 10 gallons of must.

Brewer's yeast is another strain of *Saccharomyces Cerevisiae*, but in this case it is a strain which has been found to be more suitable for brewing than for baking. Most yeasts of this type, particularly those used in this country, prefer to ferment from the top of the must with the result that a thick creamy head of yeast is formed on the surface of the fermenting liquid, and dealing with the froth may prove troublesome. Other species of yeast which are used for brewing lager, e.g. *Saccharomyces Carlsbergensis*, are bottom fermenting varieties which in this respect are preferable for winemaking. Brewer's yeasts often smell strongly of beer due to the presence of hop residues, however, and consequently an undesirable beery bouquet and flavour may develop in the wine. Hence, it is advisable to reserve brewer's yeast for brewing beer and not for making wine.

The yeast responsible for the fermentation of grape musts in the major wine producing countries of the world is botanically very closely related to baker's and brewer's yeasts. Thus, it is properly classified as *Saccharomyces Cerevisiae* variety *Ellipsoideus*, although nowadays the simplified name *S. Ellipsoideus* seems to have won general acceptance. *S. Ellipsoideus* is therefore actually a variety or sub-species of *S. Cerevisiae*, but despite this close taxonomic relationship these two yeasts show surprisingly different behaviour patterns. The disadvantages associated with the use of baker's yeast for winemaking purposes have already been discussed, but it has been found that *S. Ellipsoideus* suffers from none of these shortcomings. Indeed, *S. Ellipsoideus* satisfies almost all the conditions laid down earlier for an ideal wine yeast, and for these reasons it is the obvious choice when selecting the species of yeast best suited for winemaking. *S. Ellipsoideus* usually dominates the yeast flora in any given wine producing region because it is better fitted than its rivals to living under the conditions normally encountered in that area where, over the centuries, the process of natural selection, which works on the principle of the survival of the fittest, has operated in its favour. This picture becomes more complicated when it is realised that even minor variations in the climate, soil composition and other environmental factors all influence natural selection. As a result, numerous strains of *S. Ellipsoideus* whose characteristics vary to a greater or lesser extent according to the differences between their natural habitats have gradually evolved. A district with a variety of environments is therefore likely to have equally as many different strains of *S. Ellipsoideus* whereas another, perhaps adjacent, region which shows no significant variations of this type may very well possess only one predominant strain of the yeast.

At first sight, it would appear that the existence of these strains of *S. Ellipsoideus* would be of little significance as in many cases there are only very subtle differences between one strain and another. In practice, however, the wine produced in a particular district has been found to owe some of its unique individuality and character to the indigenous strain of yeast. The yeast often plays only a minor rôle in this respect, but at times its influence can be an important factor in determining the quality of the wine. When this is the case, two identical musts fermented under identical conditions by two different strains of *S. Ellipsoideus* may be noticeably different in both bouquet and flavour.

The discovery of these different strains of *S. Ellipsoideus* and the recognition of their importance in commercial wine production stimulated a great deal of research in this field which eventually led to the introduction of the modern selected wine yeasts. The strains of *S. Ellipsoideus* indigenous to many of the principal wine producing regions of the world were collected from the districts of their origin and grown as laboratory cultures. The latter were then submitted to a thorough scientific screening designed to isolate those strains of *S. Ellipsoideus* as pure cultures free from all the unwanted wild yeasts, moulds and bacteria normally found closely associated with the yeast in nature. This original work ranks as one of the major contributions science has made to winemaking, for its final result can now be seen in the wide range of pure wine yeast cultures which are readily available even to amateur winemakers for a very small outlay.

It is therefore clear from these remarks that a wine yeast described as, say, a Sauternes yeast, is simply a strain of *S. Ellipsoideus* which has been isolated from the Sauternes region of France, and not a yeast which will produce a Sauternes from any must to which it is added. Under appropriate conditions, a wine yeast will certainly tend to promote the development of the bouquet and flavour typical of the wine produced in the region of its origin.

Even then, however, its influence is usually relatively unimportant, although it has already been mentioned that some strains are more versatile than others in this respect. Sherry yeasts are noted for this ability, but it has also been established that many commercial German wines owe much of their unique character to the yeast. Indeed, the German wine producers became so alarmed by the ready availability of selected wine yeasts, which in their opinion would enable amateur winemakers to produce ersatz wines virtually indistinguishable from commercial grape wines, that strict laws were passed forbidding their use by the general public. Although this legislation has now been repealed, it does illustrate the importance attached to selected wine yeasts in the commercial world. A great deal of skill is usually required to imitate grape wines with any degree of success, however, for in most cases it is essential to prepare a must which closely complements the yeast. This aspect of amateur winemaking is more fully discussed in the chapters on commercial wines.

The real value of wine yeasts lies in their ability to bring out the latent qualities of a must. Few winemakers can honestly dispute the statement that better wines are obtained when the fermentation is conducted by a wine yeast rather than by baker's yeast. The fermentation itself is quiet, slow and steady, up to 16% alcohol can normally be produced without difficulty, racking is easier because the yeast forms a firm compact deposit and the dangers of off-flavours developing through the wine standing on its lees for too long are slight, since the yeast autolyses comparatively slowly. Moreover, a wine yeast preserves and enhances the natural bouquet and flavour of the ingredients. In this respect, the influence of the yeast becomes more important and pronounced when the ingredients of the must have little character of their own

When wine yeasts were first introduced to Britain, it was found that the fermentation would stick during spells of cold weather simply because these yeasts were accustomed to the higher temperatures normally encountered in the countries of their origin. To ensure a smooth uninterrupted fermentation, the winemaker was therefore obliged to maintain it at a temperature of at least 60°F. This rather serious disadvantage of wine yeasts has now been overcome. Recent work on the cross-breeding of different strains of yeast has resulted in the introduction of hybrid yeasts which are virtually identical with the original strains of *S. Ellipsoideus* except for the fact that they will continue to ferment, albeit slowly, at temperatures down to 42°F.

Wine yeasts can be purchased in the form of dried granules or tablets, as quiescent cultures suspended in a sterile nutrient solution or as agar slopes, i.e. cultures grown on nutrient agar jelly. The agar slopes are said to give the best results but liquid cultures are also excellent and both can be highly recommended. The same cannot be said of dried wine yeasts. The act of drying may have undesirable effects on the yeast and the culture may also become contaminated with other micro-organisms during the drying or packaging operations. Dried wine yeasts are therefore best avoided if other types of culture are available.

The quantity of yeast supplied in these cultures is generally insufficient to induce a sound fermentation within a short time. Even when using liquid cultures which can be added directly to the must, it is always better to prepare a starter from the culture first of all. The purpose of a starter is simply to activate and propagate the yeast in a small volume of must until a thriving and vigorous colony has been built up. Once this object has been achieved, the starter can be added to the must in the sure knowledge that a sound fermentation will begin within a comparatively short time, thus giving any other micro-organisms which may be present little chance to develop in opposition to the wine yeast.

Yeast starters are very easy to prepare and no difficulties should be encountered if the following directions are observed. A wine bottle is first sterilised with the stock sulphite solution mentioned in an earlier chapter and then thoroughly rinsed out with boiled water to remove any residual sulphite. About half a pint of must or an alternative basic starter medium to which about a tablespoonful of sugar, a teaspoonful of citric acid and a little yeast nutrient have been added is next sterilised by boiling it for a few minutes, after which it is cooled to room temperature under the tap. The cooled sterile solution is then poured into the wine bottle, the yeast culture added and the bottle immediately stoppered tightly with a plug of cotton wool. This starter is finally stood in a warm place at a temperature of about 75° to 80°F. for a few days until active fermentation begins when it is ready for use.

Many media are suitable for the preparation of yeast starters, but is is often advisable to use a bottle of must as the basis of the starter so that the yeast becomes acclimatised from the outset to living under the conditions it will experience during the fermentation of the must. If a small quantity of must cannot conveniently be obtained, pure strained fruit juices, particularly orange juice, or a solution containing a tablespoonful of malt extract dissolved in about half a pint of water can be used as alternative basic starter media. Several proprietary starter media are also available and give good results, most of these having a malt basis.

Since yeast starters are often the key to a successful fermentation, the salient features of their preparation are worth a more detailed discussion to ensure that the winemaker has a clear understanding of the principles involved. The importance of sterilisation in the preparation of starters must first be emphasised. Since the starter medium is a solution rich in nutrients which can equally well support the growth of many moulds and bacteria other than yeast, the latter may become contaminated with undesirable spoilage organisms if steps are not taken to prevent their growth. The starter medium and its container must therefore be sterilised before introducing the yeast culture to avoid mishaps of this nature. The container, usually a wine bottle, is most conveniently sterilised with strong sulphite solution. Sulphiting the actual starter medium is less satisfactory because the normal maximum dose of sulphite will kill only a proportion of the micro-organisms which may be present. The rest will merely be temporarily inhibited from further growth and may cause trouble later. Sulphite may also retard the development of the yeast during this early stage in the formation of the colony. Boiling is thus a much better method of sterilising the starter medium because it sterilises the solution more efficiently than sulphite and because no substances inhibitory to the yeast subsequently remain in it.

The growth of the yeast is also favoured by adding acid to the starter, for many micro-organisms do not grow well under strongly acid conditions which are readily tolerated by yeast. Citric acid is therefore an essential ingredient of starters for this reason. Tartaric acid may also be used, but it is less satisfactory because its inclusion somehow seems to prolong the induction period normally experienced before the first visible signs of fermentation are observed. The acid content of the starter should not, of course, be overlooked if the acidity of the must is checked prior to its addition.

It has already been mentioned that active growth and reproduction of yeast is only observed when it has a plentiful supply of oxygen. The effect of temperature upon the metabolism of the yeast has also been noted. Since a starter is prepared solely for the purpose of transforming the original dormant yeast culture into an actively fermenting nucleus colony before it is added to the must, warm aerobic conditions must be established in the starter medium to permit rapid propagation of the yeast. The starter bottle is therefore plugged with cotton wool which allows air to enter freely to replace that used up by the yeast but which at the same time excludes undesirable moulds and bacteria, and is stored in a warm place at a temperature of 75° to 80°F. The bottle may also be shaken occasionally to promote aeration.

The final important feature of yeast starters concerns the addition of nutrients and sugar. The basic starter medium normally contains a fair proportion of nutrients, but it is as well to augment this supply with a pinch each of ammonium and potassium phosphate and a vitamin B_1 tablet or a little marmite, since yeast growth would seriously be retarded by a shortage of these essential nutrients. In areas where the water is soft, a few crystals of magnesium sulphate may also be included if the starter medium is based on a malt extract. A small amount of sugar must also be added to act as a food reserve for the yeast, but in view of the fact that yeast grows better in dilute sugar solutions about 1 tablespoonful of sugar is adequate. If the starter begins to ferment before the must is ready, it can always be kept active by the addition of a little more sugar.

Although wine yeasts are rather more expensive and troublesome to use than baker's yeast, it is often overlooked that the starter prepared from a single culture can be made to ferment many gallons of wine. Only about three-quarters of the starter needs to be added to any one must. If the remaining solution is topped up with more freshly sterilised starter medium (and a fresh plug of cotton wool inserted in the bottle), further yeast growth will take place and the starter will again be in full fermentation a few days later. This procedure can be repeated *ad infinitum* provided the starter remains free from bacterial or fungal infection, but for this and other reasons it is advisable to renew the culture at least once a year. Starters can also be kept in a viable but quiescent state for several weeks by storing the starter bottle in a cool place at about 35° to 40°F. once the initial short fermentation has ceased. They can later be re-activated simply by adding a little sugar syrup and standing the starter bottle in warm surroundings.

In conclusion, it is worth noting that in an emergency the deposit removed at the second or later rackings can be used to start another fermentation, since this sediment is comprised mainly of viable yeast cells which have been inhibited from further activity either through a lack of sugar or by the high concentration of alcohol in the wine. The lees from the first racking should not be used for this purs pose, because it is heavily contaminated with dead yeast cell- and other unwanted debris. At subsequent rackings, the deposit will contain a much higher proportion of yeast and will therefore give much more reliable results.

CHAPTER X

YEAST NUTRIENTS

ALTHOUGH wine yeasts obtain their metabolic energy by the anaerobic fermentation of sugars, a yeast colony cannot normally be established in a pure solution of sugar because certain substances essential for its growth and well-being are absent under these conditions. Small amounts of potassium, magnesium, copper, iron, phosphates, sulphates, nitrogenous compounds and such accessory growth factors as vitamins and meso-inositol are required for yeast growth alone, but when active fermentation is proceeding a supply of calcium, cobalt, zinc and iodine is also necessary.

These minor growth factors are usually collectively known as yeast nutrients and may be regarded in much the same light as fertilisers are in gardening. In other words, fermentation will proceed much more satisfactorily in all respects if the yeast is adequately supplied with nutrients, although massive overdoses of them should be avoided for obvious reasons.

A shortage of yeast nutrients can prove quite serious and may even cause fermentation to stick in extreme cases. Any nutrient deficiency has some effect, however, for then the yeast colony may lack its customary vigour and fail to reach its normal maximum alcohol tolerance. The yeast must therefore always be provided with sufficient nutrients to ensure a sound fermentation, particularly if a high yield of alcohol is desired. It goes without saying that a sound fermentation leads to better quality wines.

The undiluted juice of ripe grapes is usually very well balanced with respect to sugar, acid, nutrients and the like. It is consequently an excellent medium for yeast growth and fermentation and rarely requires the addition of yeast nutrients because it is naturally endowed with ample amounts of the necessary trace elements. Few other fruit juices are quite so well balanced in this respect. Moreover, most fruit juices, vegetable extracts and so on are diluted with water, often to a considerable extent, during the preparation of the must. The concentration of the natural nutrients which are present in the must is thus often reduced by dilution with water to far too low a level for unrestricted yeast growth and reproduction to occur and fermentation is adversely affected.

In view of these facts, it is clearly inadvisable for the winemaker to assume that sufficient natural nutrients will normally be present in the must. Indeed, the converse is more often true. As a result, most experienced winemakers nowadays automatically add a supply of yeast nutrients when preparing the must to ensure that no nutrient deficiency can occur. This practice has much to recommend it. Even if ample natural nutrients were present and more were added, the resulting slight excess would have little or no detrimental effects on the quality of the wine. The problems which could arise from fermenting musts inadequately supplied with nutrients are therefore never encountered when this technique is adopted.

Many of the elements mentioned earlier are required in such small amounts that sufficient is normally present even in heavily diluted musts to permit a satisfactory fermentation. Copper, iron, cobalt, zinc and iodine may be included in this category and so too may most of the accessory growth factors, except perhaps for vitamin B_1. Magnesium and sulphate are usually available in adequate quantities in hard water districts, but if soft water has been used to prepare the must a pinch of magnesium sulphate (Epsom salts) per gallon is best added.

Since potassium salts constitute a major part of the mineral content or ash from yeast cells, this element is required in relatively large amounts. Many musts do contain enough potassium salts to support yeast growth, but a potassium deficiency is nevertheless quite frequently encountered. The addition of a quarter to half a level teaspoonful of potassium phosphate K_2HPO_4 per gallon is therefore advisable. Admittedly, an excess of potassium salts can subsequently cause persistent hazes due to the incipient precipitation of cream of tartar, but this risk is worthwhile if it means avoiding a nutrient deficiency. In any case, cream of tartar hazes are easily removed by chilling the wine.

A common feature of amateur wine musts is a shortage of nitrogenous substances. Some organic nitrogen will invariably be present in the form of amino-acids, proteins and the like, but often the quantity is insufficient and more must be added. Urea $NH_2.CO.NH_2$ or ammonium phosphate $(NH_4)_2HPO_4$ are normally employed for this purpose since both substances act as sources of readily available nitrogen for yeast. About half a teaspoonful of one or other of these two compounds will usually suffice. It is worth noting in the passing that the addition of urea or ammonium phosphate also has the advantage of reducing the amount of fusel oil produced during fermentation.

An adequate supply of phosphate is essential for a sound fermentation since many of the enzymic reactions concerned in fermentation involve the interconversion and degradation of complex organic phosphates. It is self-evident that these reactions could only proceed with difficulty if the available supply of phosphate was limited. Any phosphate deficiency is easily remedied by adding an inorganic phosphate to the must. Ammonium phosphate is ideal for this purpose since it provides the yeast with both nitrogen and phosphate simultaneously. The half teaspoonful of ammonium phosphate per gallon recommended above thus fulfils a double function and is preferable to urea for this reason.

It is also advisable to add some vitamin B_1 (alternatively known as aneurin hydrochloride or thiamine hydrochloride) to the must. This substance is an important accessory growth factor for yeasts and may often be absent or deficient in certain musts. Vitamin B_1 can be purchased cheaply in the form of 3 mgs. tablets, one of which per gallon will normally be adequate. Alternatively, about half a teaspoonful per gallon of marmite, which is a concentrated extract of yeast rich in this vitamin, may be used.

These nutrients should always be added at the time the must is being prepared and prior to its inoculation with the yeast to be fully effective, since the period of maximum yeast growth and reproduction occurs just before fermentation starts and for the ensuing few days. The colony which is established at this time must then be capable of taking the fermentation to completion since the yeast population will decrease rather than increase once anaerobic conditions are established. It is therefore very important to provide the optimum conditions for yeast growth and reproduction before the yeast starter is added to the must. Some yeast nutrients may also be added to yeast starters for this reason although the medium chosen for this purpose should normally contain ample natural nutrients in any case. Even if this practice is adopted, however, more nutrients should still be added to the must since most of those in the starter medium will be used up during the period of yeast growth in the starter itself.

Chapter XI

PREPARATION OF THE MUST

THE initial phase in the production of any wine is, of course, the preparation of the must. It is in fact a very critical stage because more can probably be done then than at any other time to influence the ultimate character and quality of the wine. The part played by many factors which make important contributions to the general wellbeing of a wine is at least partly but sometimes irrevocably determined at the time the must is being prepared. Proper control over these variables certainly cannot be exercised at a later stage once fermentation has commenced. Since the effect is the same whether the final balance of the must is achieved by accident or design, a sound knowledge of the basic principles and techniques of must preparation clearly offers the winemaker many advantages.

Perhaps the first point which should be emphasised is the importance of using the best and hence the ripest grade of ingredients available. Although it is often quite rightly said that good wine can be made from windfall apples and the like, it is equally true to say that such wines rarely attain the excellence which can (or should) consistently be achieved with top quality fruit. Admittedly, the twin problems of availability and cost must be considered in this connection particularly by city dwellers. Nothing can, of course, be done to improve matters if the choice is simply to take or to leave what is offered. When financial outlay is the limiting factor, however, the winemaker should always try to strike a balance between the cost and quality of the ingredients. It usually pays in the end to make smaller quantities of good wine from a more expensive grade of ingredients than large amounts of mediocre wine from a cheaper but poor quality version of the same ingredient. Price alone is nevertheless not the sole criterion of quality since many fruits are grown specifically for eating and often do not make good wine despite their high cost. Table grapes and dessert apples are typical examples of fruits belonging to this category. Bearing these exceptions in mind, however, the golden rule here is never to sacrifice quality for quantity (except perhaps when making a vin ordinaire where high quality is not required).

The winemaker who is also a gardener has enviable opportunities in this direction. At least a few selected ingredients can be grown fairly cheaply and in reasonable quantities even in a relatively small garden, and with careful tending their quality can often attain quite a high standard. Most important of all is that each ingredient can be harvested the moment it reaches its peak of condition and immediately converted into wine before any hint of deterioration has had a chance to occur. Such ingredients are obviously ideally suited to winemaking purposes and the high quality of the wine produced by many winemakers-cum-gardeners bears mute testimony to how much can be gained by combining the two activities.

Since this chapter is devoted to the preparation of the must, it may now be assumed that the winemaker has already chosen or devised a suitable recipe and obtained the necessary ingredients. The next step is to examine these ingredients carefully for soundness and then, where applicable, wash them thoroughly in warm water to remove dirt, dust, spray residues and so on. Completely rotten or mouldy fruits and vegetables should normally be rejected out of hand as their inclusion in the must would taint the wine. Minor bruised or otherwise damaged parts should be cut out and discarded for the same reason. Grain is sometimes contaminated with rat or mice droppings which must obviously be picked out before it is used as a wine ingredient. The green parts of flowers, notably sepals and pieces of stem, confer a bitter flavour on wines and are thus best removed. Similarly, other ingredients should be inspected, sorted and cleaned prior to use to avoid introducing undesirable constituents into the wine.

The ingredients are now ready to be incorporated in the must, and there are two basic techniques by which this object may be accomplished. Since the manner in which the must is prepared depends very much upon which of these two procedures is followed, each will be discussed in some detail so that the winemaker can compare and contrast their relative merits. A table suggesting suitable ways of handling some of the ingredients more commonly encountered in amateur winemaking has also been included later in this chapter for guidance and quick reference purposes.

The first and simpler of these two procedures is known as juice fermentation. As its name implies, juice fermentation utilises only the juice or a pulp-free extract of the ingredients and is generally employed when such a juice or extract can readily be obtained. It is the technique which should always be adopted for the production of wines where delicacy and finesse rather than fullness of body and flavour are sought. White table and sparkling wines are typical examples here because these wines almost invariably attain a higher standard of quality when produced by juice fermentation. Pulp fermentation not only tends to impart a coarser character but may also provoke difficulties with clarification under these circumstances.

It is consequently rather fortunate that the majority of fruits and vegetables commonly employed for white table wine production are amenable to juice fermentation techniques. Fruits are usually best dealt with by pressing out the juice directly either by hand or with the aid of a juice extractor or press. Since hand pressing is both laborious and inefficient, however, any winemaker dealing with more than a few pounds of ingredients at a time will clearly find it advisable to purchase or make some equipment for this purpose if none is already available. The chapter on equipment can, of course, be consulted for guidance in this connection.

There are otherwise no real practical problems. The fruit is merely stoned, crushed, sliced, milled, etc., as the case may be and its juice then pressed out. The freshly extracted juice should next immediately be treated with 100 p.p.m. sulphite both to prevent oxidative browning through the action of certain enzymes in the juice and to inhibit the growth of undesirable micro-organisms. The sulphited juice is finally transferred to a suitable container (preferably glass) which is sealed from the air and left to stand undisturbed in a cool place for 24 hours.

This waiting period serves a double purpose. In the first place, the potency of the sulphite will by then have diminished to a point where it scarcely affects the cultured yeast introduced when the preparation of the must has been completed. Secondly, a large proportion of the fine pulp particles inevitably present in any freshly expressed fruit juice will have had time to sink to the bottom of the container and there form a fairly loose but well-defined deposit of unwanted pulp debris. The relatively clear supernatant juice may thus be carefully racked off this sediment and transferred to another container in readiness for its incorporation in the must.

The lees remaining after this operation may be strained through a jelly bag into a smaller jar and left to settle further for another 24 hours. If several primary settling containers have been employed, the pulp deposit from each may, of course, conveniently be combined at this stage. The clear juice obtained in this manner should be racked off as before, but it is best fermented separately and reserved for topping up purposes. What pulp deposit still remains should be discarded as little if anything will be gained by attempting further settlings.

The volume, gravity and acidity of the bulk of the juice should be determined as soon as it is racked off the pulp deposit and these results entered in a record book together with all other relevant details, e.g. type and variety of the fruit, yield of juice per 10 lb. of fruit, cost per gallon of juice, pressing procedure and so on. Only the volume of the juice obtained from the secondary settling need be noted, however, as in other respects it should be the same as before. The amounts of sugar and acid contributed to the must from these sources can then easily be evaluated.

This data will also prove immensely useful in many other ways. For example, it will enable the winemaker to compare some important basic characteristics of various fruits and fruit juices. Such comparisons can, of course, be made between either different fruits and/or juices or different samples of the same fruit or fruit juice. In the latter case, the effects of varietal, regional, climatic and similar variable factors can immediately be detected and their significance fully comprehended. When careful records of this nature are kept in conjunction with a similar résumé and appraisal of the history and development of the wine from the preparation of the must to its final consumption, the winemaker will gradually accumulate a great deal of information which will prove invaluable for reference purposes. Its function may be regarded as that of a memory bank from which the broad ideas gained from past experience can be refreshed and rendered more specific as the occasion demands. The decision as to the purpose for which a given type and quality of ingredient is best suited can then be made with much more confidence and assurance than would otherwise be possible.

Vegetables normally require rather different handling from fruits. Although many vegetables can be cut up and pressed directly, especially by means of an electric juice extractor, this procedure is often unsatisfactory because some vegetable juices contain minor constituents which tend to coarsen the bouquet and flavour of wines. The inclusion of these substances in the must is consequently highly undesirable. Fortunately, their removal is facilitated by their appreciable volatility in steam. The vegetables should therefore be cut into chunks or slices and boiled vigorously in water in an open saucepan for some 10 to 30 minutes to dissipate as much of these volatile substances in the steam as possible. The extracted pulp need then only be strained off, pressed lightly and the spent residue discarded, this extract being added to that already obtained prior to pressing. It hardly need be added that the period of boiling also softens the pulp and thus makes pressing easier.

The vegetable extract obtained in this manner should subsequently be treated almost exactly as recommended for freshly expressed fruit juices. The only difference is that sulphiting is unnecessary in this case since the period of boiling will have effectively sterilised the extract and denatured any enzymes which could have caused oxidative browning. The addition of 50 p.p.m. sulphite will nevertheless do no harm and may be practised at the discretion of the winemaker as an extra precaution. Otherwise, settling and removal of the resultant pulp deposit are carried out exactly as before.

A number of fruits can also be treated according to the procedure just outlined for vegetables, but on the whole it is not advisable to do so. Bananas are the one notable exception to this rule. The most convenient method of dealing with this fruit is to peel it, cut it into slices and boil the latter (with or without the skins as the case may be) in water for about 30 minutes. After straining off the pulp, the banana extract should subsequently be handled in the same manner as a vegetable extract.

One important point about this method of preparing vegetable extracts should be very carefully noted. Some vegetables, particularly parsnips, contain quite large amounts of a substance called pectin which is readily extracted by boiling water. Although pectin is more fully discussed elsewhere, it may be remarked here that wines containing significant amounts of pectin may clear only with difficulty and occasionally may not clear at all. Since any natural pectin-destroying enzymes (collectively called pectinases) present in the vegetable are inactivated by the period of boiling, none remains in the must to degrade the pectin during fermentation as usually happens. It is therefore essential to make good the deficiency of natural pectinases observed under these circumstances by adding some enzyme preparation such as pectozyme or pectinol to the must at the rate of 1 oz. per 5–30 gallons according to how much pectin the ingredients contain.

Pulp fermentation is the alternative procedure to juice fermentation and naturally enough involves a period of fermentation on the pulp of the ingredients. This technique may be adopted with any ingredients which do not lend themselves to juice fermentation, as will be discussed shortly, but its principal application originally lay in the field of red wine production. Since the procedure to follow is the same in all cases, however, its main points will be discussed with reference to the preparation of red wine musts which have unique features not encountered with white wine ingredients.

The colour of many red fruits is localised or at least concentrated in the skins and is relatively insoluble in the cold juice so that very little can normally be extracted simply by pressing. Indeed, even when a fruit does yield a red juice, its colour is generally too pale to permit its direct conversion into red wine even if dilution with water can be avoided, which is rarely possible except with ripe grapes. Some means must therefore be devised to extract the colour from the skins of red fruits when red wines are sought.

One way of achieving this object is to crush the fruit and heat the mass of the juice and pulp to about 130°F. for some time. This method is employed for the production of red grape juice or concentrate, but it is really none too satisfactory as a winemaking technique. For example, a common objection to heating procedures is that they often introduce a "cooked" flavour into the wine, but whether this point is valid in amateur winemaking is open to question. What is certain, however, is that the flavour of the wine is different when heat has been applied to the crushed fruit to extract colour.

In actual fact, the only acceptable method of producing red wine is by pulp fermentation. Its success depends upon the fact that the red pigments in the skins of the fruit are relatively soluble even in quite dilute solutions of alcohol. The alcohol produced during the fermentation therefore leaches out colouring matter from the fruit pulp which is left in the must until a satisfactory depth of colour is achieved. Once this stage is reached, the pulp is strained off, pressed lightly and the spent residue discarded.

This brief description suggests that pulp fermentation offers greater practical difficulties than juice fermentation, but while it undoubtedly does call for more care and attention and finer judgment on the part of the winemaker, the basic technique is nevertheless quite simple and straightforward.

The first step is to stone the fruit, where possible, or at any rate to crush it, for the skins must be broken prior to fermentation or colour extraction may proceed rather slowly in many cases. The fruit is then placed in a wide-necked container such as a plastic bucket. The reason for stipulating a wide-necked vessel is, of course, to permit easy removal of the pulp when the time comes to strain it off. Sufficient water at least to cover the crushed fruit is next added. This mixture is finally treated with 100 to 150 p.p.m. sulphite, covered with a cloth or tight fitting lid and left to stand undisturbed in a cool place for 24 hours to allow the effects of the sulphite to moderate. It seems scarcely worth adding that the must should be kept closely covered from this point until the pulp is removed to prevent the ingress of dust, insects and airborne micro-organisms which would cause contamination and spoilage.

After 24 hours, the preparation of the must should be completed as described later and a suitable yeast starter added. Once active fermentation begins, the carbon dioxide evolved during this period will force the pulp to the surface of the must where it will form a thick, compact layer called a "cap." Fermentation proceeds very rapidly in this cap, but so too will the growth of any vinegar bacteria and related micro-organisms which may be present. Consequently, spoilage can all too easily occur if steps are not taken to inhibit the development of these highly undesirable micro-organisms. In addition, colour extraction will proceed rather slowly unless good contact is maintained between the pulp and the fermenting must. Hence, in order to minimise the risk of spoilage and to achieve a rapid rate of colour extraction, it is essential to break up the cap and mix it thoroughly with the rest of the must at least once but preferably twice or thrice daily. Indeed, the prescription for success here could well read "One vigorous stir morning, noon and night"!

The must should be checked regularly during the period of pulp fermentation to determine how much colour has been leached out of the fruit. The best way of assessing progress in this direction is to take a small sample of the must, strain out any suspended pulp particles through muslin and then examine its colour in a wineglass held in front of a strong light. If the must is subsequently going to be diluted with water, the sample should also be diluted to approximately the same extent before inspecting its colour, otherwise the pulp may be removed prematurely and a rosé rather than a red wine obtained.

The pulp is strained off as soon as this test shows that the must has achieved a satisfactory depth of colour. It is then pressed and the spent residue discarded (unless it still contains ample reserves of colour when it may be added to another must purely as a colouring agent). The point to note is that the pulp should be removed immediately the must is considered to be sufficiently deep red in colour. Failure to do so can result in a harsh astringent wine which lacks refinement due to the extraction of too much tannin from the fruit.

Unfortunately, it is impossible to be precise about the length of time required to reach this stage, for the ease with which different fruits donate their colour to the must varies very widely. For example, as little as 12–24 hours on the pulp will often suffice for elderberries whereas some varieties of cherries will barely attain even an acceptable depth of colour after a week or more, which is about the maximum time that a pulp fermentation should be allowed to continue with this type of ingredient.

The winemaker must therefore exercise careful judgment to decide when the time is ripe to strain off the pulp in red wine production.

Although pulp fermentation was originally developed primarily as a convenient means of producing red wines (which is still the case commercially), it also serves a number of other useful functions in amateur winemaking. Here, of course, the variety of ingredients is such that the standard fermentation techniques employed in commercial white wine production cannot always be applied. Some ingredients are simply not amenable to this type of approach either because their juice is difficult to obtain by direct pressing or because little or no juice as such is present. Certain fruits, flowers, herbs and grain are typical ingredients of this type.

Dried fruits, gooseberries, yellow plums, greengages and rosehips are some common fruits employed in white wine production which do not lend themselves to juice fermentation procedures. These ingredients can be treated in the same manner as vegetables, but this method of preparation is not particularly conducive to quality under these circumstances. Pectin extraction is but one of the problems which must then be overcome. Soaking the fruit in water for a specified period of time prior to fermentation is another frequently suggested approach which is certainly superior to boiling in water but suffers from the grave disadvantage of providing conditions eminently suitable for the growth of undesirable micro-organisms, especially moulds and wild yeasts. On the other hand, it must be admitted that mould growth on the surface of certain musts prior to fermentation has been claimed to have a beneficial effect on wine quality. Unfortunately, no reliable evidence supporting this theory has yet been obtained. Hence, until the facts of the matter have been established, it seems preferable to avoid this practice except possibly on an experimental basis. Any surface mould which may grow prior to or during fermentation should therefore be removed very carefully, the pulp strained off and the must fermented as quickly as possible to a fairly high alcoholic strength to kill the remaining fungal spores. In view of these remarks, procedures which involve soaking the fruit in water seem to possess no real advantage over pulp fermentation techniques. Indeed, the former would appear to be less attractive if the development of spoilage organisms is thereby encouraged. The winemaker therefore has every reason to conclude that pulp fermentation offers the best means of dealing with fruits whose juice is not readily obtainable.

In practice, these fruits should be treated in the same manner as already outlined for the preparation of red wine musts, but with one important difference. The purpose here is primarily to extract bouquet and flavour, not colour, from the ingredients. Once again, the duration of the pulp fermentation should be kept as short as possible commensurate with achieving this object to avoid producing a coarse white wine. The point is that the rate of colour extraction was the unknown factor which made it impossible to specify how long a red wine pulp fermentation ought to last, whereas no such restriction operates in this case. Much closer limits can thus be set on the length of a white wine pulp fermentation and for most fruits a period of 2–4 days will normally be quite adequate. The pulp is then strained off, pressed and the spent residue discarded as before.

Grain is another class of ingredient which requires pulp fermentation. In this instance, however, the most convenient procedure is to soak the grain in sulphited water (50 to 100 p.p.m.) for some 24 to 48 hours so that it can absorb water and soften. The individual grains can then more easily be crushed by means of a coarsely set mincer before being added to the must. Cracked grain such as flaked maize may, of course, be incorporated directly into the must without a preliminary soaking in water since it is already crushed. Thereafter, grain is dealt with according to the same principles as before except that the pulp fermentation should be extended to 4–5 days.

Many amateur winemakers have now begun to use flowers to improve the bouquet of their wines. This technique has much to recommend it and is particularly valuable in white table wine production where many ingredients fail to provide a sufficiently powerful and fragrant bouquet. The basic bouquet of a fruit together with the heady perfume of a flower provides a wholly delightful combination which adds greatly to the character of a white wine.

Since flowers contain a negligible amount of juice, it is clear that juice fermentation procedures are again unsuitable for these ingredients. A common method of dealing with flowers is to pour boiling water over the petals or even the whole flower heads and leave this mixture to infuse until it is cool. The flowers are then strained off and discarded and the floral extract added to the must. Sometimes the flowers may actually be boiled in water as a more rapid means of achieving this end, but the basic idea is still the same. Neither of these procedures, particularly the latter, should be adopted except in special instances. The reason is that many of the fragrant floral constituents whose presence in the must confers bouquet are relatively volatile esters and related compounds. Any form of heating can consequently cause a substantial loss of these components, but boiling or even hot water is especially hazardous in this respect since many volatile substances are very easily vaporised and dissipated in steam. Extraction procedures utilising boiling water thus unnecessarily deprive the wine of important bouquet-enriching substances and are therefore best avoided entirely.

Pulp fermentation techniques permit the retention of a much higher proportion of these volatile floral constituents. Even then, there is a danger that some of the more volatile components may be lost because the gas evolved during fermentation entrains and carries off water, alcohol and so on as it escapes to the atmosphere. The ease with which floral esters and the like are vaporised naturally makes their removal in this manner all too simple a task. These losses can fortunately be minimised by delaying adding the flowers to the must until the initial violent primary fermentation, which releases enormous volumes of gas in a very short time, has abated. This stage will normally be reached some 7–10 days after fermentation has commenced. The flowers can then be introduced and the gentler fermentation coupled with the higher alcohol content of the must will both extract and retain their fragrance much more efficiently. A period of 2–4 days will normally be ample for this purpose, after which the flowers should be strained off, pressed lightly and the spent residue discarded.

Once the winemaker has prepared a juice, extract or mash of crushed pulp it is usually necessary to wait for 24 hours before completing the preparation of the must. Sulphiting and/or cooling and/or settling are the main reasons for this delay according to which basic procedure is being followed. Thereafter comes the final balancing of the must prior to introducing the yeast starter. The essential features here are the same for all musts and include the addition of nutrients, checking and adjustment of sugar content and acidity and, for some white wines, the addition of tannin.

The first step is to blend the primary ingredients of the must unless, of course, only one ingredient is employed or there are good reasons for not doing so until later, e.g. flowers. Water may also be added at this stage according to the degree of dilution desired, but it is advisable to make allowance for the volume occupied by sugar and any other ingredient which has still to be added (2 lb. of sugar occupy a volume of 1 pint). For this reason, only about half to two-thirds of the total quantity of water needed should be added at this point, especially when carrying out a pulp fermentation where it is very difficult to judge the volume of must accurately.

Since the natural sugar content of most amateur wine musts is usually comparatively low, considerable augmentation with cane sugar, honey or some other suitable sweetening agent can rarely be avoided. The first task is nevertheless to check the gravity of the must and determine its natural sugar content. The amount of sugar needed to attain a specified alcohol content may then be calculated as indicated in the chapter on the hydrometer. As an initial gravity much in excess of 100 is not normally encountered in table wine production, it is simplest and most convenient to add the whole of the sugar at the outset. For dessert wines and the like, however, the technique of feeding the yeast regularly with small doses of sugar is infinitely preferable so that the initial gravity of the must is kept within the range 60 to 100. Feeding is subsequently carried out as explained in the hydrometer chapter.

Once the sugar requirements of the must have been satisfied, the winemaker can often dilute it directly to its final volume with water. Some space may be left in the container if feeding is practised, but it is by no means essential to do so even under these circumstances since any excess wine can be utilised for topping up purposes after rackings. The same is not true for pulp fermentations where the volume of the must cannot properly be assessed until the pulp is removed and pressed. In this latter instance, it is better to add initially just enough water to dilute the must to approximately three-quarters of the required final volume. Any error of judgment will not then result in excessive over-dilution, and the volume of the must can be accurately adjusted later when the pulp has been strained off.

Yeast nutrients are the next important item. The actual amounts of the various nutrients required can be ascertained from the chapter on this subject and need not be further discussed here. It is worth noting, however, that if the intention is to dilute the must considerably at a later date, a further small supply of nutrients should really be provided at this time since the existing yeast colony has to grow in size to ferment the larger volume of must successfully. This procedure is often advisable after the pulp has been removed from a pulp fermentation and the must diluted to its final volume. Otherwise, the initial supply of nutrients ought to be adequate to sustain the yeast throughout the entire fermentation.

All that now remains is to check and adjust the acidity of the must according to the recommendations in the acidity chapter. Allowance must again be made if subsequent dilution is intended. For example, if a must containing 3.5 p.p.t acid had an initial volume of 4 gallons but was later diluted to 5 gallons, the acidity of the latter would be proportionately reduced to 2.8 p.p.t. Hence, acidity adjustments should always be based on the final volume of wine which will be produced and not on the initial volume of the must. This problem can fortunately be avoided when juice fermentation techniques are employed since the must can be diluted directly to its final volume immediately its sugar requirements are satisfied but before its acid content is checked and adjusted. Pulp fermentations are usually less easy to deal with. Since the initial volume of the must is but inaccurately known, the effect of dilution on its acid content cannot be calculated. Moreover, acid will be extracted from the ingredients during the course of the fermentation so that any earlier acid determination will be rendered invalid in any case. Under these circumstances, the winemaker cannot and should not try to check and adjust the acidity of the must until the pulp is removed. It is then convenient to dilute the must to its final volume before doing so. On the other hand, some acid may be added initially to pulp fermentation musts prepared solely from ingredients known to lack acid, e.g. flowers, grain, bananas, to prevent the development of off-flavours associated with acid deficiency. This preliminary adjustment should subsequently be checked and the acidity balanced properly as soon as the pulp is strained off. It hardly need be added that the inclusion of flowers for bouquet purposes will not affect the acid content of the must and may therefore be ignored in this connection.

Tannin may be added at this stage if any is required, but otherwise the must should now be ready for inoculation with the selected yeast culture. The latter should be introduced in the form of an actively fermenting starter so that the must itself begins to ferment as soon as possible thereafter. The only point to note here is that the container of the must should not be completely filled at first in case frothing occurs and the fermenting must overflows. If necessary, some of the must should be placed in a separate container until the initial vigorous primary fermentation moderates to some extent and there is little danger of frothing. From then on the winemaker should conduct the fermentation, rack, clarify and mature the wine as suggested in the following chapters.

RECOMMENDED PROCEDURE FOR HANDLING SOME COMMON INGREDIENTS

Ingredient	*Juice Fermentation*	*Pulp Fermentation*
APPLES	Extract juice with electric juicer or mill the fruit to a fine pulp and press out the juice in a conventional press.	Preferably avoided due to superiority of juice fermentation. If there is no alternative, cut the fruit into slices and pulp ferment for four days.
APRICOTS	Stone the fruit and extract the juice in a conventional press. Fruit handled in this manner should be fully ripe and fairly juicy.	Less satisfactory than juice fermentation but may prove necessary if the fruit lacks juice. Stone the fruit and pulp ferment for two or three days.
BANANAS	Peel the fruit and cut into slices. Boil the latter in water with or without some or all the skins for half an hour. Strain off the pulp carefully but do not press as little will be gained by doing so.	None too satisfactory owing to the ease with which the pulp completely disintegrates. Extraction with boiling water is simpler and more effective.
BERRIES, e.g. blackberries, raspberries, mulberries and similar fruits	Crush and extract the juice directly in a conventional press if fruit is required mainly for flavouring purposes and not as a source of colour.	Probably the better procedure for most purposes. Crush the fruit and ferment on the pulp until sufficient flavour and/or colour is extracted.
CHERRIES	Normally unsuitable due to impossibility of removing stones and because most varieties are used for red wine production and hence require pulp fermentation.	Crush the fruit to break the skins but do not stone unless only a few pounds of fruit are used. Pulp ferment until the must attains a satisfactory depth of colour.

Recommended Procedure for handling some common ingredients—*cont.*

Ingredient	*Juice Fermentation*	*Pulp Fermentation*
CITRUS FRUITS, e.g. lemons, oranges, grapefruit, etc.	Cut the fruit in half and express juice with a citrus fruit juicer. Alternatively, stand the fruit in boiling water for five minutes, peel and extract juice from segments with electric juicer or press.	Unsuitable. Procedures advising slicing the whole fruit and pulp fermenting should be avoided. If desirable, however, some peel (no pith) may be included in the must for flavouring.
CURRANTS (black, red and white)	Can be crushed and pressed, but the juice yield may be rather low. Colour extraction is also usually required which necessitates pulp fermentation.	Crush the fruit to break the skins and pulp ferment to extract colour. Redcurrants will not normally give more than a deep rose wine. White currants should be removed after 2–4 days since only flavour will be extracted.
DRIED FRUITS, e.g. raisins, apricots, elderberries, dates.	Inadvisable even if the fruit is first soaked in water.	Crush the soaked fruit and pulp ferment for 2–4 days if the main intention is to extract flavour. If colour is also required, pulp ferment until a satisfactory depth of colour is attained.
ELDERBERRIES	Extract the juice directly in an electric juicer or crush the fruit and press in a conventional press. Since the juice on dilution will normally give a rose or light red wine, a short pulp fermentation is generally required for red wine production.	Crush the fruit and pulp ferment until a deep red must is obtained. As little as 12–24 hours is often sufficient to achieve this object.
FLOWERS AND LEAVES	Impossible since there is no juice to extract.	Leaves should be added to a must as soon as fermentation begins, but flowers should not be included until the primary fermentation has abated after 7–10 days.

Recommended Procedure for handling some common ingredients—*cont.*

Ingredient	*Juice Fermentation*	*Pulp Fermentation*
GOOSEBERRIES	Fully ripe fruit may be crushed and pressed directly but it is usually better to pulp ferment. Green gooseberries are not amenable to juice fermentation.	Crush the fruit and pulp ferment for 2–4 days. Green gooseberries may be crushed more easily if left to soak overnight in sulphited water to soften.
GRAIN	Impossible since there is no juice to extract.	Soak in water for 24–48 hours to soften the grain, then crush in a coarsely set mincer. Flaked grain does not require this treatment. Pulp ferment for 4–5 days.
GRAPES	White grapes should be crushed and pressed directly as may red grapes used for white wine production.	Crush red grapes and pulp ferment until a satisfactory depth of colour is attained. White grapes can also be pulp fermented for 2–4 days but it is much better not to do so.
PEACHES	Stone and press the fruit directly in a conventional press.	Preferably avoided, but if no other alternative stone fruit and pulp ferment for 2–3 days.
PEARS	Crush or slice fruit and press in a conventional press.	Unsuitable owing to poor flavour obtained in this manner.
PINEAPPLES	Top the fruit, cut into slices and extract juice with electric juicer. Mince or mill fruit if a conventional press is employed.	Moderately satisfactory but preferably avoided. If necessary however, slice fruit and pulp ferment for 2–3 days.

Recommended Procedure for handling some common ingredients—*cont.*

Ingredient	*Juice Fermentation*	*Pulp Fermentation*
RHUBARB	Crush the "fruit" and extract the juice by means of an electric juicer or conventional press. The crushed fruit may also be extracted twice with cold water if pressing is inconvenient, but hot water should never be used as the must may then contain rather too much of the poisonous oxalic acid.	Preferably avoided since too much poisonous oxalic acid tends to be extracted under these conditions.
PLUMS, GREENGAGES, SLOES, DAMSONS AND RELATED FRUITS.	Normally impossible due to the difficulty with which the fruits yield their juice.	Stone the fruit and pulp ferment for 3–4 days in the case of white or yellow varieties where flavour extraction is desired. Red varieties should be pulp fermented until a satisfactory depth of colour is attained.
VEGETABLES	Cut the vegetable into chunks or slices and boil in water until tender. Strain off and press the pulp. Care should be taken not to overboil or the pulp may disintegrate.	Unsuitable since the raw vegetable tends to impart a coarse flavour to the wine.

CHAPTER XII

FERMENTATION

THE term fermentation is nowadays understood to describe almost any process which enlists the aid of micro-organisms as a means of preparing useful products, very often difficult to obtain by any other method, from more readily available materials. It therefore embraces the production of such diverse and commercially important substances as alcohol, acetone, acetic acid (vinegar), citric acid, n-butanol, numerous antibiotics (e.g. penicillin and aureomycin) and so on. In winemaking, however, fermentation is generally assumed to refer only to alcoholic fermentation, i.e. the process by which yeast converts the sugar in a must into alcohol and carbon dioxide together with minor amounts of various by-products, and thereby creates wine. It follows from this definition that successful winemaking is fundamentally dependent upon conducting a sound fermentation and that a clear understanding of at least the elementary principles of fermentation is obviously a great aid towards improving wine quality.

In the past, a great aura of mystery surrounded the process of fermentation. As long ago as 1810, the French chemist Gay-Lussac correctly advanced the following equation to account for the formation of alcohol and carbon dioxide from sugar during fermentation, but at that time no satisfactory explanation or reason for this occurrence had been suggested. Various improbable theories had been proposed to explain this phenomenon, but because yeasts were then not considered to have any significance in this respect no further progress was made for many years.

$$\underset{\text{Glucose or Fructose}}{C_6H_{12}O_6} \longrightarrow \underset{\text{Ethyl Alcohol}}{2CH_3CH_2OH} + \underset{\text{Carbon Dioxide}}{2CO_2}$$

Following the pioneering work of Pasteur in the latter part of the nineteenth century, the fact that yeasts were responsible for causing fermentation gradually won general acceptance. It then became clear that the Gay-Lussac equation, as it is called, merely represented an overall picture of alcoholic fermentation. Thus, it cannot account for the formation of small amounts of certain by-products which are invariably produced during a normal fermentation in addition to alcohol and carbon dioxide. This discovery naturally stimulated a great deal of research work in this field designed to elucidate the mechanism by which fermentation proceeds.

Eventually, as a result of much sustained scientific investigation, it was shown that fermentation, far from being a simple process, proceeds by a complex series of stepwise inter-related chemical reactions initiated and controlled by substances called enzymes which are secreted by the individual yeast cells. Enzymes are actually special proteins which can promote or catalyse specific chemical reactions in living cells without undergoing any permanent change themselves. In the case of yeast, a group of enzymes collectively known as the zymase complex is responsible for controlling fermentation.

The fact that enzymes secreted by the yeast cells rather than the actual living cells themselves are the active agents in fermentation was proved shortly before 1900 when Buchner showed that an extract prepared from yeast containing neither living nor dead cells but only the enzymes of the zymase complex (and other water-soluble matter) could induce fermentation on its own. Each individual enzyme in this enzyme complex was also found to govern one and only one of the intermediate stages of fermentation. Once its task has been completed, another enzyme takes over and so on, the process continuing in such a way that each sugar molecule undergoes a progressive series of enzymic reactions which finally result in its degradation to alcohol and carbon dioxide with the release of a small amount of metabolic energy.

The introduction of modern techniques such as radioactive tracer studies provided further valuable information regarding the mechanism of fermentation. Consequently, the chemistry of this process is now known in considerable detail . Although few winemakers are likely to want a more detailed exposition of this particular subject, this chart showing the general scheme of the principal chemical reactions occurring during fermentation and accounting for the formation of the important by-product glycerol (glycerine) has been included for the sake of completeness.

PRINCIPAL CHEMICAL REACTIONS OF ALCOHOLIC FERMENTATION

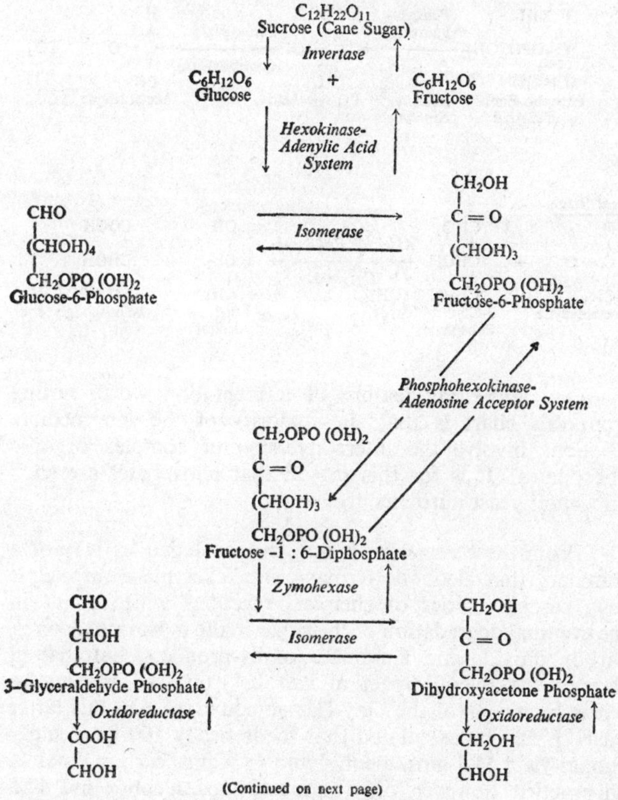

(Continued on next page)

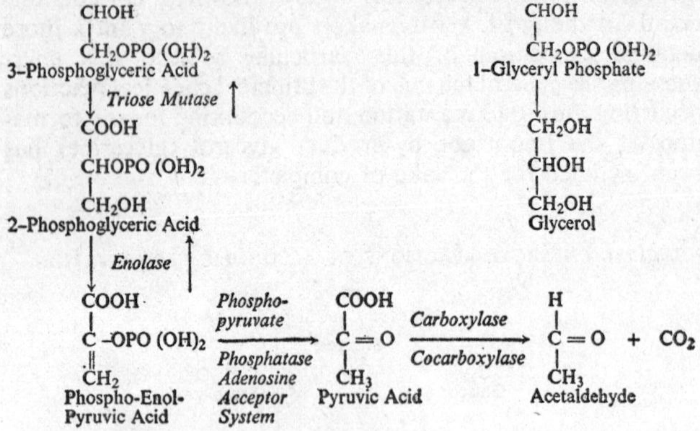

Final Stage

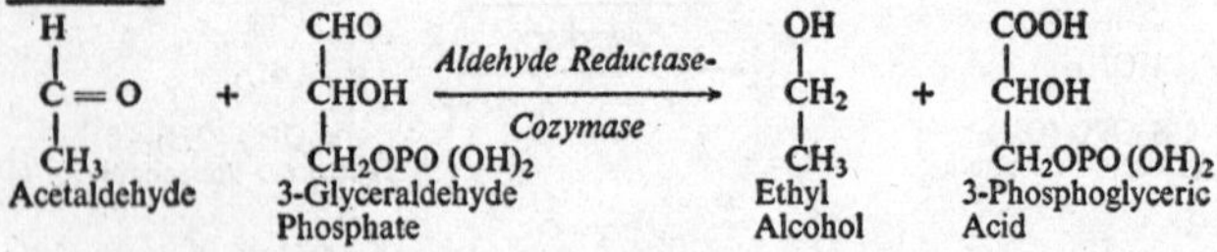

One interesting feature of fermentation worth noting from this chart is that the majority of the intermediate reactions involve the interconversion of complex organic phosphates. It is for this reason that phosphates are such important yeast nutrients.

From these remarks, it may be concluded by way of a summary that alcoholic fermentation takes place through a long complex series of chemical reactions which result in the eventual degradation of the sugar in the must into alcohol, carbon dioxide and a number of by-products, but that in essence the overall reaction can be expressed in simpler terms by means of the Gay-Lussac equation. On this latter basis, it can be calculated that theoretically 100 gms. sugar should yield 51.1 gms. alcohol and 48.9 gms. carbon dioxide. In practice, however, only about 48 gms. alcohol and 47.5 gms. carbon dioxide are actually obtained from this weight of sugar. A number of factors are responsible for this difference, but usually the losses of alcohol sustained during fermentation can be attributed to the fact that a small amount of sugar is used up in the formation of by-products and a little more sugar is metabolised completely to carbon dioxide and water and/or converted into storage carbohydrate glycogen by the yeast. Further small losses of alcohol also occur by its evaporation or entrainment in the gas evolved during fermentation. It therefore follows that secondary factors such as temperature, rate of fermentation, availability of oxygen and so on which influence these primary factors must also have some bearing on the final yield of alcohol. On the average, however, the winemaker may reasonably expect to obtain 90%–95% of the theoretical yield of alcohol from a given weight of sugar. The potential alcohol tables in the chapter on the hydrometer have accordingly been calculated on this assumption.

In addition to the principal products alcohol and carbon dioxide, a number of by-products are also always formed during a normal alcoholic fermentation, notably the trihydric alcohol glycerol (glycerine) which is usually present in wines to the extent of 1%–2%. Most of this glycerol is produced near the beginning of the fermentation. The presence of a small amount of acetaldehyde, a substance formed by one of the last enzymic reactions in the complete fermentation series, is essential if the overall reaction is to yield alcohol. Acetaldehyde is important in this respect because it acts as a hydrogen acceptor for an oxidation-reduction enzyme system. The reduced enzyme is converted back into its oxidised form by the acetaldehyde which is consequently itself reduced to alcohol. During the early stages of fermentation, no acetaldehyde is present so that the whole series of enzymic reactions leading finally to the formation of alcohol is delayed until sufficient acetaldehyde is produced to allow these reactions to proceed. In the meantime, another substance called dihydroxyacetone acts as an alternative hydrogen acceptor with the result that it becomes reduced to glycerol. Once sufficient acetaldehyde has accumulated, the latter reaction is discontinued and fermentation proceeds normally to yield alcohol. Subsequently, little more glycerol is formed.

It follows from this discussion that any substance which reacts with acetaldehyde to form an inactive complex would promote the production of glycerol by extending the duration of the dihydroxyacetone reduction reaction. Indeed, in extreme cases, the fermentation could even be adjusted to yield glycerol rather than alcohol as the major product, and this was in fact practised during the last war to augment glycerol supplies from other sources. One substance which complexes acetaldehyde in this way is sulphite. The practice of sulphiting the must prior to fermentation thus almost invariably leads to wines with a fairly high glycerol content. Sulphiting after racking will also increase the glycerol content of a wine if fermentation is subsequently renewed. Any acetaldehyde already in the wine at the time of racking will be bound by the sulphite and further glycerol will be produced until the deficit of acetaldehyde is made up and fermentation again gets under way. Other factors which favour glycerol formation include lower fermentation temperatures, and a higher proportion of tartaric acid in the must, but the strain of yeast used to conduct the fermentation also seems to have an important influence in this respect.

Pure glycerol is a dense, viscous, rather oily liquid (specific gravity 1.260) with a distinctly sweet taste. In view of the fact that wine usually contains some 1%–2% of this substance, its effects on the flavour and general quality of the wine obviously cannot be ignored. Apart from adding slightly to the sweetness of a wine, glycerol also adds body and helps to create a smoother flavour by virtue of its oleaginous properties. Indeed, the addition of glycerol to wines containing too much tannin or too much acid is a recognised means of reducing their harshness or tartness to a more palatable level. Wines which have been produced from grapes infected by the mould *Botrytis Cinerea* usually have an exceptionally high glycerol content. In this rather special case, some of the glycerol is formed in the grapes as a result of the fungal attack and the remainder is subsequently produced as a fermentation by-product in the normal way.

A second important by-product of fermentation is fusel oil. This material is not a single substance but a mixture of higher alcohols, mainly isomeric amyl alcohols. Unfortified wines normally contain less than 0.5% of these constituents.

Most of this fusel oil is formed by the de-amination of amino-acids, especially leucine and isoleucine, during the nitrogenous metabolism of the yeast. It has now been established that by no means all the fusel oil found in wines is derived from this source, however, and that some must be produced by alternative routes, possibly from sugars. In general, fusel oil is an undesirable constituent of wines except in very low concentrations, otherwise its powerful aroma and rather harsh flavour, not to mention its poisonous properties, may prove objectionable. The addition of readily available sources of nitrogen, e.g. ammonium salts, to the must prior to fermentation helps to decrease the amount of fusel oil formed. The use of yeast nutrients containing ammonium phosphate thus will automatically aid in keeping fusel oil production at a low level.

The only other notable by-product of fermentation is succinic acid, which is formed in quantities amounting to about 1% of the alcohol, e.g. a wine containing 15% alcohol would also contain about 0.15% succinic acid. This substance is important in wines because it helps to promote vinous character. It is derived at least in part by de-amination of the amino-acid glutamic acid.

Mention may also be made of the fact that very smal- amounts of acetaldehyde, 2 : 3-butylene glycol, acetyll methylcarbinol, diacetyl, acetic acid, lactic acid, methyl alcohol (from pectin degradation), hydroxymethylfurfural (in heated wines) and so on are all recognised by-products of fermentation. With the exception of acetaldehyde which has a strong aroma and may therefore add to the bouquet of a wine, these substances make little difference to the quality of a wine, mainly because they are present in such small quantities. Admittedly, lactic acid can be the principal acid present in some red wines, but in such cases it has been produced by a malo-lactic fermentation and cannot therefore be classified as a true yeast fermentation by-product. Similar remarks apply to acetic acid formed by bacterial infection.

Studies of fermentation other than from the chemical standpoint have shown that it can be divided into three principal phases of activity called the lag phase, the primary fermentation and the secondary fermentation respectively. The lag phase may be defined as the induction period or time lapse which is observed between the inoculation of the must with the yeast and the first visible signs of fermentation. The duration of this lag phase can vary from a few hours to several days, for it is dependent upon a number of factors, one of the more important of which is the initial concentration of yeast in the must. Fermentation normally cannot commence until the must contains about 30 million cells per fluid ounce. Because it is rare to find such a high initial concentration of yeast in a must, the original colony must increase in size until this critical population density of 30 million cells per fluid ounce is reached before fermentation can begin. The lag phase therefore represents a period of active yeast growth despite the apparent lack of activity at this time. Its duration is clearly dependent upon factors influencing yeast growth, e.g. temperature, availability of nutrients and oxygen, presence of sulphite and so on as well as the initial yeast concentration.

It follows from these remarks that, provided other conditions are favourable, inoculation of the must with an actively fermenting yeast starter should make for a short lag phase. Not only does this procedure ensure a fairly high initial yeast concentration but it also means that the yeast is already in an active state of growth and reproduction at the time of its introduction and does not have to be awakened from a period of dormancy, as would normally be the case if a culture were added directly to the must. The duration of the lag phase can usually be further decreased by ensuring that the optimum conditions for yeast growth and reproduction are established in the must. Thus, the effects of any sulphite should have been allowed to ameliorate by delaying inoculation with the starter for 24 hours, a plentiful supply of nutrients and oxygen should be available (the latter by stirring the must vigorously to promote aeration) and a temperature of 70°F.–80°F. should be maintained. Fermentation will then normally begin within a few hours, but even if it does take several days before this stage is reached no real harm will be done. It is, of course, advisable to avoid a lengthy lag phase whenever possible to minimise the risk of spoilage organisms developing and interfering with or even suppressing the growth of the yeast.

During the lag phase the yeast absorbs a great deal of the nutrients and dissolved oxygen from the must. It also oxidises a little of the sugar completely to carbon dioxide and water in order to obtain energy required for the rapid growth and reproduction which occurs at this time. Very little alcohol is produced under these circumstances, but because the amount of sugar lost in this way is relatively small, the loss of alcohol sustained as a result of this occurrence is also slight. The lag phase is thus a period of aerobic yeast respiration which lasts only for as long as oxygen either dissolved in the must or trapped in an air space above the must is available to the yeast. Once this supply of oxygen is exhausted, the yeast must obtain its metabolic energy solely from anaerobic fermentation. Should the oxygen supply fail before the yeast colony achieves a population density of 30 million cells per fluid ounce, active fermentation will be considerably delayed or may even fail to begin because yeast growth and reproduction become very slow under anaerobic conditions. It is therefore essential to provide the yeast with sufficient oxygen during the lag phase to permit rapid expansion of the colony. An unduly long lag phase may sometimes be observed simply because the yeast is becoming starved of oxygen. Aeration of the must by vigorous stirring may rectify matters in such cases, but the position with respect to nutrients, temperature, sulphite, etc., should also then be checked.

The end of the lag phase is usually marked by the appearance of tiny bubbles of carbon dioxide rising through the must and showing that active fermentation has commenced. The primary fermentation is considered to begin once carbon dioxide is being visibly evolved. Although at first only a gentle effervescence is observed, fermentation very quickly becomes extremely rapid and vigorous and large volumes of gas are given off. The reason for this sudden burst of activity is not difficult to determine. The primary fermentation, at least initially, is also a period of rapid yeast growth as well as the lag phase. The rate of expansion of the yeast colony during the lag phase reaches its maximum just before the primary fermentation begins. Since the yeast cells are then growing and reproducing very rapidly, they continue to do so during the initial stages of the primary fermentation, aided by any residual oxygen which was not used up during the lag phase. As the onset of the primary fermentation automatically introduces anaerobic conditions, by forming a blanket of carbon dioxide over the now oxygen-free must, this extremely rapid growth of the yeast colony can only continue for a limited period of time. The yeast cannot maintain a fast growth rate with the energy obtained solely from anaerobic fermentation. Hence, the primary fermentation becomes progressively more vigorous only for a few days, the actual duration depending upon the availability of oxygen and nutrients, temperature and so on. Thereafter its vigour will moderate considerably within the next few days for reasons which will become clear shortly.

The overall picture can be seen even more clearly by studying the actual growth of the yeast colony itself. During the whole of the lag phase, the yeast population increases smoothly, the number of yeast cells doubling every few hours. This phase of activity continues unchanged into the initial primary fermentation. Up to this time, many more new cells are produced for each cell which dies, i.e. the birth rate considerably exceeds the death rate. As very much less energy is available for yeast growth and reproduction once anaerobic conditions have been established, the must is then unable to support this rapid population expansion any longer. Consequently, further yeast growth is severely curtailed. The duration of the vigorous primary fermentation is thus partly dependent upon how long a period elapses before all the available oxygen in the must becomes exhausted. Even when this stage is reached, however, fermentation continues for a few days with almost unabated vigour because at first the number of viable yeast cells remains fairly constant. The size of the colony will, of course, show no further marked increase during this time since yeast growth is now very restricted due to the onset of anaerobic conditions.

As a result, later in the primary fermentation the energy available for yeast growth and reproduction is insufficient to permit even the replacement of all the cells which die so that for a time the death rate exceeds the birth rate. After a few days, a balance is struck between the birth and death rates and the yeast population attains its optimum density commensurate with the prevailing conditions. It follows that the primary fermentation reaches a peak of activity in its early stages and subsequently becomes slower and more moderate according to the size of the yeast colony which the must can support.

The primary fermentation is also a period of rapid alcohol production, for large amounts of sugar must be fermented to maintain the vigour of the yeast colony. Hydrometer measurements made at this time will, of course, show this effect in the form of a very rapid gravity decrease. Little loss of alcohol is sustained as a result of the yeast oxidising sugar completely to carbon dioxide and water during this period. Not only is the supply of oxygen essential for this purpose strictly limited but the metabolic rate of wine yeasts and to a slightly lesser extent that of baker's yeast (but not that of poorly fermenting wild yeasts) is also so high that a good supply must be maintained before the alcohol yield is seriously depleted in this manner. The presence of ever-increasing quantities of alcohol in the must has other effects, however, for alcohol acts as an enzyme poison and slows down the metabolism of the yeast, thus decreasing the rate of fermentation. The increase in alcohol concentration and decrease in the size of the yeast colony observed during the latter stages of the primary fermentation therefore both help to moderate its initial speed and vigour.

It is now clear that the rate and vigour of fermentation diminish fairly soon after primary fermentation begins, usually within about 5–10 days, and subsequently a slower and more sedate fermentation is observed. This quieter and steadier phase of activity marks the beginning of the secondary fermentation. In view of the fact that this change is progressive rather than sudden in nature, however, the primary and secondary fermentations merge imperceptibly together so that no sharp demarcation line can be drawn between the two stages.

The rate of fermentation is slower during the secondary fermentation than in any previous stage. It may in fact become so slow that the only signs showing fermentation is proceeding at all are the presence of a ring of tiny bubbles round the perimeter of the must and a gradual but steady gravity decrease. Sugar is nevertheless slowly but surely being converted into alcohol and the amount of alcohol produced during this period approaches the theoretical yield more closely than at any other phase of fermentation. This behaviour is typical of most strains of wine yeast and the slowness of the fermentation should be no cause for concern if periodic checks with the hydrometer show that a steady gravity decrease is occurring. On the other hand, if the gravity remains constant over an interval of 7–10 days then fermentation may have stuck for one of the reasons discussed later. In general, the winemaker should welcome a long slow fermentation since it has repeatedly been demonstrated that better quality wines are usually obtained under these conditions.

The secondary fermentation may continue for several months, but as time passes the rate of fermentation gradually decreases until finally it ceases completely and no further yeast activity is observed. Moreover, the accepted methods of stimulating fermentation, e.g. aeration, addition of nutrients, etc., become progressively less effective as the secondary fermentation proceeds towards completion. It follows that the alcohol produced during the fermentation must be exerting a stronger and stronger inhibitory action on the metabolism of the yeast as its concentration increases. Eventually, so much alcohol has been formed that the enzyme system of the yeast becomes completely poisoned and fermentation consequently ceases. The rate of fermentation therefore gradually decreases with increasing alcohol production, and the alcohol concentration at which all yeast activity terminates is called the maximum tolerance of the yeast. Most wine yeasts have a high alcohol tolerance and will normally produce 12%–15% alcohol by volume with little difficulty, but certain strains, e.g. Madeira yeast, can tolerate even higher alcohol concentrations. Indeed, up to 20%–22% alcohol by volume has been claimed in some cases although more than about 18% alcohol by volume is rarely produced by natural fermentation. The increasing alcohol content during this period also serves to kill off the weakest cells of the colony so that the death rate may slightly exceed the birth rate in the secondary fermentation, particularly in its later stages. This decrease in yeast population also, of course, makes for a slower rate of fermentation.

The rate of fermentation thus begins to decrease soon after the primary fermentation has commenced. Thereafter a progressive decrease in its rate is observed until finally fermentation ceases altogether because either the yeast has converted all the available sugar in the must into alcohol or it has reached its maximum alcohol tolerance. It has already been shown that this pattern of activity arises because the yeast population decreases and the alcohol concentration increases as fermentation proceeds towards completion.

In addition, it must be remembered that fermentation is essentially a series of chemical reactions. Thus, its rate will also be dependent to some extent upon the temperature of the must for the simple reason that the rate of most chemical reactions approximately doubles with every 10°C. (18°F.) rise in temperature. Although this statement is also true for fermentation, it requires rather more careful interpretation in this case since living cells and their enzymes provide the motivating power for its occurrence. Enzymes are delicate and rather unstable substances which are easily inactivated or denatured by heat so that the activity of all living cells shows a marked dependence upon temperature. Different organisms can tolerate different temperature levels and even the various strains of wine yeast show minor variations between themselves in this respect. In the case of most wine yeasts, however, their fermentative ability becomes seriously impaired if the cells are exposed to temperatures above 85°F.–90°F. for any length of time. Hence, any increase in the rate of fermentation which would be expected on purely chemical grounds is more than offset by the denaturation of the enzymes which occurs under these conditions. It follows that the rate of fermentation reaches a maximum at a temperature slightly below that at which the enzymes in the yeast cells become inactivated. In the case of most wine yeasts, the maximum temperature at which fermentation should be conducted is around 75°F.–80°F.

Conversely, lowering the temperature of the must would be expected to cause a decrease in the rate of fermentation, and this is indeed found to be the case. Musts held at low temperatures ferment very much more slowly than musts maintained at higher temperatures. Again, however, because fermentation occurs through the agency of living cells, it is found that yeast activity ceases if the temperature becomes too low. In this instance, the metabolism of the yeast has been so reduced by the low temperature that the cells cannot produce sufficient energy to support their continued growth. The yeast is then forced to hibernate until more favourable conditions are again established. Although the introduction of cross-bred hybrid yeasts now permits fermentation to continue at temperatures as low as 40°F.–45°F., the rate of fermentation even when these yeasts are employed becomes rather slow at temperatures below about 50°F.–55°F. simply because the enzymic reactions responsible for fermentation proceed somewhat slowly under these conditions. The higher concentration of dissolved carbon dioxide attained at low temperatures also inhibits yeast activity slightly, but this factor alone is of minor importance.

It follows from this discussion that wine yeasts usually ferment most satisfactorily if the temperature of the must lies between about 55°F. and 80°F., and that a more rapid fermentation will occur the more closely the temperature approaches to about 80° F. The value of a long slow fermentation in connection with wine quality has already been mentioned, however, and for this reason it is clearly inadvisable to conduct the fermentation at or near 80°F. Moreover, the alcohol tolerance of the yeast is somewhat reduced at higher temperatures. Since fermentation is an exothermic, i.e. heat-producing process, there is also the danger that a must held at 80° F. may reach too high a temperature because the excess heat produced during the very rapid fermentation occurring under these conditions cannot be lost quickly enough to the surroundings. Unless the must is cooled in some way to maintain its temperature below 80°F.–85°F., fermentation may cease due to the yeast becoming inactivated by the heat. On the other hand, during the lag phase when active yeast growth and reproduction is taking place, it is clearly desirable to promote expansion of the yeast colony as quickly as possible in order to get the primary fermentation under way with the minimum of delay. Hence, a temperature of 75°F.–80°F. should be maintained during the lag phase (and during the preparation of yeast starters for the same reasons). As soon as the primary fermentation begins, the temperature should be reduced to 60°F.–70°F. partly to prevent an unduly vigorous primary fermentation but mainly to ensure the long slow fermentation conducive to good quality is obtained.

When the fermentation is nearing completion, however, it is often advisable to raise the temperature to 75°F.–80°F. until all yeast activity finally ceases. This technique enables the yeast to utilise the maximum possible amount of sugar before it becomes exhausted and thus helps to stabilise the wine by reducing the chances of an inconvenient refermentation occurring later should the young wine be exposed to warmer temperatures at any time during storage. Sweet wines in particular should be treated in this manner.

Almost all fermentations will follow this pattern of activity as they progress from inception to completion. The actual rate at each stage will depend upon the yeast population density, the alcohol concentration and the temperature. Marked deviations can nevertheless occur if other factors which influence yeast growth are unfavourable. For this reason, it is important to add an adequate supply of nutrients to the must prior to fermentation and to avoid too high an initial concentration of sulphite or sugar. Surprising as it may seem, an excessive amount of sugar can prevent ferment tation (the yeast cells are unable to withstand the osmotic pressure developed between the cell contents and the mus- and exhibit the phenomenon of plasmolysis). Fortunately, the must needs to contain about 4 lb. or more of sugar per gallon before this effect is observed and most winemakers would regard this quantity as excessive in any case.

At times, fermentation will cease long before all the sugar in the must has been converted into alcohol. The fermentation is then said to have stuck. This condition can easily be detected by means of the hydrometer, for a high gravity reading of 25 or above which shows no change over a week or ten days will be recorded. Fermentation can stick for a variety of reasons, all of which result in either the death of the colony or in its hibernation because the prevailing conditions are inimical to its continued normal existence. For example, too high or too low a temperature, an inadequate supply of nutrients, an excessively high concentration of sugar, over-sulphiting and so on can all have this effect. Sometimes fermentation sticks because the yeast has reached its maximum alcohol tolerance without being able to deal with all the sugar in the must and a sickly oversweet wine results. At other times so much sugar may be present initially that fermentation hardly occurs at all and only a slightly alcoholic cordial is produced. Care must be taken to distinguish between these two extremes. A strong but over-sweet wine can and should always be used for blending and not treated as a stuck fermentation whereas a weakly alcoholic syrup is quite unsuitable for this purpose. In most cases, however, a stuck fermentation signifies that little alcohol has been formed and much unfermented sugar remains in the must. For this reason, stuck wines are very susceptible to bacterial infection and spoilage.

A stuck fermentation is obviously a highly undesirable occurrence which should be rectified as soon as possible. Unfortunately, any steps which are taken to remedy matters in the original must are unlikely to induce fermentation to restart even if the yeast colony is merely hibernating. A fresh yeast starter should therefore be introduced according to the following technique. The gravity of the must should first be reduced to about 80 or less with a similar sugar-free must or water if too high an initial concentration of sugar is responsible for sticking. In all cases, a fresh supply of nutrients should be added and the must stirred vigorously to promote aeration. An equal quantity of the must should next be mixed with an actively fermenting yeast starter and allowed to stand at a temperature of 75°F.–80°F. until active fermentation is observed. This procedure must then be repeated, mixing an equal quantity of stuck wine and actively fermenting must each time, until the whole of the stuck wine is again fermenting. This rather laborious procedure is usually necessary when restarting a stuck fermentation. The new colony otherwise not infrequently fails to establish itself if it is added directly to the stuck must, even though an actively fermenting starter is employed, because the sudden change of environment may be too drastic under these rather unusual conditions.

CHAPTER XIII

RACKING AND CLARIFICATION

RACKING is the term used to describe the decantation of clear or clearing wines from the deposit of yeast cells and other insoluble matter which has gradually built up during the fermentation of the must and the subsequent storage of the new wine. This deposit of unwanted material is known as the lees, and it must be removed regularly by racking, otherwise off-flavours may develop in the wine due to excessive autolysis of dead yeast cells and/or to the decomposition of any other debris which may be present. Periodic racking also stimulates the clarification and maturing of new wines.

Since all too few winemakers understand what actually happens when dead yeast cells autolyse, a few words at this point will help to clear the air of any confusion which exists over the subject. When a yeast cell becomes exhausted and dies, it slowly sinks to the bottom of the fermenting or storage vessel where a very complex series of chemical reactions collectively known as autolysis, i.e. self-destruction, begins. Proteolytic enzymes secreted within the yeast cell itself become active and gradually degrade the cell into its basic constituents, these products of decomposition being released into the bulk of the wine. Although many of these substances are utilised by the living yeast cells still active in the wine, certain nitrogenous substances liberated at the same time are less desirable, except in relatively small controlled amounts, since they may otherwise impart a peculiar and unpleasant musty off-flavour to the wine.

In general, a limited degree of yeast autolysis is beneficial to a wine, but this process must not be overdone otherwise the flavour of the wine may be seriously impaired. Racking at regular intervals avoids this latter danger by removing accumulated dead yeast cells before autolysis has progressed too far. It must be admitted here that exceptions to this rule do occur, notably in the case of sherry yeast, but for the present purposes such deviations from normal behaviour will not be considered.

The simplest and most satisfactory method of racking is to siphon the wine through a rubber or plastic tube from the original container into a second clean and sterilised container. Care must be taken not to carry over any of the deposit with the wine by keeping the end of the siphon tube just below the surface of the wine, tilting the container carefully as the level drops near the bottom, until the force of the suction just begins to draw up some of the lees into the stream of wine when racking should at once be discontinued. Any wine left with the lees may be recovered by keeping the deposit in a bottle or other suitable container for a few days, after which the clear wine may be racked off as above. This extra trouble is usually only worthwhile when dealing with the sediment from larger bulks of wine, say five gallons or more. A rather more elaborate siphon tube consists of a rubber tube to which is attached a glass tube with a very short U-bend at one end. The latter should be long enough to keep the inlet just above any normal deposit in a wine. This device sucks wine down from the direction of the surface, then up into the siphon tube rather than drawing it straight up from the bottom of the container. The sediment is therefore less likely to be disturbed and carried over with the wine during racking operations.

Any racking results in a considerable reduction in the size of the yeast colony, for most wine yeasts are sedimentary and settle to the bottom of the container during the quieter secondary stage of fermentation. Consequently, many viable yeast cells are removed along with the unwanted sediment by the act of racking. Further yeast growth must therefore take place before fermentation can be resumed. Under the conditions normally existing in the newly-racked wine, however, the yeast can only reproduce to a limited extent so that the yeast population rarely regains its former density following racking. Fermentation always ceases at least temporarily after racking, but even if yeast activity is renewed within a

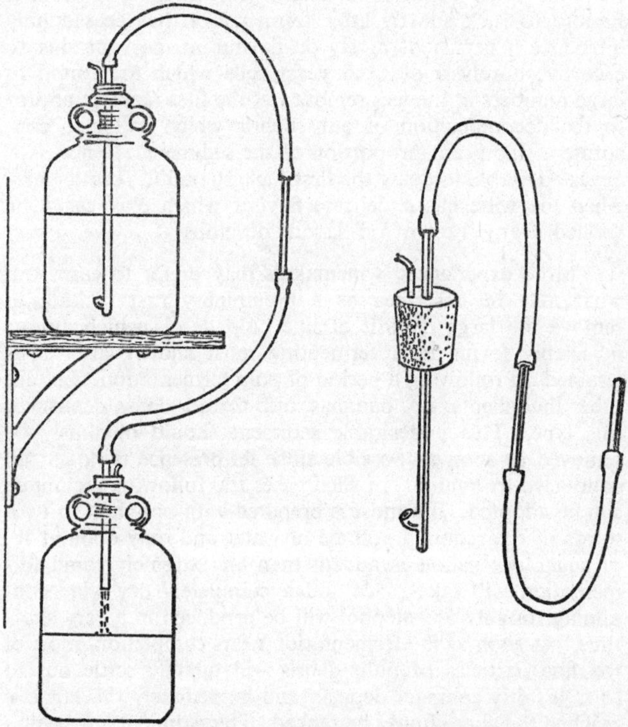

Racking, or siphoning wine.

few days, the rate of fermentation is usually rather slower than before because the new yeast colony is rather smaller than it was previously. Consequently, the overall period of fermentation is prolonged, occasionally by as much as several weeks, if the wine is racked before all the sugar has been converted into alcohol.

A wine should normally be racked for the first time at or near the end of fermentation to remove the large deposit formed during this very active phase. This first racking is undoubtedly the most important of all since the quality of the wine often depends to a large extent upon its timing. Failure to rack shortly after fermentation has ceased may introduce a persistent musty off-flavour in the wine due to excessive autolysis of dead yeast cells which are found in large numbers in the lees removed at the first racking, and/or to the decomposition of pulp debris which will also constitute a significant proportion of the sediment. Hence, it is never advisable to delay the first racking unduly, particularly when the wine has a delicate flavour which may easily be spoiled if any trace of off-flavour develops.

More experienced winemakers may prefer to carry out what may be described as a preliminary first racking to remove the large deposit of fine pulp debris which almost invariably forms in a fermenting must shortly after it is strained off following a period of pulp fermentation. Certain other ingredients, e.g. bananas, also form a dense deposit of this type. This undesirable sediment should obviously be removed as soon as possible since its presence is not at all conducive to quality. In such cases the following technique can be adopted. If a must is prepared with only half to two-thirds of the required volume of water and only about 1 lb. of sugar per gallon is added, then an extremely rapid fermentation will take place and a completely dry wine containing roughly 5% alcohol will be produced in a very short time. As soon as the fermentation nears completion, most of the fine particles of pulp debris will quickly settle out to form a fairly compact deposit, and immediately this stage is reached the wine should be racked. The sediment left behind may be allowed to settle further for a few days in a smaller container and any clear wine may be recovered by racking, but this operation should be carried out no later than a week after the previous racking because off-flavours develop very rapidly under these circumstances.

Since this racking will have considerably reduced the size of the yeast colony, steps must then be taken to establish the optimum conditions for the growth of the new yeast cells. The wine should be thoroughly aerated and a plentiful supply of yeast nutrients, particularly nitrogenous substances, must be added. The alcohol content should be reduced by adding up to half a volume of water and sugar syrup, sufficient of the latter being included to establish a gravity of between 60 and 80. Finally, the diluted syruped must should be kept at a temperature of 65°F.–75°F. until a vigorous fermentation is again observed. Fermentation is usually renewed within a week or ten days, but it must be emphasised that this procedure can cause fermentation to stick, particularly in inexperienced hands, so that beginners are advised to stick to the more conventional paths. The rate of fermentation may subsequently be rather slower than normal, but because a slow fermentation almost invariably produces a superior wine, the winemaker gains rather than loses in this respect by carrying out a preliminary first racking.

The second and later rackings are usually performed at intervals of two to three months unless a heavy lees has formed within this time, for such a deposit must be removed as soon as possible for the same reasons as before. Indeed, the time interval between the first and second rackings is often only a few weeks because a heavy sediment is commonly formed quite soon after the first racking. At least three and preferably four rackings are required to clarify and stabilise most wines, but even then the wine is best stored in bulk for a further period of time during which it need only be racked occasionally to remove any small sediment that may be observed.

A slightly different routine is followed when making sweet wines with a medium alcohol content. In such cases, the maximum alcohol tolerance of the yeast will not be reached so that fermentation must be terminated while the wine still contains some residual sugar. The first racking should be carried out at a gravity of about 20 to reduce the size of the yeast colony and decrease the rate of fermentation. Subsequent rackings at intervals of a fortnight to three weeks then give the yeast little chance to increase in numbers sufficiently quickly to counteract the continued removal of viable yeast cells. Consequently, fermentation ceases in a very short time, usually before the gravity has dropped below 10. A little sulphite, say 50 p.p.m. (1 Campden tablet per gallon), added after each racking, will also help to clarify and stabilise the wine. This technique is widely used to produce sweet table wines, but it is also of great value in the production of light imitation German wines which frequently contain a small but significant proportion of unfermented sugar. It is certainly far superior to terminating fermentation abruptly by means of an unduly heavy dose of sulphite, a procedure which has little to recommend it except in emergencies.

After each racking a small quantity of wine will be left with the lees, but because no more than a very small air space should be left above a wine to minimise the risk of bacterial infection, this loss must somehow be made good. The most obvious solution is to rack the wine into a number of smaller containers which can be completely filled, but then the advantages of bulk storage are lost. An alternative and far more satisfactory procedure adopted by many winemakers is to prepare what is known as a top-up bottle. Slightly more must than the fermenting vessel can hold is prepared and the excess is allowed to ferment separately in a smaller container, kept beside the main bulk of the wine. After the first and subsequent rackings, this spare wine in the top-up bottle can be used to replace the wine lost when the bulk of the wine is racked. The top-up bottle itself should, of course, also be racked regularly and checked to make sure that it is still sound! Some older wine, preferably but not necessarily of the same type, can be used if a top-up bottle is not available or becomes prematurely exhausted or infected. Topping up with sugar syrup of the same gravity as the wine or with water is best avoided because of the dilution effects.

As fermentation proceeds towards completion, the suspended yeasts and other insoluble matter gradually settle out and the process of clarification begins. Sediment usually builds up during the quieter secondary stage of fermentation and by the time this phase nears its close quite a heavy deposit will be observed. Until this has been removed by racking further clarification proceeds rather slowly, but after the first racking another fairly thick deposit is generally formed within quite a short time. Periodic racking helps a wine to clear as well as benefiting it in other ways. Most wines will clear to brilliance naturally within a month or two, although in certain cases complete clarification may take considerably longer and the winemaker may feel obliged to hasten matters.

Sulphiting after racking assists in the clarification of new wine in addition to performing several other important functions. The effect of sulphite on clarification can be at least partly attributed to its property of causing the coagulation and precipitation of suspended colloidal particles, by neutralising the electrical charges on the individual particles. Since the stability of a colloidal sol depends upon the mutual repulsion of its similarly charged particles, the loss of these electrical charges allows the particles to agglomerate and form larger particles which then settle out in the normal manner. Sulphite thus helps to prevent cloudiness due to persistent colloidal hazes. Clarification is also aided by the sulphite hindering the growth and development of a new yeast colony under the already relatively unfavourable conditions existing in a new wine. Its influence here is, however, probably of minor importance in most instances. The optimum dose of sulphite for all purposes is some 50 to 100 p.p.m. (1 to 2 Campden tablets per gallon), the exact amount employed within these limits being a matter for the individual winemaker to decide.

A useful trick which may promote more rapid clarification is to stir up the sediment which has formed after the first, or better still, after the second racking, and delay the next racking until a firm deposit has again been laid down. Here, the yeast is being used as a fining agent. Certain hazes, especially those due to the incipient crystallisation of cream of tartar, can sometimes be persuaded to settle out by a short period of refrigeration since cold conditions favour the deposition of these substances.

It is quite common to find that the clarification of wines based upon fruits and vegetables may be delayed or even prevented completely when minor amounts of a group of substances collectively known as the pectins are present. Wines employing parsnips as a major basic ingredient are particularly notorious on this account, but what many winemakers are only now beginning to realise is that the same problem is frequently encountered to a less severe extent in numerous other wines. Perhaps the main reason why the importance of pectins to wine quality is still poorly appreciated can be ascribed to the fact that the rapid clarification of amateur wines is presently the exception rather than the rule. The point is that this is usually the case only because pectins are present. Wines produced from ingredients naturally low in pectin clear comparatively quickly and easily and often fall bright within a few weeks of fermentation ceasing, e.g. those based on such fruits as bananas and choke cherries (a N. American wild cherry eminently suitable for port production) are often brilliantly clear by the time the second racking is carried out. It therefore follows that controlling the amount of pectin in a wine is one of the keys to good clarification.

What, then, are pectins and how do they influence the clarification of wines? Broadly speaking, the pectins constitute a group of closely related carbohydrates allied to such polysaccharides as starch and chemically defined as complex, methylated polygalacturonic acids. Their aqueous solutions possess colloidal properties and will gel, i.e. set to a jelly, in the presence of high concentrations of sugar and acid. Calcium salts also influence their gelation. The essential rôle of pectins as setting agents for jams and jellies has long been recognised, and nowadays commercial preparations of fruit pectin are readily available for addition to jams which normally do not set firmly owing to a shortage of this commodity, e.g. strawberry jam. Hence, for making jam, fruits which are naturally rich in pectin process easily and set well so that their high pectin content is here a decided advantage. Exactly the opposite is true in winemaking where even a small amount of pectin can cause many problems.

Although winemakers rarely encounter conditions which cause musts and wines high in pectin to gel, the fact that some is present can have other equally undesirable effects. Thus, wines containing pectin are exceptionally difficult to clear because the pectin acts as what is termed a protective colloid and stabilises the haze. The minute suspended particles which are responsible for wines appearing cloudy are too small to settle out naturally, no matter how long a period of storage is allowed. The molecules of water, alcohol and the like which constitute a wine are continually moving arnund and colliding, and this unending activity observed in all solutions is called Brownian movement. The latter is sufficiently vigorous to maintain minute particles of insoluble substances, such as those giving rise to hazes in wines, in suspension indefinitely because the gravitational forces promoting their settling are opposed and nullified by the restless activity of the surrounding molecules. Wines only clarify because the tiny suspended particles constituting the haze are mutually attracted and agglomerate or combine to form larger particles whose size thus eventually increases sufficiently for them to begin irrevocably settling under the action of gravity. As more and more agglomeration occurs, the lees gradually grows and the wine becomes progressively clearer until ultimately nothing remains in suspension and brilliant clarity is achieved. Racking helps clarification to proceed more rapidly and so too does judicious sulphiting which may neutralise the electrical charges on suspended colloidal particles and thereby permit their accretion. The action of a protective colloid such as pectin (and starch) is to oppose these processes of clarification by stabilising the haze forming particles and preventing their agglomeration. Since there is then no tendency for the particles to attract each other, no particle growth and hence no settling is observed so that the wine remains stubbornly cloudy indefinitely. Moreover, pectins stabilise hazes so efficiently that neither fining nor filtration is likely to be effective and may in fact only make matters worse.

How, then, can cloudy wines whose haze forming particles are stabilised by pectin be clarified? The first step in accomplishing this objective is to ascertain that pectin is really the culprit, for remedial measures appropriate in this case may not help much if the wine is hazy for some other reason. Fortunately, a very simple test will quickly provide the answer to this problem. A small sample of wine, say 1 fl. oz., is treated with 3–4 volumes methylated spirits and shaken vigorously. If pectin is present in any quantity, the alcohol will precipitate it in the form of gelatinous clots and strings almost immediately. Minor amounts of pectin may not appear at once, however, so that no test should be discarded as negative until the sample has been allowed to stand for an hour or two. The formation of an opalescent haze is not usually due to pectin and should therefore be ignored. To see what a positive test actually looks like, a solution high in pectin may be prepared by boiling a dried apricot in a little water for 5–10 minutes and then treated with methylated spirit once it has cooled. So much pectin will sometimes be precipitated that the solution will set solid unless it is vigorously shaken!

The only satisfactory way to clear pectin clouded wines is to degrade the pectin so that its protective action on the particles causing the haze is destroyed and agglomeration can then occur in the normal manner. At least three products, viz. Pectozyme, Pectinol and Pektolase are currently available for this purpose and all are sources of enzymes whose essential function is to break the long pectin chain into shorter units which are unable to act as protective colloids. (This statement is naturally a gross over-simplification of what actually happens, but it does give a simple picture of the situation). About 10–15 gallons of wine can be clarified with 1 oz. Pectozyme which is most conveniently added directly to the wine rather than extracted with water, as is generally recommended, because the insoluble residues tend to sink and will be removed at the next racking. A more refined technique is to place the Pectozyme in a muslin bag which may then be suspended in the wine for a few days so that all the enzyme it contains is extracted. Pectinol will be discussed in more detail later, but it may be noted here that 1 oz. Pectinol 10M will clear 30 gallons of wine.

Although enzyme preparations of the type just described can be used with great success for clearing wines with pectin stabilised hazes, it is obviously preferable to avoid encountering such difficulties at so late a stage in the production of the wine. Far less trouble would arise if the pectin could be destroyed prior to and/or during fermentation so that it is completely degraded by the time the first racking falls due. The wine would then clear more quickly and more completely and would require less attention at a stage when its quality is most likely to suffer from too much handling.

Several factors must be taken into account when adopting this approach. To begin with, most of the ingredients commonly employed by amateur winemakers contain some pectin. Certain fruits and vegetables such as apricots and parsnips are particularly well endowed with this commodity, whereas others possess very little, bananas and choke cherries containing hardly any at all. In addition, these ingredients contain enzymes which will degrade pectin, but often the amounts of these natural pectinases are quite small and may be inadequate to destroy all the pectin found in the must. Under favourable conditions, however, some or even all the pectin derived from the ingredients of the must will be degraded through the action of the natural pectin destroying enzymes obtained from the same source.

The unfortunate fact which many winemakers fail to realise is that enzymes, being proteins, are very delicate substances easily denatured or inactivated by relatively minor changes in their environment. Heat has a disastrous effect in this respect, for few enzymes remain active after being exposed to boiling water or even, in many cases, when held much above room temperature for any length of time. Moreover, this denaturation is permanent because enzymic activity is not regained when normal conditions are restored. An analogous situation obtains when eggs are cooled after boiling, for the white of an egg is a protein which coagulates on cooking and does not revert back to its original state on cooling. The natural pectinases found in winemaking ingredients are likewise inactivated by heat so that any pectin destruction which they may have caused is never observed when hot or boiling water has been employed to prepare the must. Indeed, to add insult to injury, pectins are more soluble in hot than in cold water with the result that hot extractions not only denature useful natural pectinases but also lead to a higher concentration of pectin in the must. If no steps are then taken to deal with this situation, it is obvious that the wine will subsequently prove difficult and perhaps impossible to clear by normal techniques.

There are occasions when the winemaker has no alternative but to boil ingredients in water, e.g. parsnips must be prepared in this manner. Usually, however, pressing or cold water extraction procedures can be applied, and preference should therefore be given to such methods whenever possible to minimise pectin extraction and the inactivation of natural pectinases. It is nevertheless advisable always to ensure that pectin will cause no future clarification problems by supplementing any natural enzymes already in the must, even when every precaution has been taken to avoid their destruction.

If heating has been involved at any stage in the preparation of the must, it becomes absolutely essential to ensure that pectin-destroying enzymes are added prior to or early in the fermentation to replace those which have been denatured. The amount of enzyme preparation required for this purpose is about 1 oz. Pectozyme per 15 gallons or 1 oz. Pectinol per 30 gallons, but it is possible to use even less quite successfully in musts whose pectin content is fairly low. Past experience is really the best guide, however, and the winemaker should be prepared to experiment to determine the optimum balance.

Although the stage at which these enzyme preparations are introduced is by no means critical insofar as their pectin degrading abilities are concerned, it is far more satisfactory from the point of view of wine quality to add them prior to or early in the fermentation. Clarification will then begin soon after fermentation has ceased and will be well advanced by the time the first racking falls due, instead of taking many months as is frequently the case when none is added. The main point to note is that enzyme preparations of any description should never be added to a must until the winemaker is certain they will not be inactivated. When pressing or cold extraction procedures have been employed to prepare the must, they are best added with the sulphite (which has no effect on their activity), especially if settling techniques are practised prior to fermentation. Otherwise, a good rule is to add them with the yeast starter because conditions suitable for inoculating musts with yeast will also be perfectly satisfactory for introducing thermally labile enzymes. There is certainly no advantage to be gained by delaying the addition of pectin-destroying enzymes until fermentation has ceased, for the wine will then simply take longer to clear and its quality may in fact suffer from it receiving undue handling at such a late stage in its production.

Apart from promoting superior clarification, the routine inclusion of pectin-destroying enzyme preparations in every must has several other advantages. Thus, a higher yield of free run juice will be obtained after a pulp fermentation, easier and more efficient pressing of the pulp or marc can be expected and a less slimy lees which facilitates racking will be deposited during and after fermentation. In addition, the wine is said to mature better and develop a finer flavour and more fruity bouquet than comparable untreated wines.

There is one final point concerning commercial enzyme preparations of this type which should be brought to the notice of amateur winemakers. As well as providing enzymes which will degrade pectins, Pectozyme, Pectinol and Pektolase also contain secondary enzyme systems which will break down starch and related polysaccharides, hydrolyse such disaccharides as maltose and sucrose (cane sugar) and destroy proteins. These extra factors can often prove very useful in winemaking, for if measures are taken on a routine basis to deal with pectins derived from the ingredients of the must, the winemaker is unlikely to be troubled with starch or protein stabilised hazes either. Hence, the inclusion of pectin-destroying enzymes in every must has many advantages and will amply repay the slight extra expense incurred in this way.

Since the amateur may become confused when faced with the choice of several different commercial products, the following notes may prove helpful in making a decision as to which to select. There are several grades of Pectinol, of which Pectinol 10M and Pectinol 100D are usually recommended for winemaking purposes. Pectinol 10M is diluted and standardised with glucose so that it dissolves rapidly and completely on being added to musts and wines, whereas Pectinol 100D utilises the insoluble diatomaceous earth as the standardising medium. As both grades are otherwise identical, it is fairly obvious that Pectinol 10M is the better grade to use. By way of contrast, Pectozyme is standardised with bran from which the active enzyme must be extracted, e.g by suspending it in a muslin bag in the must, so that it is less satisfactory than Pectinol 10M in this respect. Pectozyme is also less active than Pectinol 10M, but its cost is correspondingly lower and there is really little to choose between the two in terms of cost and convenience. Pektolase is a liquid preparation whose cost and activity seem comparable with Pectozyme and it is, of course, conveniently measured out for any quantity of must. The main point to note with Pektolase is that liquid enzyme preparations are generally less stable than their solid counterparts even when stored in a cool place, so that it should probably not be kept for more than a few months before being used.

Persistent hazes may also be caused by starch, which can function as a protective colloid in the same way as pectins. Alternatively, minute self-stabilised particles of starch itself may be responsible. This condition is most frequently encountered in grain or apple wines. It is readily detected by the deep blue-black colour which developes when a few drops of a dilute solution of iodine (in aqueous potassium iodide) is added to a small sample (say 10 mls. or ½ fl. oz.) of the wine. In such cases, treatment with a starch-reducing enzymic preparation Amylozyme 100 will allow clarification to proceed. As before, the Amylozyme 100 can be mixed into the wine directly at the rate of 1 oz. per 5 gallons and the wine left in a warm place until signs of clarification are observed. It may then be racked and treated in the normal manner. This procedure is equally as effective as the much more troublesome method usually recommended for using this enzymic preparation. Although it does take rather longer to complete, it also considerably lessens the risk of damaging the quality of the wine.

Occasionally, a wine will remain obstinately cloudy or hazy despite all efforts to induce clarification, and under these circumstances it may be necessary to resort to fining or filtration. Neither procedure should normally be employed until all other measures have failed. Even then, the fining should always be attempted first since this method is much less likely to prove harmful to the quality of the wine than filtration for reasons which will become apparent later. The danger of fining is that more than just the haze may be removed so that the overall quality of the wine may suffer from this treatment. Moreover, great care must be taken not to overfine a wine, otherwise the haze may be stabilised instead of being removed. A permanently cloudy wine could then result. The secret of fining is to use the minimum amount of fining agent and to ensure that the latter is always very thoroughly mixed into the bulk of the wine undergoing treatment.

Some of the commonest fining agents used for this purpose include white of egg, fresh ox blood, isinglass, gelatine, casein, bentonite and a host of other materials including proprietary finings. All these fining agents are substances which react with some constituent of the wine to form a loose flocculent precipitate which attracts and entraps any suspended insoluble particles already present in the wine as it sinks to the bottom of the storage vessel. Although the exact mechanism of how a fining agent works is still not completely understood, it seems that the precipitate formed by the fining agent carries a positive electric charge which attracts the negatively charged particles of the other suspended matter in the wine. Both precipitates then settle out together to leave a clear supernatant wine. Simple mechanical entanglement which does not depend upon the mutual electrical attraction of oppositely charged particles may also play a part, but this factor is probably of minor importance.

White of egg and ox blood are both sources of albuminous proteins which interact with the tannins in wine. These finings are therefore best reserved for red wines, particularly those which are harsh due to an excess of tannin, since they do not act so well with white wines even when extra tannin is added prior to their use. One egg white will fine ten gallons of wine, but it must be beaten into a stiff froth before being mixed thoroughly with the bulk of the wine. This type of fining is frequently employed by commercial red wine producers in France. It is well worth trying with excessively astringent red wines since it will reduce the tannin content to a more palatable level as well as removing any haze which may be present. Indeed, white of egg may be used simply to reduce the astringency of harsh red wines whether they are hazy or not, e.g. elderberry wines respond very well to this treatment.

Isinglass, a purified fish gelatine extracted from the swim bladders of sturgeon, is a fining agent mentioned in many traditional recipes. Nowadays, however, it is rarely recommended because of its temperamental nature. Since 1 oz. isinglass is sufficient to clear about fifty gallons of wine, there is little point in using this fining agent for clarifying less than five or ten gallons of wine at a time. The isinglass must first be finely powdered and soaked overnight in a little water containing some tartaric acid so that it can absorb moisture and swell up to a gelatinous consistency. This jelly should be rubbed through a fine sieve to remove any lumps and then whisked briskly with about a pint of the wine to form a fine dispersion before being mixed with the bulk of the wine. If these directions are followed carefully, a brilliantly clear wine should be obtained a few weeks later, but isinglass is tricky to use and success cannot be guaranteed every time even under apparently ideal conditions.

The wines of commerce are sometimes fined with gelatine, a collagenous protein extracted principally from hide and bone, which, like the albuminous proteins, reacts with the tannins in wine. Tannin must therefore be added to white wines prior to fining them with gelatine, but normally it need not be added to red wines which should contain sufficient tannin of their own. Preliminary trials are necessary to determine the amount of gelatine required to fine a particular wine. A 1% solution of gelatine should be prepared by soaking 1 gm. high-grade edible gelatine in about 25 mls. cold water for a few hours to allow it to absorb moisture and swell up to form a soft mass which is then dissolved by adding sufficient hot water to make the final volume up to 100 mls. A 1% solution of tannin will also be required for white wines and can be prepared by dissolving 1 gm. grape tannin or BP tannic acid in 100 mls. water.

A number of 100 mls. samples of wine should be placed in identical containers to allow a fair comparison, and if necessary treated with 1 ml. 1% tannin solution and left to rest for 24 hours. Four 100 mls. samples of wine should then be treated with 1 mls., 2 mls., 3 mls. and 4 mls. of 1% gelatine solution and allowed to stand in a cool place for 24 hours, after which the sample showing the best clarification can be selected by visual inspection. From this data, the volumes of tannin and gelatine solution required to fine the bulk of the wine can easily be calculated. Should none of these samples show any satisfactory clarification, a second test using 2 mls. 1% tannin solution and the same volumes of 1% gelatine solution as before may be carried out. If this trial also proves valueless another fining agent should be used.

Casein, the principal protein found in milk, is another fining agent used by commercial wine producers, but because pure casein itself is virtually insoluble in water it must be dissolved in alkali before use. About 5 mls. strong ammonia are mixed with 100 mls. water and 6 gms. casein dissolved in this solution which should then be boiled until very little odour of ammonia can be detected in the steam. Dilution with water to a total volume of 300 mls. will finally give an almost neutral 2% casein solution. If sodium or potassium caseinate is available, however, a 2% casein solution can be prepared directly by dissolving two grams of this salt in 100 mls. of water.

White wines are again best treated with tannin before attempting to fine them with casein. Preliminary trials are also once more necessary to determine the correct amount of casein required. A number of 100 mls. samples of wine in identical containers should be treated with 1 ml. tannin solution and left to rest for 24 hours before adding 1 ml., 2 mls., 3 mls., 4 mls. of 2% casein solution. After 24 hours the sample showing the best clarification can be selected by visual inspection, and the volumes of tannin and casein solution required to fine the bulk of the wine can be calculated from this data. If none of these samples shows a satisfactory clarification, a second test using 2 mls. of 1% tannin solution and the same volumes of 2% casein solution may be carried out, but in the event of this test again proving indeterminate another fining agent should be chosen.

Bentonite, a montmorillonite clay with enormous swelling properties in water, is a fining agent very widely used in America. It is normally employed as a 5% suspension in water or wine which is easily prepared by mixing 5 grams of powdered Bentonite with 100 mls. of water or wine. This slurry should be rubbed through a fine sieve to remove any lumps which may be present. Between 20 mls. and 100 mls. of this suspension is generally required to clarify a gallon of wine, depending upon its cloudiness. Although preliminary trials are probably advisable to determine the correct amount of Bentonite required, an excess of this fining agent does no harm and it can be employed with considerably more freedom than almost any other substance used for this purpose.

Bentonite will normally clarify the most stubbornly cloudy wine and it will even clear a wine which has been treated unsuccessfully with one of the fining agents previously described. It follows that Bentonite is one of the best and safest fining agents for amateur winemakers, but unfortunately it does not seem to be readily obtainable in this country at present.

Although all these fining agents usually give satisfactory results when they are used properly, most of them are best reserved for fairly large quantities of wine. For winemakers who wish to fine only single gallons of wine at a time, proprietary wine finings offer the simplest and safest choice of a fining agent. A number of these preparations are currently available, but Serena wine finings have been found to give the best results and rarely fail to clarify hazy wines. Full instructions are included with these finings, however, so that no further description need be given in detail here.

Filtration can also be employed to clarify stubbornly cloudy or hazy wines. Although filter papers can be used for this purpose, either a proprietary rapid wine filter or asbestos pulp is infinitely preferable. Since full instructions are always provided with rapid wine filters, no further remarks need be made beyond saying that the winemaker should take great care to follow the directions of the manufacturer very strictly.

Asbestos pulp is very easy to use, and a small handful will normally suffice for at least five gallons of wine provided it is not too cloudy. The pulp is first whisked into a froth with a little wine to effect complete flocculation. The mixture is then poured carefully into a large funnel whose outlet has been lightly plugged with a small piece of cotton wool. Since the bed of the pulp should be disturbed as little as possible during the filtration, a saucer may be placed in the upper part of the funnel to prevent a direct flow of wine from impinging upon the filter bed. The wine can then be poured on this saucer so that it overflows gently down the sides of the funnel to the pulp below with the minimum disturbance.

The first few ounces of wine passing through the filter may be cloudy and/or may possess a peculiar flavour. These are therefore best rejected. Thereafter brilliantly clear wine should be obtained. During the filtration, the funnel should be kept topped up with wine and covered with a cloth to exclude dirt and insects. Normally a filtration can be left to its own devices except for an occasional topping up, but at times so much insoluble material is removed that the filter clogs up and no more wine can pass through. This difficulty rarely arises except when dealing with very cloudy wines, but should such a situation be encountered there is no alternative but to prepare a new filter bed.

Although the above procedure is simple and requires little more equipment than a large funnel, it is somewhat unsatisfactory in that the winemaker must top up with wine at intervals. The filtration cannot be left unattended overnight to complete itself automatically. Were this possible, of course, it would be much easier and considerably less time-consuming to filter even comparatively large quantities of wine. The equipment would merely have to be assembled, the filtration started and, once things were proceeding satisfactorily, it could then be allowed to continue on its own until all the wine had been filtered. The advantages of such an arrangement are numerous. Since necessity is said to be the mother of invention, several types of continuous wine filters have recently been designed. The construction and operation of one of the most effective of these continuous filters have therefore been described in the next chapter.

Vacuum filtration is another means of clarifying hazy wines. This procedure has the advantage of increasing the rate of filtration, often quite considerably, and will frequently permit the clarification of many gallons of wine within a relatively short period of time. Here the bed of asbestos pulp or similar filter aid is formed in a special filter funnel called a Buchner funnel which sits on a rubber gasket in the mouth of the receiving vessel. The latter is so designed that a vacuum can be established within it by means of a simple water pump powered by the domestic water supply. The wine is sucked through the filter bed by the vacuum within the receiver and consequently can be filtered much more rapidly than would otherwise be possible. Vacuum filtration has one main drawback. Because better clarification is usually achieved by slower rates of filtration, it is not uncommon to find that stubbornly cloudy wines may require several passes through the filter before their clarity reaches a satisfactory level.

Filtration is generally a very effective means of clarifying cloudy wines, but it does suffer from one very grave disadvantage. The procedures described above unavoidably expose the wine to the air during filtration, particularly at the moment it passes through the filter bed and drops into the receiving vessel below. Consequently, every drop of wine has ample opportunity to absorb excessive amounts of oxygen from the air during filtration. The use of a vacuum filter helps to reduce the oxygen absorption to some extent but by no means prevents its occurrence. Filtered wines therefore tend to become over-oxidised and contain unduly large amounts of acetaldehyde. Too much of this substance causes most wines to acquire a flat, lifeless and uninteresting character, until the excess disappears through further chemical reaction. The so-called "bottle-sickness" encountered in many recently bottled wines is caused in a similar manner.

The effects of over-oxidation may be temporary or permanent depending upon how much oxidation has actually occurred. Several weeks or even months may elapse before the wine does finally recover, but it is common to find that the wine never does completely regain its former quality. Delicate wines are particularly susceptible to loss of quality on filtration, but as a general rule all good wines are best not filtered otherwise much of their delicacy and finesse could be irretrievably lost. Indifferent or mediocre wines can be treated in this way with more confidence, but only because such wines have little to lose through over-oxidation in any case. Winemakers should therefore never filter their best wines except as a last desperate resort. Fining is infinitely preferable in such instances. Lesser quality wines can be treated in the same manner at the discretion of the winemaker, although it would be advisable to consider fining prior to filtering whatever the quality of the wine.

It is worth noting here that many commercial wines are very carefully filtered immediately prior to bottling. In case the winemaker considers this information contradicts the remarks made above, the following point must be remembered. The wine is not exposed to the air in commercial practice because such equipment as filter presses is employed. The filtration is carried out by pressurising the wine through the filter with the aid of nitrogen or some other inert oxygen-free gas. Hence, commercial producers can filter their wines without the slightest risk of causing over-oxidation whereas amateur winemakers cannot readily do so due to equipment limitations.

There are nevertheless some precautions which can be taken to minimise the degree of oxidation experienced by a wine during filtration. For example, the addition of 100 p.p.m. sulphite prior to filtration will prove beneficial. In this connection, the sulphite is acting in the capacity of an anti-oxidant since it, rather than the constituents of the wine, will combine with the oxygen absorbed during the operation. Admittedly, oxidation will not be suppressed entirely by the prior sulphiting, but its deleterious effects will at least be reduced. An alternative but less satisfactory procedure is to add 100 p.p.m. sulphite after filtering the wine. Since sulphite combines with acetaldehyde, some of the excess of the latter formed during the filtration will be neutralised and the wine will have a better chance of recovering its former quality.

An even more useful technique is to replace the air in the receiving vessel with a harmless inert gas such as carbon dioxide. The wine passing through the filter cannot then absorb any oxygen because none is available and oxidation is therefore prevented. Since large amounts of carbon dioxide are available to amateur winemakers as a by-product of fermentation (the fermentation of 1 lb. sugar will yield over 100 litres of carbon dioxide), it is a very simple matter to establish the desired inert atmosphere in the receiver. A piece of rubber or plastic tubing is connected to the outlet of an air-lock fitted to an actively fermenting must. The other end is inserted into and pushed to the bottom of the receiving vessel which will be used for the filtration. The carbon dioxide evolved from the fermenting must, being heavier than air, will then displace all the air already in the receiver. The time required to do this will naturally depend upon the rate of fermentation and the capacity of the receiving vessel, but usually at least an hour should be allowed for this purpose. Once the inert atmosphere has been established, the rubber tube may be removed and filtration can be carried out in the normal manner. The receiver should not, of course, be turned upside down once it contains carbon dioxide otherwise the gas will be lost. Ingenious winemakers may also devise an arrangement which will permit a continuous flow of carbon dioxide to pass through the receiver during the whole period of filtration. Unfortunately, this technique cannot be employed with a vacuum filter, but it is an extremely valuable adjunct to other filtration procedures and will amply repay the little extra work its adoption entails.

CHAPTER XIV

A CONTINUOUS WINE FILTER

VERY little equipment beyond that normally possessed by the average amateur winemaker is required to set up the simple yet efficient continuous wine filter illustrated in the accompanying diagram. Indeed, the only item which at first sight may appear to present a problem is a wine bottle with its base removed, but fortunately this difficulty is more apparent than real. It is actually very easy to remove the bottom cleanly from a bottle, even at home, and the following method rarely fails to achieve the desired result.

A little water, sufficient to give a depth of ½″–1″, should be poured into the bottle and a piece of string soaked in paraffin tied tightly round it at the surface level of the water therein. The string should then be set alight, and a few minutes later the bottle will crack cleanly along the line of the string. A few notches made round the bottle with a file will hold the string more firmly in place and help to achieve a cleaner break. Any rough edges which do remain may finally be smoothed off with a file. A glass cutting wheel may also, of course, be used to remove the bottom from a bottle, but few winemakers are likely to have such equipment at their disposal.

The filter should be assembled essentially as shown in the diagram, but the following points should be carefully noted. The syphon tube should reach to within ¼″ of the bottom of the reservoir so that almost its entire contents will automatically syphon into the filter bottle. The bottom of the reservoir must also be slightly higher than the top of the filter bottle for the same reason. The lower end of the syphon should project about two inches into the filter bottle so that it remains below the surface of the wine therein during the filtration. This arrangement prevents an air bubble from entering the syphon tube and causing an air-lock which could seriously interfere with the flow of wine from the reservoir. The bungs in the filter bottle must be tightly fitted or leaking will occur. Care is also necessary to ensure that one of the washed pebbles which fill the filter bottle to just above the shoulder does not lodge directly over the exit tube and thus partly block the outlet to the receiver.

One of the great advantages of this filter is the flexibility permitted by the rubber tubing connections between the reservoir, filter bottle and receiver. Only the filter bottle must be clamped securely in a fixed position. Most wine-makers will therefore find it convenient to place the reservoir on a table or bench and the receiver on the floor, adjusting the length of the rubber tubing connections to suit their own requirements. The filter bottle can then be secured to a chair or stool. Alternatively, of course, a special stand may be constructed for the entire filter should this be considered worthwhile.

The operating procedure is extremely simple. A few hours before the filter will be used, displace the air in the receiver with carbon dioxide as described near the end of the racking and clarification chapter. Next prepare the asbestos pulp or other filter aid in the normal manner (a small handful of asbestos pulp will be ample for this purpose). After assembling the equipment, close screw-clip 10B and pour the asbestos pulp or filter aid suspension into the filter bottle Keep the clip closed and open screw-clips 10A and 10C. Apply suction to the rubber tube to which screw-clip 10A is attached in order to start the syphon. Shut screw-clip 10A once the level of wine in the filter bottle is about an inch above the lower end of the syphon tube in the filter bottle (as in diagram). Allow the asbestos pulp or filter aid to settle for a few minutes before opening screw-clip 10B to start the filtration. The first few ounces of wine emerging into the receiver will probably be cloudy and may possess a peculiar taste so that this initial amount is best discarded. Thereafter filtration should proceed satisfactorily and automatically until all the wine in the reservoir has been filtered.

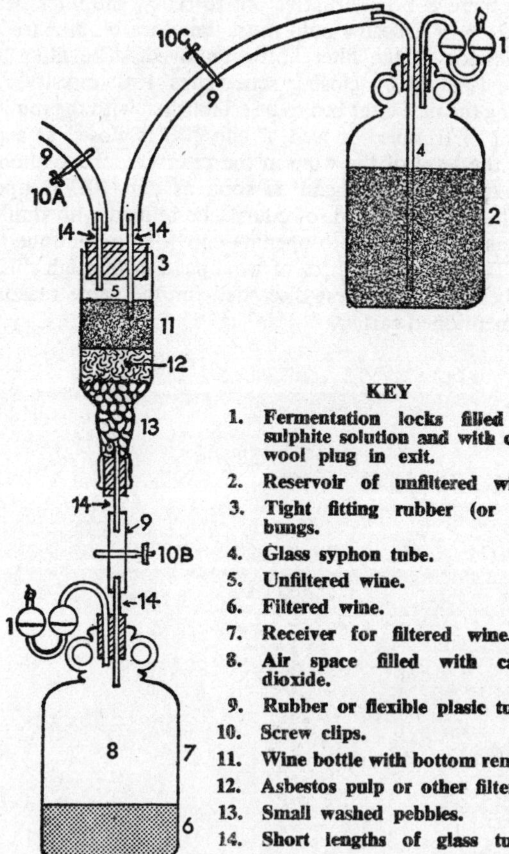

KEY

1. Fermentation locks filled with sulphite solution and with cotton wool plug in exit.
2. Reservoir of unfiltered wine.
3. Tight fitting rubber (or cork) bungs.
4. Glass syphon tube.
5. Unfiltered wine.
6. Filtered wine.
7. Receiver for filtered wine.
8. Air space filled with carbon dioxide.
9. Rubber or flexible plasic tubing.
10. Screw clips.
11. Wine bottle with bottom removed
12. Asbestos pulp or other filter aid
13. Small washed pebbles.
14. Short lengths of glass tubing.

At times, the wine undergoing filtration may contain so much suspended matter that the filter eventually becomes plugged and little or no wine passes through. Should this occur, there is no alternative but to renew the filter bed. A new batch of asbestos pulp must therefore be prepared and that already in the filter bottle removed. The filter bottle can be isolated by closing screw-clips 10B and 10C, thus enabling the new filter bed to be established with the minimum amount of trouble. Indeed, if clip 10C is closed at a point below the level of the wine in the reservoir, the syphon will automatically begin again as soon as clip 10C is opened. The filter bottle should, of course, be refilled with unfiltered wine (as before) prior to opening clip 10B to continue filtration. The first few ounces of wine passing through this new filter bed are again best discarded for the same reasons as were mentioned earlier.

CHAPTER XV
MATURING

A WINE sampled soon after fermentation has ceased is almost certain to taste raw and harsh or even downright unpleasant and may possess a poor bouquet simply because at this stage in its production the wine is young and still very much in its infancy. All new wines must be given an adequate period of storage prior to consumption in order that time can polish smooth these rough edges of their youth and develop their bouquet to its fullest extent. In other words, a wine must be allowed to mature if its latent quality is to have any chance of coming to the fore, since its bouquet and flavour can often improve to an astonishing degree as it grows older. Maturing is therefore the final important phase in quality wine production.

New wines mature during storage as a result of what is poetically called the marriage of their various major and minor constituents. In actual fact, wines improve and mellow with age because innumerable complex chemical reactions continue to take place indefinitely after fermentation has ceased, even though they are apparently quite lifeless. The tranquil appearance of a maturing wine is thus very misleading since slow but hidden changes as important in their own right as those wrought more rapidly and visibly by fermentation are continuously occurring beneath this outwardly calm surface, to the ultimate benefit of the wine.

Although the chemical reactions which take place in a maturing wine are extremely complex and as yet poorly understood, it does seem fairly certain that concurrent and consecutive oxidation, reduction and esterification reactions involving surprisingly small amounts of the various constituents of the wine predominate. Traces of ethyl alcohol are oxidised to acetaldehyde and acetic acid while a proportion of the higher alcohols, notably those which constitute the fusel oil formed as a by-product of fermentation, are similarly converted into their respective aldehydes and acids. Acetaldehyde and these other aldehydes may then combine with the alcohols to form acetals, and since both aldehydes and acetals are on the whole fragrant, pleasantly aromatic, volatile substances, they make a direct contribution to the bouquet of the wine. Combination between the various acids and alcohols in the wine also occurs with the formation of esters whose fresh fruity aroma once again appears in the bouquet. These chemical reactions are but a few of the numerous changes which take place in a maturing wine, but they do serve to illustrate the complexity of the marrying process and give at least some small indication of how the flavour of a wine mellows and its bouquet develops with age.

A maturing wine obviously requires an adequate supply of air to allow these oxidation reactions to proceed, but on the other hand too generous a supply of oxygen should be avoided, otherwise the quality of the wine will be impaired by over-oxidation. The formation of excessive amounts of acetaldehyde in this way is one of the commonest reasons why some wines acquire a flat, lifeless flavour, particularly when filtering has been employed for clarification purposes, since this operation inevitably exposes a wine unduly to the air from which it avidly absorbs oxygen with subsequent detrimental effects on its quality.

The effect of light on wine may be advantageously considered at this point. Exposing a wine to light, particularly direct sunlight, promotes undesirable photochemical reactions which can quickly ruin its quality. Both flavour and bouquet are adversely affected by the products of these reactions and the wine rapidly becomes stale. Light will also bleach the colour of red wines which are usually stored in amber or green bottles to prevent or at least minimise the risk of spoilage in this manner. The amateur must therefore take every precaution to exclude light from storage areas, especially where red wines are kept, and a permanently dark cellar or similar location is obviously ideally suited for this purpose.

Since the rate of a chemical reaction is a function of the temperature at which it proceeds (a rise in temperature of about 10°C. usually about doubles the reaction rate), this latter factor is clearly of great importance in the maturing of wine, for the majority of wines show a greater improvement in quality if they are allowed to mature fairly slowly. The so-called rapid methods of ageing wine are therefore of limited value because they achieve their end partly at the expense of quality. It follows that wine is best matured under cool conditions, and commercial winemakers consider that an even temperature of about 55°F. is ideal for this purpose.

Another important factor which affects the rate of maturing is volume, for small quantities of wine mature more rapidly than larger volumes under otherwise identical conditions. Bearing in mind the fact that the best quality wines are matured fairly slowly, it is obviously advisable to allow a wine to mature in bulk rather than bottle it immediately after fermentation has ceased, and this point will be discussed in more detail shortly.

Bulk storage in wood undoubtedly brings out the best in a wine because not only can the wine absorb substances from the wood and vice versa, but the finely porous nature of wood also permits the slow but continuous entry of air from which all dust and bacteria have been removed during its passage through the minute pores of the wood. The wine is therefore assured of an unbroken supply of oxygen throughout its maturing period in the cask, usually in quantities sufficiently small to cause no problem of over-oxidation. Indeed, in the case of large casks with a capacity greater than about 16 gallons, the supply of oxygen entering through the pores of the wood will almost certainly need to be augmented slightly by the aeration the wine receives at rackings. Many commercial winemakers regard casks containing about 50 gallons as the maximum size commensurate with adequate maturing for this reason.

Most amateur winemakers are interested in rather smaller cooperage, however, and casks with a capacity of nine gallons or less seem to be the most popular size in this country although some enthusiasts do possess 56-gallon casks. The most important feature of these small casks is the ratio of their surface area to their volume, for if this ratio is too large the wine will receive too generous a supply of oxygen and may oxidise rather too rapidly. From this consideration, it has been generally concluded that a 3-gallon cask is the absolute minimum in which to mature most wines, and even these casks are probably best reserved for sherries and similar oxidised wines. Casks with a capacity of 4½ to 6 gallons are much more satisfactory but still rather on the small side. Red wines can often be successfully matured in such casks if racking is kept to a minimum (say once every six months) or even avoided entirely once the wine has been clarified and no more sediment is deposited. Only the most robust white wines will not become over-oxidised under these conditions, however, so that it is generally inadvisable to consider maturing white table wines in cooperage of this size. Strong sweet white dessert wines which resemble Sauternes in character may be permitted a short period of maturing (up to six months) in a 4½–6 gallon cask provided racking is avoided except when it is absolutely essential in order to remove a deposit, but other white wines should not spend more than a month or two at the most in such casks. Experience indicates that 9–16 gallon casks are in fact the optimum size for most amateur winemaking purposes. Their capacity is not so large that racking becomes a serious problem, yet at the same time their ratio of surface area to volume is such that a wine will normally mature reasonably slowly. Indeed, with the exception of most white table wines, regular racking every 4–6 months is generally necessary after clarification is complete to augment the supply of oxygen reaching the wine by diffusion through the wood. Suitable wines may therefore be safely matured for some years in 9–16 gallon casks. Still larger cooperage is also perfectly satisfactory if the winemaker can handle the quantities of wine involved, but racking at intervals of 3–4 months is then usually essential to ensure that the wine receives sufficient oxygen for its development. At all times, of course, excessive aeration during racking should be avoided because it is not only unnecessary but also often proves detrimental to quality by causing over-oxidation of the wine.

At present, a great deal of wine produced by amateur winemakers is matured in glass containers instead of wooden casks. Although this practice is quite in order, a wine matured in glass will rarely if ever attain the standard it would reach if it were matured in wood, unless the winemaker is prepared to devote a great deal of time, care and attention to ensure that it does so. The reasons for this difference between maturing in glass and in wood are still rather obscure, but the following suggestions may at least partly explain matters. A wine stored in a cask can absorb small amounts of air continuously through the pores of the wood, and thus can satisfy its oxygen requirements to a greater or lesser extent without any interference or aid from the winemaker. On the other hand, glass is impermeable to air so that the oxygen required by the marrying process can only be supplied by racking the wine regularly at intervals of about 2–3 months. As a result, wines matured in glass receive the whole of their oxygen supply in a series of massive doses, a far from ideal situation which must exert some disturbing influence upon the course of the marrying process. Again, when a wine is stored in a cask there is an interchange of substances between it and the wood which almost certainly has some beneficial influence on its development, but the impervious nature of glass prohibits any such exchange so that the quality of the wine may be impaired, e.g. by the retention of certain undesirable constituents which adversely affect the flavour.

Since bulk maturing, particularly in wood, favours oxidation reactions rather than esterifications, there will eventually come a time when the wine is approaching maturity insofar as oxidation is concerned, yet it is still very young with respect to ester formation. Once this stage has been reached, steps must be taken to store the wine under conditions which will allow ester formation and allied reactions to proceed at least as rapidly as before but which will reduce the rate of oxidation very considerably so that the wine does not become over-oxidised before esterification has had time to add a final refined character to the wine. This problem is very neatly solved by bottling the wine immediately oxidation is judged to be sufficiently far advanced. Bottling effectively seals a wine from the air and prevents the access of oxygen, thus seriously curtailing further oxidation of the wine once the small amount of air which is always trapped in the wine during bottling operations has become exhausted. Oxidation-reduction reactions in which one substance oxidises another and is itself simultaneously reduced can, of course, still take place, but these reactions usually proceed comparatively slowly in wines and are governed mainly by an electrical property of the wine known as its oxidation-reduction potential or rH value. Ester formation therefore proceeds more rapidly than oxidation under these conditions until eventually both types of reaction become about equally far advanced. Provided the winemaker has judged the bottling time correctly, the wine should then be at the height of its development.

It is extremely difficult to judge exactly when a wine is ready for bottling and really this decision can only be based upon past experience. Apart from assessing the maturity of the wine, however, it must also be examined for clarity and tested for bottle ripeness before bottling is attempted. Any slight residual haze in the wine would eventually settle out and form a deposit in the bottle so that such wines should be given a polishing filtration or preferably fined before they are bottled to minimise this risk. Again, a wine ready for bottling should be completely stable. Thus, a small sample of wine exposed to the air overnight in a wineglass should not darken, otherwise the addition of one Campden tablet or its equivalent per gallon is indicated and bottling should be postponed for a few months. A larger sample of wine, sufficient to half-fill a wine bottle, should not throw a deposit nor begin to referment when it is left in a bottle plugged with cotton wool at a temperature of 75°F.–80°F. for several days. A positive result in this latter test means that fermentation is incomplete and the bulk of the wine should be stored at 75°F.–80°F. until no further activity is observed. It may then be concluded that the wine will probably not be ready for bottling for at least another six months when its bottle ripeness may again be checked.

At this point, it is worthwhile noting that recently bottled wines usually suffer from what is called "bottle sickness," i.e. the wine tastes flat and uninspiring as a result of the aeration it received during the bottling operation, possibly due to the formation of acetaldehyde. Fortunately, these effects are only temporary since after a few weeks the wine will normally regain its former quality, but it should not be drunk for at least three months after bottling and preferably not within six months of this time to allow it to recover from this bottle sickness.

Most wines will continue to improve during storage for several years, but eventually a wine attains a certain peak of perfection beyond which no further improvement will take place however long the wine is kept. Indeed, if the wine is not consumed fairly soon after it reaches this summit of its development, a gradual deterioration with age will begin until ultimately the wine becomes flat, lifeless and uninspiring. Although it has already been emphasised that a wine will not develop to its fullest extent unless it is matured for an adequate period of time both in cask and in bottle, because different types of wine and even different wines of the same type vary enormously in their longevity, the maturing cycle for individual wines can usually only be decided on the merits of each wine.

The maturing of the various wine types cannot therefore be discussed in detail for this reason, but nevertheless it is possible to formulate some general rules, for wines high in alcohol, tannin and acid tend to live the longest because these substances act as insurances against deterioration with age. Light, well-balanced white wines thus mature quite rapidly and are normally ready for bottling by the time they are 6 to 12 months old, but they should be kept for at least a further 3 months in bottle before drinking to recover from bottle sickness and to round off their character. Certain wines of this type therefore may be mature within about 9 months. The more acid white wines, e.g. German wines, tend to follow much the same pattern, although they may take slightly longer to mature because of their high acidity, but the better quality German wines may require between 6 and 18 months in cask and several more years in bottle before they are at their best. Strong, full-bodied white wines like Sauternes are very long-lived, however, mainly because their alcohol content is high, and after spending between 1 and 3 years in cask wines of this type will keep and improve for many years in bottle if properly stored.

Red wines usually mature comparatively slowly due to their high tannin content, and certain red wines, notably clarets, may take as long as 20 years to reach their peak quality. On the other hand, some other types of red wines, e.g. Beaujolais, are ready for drinking much sooner and are best consumed while they are comparatively young, so that it is extremely difficult to suggest even very general rules for maturing red wines. Since a hard and harsh claret is known to take longer to mature but in the end turns out to be superior to a comparable but initially better-balanced wine of the same type, however, it may be concluded that red wines high in acid and tannin should be given the longest period of maturing both in cask and in bottle. For similar reasons those red wines with a fairly high alcohol content should also be kept for a rather longer time. Red wines may therefore require anything between 1 and 3 years in cask and a further 1 to 20 years in bottle according to how much tannin, acid and alcohol they contain before they can be considered fully mature.

Fortified wines such as port, sherry and madeira will keep and continue to improve for decades because their high alcohol content prevents the growth of most micro-organisms and considerably delays the normal deterioration of a wine with age, cf. tannin in red wines. No details regarding the cask ageing of these wines can be given, however, for the period required by each type and its sub-types varies very widely indeed, e.g. tawny port is matured in cask very much longer than vintage or ruby port. After a fortified wine is bottled, of course, it may be kept for very many years if it is properly stored.

It is clear from this discussion that few amateurs store their wines long enough to allow them to reach their peak of perfection, but most people will be appalled at the thought of keeping their wines for some years before they are consumed, even if the necessary will-power to do so should be raised. Some compromise must obviously be made. Since high quality wines always improve to a considerably greater extent than mediocre wines with age, the solution to this problem is comparatively simple. Any fairly young wine which is thought to show promise should be kept and tasted at intervals of three or four months to see whether or not it is living up to its expectations until, by the time the wine has spent between six months and a year in cask, the wine-maker, basing his judgment mainly upon past experience, should be able to confirm or reject his initial impressions. Any high-quality wine can thus be matured further in cask and in bottle according to its type. Wines which fail to reach the required standard after a year in cask or younger wines which are obviously mediocre and unlikely to show any outstanding improvement with age, can then be drunk at any time and will cover the daily requirements for table wines, i.e. they will fulfil the same function as does vin ordinaire in France. By adopting this system, the winemaker will gradually build up a cellar of top-quality mature wine which can be reserved for special occasions, yet at the same itme there should still be an ample supply of various types of wine to satisfy the daily household demands. Nevertheless, it is advisable to try and keep most wines for a minimum period of six months, preferably in cask, to round off any initial harshness in their flavour and also to see if any hidden and unsuspected quality will appear.

CHAPTER XVI

BLENDING FOR QUALITY

THE principal aim of every winemaker is basically to produce wines whose quality remains consistently high from year to year. Few succeed in achieving their objective, however, for it is wellnigh impossible to avoid making a small proportion of mediocre wines and experiencing an occasional failure which is best not even mentioned! Hence, the difficulties facing the winemaker are how to minimise the chances of producing inferior wines in the future and what to do with those which have already been made. These two problems can, of course, be tackled in several ways, but perhaps the first point to note is that a thorough understanding ot the basic principles of winemaking goes a very long way towards reducing the incidence of failures. The less experienced winemaker is therefore well advised to bear this fact in mind before proceeding any further. By the same token, experienced winemakers whose basic knowledge is or should be quite sound, will generally find that blending either before or after fermentation offers the least drastic yet most effective solution to both questions.

These brief introductory remarks clearly indicate that blending is an extremely valuable technique which can be of great and lasting service to the winemaker. Some amateur winemakers who favour a more traditional approach nevertheless disagree with and strongly oppose blending of any description although their reasons for doing so seem rather inconsequential in the light of modern ideas. One view which receives a surprising amount of support is that every wine should have a name indicative of its origin, e.g. elderberry wine, parsnip wine and so on, whereas no such means of identification is feasible when extensive blending is practised. This contention is certainly quite valid, but in itself it seems a very trivial reason for condemning blending out of hand.

Surely the bouquet, the flavour and the overall quality of the wine are what really count? What it is called can only properly be regarded as a minor consideration in comparison with these other features. It seems incredible that any winemaker could even contemplate sacrificing quality by refusing to recognise the great value of blending solely because it does not permit the unequivocal naming of a wine. After all, blended wines can always be called aperitifs, table wines, dessert wines and the like, and it may even justifiably be argued that these names are more sophisticated! Whatever else, there can be no real grounds for disputing that a good quality "nameless" blended wine is infinitely preferable to a mediocre elderflower or carrot wine.

A second more sensible objection to blending is often raised when the subject of shows comes under discussion. The classes in many shows are still based upon a system of naming wines according to their principal ingredient which does tend to make it difficult to decide where a blended wine should be entered. Perhaps the main point to note here is that this classification was originally adopted because winemakers were traditionally accustomed to naming their wines in this fashion. In other words, show schedules were designed to suit the ideas current at the time of their inception so that wines were conveniently distinguished and classified on the basis of their principal ingredients. Nowadays, however, more and more blended wines which do not fit well, if at all, into ingredient classes are being produced and the tendency is to classify wines according to the purpose for which they are intended, e.g. as aperitifs, table wines, dessert wines and the like.

It is therefore hardly surprising that increasing pressure is being exerted to alter show schedules to take cognizance of this fact and offer purpose as well as ingredient classes with the ultimate aim of eliminating the latter almost entirely. The first steps in this direction have in fact already been taken, for the National and some of the larger regional shows have now introduced a few purpose classes and more are appearing every year. The transition to this type of class will, of course, be gradual and must inevitably incur some criticisim, but if the present rate of progress is maintained it seems reasonable to hope that the time when purpose classes will predominate may not be too far distant in the future. The superiority of this system of classification is certainly not hard to demonstrate. Its principal virtue is that it lays emphasis on the quality of a wine without overestimating the importance of its ingredients. A technique such as blending is not then restricted by the scope of show regulations, as tends to be the case at the moment, but rather is encouraged because it is an invaluable aid to quality.

Until these ideas gain general acceptance, however, winemakers who produce a high proportion of blended wines can only submit entries to purpose or general ingredient classes which make provision for such wines. Fortunately, the number of classes of this type is now growing apace. Purpose classes are still in the minority, but general ingredient classes, e.g. for fruit wines, which undoubtedly represent a transitional stage in the trend towards classification by purpose, are displacing single ingredient classes at a gratifyingly rapid rate. In areas where these more advanced ideas have not yet been approved, it may be noted that one other alternative does present itself. If much of the character of a blended wine is due primarily to one ingredient, there is nothing in most show regulations to prohibit the entry of that wine into the appropriate ingredient class. Indeed, numerous precedents can be cited here. To quote but one example, many flower and vegetable wines contain raisins yet are nevertheless accepted without question as entries for flower and vegetable wine classes.

BLENDING INGREDIENTS

Blending is theoretically an extremely simple technique, but in practice proficiency only comes with experience. Perhaps the most difficult problem which arises is to decide when to blend, for it is perfectly feasible to do so either before or after fermentation and each procedure has its merits. In general, preference should be given to blending ingredients prior to fermentation. The reason is that many single ingredients such as flowers and vegetables tend to give wines which are inherently unbalanced in some respect. Since their shortcomings are already known in advance, there seems little point in going to the trouble of making such a wine if its imperfections can be eliminated at the outset, long before the wine is ready for critical appraisal, simply by preparing the must from a carefully selected blend of ingredients. In other words, the idea is to anticipate and eradicate beforehand the faults to which experience indicates the wine is liable. The technique of blending ingredients consequently helps to reduce the number of mediocre or inferior wines which the winemaker is likely to produce and thereby leads to a higher average standard of quality. Furthermore, a greater proportion of superior wines than was previously obtained can be expected because the must will be better balanced initially than it was before. As fermentation and maturing both proceed more satisfactorily under these circumstances, a higher alcohol yield, finer flavour and fuller bouquet will usually be achieved and the wine will benefit accordingly. A final advantage is that the character of the individual ingredients will blend much more quickly and harmoniously during the fermentation than would otherwise be the case.

What, then, are the principles which the winemaker should follow when preparing a must from a blend of ingredients? Basically, the aim is to select two or more ingredients, each of which possesses some attribute that the others lack, so that the must is well-balanced in every respect and its character is in keeping with the type of wine being produced. Several factors need careful consideration here. The quality of a wine depends largely upon how well it is balanced as regards bouquet, flavour, body, alcoholic strength, acidity, astringency and so on, which themselves are determined mainly by the composition of the must. Grape juice illustrates these remarks very well. In poor years when too much acid and too little sugar is present, grapes produce inferior wines unless measures are taken to correct these defects. In good years, however, grape juice is generally so well-balanced that it can be converted directly into wine as soon as it is expressed from the berries. Since few if any other fruits can match the grape in this respect, amateur winemakers are forced to adjust the balance of their musts, often quite extensively, and have consequently come to regard the composition of grape juice as a very useful and proven standard on which to base their ideas.

It is therefore fortunate that the acidity, sweetness and alcohol content (and to a lesser extent, the tannin content) of a must can be controlled without too much difficulty by means of the hydrometer and acid testing equipment whose use has already been described in considerable detail elsewhere. The amount of acid and sugar in a must and hence the alcoholic strength and sweetness of the wine can therefore be adjusted to within comparatively close limits to suit the type of wine required. The astringency too can usually be kept within bounds either by adding tannin to musts or wines deficient in this commodity or by avoiding unduly long pulp fermentations with tannin-rich ingredients. Adequate maturing also plays a prominent part in mellowing astringent wines. On the other hand, body, bouquet and flavour are more elusive quality factors which defy precise measurement, and it is probably for this very reason that many wines fail to come up to expectations on these grounds alone.

It follows from these remarks that the first task of the winemaker should be to select a blend of ingredients which will provide the body, bouquet and flavour best suited to the character of the desired type of wine. Acidity, astringency and the like also deserve some attention, of course, but are much less important in this connection because any imbalances of this nature can normally be corrected at the time the must is prepared. The only real danger to avoid here is introducing excessive amounts of acid or tannin into the must.

Although there is a justifiable tendency to assume that these ideas are quite easy to put into practice, in reality it needs no little skill to do so successfully on a routine basis. Amateur winemakers certainly have a vast range of ingredients at their disposal, but nothing is gained merely by blending a few at random. To begin with, it is very important to pause and consider what type of wine is required. Its principal characteristics should be elucidated so that the winemaker has from the outset a broad appreciation of the objectives at which to aim. The advantages and disadvantages of the available ingredients which seem potentially suitable for this purpose should next be carefully evaluated. The final blend of ingredients is then selected by a process of elimination designed to reject every potential ingredient which would not make an essential or at least useful contribution towards achieving a must appropriate for the end in view. Unfortunately, there are relatively few rules to guide the winemaker here, for it is very much a matter of skilful judgment based upon experience. Every case has to be treated on its merits according to what ingredients are available and the type of wine desired. Since it would obviously be impossible to discuss even the main features of every situation which could conceivably be encountered, perhaps the best compromise under these circumstances is to review fairly extensively some of the most important quality factors to which due attention should always be paid.

BODY

Body is a convenient subject with which to begin. The origins of the term "body" are now rather obscure, but there is reason to believe that it arose from the traditional practice of throwing pieces of meat or even at times dead rats into vats of fermenting cider or wine musts quite literally to add body, and thereby, it was hoped, improve their character. Nowadays, of course, such a procedure would be regarded as unhygienic to say the very least! What, then, is the modern conception of body? In the first place, it is certainly related to the amount of involatile substances such as acids, salts, tannins and sugars present in the wine, fuller-bodied wines containing more of these constituents than lighter types, but even at the best of times only a very approximate correlation of this nature can usually be established. The same applies to the observation that the more alcohol a wine contains the fuller or heavier in body it is likely to be, for numerous exceptions to this rule can easily be found. In short, there is no precise definition nor any simple method of assessing the body of a wine except by the impressions it makes on the senses.

Perhaps the best approach from the practical point of view is to consider body in relation to different types of wine. Both red and white dry table wines, but particularly the latter, range from light to medium in body although a few are rather heavier than the average in this respect, white burgundies and red Rhône wines being especially notable for their full body. Slightly sweeter table wines, often described as medium dry, of which certain Graves and German wines are typical examples, usually possess a little more body than their drier counterparts by virtue of their small sugar content, but on the whole the latter is too low to have any appreciable effect. By way of contrast, the relatively large amounts of unfermented sugar present in dessert and after-dinner wines increases their body quite considerably with the result that wines of this type are invariably full-bodied or even very heavy in character. Aperitifs too are often well-endowed with body, but it is difficult to generalise with this group of wines since it embraces a very heterogeneous mixture of different types. The austere yet delicate dryness of a fine Fino sherry can hardly be compared with the fullness and vigour of a dry white Port, but both can serve equally well as aperitifs on almost any occasion!

The amateur can normally meet these requirements without undue difficulty. Table wines possibly offer the greatest challenge because no real guidance can be expected from traditional recipes which are mostly designed to produce strong, sweet dessert wines. Indeed, it is probably for this very reason that there is a distinct tendency for winemakers to make table wines rather too strong and full-bodied to be entirely acceptable for this purpose. At the other end of the scale, it is not uncommon to discover wines which taste very thin and watery and consequently lack appeal due to a pronounced deficiency of body. In many cases, the basic cause of the trouble lies in using, as the main constituent of the must, such ingredients as flowers and leaves which make no significant contribution to the body of the must but only to its bouquet and/or flavour. A similar situation may also be encountered when the principal ingredient of the must is a highly acid fruit such as red or blackcurrants whose juice has required so much dilution with water to reduce its acidity to a tolerable level that the must has simultaneously been deprived of much of its body. These faults can generally be avoided by employing fruit or fruit/vegetable blends as the basic ingredients for all table wines at the rate of 3–4 lbs. per gallon for a light to medium-bodied wine or slightly more if a fuller-bodied wine is desired. Highly acid fruits may then be used sparingly and the deficit in the total quantity of basic ingredients made good with vegetables and/or mildly acid fruits so that the problem of dealing with an excessively acid must never arises.

Dessert and allied types of wine naturally demand a larger quantity of ingredients per gallon than table wines in order to obtain the requisite fullness of body. Fruit or fruit/vegetable blends should again be employed as the basic ingredients, but in this instance some 4 lbs. per gallon should be regarded as the minimum quantity commensurate with achieving adequate body. In actual fact, it is usually advisable to include at least one ingredient specifically to provide the must with body and depth of character. Grain is often recommended for this purpose, but its use in this capacity rarely proves acceptable because even a small proportion of grain can have a marked effect on the bouquet and flavour of a wine. Bananas are far superior to grain as an ingredient for improving the body of a must. Not only does this fruit provide a great deal of body, but, unlike grain, it does so without introducing a noticeable bouquet or flavour of its own into the wine, especially if the skins are discarded prior to extracting the sliced fruit with boiling water. The low acid and tannin content of bananas is another factor which favours their being used to increase the body of a must. The amount of bananas to include in a blend obviously depends upon how much extra body is required, but in general ½–2 lbs. per gallon will prove adequate. As already mentioned, the skins are best discarded if as little banana character as possible is desired, but some or all may be included when this consideration is unimportant, as is often the case with sweet red wines.

BOUQUET

Attention may now be turned to the important matter of bouquet. There can be little doubt that a fine bouquet does a great deal to enhance the quality of any wine, for even the most exquisitely flavoured wine loses much of its appeal unless it is complemented by an equally outstanding bouquet. Although it goes without saying that all wines should possess a good bouquet, white and to a lesser extent red table wines are particularly demanding in this respect. Thus, the almost unbelievable power and fragrance of the bouquet of such famous white table wines as those from Germany and the Burgundy region of France has indisputably played a major part in leading to their acknowledgment as the finest wines of this type which the world can produce. The delicate subtlety of clarets too lies as much in their bouquet as in their flavour, while the perfumed elegance of Sauternes harmonises perfectly with their aristocratic richness. Similar remarks could also be passed about many other wines, but enough has already been said to illustrate the profound influence that bouquet can exercise over wine quality. Indeed, it can often spell the difference between greatness and mediocrity, especially in the case of white table wines.

In view of these remarks, it is perhaps unfortunate that traditional recipes still enjoy wide popularity since the majority fail to make any provision to ensure that the wine possesses a refined and pleasing bouquet. As a result, all too many amateur wines suffer from a pronounced lack of bouquet which lowers their quality and detracts greatly from their enjoyment. Wines produced primarily from vegetables, grain and allied ingredients are probably the worst offenders in this respect as their bouquet may at times be almost non-existent, but it is rather unfortunate that many wines based upon fruits are not very much better. Admittedly, relatively few fruits can hope to match, much less surpass, the power and fragrance of bouquet which the grape can provide, but the winemaker can do a great deal towards improving the bouquet of fruit wines simply by handling the fruit properly. Grapes are always picked in the peak of condition and used as soon as possible after harvesting. These two facts go a long way towards explaining why grape wines possess such magnificent bouquets, for wine produced from unripe grapes or berries which have been stored for some time after picking (even under refrigeration) do not reach the same high standard of bouquet as that made from otherwise identical grapes picked fully ripe and converted into wine immediately. This behaviour is also observed with other fruits, often to an even more marked degree than with grapes, so that the winemaker should always endeavour to allow fruits to ripen fully before picking them and then begin to prepare the must without delay once the fruit has been harvested. Failure to do so will almost invariably result in a poorer bouquet and hence a lesser quality wine than the fruit is potentially capable of producing.

Maturing also has a profound influence on bouquet development. The natural bouquet conferred by the ingredients is modified and reinforced during maturing as a result of certain chemical reactions which lead to the formation of fragrant volatile esters, acetals and related substances. Although relatively little is known about the factors governing the development of bouquet in a maturing wine, it does seem that the acid balance of the wine is important in this respect because the alcohols combine more readily with some acids than others to form the esters which contribute so much to the bouquet of a wine. Thus, citric acid does not readily participate in esterification reactions in maturing whereas malic acid does so much more easily and is therefore preferable to citric acid for this reason. Succinic acid, one of the more prominent by-products of fermentation, appears to esterify more completely than any other of the common acids in wine so that the inclusion of up to $\frac{1}{8}$ of an ounce per gallon of this acid in the must is likely to promote the development of a superior bouquet. Experimental wines to which succinic acid has been added certainly seem to support this idea, but the potential of succinic acid in this direction has not yet been fully evaluated. In addition to these remarks, however, the winemaker should also remember that esterifications and related reactions proceed at comparatively slow rates and need more than a few months to make any significant contribution to the bouquet of a wine. Hence, unless a wine is matured for a reasonable length of time, its bouquet is unlikely to show any worthwhile improvement over that supplied by its ingredients.

Flowers constitute one major class of ingredients consistently able to produce wines whose chief attraction lies in the strength and fragrance of their bouquet. The inclusion of flowers in the blend of ingredients used to prepare a must therefore appears a very simple yet highly effective means of improving the bouquet of a wine. Flowers certainly seem well suited to this task. The acid and tannin balance of the must is unaffected by their presence because flowers contain very little of either of these commodities. Nor is the flavour of the wine usually modified to any great extent, for the contribution made by the floral constituents of the must generally remains discreetly in the background and can only be detected as a fleeting but pleasant nuance in all except the lightest and most delicate table wines. Flowers can nevertheless provide a wine with more than just bouquet and delicate flavours. Colour can also be extracted from this source if red or other deeply tinted flowers are included in the must, particularly if the pulp fermentation procedure recommended in a previous chapter is followed. Admittedly, it is rarely possible to obtain a dark red wine in this way, but a fairly deep rosé can be produced without undue difficulty. The winemaker can certainly rest assured that the wine will acquire a distinct pink tinge under these circumstances. Hence, red flowers should always be reserved solely for incorporation into red or rosé wine musts whereas white or yellow flowers may safely be used for the production of any kind of wine.

It is often quite a difficult task to decide just what type and quantity of flowers should be selected to provide a bouquet which will harmonise well with the general character of the wine. This problem is further aggravated by the fact that the majority of flowers normally employed as wine-making ingredients are very satisfactory for this purpose. A few do have very little to offer a wine in the way of bouquet and can therefore be eliminated immediately, but no real progress can be made in this way since dandelions and broom flowers are about the only common varieties which fall into this category. Fortunately, certain flowers excel in their ability to enrich the bouquet of a wine, so that many wine-makers find it convenient to limit their attention exclusively to dealing with these ingredients. This practice has much to recommend it, for the virtues, defects and idiosyncrasies of the chosen types of flower can very quickly be assessed and each may then be used to its best advantage. There is consequently less danger of lowering the quality of the wine by misjudging the amount of flowers required when this approach is adopted. In particular, the chances of adding too many flowers to the must and thereby giving the wine such a strong and/or scented a bouquet that all its delicacy and finesse is entirely obliterated are very considerably reduced.

Elderflowers unquestionably figure predominantly among the flowers which first spring to mind when the subject of bouquet comes under discussion. Nor can it be denied that their high standing in this respect is richly deserved, for elderflowers have long been acknowledged to impart a bouquet which can rarely be surpassed for fragrance and elegance. The bouquet of almost any wine can in fact hardly fail to benefit from their inclusion in the must. Elderflowers also have the advantage of being extremely economical to use. Their heady perfume is so powerful that as little as a quarter of a pint per gallon may sometimes prove adequate, but ½ to ¾ of a pint per gallon should really be regarded as the normal average quantity which will suit most wines. Care should be taken not to add more than about ¾ to 1 pint per gallon, however, otherwise the wine is liable to develop an unpleasant "catty" bouquet which will completely spoil its enjoyment. It should also be noted that some eminent winemakers assert that there are some types of elderflowers which invariably confer a catty bouquet on a wine, no matter how few flowers are added. Since a number of sub-species of the elder tree undoubtedly do exist (even one whose berries are green when fully ripe), this view is probably quite correct. Soil conditions and composition may also be significant in this respect. The best elderflowers actually seem to be those which are pure white rather than creamy in colour and which grow relatively sparsely in fairly small heads. Large creamy coloured heads on a tree literally covered with blooms should therefore be avoided or at least viewed with suspicion for this reason unless previous experience dictates otherwise.

Dried elderflowers are also available at a moderate cost and can be used as a substitute for the fresh flowers when the latter are out of season. In common with other dried ingredients, however, dried elderflowers are not as satisfactory as their fresh counterparts so that another fresh flower such as rose petals should preferably be employed instead of dried elderflowers if such an alternative does present itself. On the other hand, if dried elderflowers must be used, it is generally considered that $\frac{1}{2}$ oz. per gallon of the dried flowers is roughly equivalent to 1 to $1\frac{1}{2}$ pints per gallon of the fresh, but some variations can be expected according to the source of supply.

Rose petals run a close second to elderflowers in their ability to enhance the bouquet of a wine. Moreover, their season is much longer since roses bloom from June to September or October so that fresh rose petals can readily be obtained for a large part of the year. Rose petals give a much more scented bouquet than elderflowers, and for this reason must be used in moderation. It is not the duty of a wine to smell like a flower garden! Roses are, of course, noted for the number of different varieties which can be grown, and each variety will provide a unique bouquet of its own. Sometimes the distinctions between the bouquets imparted by one rose and another are very subtle and insignificant, but more often than not certain differences are readily apparent. These varietal variations make it almost impossible to be specific about the amount of petals which will be required, but, depending upon the strength and nature of their perfume, one-quarter to three-quarters of a pint per gallon will usually turn out to be ample. Colour must also be taken into account when rose petals are employed and only yellow varieties included in white wine musts.

Blends of elderflowers and rose petals frequently offer many advantages. These two flowers complement each other very well to give a bouquet which combines the best attributes of both and is consequently superior to that achieved by either alone on many occasions. At the same time, the danger of a "catty" or overly-scented bouquet developing in the wine is significantly reduced because smaller amounts of the individual flowers are added to the must. In general, a blend consisting of $\frac{1}{4}$ to $\frac{1}{2}$ pint per gallon each of elderflowers and rose petals will prove eminently satisfactory, the proportions of the two flowers in the blend depending upon the type of bouquet preferred.

Numerous other flowers can be included in the must for bouquet purposes, but few come into the class of elderflowers and rose petals. Some which may be rated as moderately good in this respect are white and pink hawthorn flowers (mayblossom) and cowslips, while gorseflowers, primroses and golden rod are reasonably satisfactory. Their main disadvantage is commonly that sufficient quantities are not readily available, for in many cases about 2 to 4 pints per gallon will be needed. The winemaker should therefore regard these flowers more as specialised ingredients which are best reserved for making small amounts of wine or for experimental investigations.

FLAVOUR

It is but a short step to pass from the subject of bouquet to that of flavour, the next topic for discussion, since the two are inseparable partners when the time comes to assess the worth of a wine. Flavour is nevertheless the most important single factor upon which wine quality depends. A wine may still be enjoyed, albeit with reservations, if it simply lacks good bouquet, but it will hold no appeal whatsoever should its flavour be found wanting. No matter how well-balanced a wine may be in other respects, it will never achieve greatness unless its flavour so decrees. Indeed, amateur wines were at one time an object of derision simply because their flavour was often so poor that it could only truthfully be described as appalling, and many recipes included spices in an effort to obtain a more palatable product. Although quality has nowadays improved tremendously, it is a regrettable fact that there is still a long way to go before the situation can be described as satisfactory, as the relatively low standard often reached by the wines exhibited at the National and other shows all too clearly indicates.

The main intention here is not so much to delve deeply into flavour *per se* but rather to discuss it in relation to different types of wine. Table wines, for example, should not be too strongly flavoured. A prominent ingredient taste is thus only rarely acceptable in this type of wine, since its purpose is to enhance the enjoyment of the food, not to dominate the meal. It is for this reason that red wines cannot successfully accompany fish, for the delicacy of the latter would be completely overwhelmed by the robustness of the wine. Hence, such strongly flavoured ingredients as grain and herbs should be avoided in table wine production. So too should fruits whose character is unmistakably retained in the wine, raspberries and blackcurrants being notable on this account. The emphasis in the case of table wines lies more towards mild fruits, flowers and vegetables which give a wine character without their own contribution being immediately apparent. Ideally, of course, all the ingredients of the must should blend together so that none can be detected individually in the wine. The latter is then forced to stand on its own merits as a wine and must be judged as such without the issue being clouded by any of the preconceived ideas which a knowledge of its ingredients would inevitably instil.

Dessert wines are less exacting than table wines insofar as flavour is concerned. Too strong an ingredient flavour should be avoided because the wine still has to accompany food, but on the other hand it must be sufficiently fully-flavoured to partner a heavy pudding or similar dessert without being overwhelmed. This object can effectively be accomplished simply by including a fairly high proportion of fruit in the must, at least 4 lbs. of fruit per gallon usually being advisable even when fruit/vegetable blends are employed as the basic ingredients. The flavour of dessert wines can also be improved in other ways. Red wines of this type often benefit from the inclusion of about ½ lb. per gallon of raspberries, loganberries, blackcurrants or related fruits whose character is normally retained prominently in a wine. This amount is just enough to provide a wine with a discreet fruity background which will greatly enhance its appeal without obtruding directly on the palate. A similar effect can be achieved in both white and red dessert wines when bananas are used to increase their body merely by retaining up to half the skins in the must.

These principles may also be extended to after-dinner or post-prandial wines which commonly resemble dessert wines except for their rather fuller body and greater alcoholic strength, many in fact being fortified at some stage in their production. Port, oloroso sherry and the sweeter types of madeira are typical examples of after-dinner wines. Thus, apart from using even larger quantities of fruit and/or vegetables in these latter wines, the approach is much the same in both cases. The only point to note is that after-dinner wines generally benefit from fortification unless an alcoholic strength of about 17% to 18% by volume can be achieved directly by fermentation. Otherwise, the quality of the wine determines whether the extra expense of fortification can really be justified. The winemaker does have one great advantage here since after-dinner wines may be tailored to meet individual tastes. Strongly flavoured wines are not out of place at the end of a meal. Indeed, a few glasses of a well-made raspberry or grain wine can provide a magnificent climax to a dinner. Hence, ingredients which are noted for their ability to produce powerfully flavoured wines may be ideal for making after-dinner wines. Herbs are about the only exception to this rule as their flavour seems better suited to stimulating the appetite.

Aperitifs need very careful appraisal from the point of view of flavour because this group of wines embraces a multitude of different types. Some, like fino sherry, are comparatively light in body, dry and delicate. Others, like white port, are full-bodied and generous yet essentially dry in character. Still others, like Martini and Dubonnet, are full-bodied, sweet (sometimes dry) wines strongly flavoured with herbs, quinine and the like. The variety of aperitifs is in fact such that there are very few features which all share in common, although the majority do have a high alcoholic strength as a result of fortification. It is consequently advisable to produce as much alcohol as possible by fermentation for the same reasons as were just mentioned in connection with after-dinner wines. Flavour is an entirely different proposition, however, for what holds true for one type of aperitif often does not apply to another. General rules simply cannot be formulated because every type of aperitif must be treated on its own merits, although it is worth noting that certain ingredients seem particularly well suited for aperitif production. Oranges, for example, are an excellent basic ingredient for the drier and more delicate aperitifs, especially if a little of the zest is included in the must to give the wine added piquancy. Fresh and dried herbs are also ideal for this purpose and can serve in a double capacity. The chosen herbs may either be used from the outset as a basic ingredient of the must or may be added to and allowed to infuse for a time in a wine which has already finished fermenting. Although the former method is usually preferable, the latter may often prove of value when a strong sweet wine has failed to come up to expectations, for in this way it can be converted into a very pleasant aperitif. Flavouring essences too may be employed in a similar manner.

VINOUS QUALITY

There is one other very important aspect of blending ingredients which has so far been completely ignored. It has been pointed out on numerous occasions that certain amateur wines, chiefly those based primarily on ingredients other than fruits, lack an indefinable "something" in their character. This rather nebulous feature has been termed vinous quality or vinosity and is really a broad appreciation of a wine as a wine as opposed to any alcoholic beverage. Unfortunately, it is almost impossible to give a more precise description since any attempt to do so would be more likely to confuse rather than clarify the issue. The winemaker may nevertheless rest assured that the palate will at once find a wine lacking vinous quality to be deficient in some respect even though the reasons for coming to this conclusion may not be immediately apparent. This serious fault can easily be prevented by including raisins or, better still, grape concentrate in the must, about 1 to 2 lbs. of raisins or ½ to 1 pint of grape concentrate per gallon usually being adequate for this purpose. Indeed, the routine use of grape concentrate as a standard ingredient of every must has much to commend it since wine quality is sure to benefit from this practice. The extra expense incurred in this way is partly offset by a corresponding saving in sugar (1 pint of grape concentrate replaces 1 lb. of sugar). In addition, the cheaper brands of grape concentrate are perfectly satisfactory for improving the vinous quality of a wine so that its cost will only be increased by a few shillings per gallon even when 1 pint of grape concentrate per gallon is employed.

DESIGNING RECIPES

It seems advisable at this stage to review what has just been said on the subject of blending ingredients and illustrate how this technique actually operates in practice. Since new ideas can often be more thoroughly understood with the aid of examples, the procedure which was followed when designing one of the recipes presented in a later chapter will be discussed here in some detail. The wine concerned is a white table wine and the quantity required is five gallons. The preparation of the must and so on will not, of course, be dealt with at this point as it is fully described elsewhere.

The first task is to summarise the principal characteristics of the type of wine which is sought. Thus, a typical white table wine will be light to medium in body, delicately flavoured, and will possess a fine fragrant bouquet. Its alcoholic strength will probably be around 10% to 12% by volume,while its acidity may vary quite widely according to the region of its origin, although 3.0 to 3.5 p.p.t. would be a fairly representative range for all but northern European wines. Some unfermented sugar may remain in the wine but rarely very much so that it will usually be dry or medium dry. These brief remarks at once provide a basis on which a recipe can be designed.

The best basic ingredients for white table wines are undoubtedly fruits although fruit/vegetable blends may sometimes be employed, especially when a fuller bodied wine is preferred. Many fruits are suitable for this purpose, e.g. peaches, pears, greengages, apricots and the like, but peaches are well known to produce excellent white wines and will therefore be chosen as the basic ingredient for this particular wine too. Since a medium-bodied delicately flavoured wine is required, large quantities of fruit should be avoided so that 4 lbs. of peaches per gallon should prove adequate. The winemaker should note at this point that the addition of a little pectozyme, say $\frac{1}{8}$ oz. per gallon, is advisable because peaches are comparatively rich in pectin which could later cause clarification difficulties were it not destroyed prior to or during fermentation.

Some raisins or white grape concentrate should also be included to provide vinous quality, but in this instance it is preferable to use grape concentrate at the rate of $\frac{1}{2}$ pint per gallon. The latter may be replaced by 1 lb. of raisins per gallon, but this substitution is worth considering only when cost is a major factor.

Bouquet is the only other factor which has not yet been taken into account. Since the ingredients so far selected are not particularly noted for supplying bouquet, which is extremely important in white wine production, about ½ pint of yellow rose petals per gallon must be added to rectify this imbalance. Elderflowers cannot be used since they are not in season at the same time as peaches and dried elderflowers should be avoided when rose petals are available.

The sugar requirements of this wine can be calculated fairly easily, for it ought to contain roughly 12% alcohol by volume which would be obtained by the complete fermentation of about 2 lbs. of sugar per gallon. In other words, the initial gravity of the must should be around 90. The grape concentrate will supply approximately ½ lb. sugar per gallon and the peaches another ¼ to ½ lb. per gallon, so that a further 1 to 1¼ lbs. of sugar per gallon will be required. Some or even all this sugar may be advantageously replaced with honey, although 1¼ to 1½ lbs. honey would be needed were it employed exclusively. In practice, of course, just enough sugar and/or honey to increase the initial gravity of the must to 90 would be added.

It is wellnigh impossible even to estimate how much acid should be introduced into the must until the latter has been prepared and its acidity checked. Both the peaches and the grape concentrate will supply some acid, possibly enough to give an acidity of 3.0 to 3.5 p.p.t. directly. If insufficient acid is obtained from the ingredients, however, the deficiency should be made good with Acid Mixture A.

The basic recipe for five gallons white table wine is therefore 20 lbs. of peaches, 2½ pints of white grape concentrate, 2½ pints of yellow rose petals, ½ oz. of pectozyme, sufficient sugar and/or honey to give an initial gravity of 90, acid mixture A (if required) to an acidity of 3.0 to 3.5 p.p.t. together with the usual nutrients and a suitable yeast starter. Several yeasts can be employed for white table wine production, notably the Graves, Bordeaux, Chablis and Steinberg strains, but Steinberg is an excellent "stock" variety and has therefore been recommended in this instance.

It is hoped that these remarks will help to give the winemaker some further insight into the principles of recipe design. Although no other recipes have been accorded such a detailed exposition, the approach is analogous in almost every case so that the reasons why certain ingredients have been selected for a particular type of wine should be fairly easy to establish simply by inspecting the recipe itself. Indeed, it should always be possible to work backwards in this way with a properly designed recipe. A careful study of the recipes presented in a later chapter will thus be useful in this respect and can be referred to for guidance when devising others for similar purposes.

BLENDING WINES

Experience has shown that a consistently higher average standard of quality can be attained when musts are prepared from judiciously selected blends of ingredients than by more traditional methods. The proportion of superior wines which can be expected is also increased when this technique is adopted. Blending ingredients prior to fermentation consequently enables the winemaker to produce more fine wines and fewer mediocre or inferior wines than has hitherto been the case. It is nevertheless obvious that the latter cannot be eliminated entirely because winemaking is very far from being an exact science and, incidentally, owes much of its appeal to this very fact. Poor quality wines will still occasionally be encountered no matter how thoughtfully the ingredients of the must are chosen or how much care is lavished on the wine at every stage in its production. There is then little choice but to regard such failures as an occupational hazard of amateur winemaking! In the main, however, some momentary lapse on the part of the winemaker can be held directly responsible for a wine being mediocre in quality. Unfortunate accidents or oversights can happen all too easily. For example, the acidity of the must may have been adjusted incorrectly or not at all, too long a period of pulp fermentation may have been allowed and so on, thereby upsetting the balance of the wine and lowering its quality to a greater or lesser extent. Alternatively, of course, the fault may be with the ingredients selected for the must, in which case a sound and reasonably well-balanced but rather unpretentious wine lacking any real depth of character may be obtained.

What, then, can be done to improve the quality of the poor wines which even the most experienced winemaker cannot avoid producing from time to time? If the wine is palatable and merely has no distinctive character of its own, the simplest answer to this question is probably to drink it young as a vin ordinaire and/or use it for cooking purposes. Unfortunately, many inferior wines have insufficient appeal to serve even in this humble capacity. Some whose balance leaves a great deal to be desired may in fact be quite unpleasant, as is often the case when too much acid or tannin is present. There are admittedly various ways and means of rendering such wines palatable, but few can truthfully be described as entirely satisfactory. Thus, sugar may be added to mask excessive acidity or astringency, but this procedure can only properly be regarded as a final desperate measure which, it is hoped, will at least make the wine fit to drink. It merely circumvents the main issue and does nothing to overcome or remedy the defects inherent in the wine.

Once again blending offers the best solution to this problem, for a blend prepared from a number of nondescript wines will often reach a far higher standard of quality than any one of its constituent wines. The principles governing the blending of wines are, as might be expected, very similar to those already described in connection with the blending of ingredients. The object here is to select a number of wines, each of which possesses some attribute the others lack, and blend them in such a way that all the defects apparent in the individual wines are mutually cancelled out to give a vastly superior composite wine. Although this undertaking may superficially look extremely easy, the winemaker should now have been warned by what has gone before that proficiency at blending of any description calls for a high degree of skill and only comes with experience. Herein lies one great advantage of dealing with wines as opposed to ingredients, for blending can be continued until the winemaker is satisfied that the best possible balance has been achieved with the wines which are available. In addition, there is no need to employ large quantities of wines initially since trial blends should first be prepared on a small scale to determine what relative amounts of each wine will be required to attain the optimum quality for the type of wine, preferred. The bulk of the wines can then be blended in those proportions to obtain the desired result.

It follows from these remarks that any wines whose quality for some reason does not come up to expectations should be kept until enough different wines are available to make blending a worthwhile proposition. The first step should then always be to evaluate critically the character and quality of each wine so that both its merits and its faults are firmly established right from the outset. In this connection, the acid content and gravity of every wine should be determined and its alcoholic strength calculated from the gravity data obtained during fermentation. Astringency, body, bouquet, flavour and the like should also be appraised by tasting and these observations carefully recorded for future reference. A comprehensive picture of all the wines destined for blending will thus be built up and will prove of immense practical value when the preparation of actual trial blends commences.

The principal characteristics of these wines should next be reviewed collectively in order to gain some idea about the type of wine at which to aim. For example, if most of the wines are fairly strong and sweet, it would be logical to make the target a dessert wine. Similarly, a number of light to medium drier wines would preferably be blended to produce a table wine. Colour too must be taken into account since red and white wines should generallly be segregated unless a rosé blend is desired. A small proportion of white wine will, of course, scarcely alter the colour of a predominantly red blend, but conversely the result would inevitably be a rosé wine of some description because very little red wine is needed to confer a noticeable pink tinge on a white wine. Some preliminary selection can therefore be carried out so that wines whose character differs markedly from that of the majority can be set aside for future blending purposes or at least used with caution. Thus, one or two strong sweet wines among a number of lighter and drier wines would normally be reserved for the future until sufficient similar wines had been accumulated to make the preparation of a dessert wine blend possible.

The golden rule when blending wines is to begin by doing so on a small scale. A 100 mls. sample is ample for assessing the potential of a particular blend, especially as the first impression gained in this way can, if necessary, be verified by preparing a larger sample. Any number of small trial blends may consequently be produced without losing much wine should the first few attempts end in failure as is commonly the case. Blending is a matter of trial and error coupled with experience and a sound basic knowledge of the individual wines concerned. An objective approach is also essential, however, for every wine and every trial blend must be very critically appraised to achieve even a moderate degree of success.

Blending wines primarily involves counterbalancing the faults in one wine by means of another wine which suffers from the same defect but to the opposite extreme, at the same time striving to obtain the type of wine which the individual constituents of the blend seem best suited to provide. Thus, a highly astringent wine would be blended with an insipid wine which lacks tannin in such proportions as to achieve a balanced whole. In just the same way, other quality factors such as acidity, body, bouquet, flavour and the like can be brought into balance by judiciously blending a number of wines. Acidity, gravity and alcoholic strength can in fact be adjusted directly from what is already known about the wines, but for obvious reasons it is advisable to supplement the conclusions drawn solely on the basis of this information by preparing and tasting trial blends. Otherwise, blending must be carried out entirely with the aid of the palate. Two or more wines are blended in proportions which the winemaker thinks should provide, say, the optimum tannin content or the best flavour or the finest bouquet. This trial blend is next tasted, its quality assessed and alterations made to the ratios of the constituent wines until the best possible balance has apparently been attained. This process is continued on a small scale until every quality factor has been taken into account and a final blend with no major and as few minor faults as possible has been produced. The bulk of the wines can then be blended in these proportions to obtain the desired composite wine. It may, of course, take some time to reach this stage, but the winemaker can rest assured that many pleasant hours can be spent preparing and weighing up the pros and cons of various trial blends. As has repeatedly been stressed, proficiency will only come with experience, but acquiring that experience can be a very rewarding and enjoyable pastime, especially during the long winter months when there is usually less to keep the winemaker occupied.

A recently blended wine should normally be regarded and treated in the same way as a young, immature wine which has just finished fermenting. In actual fact, this may very well be the case since a short period of refermentation is quite often observed soon after a blend of wines has been prepared. Nor should the winemaker attempt to prevent such a refermentation by sulphiting. Indeed, its occurrence should rather be welcomed and actively encouraged whenever possible, for there is no better way than even a brief fermentation to bring about the harmonious marriage of the individual wines from which the blend was produced. Whether refermentation takes place or not, however, the blend will almost certainly throw a surprisingly large deposit during the first few weeks or months following its preparation, despite the fact that it may have been perfectly clear from the very outset. The formation of such a sediment is a natural consequence of blending different wines, but it does mean that periodic racking is necessary to remove the unwanted lees as well as to aerate the wine. Maturing in cask and/or bottle is then carried out exactly as it would be for any new wine of the same type as the blend.

In conclusion, it is worth mentioning that blending should not by any means be considered to be limited only to poor wines. Good quality wines may frequently be improved still further by being blended with other comparable wines of the same type. Port, sherry and champagne are typical examples of commercial wines whose consistently high quality is maintained in this manner. No wine, no matter how excellent it may be, can ever be rated as perfect. Some minor though perhaps very subtle imperfections apparent only to an experienced palate will inevitably mar its greatness. The more advanced winemaker should therefore try blending several superior wines of the same type in an effort to eliminate their more obvious minor defects.

It may turn out that nothing can be gained by doing so, but usually some improvement can be wrought when the winemaker will be rewarded with a really superb wine. The old adage "nothing ventured, nothing gained" aptly describes the situation here and, indeed, may be applied to the entire subject of blending so that the winemaker is well advised to adopt blending as a standard procedure without further ado.

CHAPTER XVII

ALCOHOL AND FORTIFICATION

WINE may basically be defined as a type of alcoholic beverage, but such a description so obviously fails to do justice to the finer qualities for which wine is renowned that it hardly merits serious attention. It is nevertheless a lamentable fact that many people in certain otherwise highly civilised countries of the world still accord wine little more respect or recognition than this pathetic definition implies. The one redeeming feature which explains its inclusion here is that it serves to emphasise the important fact that all wines contain alcohol. Indeed, alcohol is almost invariably second only to water as a major constituent of wine. Up to 20% alcohol by volume may at times be present, and water and alcohol together often account for well over 90% of the total volume of a wine.

These brief introductory remarks show that alcohol occupies an eminent position in winemaking. What, then, is this substance to which wine owes much of its stimulating and mellowing effects? Although the name alcohol is used as a generic term in chemistry to describe a large family of related compounds, it has a much more specific meaning to the winemaker. Here, it refers almost exclusively to ethyl alcohol or ethanol, chemical formula CH_3CH_2OH, which is the principal alcohol found in wine. Ethyl alcohol is a colourless, mobile liquid, miscible with water in all proportions, which boils at about 78° C. and has a specific gravity of approximately 0.79. In other words, it is both lighter than water and boils at a lower temperature. Pure alcohol has a burning taste and is extremely unpalatable in the undiluted state. Some idea of its fiery nature can be gleaned by drinking a little neat whisky or brandy. The burning sensation caused by these spirits is quite pronounced, yet their alcohol content is usually only around 40% by volume.

The main interests of the winemaker do not lie with pure alcohol, however, but rather are centred around the alcoholic strength of wines. Since the exact amount of alcohol in a wine can only be determined by means of such complicated and expensive equipment as the ebullioscope, it it fortunate that its approximate alcohol content, which is much more easily estimated, is sufficiently accurate for almost any purpose the amateur may have in mind. Both the hydrometer and the vinometer can be employed to obtain this information, but their use and limitations in this connection have already received detailed attention in previous chapters and so need not be further discussed here.

The data provided by the hydrometer is usually handled in such a way that the strength of the wine is expressed as the percentage of alcohol by volume. The vinometer is also calibrated to provide a direct reading of the alcohol content in the same units. The amateur is therefore educated from the start to think in terms of percentage alcohol by volume as a measure of alcoholic strength. The same also applies to commercial wine producers in many parts of Europe. There, the alcohol content of a wine may be expressed in degrees Gay-Lussac, but the difference is one of name only since the two terms percentage alcohol by volume and degrees Gay-Lussac are synonymous. Thus, a wine containing 12% alcohol by volume also has an alcoholic strength of 12° Gay-Lussac.

The amount of alcohol in a wine can in fact be expressed in several different ways. Many of these alternative scales of measurement have very limited applications and may therefore be ignored, but there is one system which does merit closer attention because it is very widely used in this country. The British Customs and Excise authorities measure alcoholic strength in terms of proof spirit, a concept which is often only poorly understood and which consequently tends to cause some considerable confusion wherever it is encountered. Since the proof spirit scale of measurement is so common that it cannot be avoided indefinitely, the winemaker is well advised to try and achieve some familiarity with its basic essentials or at least be able to convert a proof spirit strength into a percentage of alcohol by volume and vice versa.

The true origins of the term proof spirit are now rather obscure, although it is said to date from the time when no accurate means of assessing the strengths of spirits were available. In those days, some gunpowder was moistened with a little of the spirit under test and, if it could still be ignited, the spirit was considered to be at least proof in strength. Proof spirit was thus that mixture of alcohol and water which would just permit gunpowder moistened with it to ignite.

Whether this fascinating anecdote is a true story or merely a legend has not been established, but in any event it would certainly help to account for the modern definition of (100) proof spirit as stated in the Customs and Excise Act of 1952. This Act says—"Spirits shall be deemed to be proof if the volume of ethyl alcohol contained therein made up to the volume of the spirits with distilled water has a weight equal to that of 12/13ths of a volume of distilled water equal to the volume of spirits, the volume of each liquid being computed at 51° F." This definition can only be described as appalling, and it is hardly surprising that most people find its meaning to be completely incomprehensible. Indeed, its translation into simpler terms is by no means too easy a task even for a person with scientific training! In practice, however, it turns out that (100) proof spirit contains 57.06% alcohol by volume at 51° F. which is at least understandable even though the figure does appear rather odd!

It may now be calculated that pure alcohol is 175.1 proof spirit. This information immediately shows that the conversion from proof spirit to percentage of alcohol by volume is not as difficult as might at first have been expected. For all but the most exact calculations, multiplying the proof spirit strength by four and dividing the product by seven will give the percentage of alcohol by volume directly, i.e. the conversion factor here is $\frac{4}{7}$. Conversely, multiplying a percentage of alcohol by volume by seven and dividing the product by four will give the alcoholic strength in terms of proof spirit, i.e. the conversion factor here is $\frac{7}{4}$, the reciprocal of the previous figure. These remarks can perhaps best be clarified by means of the following examples. Many spirits such as whisky, rum and gin are labelled as being 70 proof, so that their alcohol content is in fact $70 \times \frac{4}{7}$ or 40% by volume. Similarly, table wines contain on the average some 12% alcohol by volume, so that their alcoholic strength is $12 \times \frac{7}{4}$ or 21 proof. A table showing the proof spirit strength corresonding to a given percentage of alcohol by volume has also been included here for reference purposes.

RELATION BETWEEN PERCENTAGE ALCOHOL BY VOLUME AND BRITISH PROOF SPIRIT

% Alcohol by volume	*Proof Spirit*	*% Alcohol by volume*	*Proof Spirit*
2	3.5	25	43.8
4	7.0	30	52.5
6	10.5	35	61.3
8	14.0	40	70.0
10	17.5	45	78.8
12	21.0	50	87.5
14	24.5	60	105.0
16	28.0	70	122
18	31.5	80	140
20	35.0	100	175

Sometimes the winemaker may come across the expressions "overproof" and "underproof" and may be unsure of their true meaning. The explanation is actually quite simple. Proof spirit itself is generally understood to mean 100 proof spirit. Hence, a spirit which is 30 overproof is simply 130 proof and one which is 20 underproof is 80 proof. In other words, the amount by which the spirit is over or under proof is merely added to or subtracted from 100 as the case may be to obtain its alcoholic strength in terms of proof spirit.

One word of warning should be heeded here. The Americans, it must be admitted on this occasion with every justification, found the British system of proof spirit to be far too complicated for their needs. As a result, proof spirit was redefined in America as that mixture of ethyl alcohol and water which contains 50% alcohol by volume at 60° F., thereby providing a very simple relation between proof spirit and the percentage of alcohol by volume. The winemaker should therefore bear this difference in mind when reading any American books on wine technology.

Wine occupies an intermediate position between beer and spirits insofar as its alcoholic strength is concerned. It rarely contains less than 6% to 8% alcohol by volume or more than 20% to 22%. These limits are really extremes, however, for table wines, which generally have an alcohol content of some 9% to 15%, far outnumber all other types put together. Furthermore, in the commerical field, the amount of sugar in the grapes rarely permits fermentation to produce more than 15% to 16% alcohol. Even amateurs, who are not limited in this respect by the sugar content of their ingredients, usually find it difficult to obtain more than about 16% to 18% alcohol because most yeasts reach their maximum alcohol tolerance at this point and are inhibited from further activity. Fermentation alone cannot therefore provide sufficient alcohol to account for the amount present in such commercial wines as sherry, port and madeira nor can it normally do so for similar amateur wines.

How, then, is it possible to produce wines containing as much as 22% alcohol by volume? The answer to this problem is very simple. Some of the alcohol is produced by fermenting the must in the normal manner, but more in the form of distilled spirit is added later, generally though not always after fermentation has ceased. Wines of this type are said to be fortified and contain about 16% to 22% alcohol by volume of which added spirit may comprise quite a large proportion.

Although almost any distilled spirit can theoretically be employed for this purpose, in practice brandy is by far the commonest. In all except name, however, fortifying brandy bears little resemblance to the cognacs and armagnacs so beloved by the connoisseur. The reason is that the term brandy has a much wider significance than is often appreciated. It is in fact used to describe any grape spirit irrespective of its quality and character and serves to distinguish these spirits from others distilled from such basic ingredients as fruits, grain, sugar cane and so on. Alternatively, of course, the winemaker may prefer to avoid any chance of confusion by referring to grape spirit as eau-de-vie.

Fortifying brandy is obtained from a number of sources. A very large proportion is produced by the distillation of wines which yield a spirit known as eau-de-vie-de-vin. The wines from which the brandy is derived may either have been fermented specifically for distilling or may be so poor in quality as to be fit for no other purpose. In Spain, for example, some of the spirit used to fortify sherry is distilled from rejected rayas which have failed to come up to expectations and are unsuitable even for blending. The lees remaining after fermentation and rackings may also be distilled into a brandy known appropriately as eau-de-vie-de-lie. Yet another source is the spent pulp or marc left after the grapes have been pressed. Water is added to this pulp and the mixture allowed to ferment for a short time to a relatively low alcohol content. It is then distilled to give marc brandy or eau-de-vie-de-marc. Surprisingly enough, some of the brandy obtained from lees or marc can achieve quite a high quality if it is carefully distilled and matured. Since such spirits are considerably less expensive than cognac or armagnac, many are produced for sale as cheap brandy rather than for fortifying purposes. Such is the case with Marc-de-Bourgogne which is generally recognised to be one of the best brandies of its kind, although its fiery nature does not always endear it to the British palate!

Contrary to popular belief, eau-de-vie need not be a neutral spirit completely lacking any bouquet and flavour of its own. Many fortifying brandies are in fact essentially neutral in character, but it is not too uncommon to encounter quite a pungent and strongly-flavoured spirit of this type. These differences between one brandy and another are obviously very important insofar as the influence of the spirit upon the character of the wine to which it is added is concerned. The type of eau-de-vie selected for fortifying a particular wine consequently depends very much upon what objectives fortification is intended to accomplish. In many cases, the principal aim is merely to increase the alcoholic strength of the wine without appreciably altering its bouquet and flavour, a purpose for which a neutral spirit is, of course, admirably suited. At other times, however, it may be desirable to modify the bouquet and flavour of the wine as well as increasing its alcohol content, and then an aromatic, full-flavoured brandy must be employed. For example, the spirit used to fortify sherry lacks any distinctive character of its own, whereas that added to port and some of the muscatel wines produced locally all over Europe has quite a pronounced flavour and aroma.

These fortifying brandies, in common with all other spirits, owe much of their character to the manner in which the distillation is conducted. The bouquet and flavour of any spirit is due primarily to the presence of small quantities of higher alcohols, esters and allied substances collectively known as the congenerics which pass over with the alcohol during the distillation. The amount of congenerics a spirit contains and hence the strength of its bouquet and flavour depends mainly upon its degree of rectification, i.e. upon the alcoholic strength to which it was distilled. The higher the alcohol content of a spirit, the fewer congenerics it will possess and the more nearly neutral in character it will become. Even when a spirit is distilled to some 90% to 95% alcohol by volume, however, traces of certain very persistent congenerics still remain so that treatment with charcoal is necessary before a truly neutral spirit can be obtained. This latter purification stage is commonly employed in the production of vodka or the basic spirit from which gin is made, but it is rarely practised with fortifying brandies where mere traces of congenerics are relatively unimportant. Such brandies are simply distilled to the degree of rectification required to provide the desired type of eau-de-vie. The almost neutral spirits used in Spain and elsewhere are thus obtained by distilling to a very high proof strength so that most of the congenerics are eliminated. Other brandies are not rectified so highly in order to retain some bouquet and flavour. In Portugal, for example, the brandy added to port contains just under 80% alcohol by volume and every effort is made during the distillation to preserve the beneficial congenerics.

The fortification of wine is a long-established practice which probably first gained favour as a means of preserving wines from bacterial and fungal spoilage at a time when the causes of such spoilage were but poorly understood or even completely unknown. Since wines which contain some 20% alcohol by volume are certainly immune to infection by most unwanted micro-organisms except for a few species of lactic acid bacteria, the addition of alcohol to a wine for the purpose of keeping it sound formerly had considerable merit Nowadays, of course, modern knowledge and techniques have made it completely unnecessary to fortify a wine on these grounds alone, so that some other reason must be sought to explain why such wines are still commonly produced in many parts of the world.

The answer to this apparently paradoxical situation is actually very obvious. Many wines have been fortified for so long that their enhanced alcoholic strength has become an accepted part of their appeal. It would consequently be decidedly harmful if not impossible to stop adding alcohol to these wines simply because there was no longer any need to do so to prevent spoilage. Port is a typical example of a wine which could not be produced were fortification not practised. In this case, most of the fortifying brandy is introduced only a few days after fermentation has started, thereby terminating yeast activity abruptly to give a strong sweet wine which retains much of the natural sugar derived from the grapes.

Nowadays, the technique of fortification is primarily employed for the production of aperitifs and after-dinner wines of which sherry, port and madeira are probably the most famous representatives, although various sweet fortified muscatel wines from many parts of Europe are also quite well known, e.g. Muscat de Frontignan. Champagne too may be regarded as a fortified wine. The ullage caused by the dégorgement of the yeast deposit is made good by adding a dosage of liqueur d'expédition which consists of a mixture of old wine, well-aged brandy and cane sugar. Here, one of the functions of the brandy is to discourage further yeast growth in the sweetened wine by increasing its alcohol content slightly.

Amateur winemakers do not normally have many opportunities to fortify their wines. In the first place, there is often no reason to do so since a suitable alcoholic strength for both table and dessert wines, which are or should be the types of most interest to the winemaker, can easily be achieved directly by fermentation. Secondly, even when fortification would undoubtedly prove advantageous, the very high cost of the distilled spirit needed for this purpose rarely makes it an attractive proposition. Nor can amateur winemakers overcome this problem by distilling their own fortifying spirit from wines, lees and so on because any such activity is strictly illegal, and quite rightly so. No winemaker should ever contemplate distillation as a means of obtaining fortifying spirit. Apart from the fact that illicit distillation is a serious offence, if it is improperly conducted the spirit which is produced will be dangerous to health because it will contain excessive amounts of such highly undesirable constituents as methyl alcohol and fusel oil.

In view of the very high cost of distilled spirits, the amateur obviously cannot afford to fortify any wine without first considering very carefully whether the extra expense thereby incurred is really justified. Several criteria can be used as guides here. To begin with, the character of the wine must be such that it could serve quite well as an aperitif or after-dinner wine without the addition of any spirit. For this purpose, of course, it should contain at least 15% alcohol by volume from the outset. Secondly, its quality must be high, for only the very best wines are worth fortifying. Finally, fortification should promote a definite improvement in quality and/or character which would not otherwise be achieved. These points can often be settled purely on the basis of past experience. If any doubt still exists, however, it is probably best to fortify one single bottle of the wine and mature it for a few months together with a control bottle of the unfortified wine. This short period of storage will give the wine and spirit some chance to marry and at the same time will allow both wines to recover from the after-effects of bottling. A critical comparison of the two will then put the winemaker in a much better position to judge if the wine is likely to benefit sufficiently from fortification to merit the cost of adding spirit to the remainder.

Once the winemaker has definitely decided to fortify a wine, some thought must be given to selecting a suitable spirit for this purpose. The first consideration is almost certainly cost. Although all spirits are expensive, the better quality brandies, whiskies and so on naturally always command premium prices. As far as fortification is concerned, however, little if anything is gained by employing high quality spirits when cheaper brands containing the same amount of alcohol are also readily available. The winemaker should therefore buy the best spirit which provides the most alcohol for the least expenditure.

Another factor which should be taken into account is the effect of the spirit upon the wine. In general, amateurs will find that a neutral spirit having little or no influence upon the bouquet and flavour of the wine to which it is added will serve their purpose best, but almost any true spirit will suffice. Here, true spirit means one which contains no flavouring or sweetening agent beyond the congenerics retained during the distillation. Gin and liqueurs are thus excluded by this definition whereas vodka, brandy, whisky, calvados, slivovitz and the like are acceptable. Of the latter, vodka is probably the first choice because most vodkas are essentially neutral in character. Furthermore, 140 proof vodka or Polish spirit which contains 80% alcohol by volume is readily available in this country, and this spirit has a double advantage in the production of fortified wines. Not only does it enable the winemaker to increase the alcohol content of a wine without impairing the existing bouquet and flavour, but it also minimises the dilution experienced on fortification since only half as much 140 proof vodka as 70 proof brandy or other spirit is required to achieve the same result. The winemaker is therefore well advised to choose 140 proof vodka or Polish spirit on the basis of its high alcoholic strength and neutral character for routine fortification purposes.

The only problem now remaining is to calculate how much spirit is required to increase the alcohol content of a wine to any desired level. Little difficulty should be experienced here if one of the procedures outlined below is followed. The important point to remember is that the alcoholic strength and volume of both the wine and the spirit must always be expressed in the same units. Thus, either the percentage of alcohol by volume or proof spirit is a satisfactory measure of alcoholic strength, but both units cannot be employed simultaneously in a single calculation. The same applies to expressing volume in terms of either pints or gallons. In actual fact, the winemaker will probably find it preferable to work with the same units all the time to avoid any chance of confusion. Under these circumstances, the percentage of alcohol by volume seems to be the most convenient unit for expressing alcoholic strengths and pints the most convenient for volumes. All alcoholic strengths and volumes must then, if necessary, be converted into the selected units before beginning the calculations.

The Pearson Square is a device which is very commonly used to determine the amount of alcohol needed for fortification purposes. The first step is to draw a square and insert the letters as shown in the accompanying diagram:—

A 80		B 51
	C 20	
5 D		60 E

A = Alcoholic strength of the spirit.

B = Alcoholic strength of the wine.

C = Desired alcoholic strength.

D = C−B.

E = A−C.

In the corner marked A is put the alcoholic strength of the spirit and at B the alcohol content of the wine. In the centre at C is written the desired alcoholic strength. Finally, at D is written the difference between C and B and at E the difference between A and C. The ratio of D to E is then the proportion of alcohol which should be added to the wine to increase its alcohol content to the desired strength.

The operation of the Pearson Square is perhaps best illustrated by means of a worked example. A typical problem would be to calculate how much 140 proof vodka (which contains 80% alcohol by volume) is required to increase to 20% by volume the alcohol content of 1½ gallons of wine whose strength is only 15% alcohol by volume. On inserting the appropriate figures in the Pearson Square as shown in the diagram, it can at once be seen that 5 volumes of spirit must be added to every 60 volumes of wine to achieve the desired result. Hence, in this case, 1 pint of 140 proof vodka must be added to the 12 pints of wine to increase its alcoholic strength from 15% to 20% by volume.

Two serious criticisms can be levelled against this procedure. First of all, it does not show directly how much spirit is required to fortify a given volume of wine except in such fortuitous cases as the example quoted above. The answer is simply a ratio which must normally be multiplied by the volume of wine to discover exactly how much spirit is needed. Thus, had there been 18 pints instead of 12 pints of wine in the preceding example, then 5/60ths × 18 or 1½ pints of spirit would have been required. Secondly, the Pearson Square does not readily permit the winemaker to calculate what increase in strength could be expected on adding, say, a pint of 140 proof vodka to a gallon of wine already containing 15% alcohol by volume.

These shortcomings are easily circumvented by using the following formula which is, of course, merely an alternative but more comprehensive algebraic expression of the principles embodied in the Pearson Square:—

$$x = \frac{b\,(c-a)}{(d-c)}$$

Where:—

a = Alcoholic strength of the wine.
b = Volume of wine.
c = Desired alcoholic strength of the wine.
d = Alcoholic strength of the spirit.
x = Volume of spirit required.

The example already studied in connection with the operation of the Pearson Square may now be evaluated by means of the above equation:—

$$x = \frac{12\,(20-15)}{(80-20)} = \frac{12 \times 5}{60} = 1 \text{ pint}$$

It follows that 1 pint of 140 proof vodka must be added to the 12 pints of wine to raise its alcoholic strength from 15% to 20% by volume, the same answer that was obtained previously. The winemaker may therefore use either method for this purpose depending upon which is considered to be the more convenient.

The preceding equation may also be rearranged to allow the winemaker to calculate the effects of adding a known volume of alcohol to a given volume of wine. Here, the final alcoholic strength *c* of the fortified wine is the unknown quantity for evaluation:—

$$c = \frac{dx + ab}{b + x}$$

The increase in alcoholic strength achieved in this manner is then simply the difference between *c* and the original alcoholic strength *a* of the wine. For example, the winemaker may wish to know by how much 1 pint of 140 proof vodka (80% alcohol by volume) will increase the alcoholic strength of 3 gallons (24 pints) of wine which already contains 16% alcohol by volume. From the rearranged equation:—

$$c = \frac{(80 \times 1) + (16 \times 24)}{24 + 1} = \frac{80 + 384}{25} = \frac{464}{25} = 18.5\%$$

Since the original strength of the wine was 16% by volume, the effect of the added spirit would be to raise the alcoholic strength by 2.5% by volume.

The winemaker will doubtless by now have realised that fortification is extremely expensive because a considerable amount of very strong and hence very costly spirit is required even for a single gallon of wine. It is consequently advisable to obtain the highest possible yield of alcohol by fermentation when producing wines which may later be fortified. The amount of spirit which must be added is then appreciably decreased with a concomitant saving in cost. The position may perhaps best be summed up by saying that fortification should only be practised with small amounts of the very highest quality wines which already contain at least 15% to 16% alcohol by volume. The winemaker may then be rewarded by a really superb wine a few years later.

CHAPTER XVIII

WINE DISORDERS AND THEIR TREATMENT

WINE is often said to be a living thing, and therefore is susceptible to many constitutional disorders of bacterial, fungal, and various other origins. Despite an awesome list of possible afflictions, however, the majority of wines somehow manage to remain in a sound and healthy condition throughout the entire course of their existence. How, then, is this seeming miracle accomplished? Modern medical science emphasises the prevention rather than the cure of disease, and this wise philosophy can equally as well be applied to winemaking as to general living standards. Wine spoilage can largely be avoided by observing scrupulous cleanliness at all times, for undesirable micro-organisms are encouraged to develop when dirt is allowed to accumulate and unsanitary conditions prevail. All likely breeding places of disease such as dirty equipment, spent pulp, splashes of wine from straining and racking operations and so on must be eliminated at the first available opportunity. Unsatisfactory equipment, notably metal strainers and containers, should also be scrapped and replaced without delay to avoid contamination. Unfortunately, occasional oversights and acts of negligence will always occur, so that some description of the cause and treatment of at least the commoner wine disorders is an essential albeit dismal feature of any book of this type.

Acetification is probably one of the commonest yet at the same time the most disastrous infections which can affect a wine. The cause is bacterial in origin and a micro-organism called *Acetobacter Aceti* (or sometimes *Mycoderma Aceti*) is commonly responsible, but at least twenty other related species as well as certain types of film yeasts can also induce acetification and more than one species may be present simultaneously in an infected wine. These vinegar bacteria attack the alcohol in a wine and convert it into acetic acid and/or the ester ethyl acetate. Since acetic acid is the principal constituent of vinegar, its formation in a wine can at once be detected by the strong vinegary taste and smell which accompanies the infection. When ethyl acetate is produced together with or instead of acetic acid, a pleasant sweetish aroma reminiscent of pear drops will also be apparent.

Vinegar bacteria can gain access to a wine in many ways, but it is usual to find that unsterilised ingredients or fruit flies are responsible. Most ingredients employed by amateur winemakers carry a varied flora of bacteria and fungi which should be killed or at least inhibited prior to fermentation. Failure to do so, especially in the case of damaged or over-ripe fruit, may allow spoilage organisms to develop in the must and ruin the wine at an early stage in its production. Tiny fruit flies are also attracted by fermenting musts and wines like moths to a candle. These insects are harmless in themselves, but due to their predilection for rotten fruit they almost invariably act as carriers of vinegar bacteria and must therefore be rigorously excluded at all times or acetification may follow in their train. Infection by airborne cells or spores can also occur, but such an event is rare and unlikely unless unsuspected bacterial colonies are already growing in the vicinity. The important point is really to keep the must closely covered at all times and leave it exposed to the air for as short a period as possible when taking samples and so on. The value of fermentation locks as a simple and effective means of protecting musts from contamination becomes apparent in this connection. Indeed, this function may rightly be regarded as one of their most useful applications.

Once vinegar bacteria have gained a hold, there is often little that can be done to save the wine unless the infection is caught and stamped out in its very early stages. It is well-nigh impossible to eliminate or even mask a strong vinegary bouquet and flavour, and under these circumstances the best plan is to allow the wine to go completely to vinegar which can then be advantageously employed in the kitchen. After all, wine vinegar is an excellent and much-prized article which gives a delightful piquancy to savoury dishes, although few winemakers will view matters in this light on discovering that a wine is turning to vinegar!

If acetification is detected before an appreciable amount of acetic acid has been formed, the wine may not be beyond redemption provided steps are immediately taken to combat the infection. The first move is to add 100 to 150 p.p.m. sulphite which will kill off the bacteria and prevent matters from becoming any worse. The vinegary taste and smell will still remain, however, and can only be satisfactorily eliminated by refermentation. This procedure is usually inconvenient and rarely worth the trouble for a finished wine which has become infected during storage. Such wines may as well be discarded directly or left unsulphited and stored elsewhere until all the alcohol has been converted into vinegar.

On the other hand, when dealing with musts which have begun to acetify during fermentation, an almost complete cure can at times be achieved by sulphiting and restarting the fermentation. The heavy sulphiting necessary to kill the vinegar bacteria will also have killed or at least seriously weakened the existing yeast colony, however, so that a fresh culture has to be introduced. The must should first be allowed to stand for 24 hours to permit the potency of the sulphite to diminish to a point where it will not harm the new yeast culture. Fermentation is then restarted gradually by the technique used to revive a stuck fermentation so that the yeast has every chance to acclimatise itself to the inimical conditions in the infected must. The principal difficulty here lies in persuading fermentation to restart since even a small concentration of acetic acid tends to inhibit yeast activity. Once the whole must is again in active fermentation, much of the volatile acetic acid therein will be carried off in the stream of carbon dioxide evolved as fermentation proceeds. Admittedly, all the acetic acid will not be removed in this manner, but often so little will remain that it will be difficult to detect in all but a dry wine.

It is quite clear from these remarks that acetification is an infection which should be avoided at all costs. Some precautions against spoilage in this manner have already been mentioned, but in addition the wine should be produced and stored under conditions which are unfavourable to the growth and development of vinegar bacteria. The latter are first of all strictly aerobic and cannot exist in the absence of oxygen. Hence, all wines should be stored in completely filled containers so that little or no air space is left above them except perhaps during fermentation when a protective blanket of carbon dioxide covers the must. Containers used for pulp fermentations should never be completely filled for this very reason, for the layer of carbon dioxide then formed above the cap helps to prevent if from becoming infected with spoilage organisms such as vinegar bacteria. Acetobacter and its allies are also thermophylic in nature, i.e. they develop better under warm conditions and a temperature of 90° to 100° F. is ideally suited to their needs. Wines should consequently never be kept at temperatures above 80° F. for any length of time in case the growth of vinegar bacteria is thereby encouraged. Fermenting musts are particularly susceptible to infection if the temperature becomes too high since the yeast is killed or seriously weakened by exposure to temperatures much above 80° to 85° F. Finally, most species of acetobacter do not grow well in wines containing more than about 10% alcohol by volume although some of the rarer species can withstand as much as 15% alcohol. Normally, however, acetification can be avoided by maintaining the alcoholic strength of the wine above 10% by volume, and this figure should be regarded as the minimum alcohol content of a wine not destined for consumption within a few months of production.

Another common though much less serious disorder called flowers of wine is caused by film yeasts. *Candida Mycoderma*, formerly known as *Mycoderma Vini*, is usually responsible for this type of spoilage, but other similar film yeasts, notably Pichia and Hansenula, may also occasionally be encountered. All are similar in appearance and behaviour, however, and normally develop only on still wines. Flowers of wine is easy to detect and identify. It first appears as a number of discrete whitish patches on the surface of the wine. These islands of film yeast gradually increase in size until eventually they coalesce to form a rather delicate grey-white wrinkled skin or pellicle which completely covers the surface of the wine. Shaking will cause this pellicle to break up and some will sink to the bottom of the container, but after a few days it will re-form.

Film yeasts (other than those responsible for sherry flors) attack the alcohol in a wine and slowly convert it to water and carbon dioxide. Other substances are also metabolised, and if the infection is allowed to proceed unchecked the wine will become flat and lifeless within a few months. Flowers of wine must therefore be eliminated as soon as the first signs of film yeast development are noted, but speed of action is less critical here because spoilage proceeds slowly. Treatment should nevertheless not be delayed unduly on this account or the quality of the wine will suffer quite needlessly.

Sulphite is again the answer to flowers of wine, and the addition of 100 to 150 p.p.m. will normally wipe out the infection. The wine should be left to settle for a few days after this treatment to allow fragments of the pellicle time to sink to the bottom of the container. It should then be racked carefully into a clean sterilised container and inspected occasionally to ensure that no reinfection has occurred. Regular sulphiting every two to three months with 50 to 100 p.p.m. sulphite may prove advisable if a light wine is attacked since flowers of wine sometimes proves difficult to eradicate under these conditions.

Flowers of wine can be avoided by taking the same precautions as were advised to keep the must or wine free from vinegar bacteria. Film yeasts are also strictly aerobic and cannot grow in the absence of oxygen. Their development is therefore very restricted if not completely prevented by storing wines in completely filled containers. Relatively light wines are also more liable to infection than stronger types so that the former should be examined regularly to ascertain their condition is still sound. An alcohol content of 10% by volume is again the minimum strength which will discourage the growth of *C. Mycoderma* and its allies, but it can develop in most table wines given the right conditions.

A large group of micro-organisms collectively known as the lactic acid bacteria can also be responsible for a number of wine disorders. Indeed, many of the peculiar off-flavours encountered in amateur wines probably occur as the result of infection by these bacteria. Sweet wines generally suffer more than dry wines because lactic acid bacteria attack sugar to form unpleasant by-products. Some species may actually be beneficial to dry acid wines because they convert malic acid to the less sour lactic acid and thereby render the wine more palatable. The same species could nevertheless ruin a sweet wine by converting sugar as well as acid into other products.

The condition known as ropiness or oiliness is caused by a species of lactic acid bacteria which under the microscope resemble short rods in shape. Colonies of these bacteria grow in long chains which are held together by a slimy gelatinous substance. An infected wine thus acquires an unusually viscous consistency and in extreme cases may pour like a thick oil, hence the term "oiliness." Fortunately, the flavour of the wine does not seem to be impaired although its appearance renders it undrinkable. The cure is also very simple. The wine is first treated with 100 to 150 p.p.m. sulphite to kill the bacteria and then stirred very vigorously to break up the bacterial chains and promote aeration. It is finally left to settle for a few days and racked carefully off any deposit which may form. Since a further period of storage is generally inadvisable, treated wines are best drunk a few weeks later when they have recovered from this rather drastic handling.

Various other species of lactic acid bacteria resembling long rods in shape may also be encountered, primarily in wines containing some residual unfermented sugar. The bacteria convert the sugar into unpleasant by-products such as mannitol which may give the wine an excessively bitter taste or cause other strange and peculiar off-flavours to develop. Tourne disease is the term commonly used to describe such infections which are probably more prevalent than most amateur winemakers realise. Sometimes the presence of these undesirable lactic acid bacteria can be confirmed by holding the wine in front of a strong light and gently swirling it. If a silky cloud or sheen is observed, it is fairly certain that the wine is affected with Tourne disease. A negative result to this test does not mean that the infection is absent, however, but unless the winemaker has access to a microscope and can identify what organisms are present it can only be assumed that some species of lactic acid bacteria has gained entry.

Although the progress of Tourne disease can be halted by treating the wine with 100 to 150 p.p.m. sulphite, it is usually difficult, sometimes impossible, to eliminate what off-flavours have already been formed. Blending may be the answer if the wine has not been too badly affected, but often there is no real alternative but to discard it. Sugar is sometimes advocated as a masking agent, but generally the wine has to be made sickly-sweet before the off-flavour is hidden, so that this "remedy" cannot really be recommended.

One rather drastic treatment has on occasions been successful in saving a wine afflicted with Tourne disease and is well worth trying as a final resort. After sulphiting, the wine should be treated with 3 teaspoonfuls of 20 vols. hydrogen peroxide per gallon (which can be obtained from any chemist), and subsequently heated to 105° to 120° F. for 2 to 3 hours. It should then be cooled and rested for a week after which it will be ready for consumption regardless of its age. The amount of hydrogen peroxide should be doubled for red wines or if a very strong off-flavour has developed, but otherwise the dose recommended above should be adequate. This procedure naturally alters the character of the wine to some extent—it was in fact originally devised as a method for the rapid ageing of wines—but this is a small price to pay for saving a wine which would otherwise be unfit to drink.

This rather brief discussion by no means covers all the infections to which wines are subject, but it does provide the winemaker with at least an insight into the more important disorders which are likely to be encountered. In actual fact, there would be little point in going deeper into the subject since the only way invading bacteria and fungi can normally be repulsed is by adding sulphite at the rate of 100 to 150 parts per million. The winemaker can then only hope that the infection has been caught in time before the bouquet and flavour of the wine have been too seriously damaged.

A final word remains to be said on the subject of chemical disorders. Persistent white or coloured hazes collectively known as casse may be formed during maturing if the wine at any stage in its production has come into contact with certain metals, notably copper, iron, lead, tin and zinc. As little as a few parts per million of some metals may be sufficient to cause a pronounced haze and a metallic flavour may also be detectable. In most cases, the addition of a little citric acid will prevent any further development of metallic casse, but the haze already present will not be dispersed by this treatment, and must be removed by filtering or fining.

Perhaps the most important point in this connection is that many metals responsible for casse are quite poisonous and their effects may be cumulative. Lead is particularly dangerous in this respect, and several cases of lead poisoning caused by drinking wine fermented in lead-glazed containers have been reported. Wines possessing a metallic taste and haze due to suspected metallic casse are therefore best discarded immediately, especially if fermentation and/or storage has been carried out in an old, possibly lead-glazed, stone container. Such situations can, of course, be avoided by ensuring that no metal equipment or lead-glazed containers come into contact with the wine at any stage in its production.

Oxidasic casse is another term which may sometimes be encountered, but in this case metals are not responsible. Wines suffering from oxidasic casse turn brown very readily because they contain large amounts of an enzyme called o-polyphenyloxidase which catalyses the oxidation of tannins and the like to brown products. This effect is commonly observed in wines prepared from over-ripe fruit or pears which are unusually rich in this enzyme. Its occurrence can be confirmed by standing two glasses of the wine, one untreated and the other treated with 50 to 100 p.p.m. sulphite, exposed to the air overnight. If the untreated wine darkens in colour but the other does not, then the wine is suffering from oxidasic casse. Citric acid should also have no influence on the rate of browning. If it does, then metallic casse is responsible. The complete test is therefore to use three glasses of wine, two as above and another to which about 1% citric acid has been added. If only the sulphited sample does not darken, then the bulk of the wine should be treated with 50 to 100 p.p.m. sulphite to prevent further browning. This treatment must then be repeated every two to three months to be effective. The function of sulphite in this case is as an anti-oxidant not as a bactericidal agent, i.e. it combines with the excess oxygen reaching the wine before the enzyme causing the browning has a chance to do so.

CHAPTER XIX

A SELECTION OF RECIPES

THE advantage of blending ingredients as a simple yet effective means of improving wine quality has already been fully discussed in a previous chapter. The adoption of this technique immediately raises certain practical problems, however, for a great many winemakers are, unfortunately, content to limit their activities to the production of wines strictly according to published recipes. Some of these recipes do advocate blending ingredients, but far too many still suffer from the defect of employing only one ingredient and little else besides yeast, nutrients and sugar. Consequently, it is quite common to encounter wines which are inherently unbalanced in one way or another, as the relatively low standard of quality of many wines exhibited at the National and other shows all too clearly demonstrates.

Many of these faults can easily be avoided by producing the wine from a blend of ingredients, but putting this advice into practice often proves difficult. The shortage of published recipes of this type is currently so acute that any winemakers wishing to adopt this technique very quickly run out of new material and are then forced to begin designing their own recipes in order to make further progress. The problem which actually requires close attention is therefore how to set about designing a recipe. Hence, although the principles of recipe design are thoroughly explained elsewhere, it was deemed advisable to include a small selection of recipes for different types of wine at this point in this book so that the winemaker can study their design and refer to them for guidance when designing others for similar types of wine.

WHITE TABLE WINE

Ingredients:

20 lb. peaches
2½ pts. White Grape Conc.
½ oz. Pectozyme
2½ pts. yellow rose petals
Acid Mixture A as required
Sugar as required (or honey)
Yeast nutrients
Steinberg yeast starter
Water to 5 gallons

Method:

Stone the peaches and press out the juice. Add 100 p.p.m. sulphite and allow to settle for 24 hours, then rack it off the pulp deposit. Add the grape concentrate, nutrients and sufficient sugar and/or honey syrup and water to give 5 gallons of must with an initial gravity of 90. Check the acidity and adjust it to 3.0–3.5 p.p.t with acid mixture A if necessary. Add the yeast starter and pectozyme.

Ferment for about seven days, then add the rose petals. Strain off the latter after three days and continue the fermentation until the gravity drops to just below 0 when the wine should be racked for the first time. Rack again when a heavy sediment forms, add 50 p.p.m. sulphite and thereafter rack at intervals of about three months. Mature the wine in the normal manner for a white table wine.

WHITE TABLE WINE

Ingredients:

5 lb. dried apricots
5 lb. sultanas
1½ pts. yellow rose petals
½ oz. Pectozyme
5 lb. sugar
Yeast nutrients
Chablis or Burgundy yeast starter
Water to 5 gallons

Method:

Add 4 gallons cold water to the apricots, sultanas, pectozyme, sugar and yeast nutrients and stir until the latter two ingredients have dissolved. Introduce the yeast starter and ferment on the pulp for three days. Strain off the pulp and press it lightly. Continue the fermentation for another four days then add the rose petals. Strain off the latter three days later and dilute to 5 gallons with water. Check the acidity and adjust it to 3.5–4.0 p.p.t (chalk will probably be required). Continue the fermentation until the gravity drops to between 0 and −5 then rack for the first time. Rack again when a heavy sediment forms, add 50 p.p.m. sulphite and thereafter rack at intervals of about three months. Mature in the manner recommended for a light table wine.

WHITE TABLE WINE

Ingredients:

25 lb. apples
4 pts. orange juice
4 pts. white grape concentrate
2 pts. fresh or ½ oz. dried elderflowers
Sugar or honey as required
Yeast nutrients
Graves yeast starter
Water to 5 gallons

Method:

Press the apples, and sufficient oranges to obtain about 4 pints orange juice. Blend the two juices, add 100 p.p.m. sulphite and leave to settle for 24 hours as described in the text. Rack the clear juice off the deposit, add the grape concentrate and nutrients and dilute with water and sugar or honey to 5 gallons so as to obtain a starting gravity of 90. Check the acidity and adjust it to about 3.2–3.5 p.p.t. Add the yeast starter, ferment for seven days then add the elderflowers. Strain off the latter after three days and continue the fermentation until the gravity drops to 5. Rack for the first time at this point and again when the gravity drops to 0. Add 75 p.p.m. sulphite after the second racking and thereafter rack every three months. Mature in the normal manner for a white table wine.

ROSÉ TABLE WINE

Ingredients:

10 lb. elderberries
4 pts. white grape conc.
2 pts. yellow rose petals
5 lb. sugar
Yeast nutrients
Bordeaux yeast starter
Water to 5 gallons

Method:

Crush the elderberries and add 4 gallons water together with the sugar, nutrients and yeast starter. Ferment on the pulp until a rosé colour is obtained (probably after a few hours) then strain off the pulp and press lightly. Add the grape concentrate, dilute to 5 gallons with water and check the acidity. Adjust the latter to about 3.5 p.p.t. using acid mixture A if any acid need be added. Add the rose petals seven days after fermentation has commenced and ferment on the flower pulp for three days before straining it off. Rack for the first time when the gravity drops to about 0 and again when a heavy sediment forms, adding about 50 p.p.m. sulphite after the second racking. Thereafter rack every three months. Mature in the same way as a white table wine.

RED TABLE WINE

Ingredients:

10 lb. elderberries	**Yeast nutrients**
10 lb. raisins	**Beaujolais yeast starter**
½ oz. dried elderflowers	**Water to 5 gallons**
4 lb. sugar	

Method:

Crush the elderberries and raisins and add 4 gallons water together with the yeast nutrients, sugar and yeast starter. The dried elderflowers may also be added at this point since their function is to strengthen the bouquet rather than provide it all. Ferment on the pulp until a deep red colour is obtained, then strain off the pulp and press it lightly. Dilute to 5 gallons with water, check the acidity and adjust it to 3.5–4.0 p.p.t. Ferment to dryness, rack and add 50 p.p.m. sulphite. Rack again when a heavy sediment is formed, again add 50 p.p.m. sulphite and thereafter rack every three months. Mature in cask for one year and in bottle for a further one-two years although the wine will be drinkable earlier.

RED TABLE WINE

Ingredients:

10 lb. sloes	**Yeast nutrients**
4 pts. red grape conc.	**Bordeaux yeast starter**
2 pts. red rose petals	**Water to 5 gallons**
5 lb. sugar	**½ oz. Pectozyme**

Method:

Crush the sloes (stone them if possible) and add 4 gallons water together with the sugar, nutrients, pectozyme and yeast starter. Ferment on the pulp until the must attains a deep red colour, then strain off the pulp and press it lightly. Add the grape concentrate and dilute to 5 gallons with water. Check the acidity and adjust it to about 3.5 p.p.t. Add the rose petals and strain them off three days later. Ferment to dryness, rack and add 50 p.p.m. sulphite. Rack and sulphite again as soon as a heavy sediment is observed. Thereafter rack every three months. Mature in cask for one–two years and then in bottle for several more years. This wine may mature fairly slowly, but its potential is high and is well worth storing for several years.

RED TABLE WINE

Ingredients:

40 lb. cherries	**½ oz. Pectozyme**
10 lb. raisins	**Yeast nutrients**
2 pts. red rose petals	**Burgundy yeast starter**
3 lb. sugar	**Water to 5 gallons**

Method:

Crush the cherries and raisins and add 2 gallons water together with the sugar, pectozyme, nutrients and yeast starter. Ferment on the pulp until a deep red colour is obtained then strain off the pulp and press it lightly. Dilute to 5 gallons with water, check the acidity and adjust it to about 4.0 p.p.t with chalk or acid mixture B as required. Add the rose petals and strain them off three days later. Ferment to dryness, rack and add 50 p.p.m. sulphite. Rack and sulphite again when a heavy deposit forms. Thereafter rack every three months. Mature in cask for one year and in bottle for another few years.

WHITE DESSERT WINE

Ingredients:

20 lb. parsnips
5 lb. bananas
4 pts. white grape conc.
2 pts. elderflowers
½ oz. Pectozyme
5 lb. Demerara sugar
Honey or white sugar as required
Yeast nutrients
Sauternes yeast starter
Water to 5 gallons

Method:

Wash the parsnips, cut into chunks and boil in 3 gallons water for ten minutes. Strain off the pulp and press it lightly. Peel the bananas, cut into slices and boil (with skins) in 1 gallon water for half an hour. Strain off the hot extract and blend it with the parsnip extract. Leave to cool and settle for 24 hours and then rack it off the deposit. Add the grape concentrate, Demerara sugar, pectozyme and yeast nutrients. Dilute to 5 gallons with water and honey or white sugar to achieve an initial gravity of 100. Check the acidity and adjust it to about 4.0 p.p.t. with acid mixture B. Add the yeast starter.

Ferment until the gravity drops to 15–20 and then rack. Rack again at a gravity of 10–15 and add 100 p.p.m. sulphite. Thereafter rack every three months unless a heavy sediment is observed within this interval. Mature in the normal manner for a white dessert wine. For cask maturing, it is preferable to make at least 10 gallons of wine otherwise regular and careful inspection is necessary to avoid over-oxidation.

RED DESSERT WINE

Ingredients:

25 lb. damsons
5 lb. bananas
5 lb. raisins
2 pts. red grape conc.
12 lb. sugar
½ oz. Pectozyme
Yeast nutrients
Port yeast starter
Water to 5 gallons

Method:

Crush the raisins and damsons (preferably stoned). Peel the bananas, cut into slices and boil the slices and skins in 1 gallon water for half an hour. Strain the hot extract over the raisins and damsons and add 3 gallons water. Add the yeast nutrients and 5 lb. sugar, stir until dissolved and allow to cool if necessary before introducing the pectozyme and yeast starter. Ferment on the pulp until a deep red colour is obtained then strain off the pulp and press lightly. Add the grape concentrate and the remaining 7 lb. sugar and dilute it to 5 gallons with water. Check the acidity and adjust it to 4.0–4.5 p.p.t. using acid mixture B if any need be added. Ferment until the gravity reaches 20, rack and again rack when the gravity has dropped to 10–15. Add 100 p.p.m. sulphite after the second racking and thereafter rack every three months unless the formation of a heavy sediment dictates otherwise. Mature in cask for one–two years and in bottle for several more years. This wine will continue to improve for many years.

WHITE AFTER-DINNER WINE

Ingredients:

40 lb. peaches	**½ oz. Pectozyme**
5 lb. bananas	**Yeast nutrients**
4 pts. white grape conc.	**Madeira yeast starter**
2 pts. yellow rose petals	**Sugar as required**
	Water to 5 gallons

Method:

Stone the peaches and press out the juice. Add 100 p.p.m. sulphite and leave to settle for 24 hours. Peel the bananas, cut into slices and boil the latter with the skins in 1 gallon water for half an hour. Strain off the pulp and leave to settle for 24 hours. Rack the peach juice and banana extract off their sediments, add the grape concentrate, pecto zyme and yeast nutrients then dilute to 5 gallons with wate and sugar to an initial gravity of 100. Check the acidity and adjust it to about 4.0 p.p.t. Add the yeast starter and after seven days add the rose petals. Strain off the latter after three days. Ferment until the gravity drops to about 5 then add ¼ lb. sugar per gallon. Continue feeding in this manner until the yeast reaches its maximum alcohol tolerance. Rack the wine off the sediment, add 100 p.p.m. sulphite and repeat this treatment as soon as a heavy deposit forms. Thereafter rack every three months unless a heavy sediment dictates otherwise. Mature in the same manner as for a white dessert wine. Fortification may be considered if the wine reaches a high standard of quality. For cask maturing, it is preferable to make at least 10 gallons of wine otherwise regular and careful inspection is necessary to avoid over-oxidation.

RED AFTER-DINNER WINE

Ingredients:

20 lb. raspberries	**Sugar as required**
10 lb. raisins	**Yeast nutrients**
5 lb. bananas	**Port yeast starter**
½ oz. Pectozyme	**Water to 5 gallons**

Method:

Crush the raspberries and raisins. Peel the bananas, cut into slices and boil the slices and skins in 1 gallon water for half an hour. Strain the hot extract over the crushed fruit and add another 2½ gallons water. Allow to cool then add the pectozyme, 5 lb. sugar, the nutrients and the yeast starter. Ferment on the pulp until a deep red colour is obtained then strain off the pulp and press lightly. Dilute to 5 gallons with water, add another 2 lb. sugar and check the acidity. Adjust the latter to about 4.0–4.5 p.p.t. Continue the fermentation until the gravity drops to about 5 then add ¼ lb. sugar per gallon. Feed the yeast in this manner with small doses of sugar syrup until fermentation ceases when the wine should be racked and treated with 100 p.p.m. sulphite. Rack and sulphite again as soon as a heavy deposit forms and thereafter rack every three months. Mature in cask for one–two years and in bottle for several more years. Fortification should be considered when the quality of the wine appears to justify the extra expense.

APERITIF WINE

Ingredients:

2 gallons orange juice	**Sugar as required**
4 pts. white grape conc.	**Yeast nutrients**
3 lb. bananas	**Sherry yeast starter**
Peel (no pith) from 20 oranges	**Water to 5 gallons**

Method:

Press the juice from sufficient oranges to obtain about 2¼ gallons of juice. Add 100 p.p.m. sulphite, leave to settle for 24 hours then rack the clear juice off its deposit. Peel the bananas, cut into slices and boil the slices only in ½ gallon water for half an hour. Allow to cool and settle for 24 hours with the orange juice. Remove the peel from about 20 oranges taking care not to include any pith. Blend the settled orange juice and banana extract, add the yeast nutrients and dilute to 5 gallons with sugar and water so as to attain an initial gravity of 100. Check the acidity and adjust it to around 4.0–4.5 p.p.t. Add the orange peel and yeast starter and ferment on the peel for about four days before straining it off. Continue the fermentation until the gravity drops to −5 or below then add ¼ lb. sugar per gallon. Repeat this procedure until the rate of gravity decrease is about 1–2 points per day, then allow to ferment to dryness. Rack the wine off the sediment, add 100 p.p.m. sulphite and rack again as soon as a heavy deposit is observed. Thereafter rack every three months. Mature in the same manner as a white table wine.

NOTE—Concentrated orange juice may be used to replace some of the fresh orange juice as long as the orange peel is not omitted by so doing.

Chapter XX

RACK AND CLOTH PRESS

THE press whose construction is described below is based upon the classic and proven rack and cloth design. Although it is by no means a cheap item of equipment to build, neither is it unduly expensive since an equivalent model would cost considerably more to buy from a supplier. The capacity of this press is sufficiently large (some 56 lb. per load) that relatively few winemakers are likely to find it too small for their needs. Indeed, most people will probably consider it too large, but herein actually lies one of its advantages. Instead of scaling down its size which, it must be added, is a most inadvisable course of action, a group of winemakers or the members of a circle should undertake its construction and operation as a joint project. The cost to each person will then be moderately small without reducing the high performance of the press.

Joint operation also offers many other advantages. Ingredients can be purchased and pressed in bulk and the juice subsequently shared out. In this way, the amount of labour involved in pressing will be considerably reduced because it will be divided among a number of people. What is more important, a significant financial gain can often be made. Not only will the press give a higher yield of juice than would otherwise be obtained but the price of the ingredients may also be lower as a result of their bulk purchase.

A list of the components required is given at the end of this chapter. Oak has been specified as the best wood to use for the main press frame, but other hardwoods such as ash are also suitable if oak is not readily available. Hardwood is probably the best material for the press bed and solid rack, but plywood is considerably cheaper and will prove eminently satisfactory provided an exterior grade is employed. The laths and cheese form for which soft wood will suffice are most conveniently constructed with white pine.

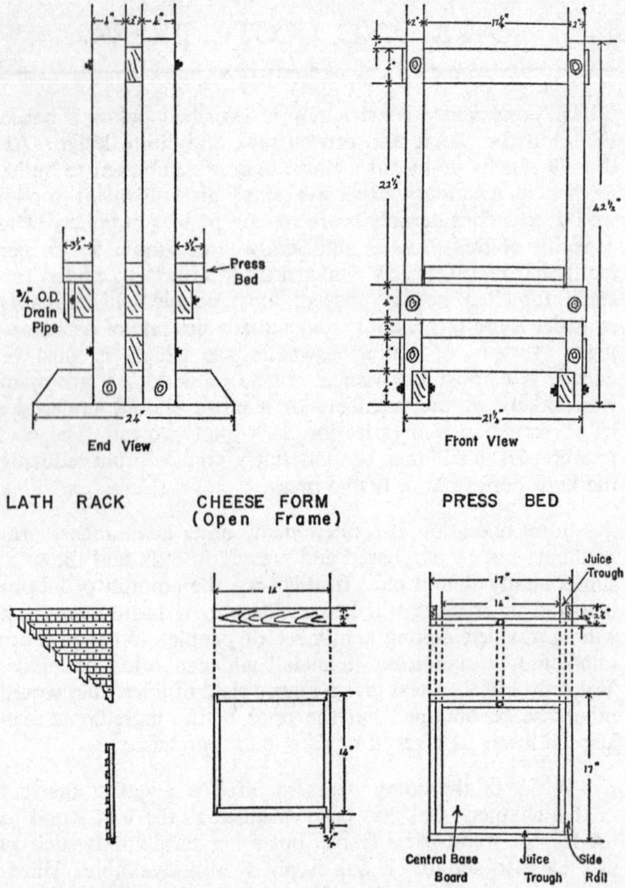

An easily made press.

The bolts which hold the main press frame will undoubtedly be expensive items to purchase and may have to be ordered specially from an ironmonger. An alternative is to use steel rods with at least three inches of thread at either end which can readily be fabricated if the winemaker has access to a well-equipped machine shop. Twenty instead of ten nuts will then be required, of course, but otherwise threaded rods are equally as good as bolts for this purpose.

The press is operated with the aid of a hydraulic car jack capable of exerting 3–5 tons pressure. Although the price of such a jack is fairly high—it may cost as much as all the rest of the components put together—the winemaker generally has two choices open. In the first place, a suitable jack may be purchased outright and its cost accepted as part of the cost of the press. This suggestion, albeit rather unattractive financially, is in fact a better solution to the problem, especially if frequent use of the press is envisaged. The alternative is to borrow a jack, which can only really be considered when pressing is likely to be restricted to a few days each year. There is, of course, much less difficulty when the winemaker owns a car. The jack may then be bought for its true purpose and its use in the press regarded as a valuable secondary function.

The first step in the construction of the press is to cut all the wood to the correct size. Next comes the drilling of the bolt holes which should be 1/16th inch greater in diameter than the bolts themselves to permit easier assembly. Great care is required at this stage to ensure that every bolt hole is drilled straight through the centre of each support, for if accurate hole alignment is not achieved considerable difficulty will be experienced when the time comes to insert the bolts. Poor workmanship here could in fact ruin everything. Accurate hand drilling will normally prove quite satisfactory, but the task will obviously be much simplified if a drill press can be employed.

The main press frame, press bed and cheese form are then assembled as illustrated in the accompanying diagrams and all the bolts tightened up to their maximum extent. The press bed is next placed centrally upon the lower cross-members of the main frame and fixed in place by means of 4 × 2½″ flat-headed wood screws countersunk into the centre base board. Finally, the drain hole is fitted with a short length of ¾″ (outer diameter) plastic tube which permits the winemaker to direct the juice into a suitable receiving vessel, e.g. a gallon jar.

The racks are constructed by forming a cross-hatch pattern of ten laths each way to give an open framework measuring 14″ × 14″. The laths are therefore spaced about their own distance apart which facilitates rack assembly. A solid rack of the same dimensions and ¾″ thick will also be required to support the jack and distribute its pressure evenly during pressing. Hardwood or exterior grade plywood are suitable for this purpose.

Once the assembly of the press and racks has been completed, the next stage is to apply a protective coating of wax to all the parts which will come in contact with the juice during pressing. In practice, of course, it is just as easy to coat the whole frame with wax as to treat discrete areas. A mixture consisting of equal parts of beeswax and paraffin wax should be employed for this purpose. Since the beeswax prevents the coating from hardening, cracking and flaking off, it is essential not to omit this component from the mixture despite its comparatively high cost. The two waxes are placed in a suitable container which in turn is placed in a saucepan of boiling water or at least melted away from a direct flame since hot wax is highly inflammable. After thoroughly mixing the two components, the melted wax may be applied by means of a paint brush as soon as its consistency reaches that of a mobile liquid. This protective coating ought to last for many months under normal conditions of use, but it should be inspected regularly for flaws and touched up when necessary to avoid contaminating the juice by direct contact with wood or metal parts of the press.

Press cloths are the only items which have not yet received any attention. The material employed for this purpose must be both strong and fairly closely woven so that it will neither burst under pressure nor permit ingredients to escape. Sacks originally used to hold sugar, flour and the like are ideally suited for conversion into press cloths and have the added merit of being readily obtainable for little or no cost. These sacks must first be thoroughly washed to clean and pre-shrink them and then cut into squares measuring roughly 30″ × 30″. The edges should next be turned over and a one inch hem sewn on with strong thread. Some auxiliary press cloths will also be required as liners when dealing with pulpy ingredients. Muslin will suffice for this purpose, but fine terylene or nylon cloth is even better by virtue of its great strength and ease of cleaning. Although the capacity of the press is such that no more than 4–5 cloths per load will normally be needed, it is advisable to have a few more available as spares in case some burst during the pressing operations. Since it would be extremely annoying to have this happen with no replacements on hand, some 8–10 main press cloths and the same number of liners should be kept in stock. New cloths can then be made at leisure to replace any which may burst in use.

The principle on which this press operates is to build up alternate layers of laths and bags of fruit (known as cheeses) on the press bed and extract the juice by applying pressure gradually with the aid of the jack. The exact mode of operation is as follows:—

Tighten up all bolts on the main press frame to their maximum extent as some relaxation will inevitably have occurred since the press was last used. Particular attention should be paid to the bolts supporting the upper cross-member which carries most of the strain. Next rinse the press thoroughly with warm water immediately prior to use (do not use hot water or the wax coating may melt). A light rub over with a cloth dipped in strong sulphite solution is also advisable as an extra precaution. The press is then ready to receive its first load of fruit.

Place a lath rack on the centre base board of the press bed and set the cheese form on top of this rack. Spread a press cloth (with or without a liner as the case may be) diagonally over the cheese form and fill the depression evenly with the prepared ingredients. Care should be taken not to overfill the press cloth, however, or it may split open during pressing. It is sufficient to pack the ingredients in tightly to the top of the cheese form and level off the surface there. Finally, fold the covers of the cloth over the layer of ingredients to make a closed bag or envelope, remove the cheese form and place another lath rack on top of the completed cheese.

Repeat this procedure several times so that a structure consisting of alternate lath racks and bags or cheeses of ingredients is built up. The number of cheeses which the press will hold naturally depends upon how much room must be left for the jack below the upper cross-bar, but in this case the maximum load will normally be 4–5 cheeses. Once the press has been loaded to capacity, place a lath rack followed by the solid rack on top of the final cheese and slip the jack into position.

Everything is now ready to proceed with the extraction of the juice. The main point to note here is that intense pressure is not required. Indeed, the exertion of too much force may have highly undesirable consequences. Not only will it not permit any more rapid or efficient juice extraction (rather the reverse is more likely), but it may also cause the press bags to split and could even break the main cross member in extreme cases. The correct idea is to apply a steady even pressure gradually to a point where the juice flows freely, maintain the pressure until the flow of juice visibly slackens and then increase the pressure again to its former level. This procedure is continued until the bulk of the juice has been extracted when the cheeses are removed, the cake of pulp broken up or repacked and finally re-pressed to obtain what juice still remains.

The practical details of this operation may be summarised as follows. Apply pressure with the jack until a moderate resistance to any further increase in pressure is encountered. By this time, a good flow of juice should be apparent. Allow the flow of juice to diminish appreciably before applying more pressure and restoring the latter to its original level. Repeat this procedure until very little juice is being extracted even by moderately heavy pressing. Once this stage is reached, release the pressure and remove the cheeses (now somewhat flattened) intact from the press-bed. Fold each cheese in half and replace it in the press. Build up racks and cheeses as before except that each new cheese now comprises two of the former cheeses folded double. Re-press this load of pulp exactly as just described. Although the yield of juice obtained in this manner will be considerably less than that from the initial pressing, it is almost invariably large enough to warrant the extra effort of re-pressing. This juice may be mixed with the first pressings, but it is usually advisable to keep and use it separately since its quality will generally be rather lower due to the more drastic extraction conditions employed. The spent pulp remaining after the second pressing will be virtually bone dry and should therefore be discarded. It need hardly be added that the freshly extracted juice should be sulphited and settled as recommended in the chapter on the preparation of the must unless, of course, the pulp has been strained off an actively fermenting must to which the juice will immediately be returned.

The press cloths and liners may be emptied and re-used directly several times during an unbroken pressing session, but they must be thoroughly washed, sterilised and dried immediately thereafter even if pressing will be resumed the next day. Failure to do so will very likely result in their contamination with undesirable micro-organisms which could later cause spoilage of the wine. The press should simultaneously be cleaned for the same reasons, with warm (not hot) soapy water and the soap rinsed off with generous quantities of clean cold or warm water. It may then be lightly sponged over with a cloth dipped in strong sulphite solution and left to dry without rinsing. The press cloths may be cleaned in a similar manner except that a dilute sulphite solution should be used for sterilisation and the sulphite rinsed out before drying to prevent the cloth from rotting.

A final word may be said about preparing the ingredients for pressing. The best results are achieved when the ingredients are mashed to a fine pulp before being loaded into the press, but a compromise which permits good juice extraction without requiring too much prior preparation can often be reached. Apples and similar fruits must really be cut into small pieces and crushed in a large mincer before pressing, but few other ingredients are quite so demanding. Grapes, gooseberries, etc., need only be crushed and each berry broken while soft fruits such as berries can often be loaded straight into the press and roughly crushed when forming the cheese. Stone fruits must be stoned which makes cherries and the like difficult to deal with properly but is comparatively simple with peaches and larger fruits of this type. The latter can often be loaded directly into the press like berries. Vegetables require preliminary softening by boiling slices or chunks in water for a short time, e.g. parsnips press very well after being boiled in water for about 10 minutes. In other words, different types of ingredients must be dealt with on their individual merits, and the wine-maker will soon learn from experience how to prepare the commoner fruits and vegetables for pressing.

LIST OF COMPONENTS

Main Press Frame

4 pieces oak 2″ × 4″ × 42½″ (Uprights)
5 pieces oak 2″ × 4″ × 22″ (Cross members)
2 pieces oak 2″ × 4″ × 24″ (Feet)
4 bolts ¾″ × 4″
4 bolts ¾″ × 12″
2 bolts ¾″ × 16″
20 washers for above bolts
10 nuts (¾″) for above bolts

Press Bed

1 piece plywood ¾″ × 17″ × 17″ (Bottom base board)
1 piece plywood ¾″ × 14″ × 14″ (Centre base board)
2 pieces white pine ¾″ × 1½″ × 17″ (Side rails)
2 pieces white pine ¾″ × 1½″ × 15½″ (Side rails)
1 piece plastic tube ¾″ O.D. short length (Drain tube)
4 flat-headed wood screws 2½″ long

Cheese Form

2 pieces white pine ¾″ × 2″ × 14″
2 pieces white pine ¾″ × 2″ × 13¼″

Lath Racks

100 pieces white pine ¼″ × ¾″ × 14″
Sufficient for five racks at 20 laths per rack

Solid Rack

1 piece plywood ¾″ × 14″ × 14″

Other items

Nails, cloth, wax, ¼″ thick steel bearing plate for jack and so on.

CHAPTER XXI

CLEANING AND CONDITIONING OAK CASKS

IT is extremely important to ensure that every cask or barrel in which wine will be stored or fermented is thoroughly cleaned and sterilised prior to use so that there is no danger of it contaminating the wine in any way. The wood of new casks which have never held wine contains quite large amounts of tannins and the like which would be leached out by a wine and would consequently coarsen its flavour were steps not taken to effect their removal beforehand. Reconditioned casks are considerably better in this respect since the wood has already been in contact with wine, but infection by spoilage organisms may have occurred and fresh wood surfaces are often exposed during recoopering so that thorough cleaning is still imperative. Secondhand casks must always be regarded with suspicion because superficial deposits, typically a thick black crust and/or spoilage organisms, may be present on, in or between the staves and must be eliminated before the cask is put into service. A standard procedure for cleaning and conditioning newly acquired casks has therefore been devised, the details of which are described below. The winemaker will find it advisable to treat all such casks in this manner to minimise the risk of contaminating or even spoiling the first few wines for which they are employed.

Fill the cask with cold water and continue to top it up regularly until any staves which may have parted due to the wood drying out have come together again and the cask is completely watertight. If leaks are still apparent after about 48 hours, further soaking is unlikely to effect any improvement and the cask should then be returned to the supplier on the grounds that it is faulty. Even when dealing with casks which are free from leaks from the very beginning, it is advisable to leave them filled with cold water for 12 to 24 hours to allow the wood to absorb water and become saturated with moisture.

After this initial soaking period, pour off the water and refill the cask with a hot solution of washing soda, using about 2 lb. of the latter per 5 gallons of water. If the cask is in very poor condition, it should be treated with a boiling hot solution of washing soda, but normally hot water drawn directly from the tap will suffice. Leave this solution in the cask overnight, then pour it off. In most cases, its colour will be a very dark brown and reconditioned or secondhand casks may give a muddy solution if any black scale has been dislodged from the interior. This treatment should be repeated with casks whose condition is poor, but normally this will not be necessary. Once the final washing soda solution has been poured off, rinse the cask briefly with one or two changes of cold water to remove any residual soda from the surface of the staves.

Next fill the cask with very hot or boiling water and allow to stand overnight. This treatment will extract the washing soda solution absorbed by the staves and will complete the removal of tannins and so forth from the wood. It should be repeated until the water emerging from the cask is either colourless or has a pale brownish tint. Two or possibly three such hot water extractions will normally be ample, after which the cask should be rinsed out with cold water. At this stage, the interior should look clean and smell sweet.

All that now remains is to sterilise and condition the cask. First of all, partially fill the cask, say to about 10% to 20% of its capacity, with dilute sulphite solution (stock solution diluted with nine volumes of water). Bung down the cask tightly and roll it around vigorously for half to one hour (with occasional rests, of course!) so that the sulphite penetrates into every corner. This procedure not only ensures complete sterility but will also neutralise any residual washing soda which may somehow have escaped removal previously. Finally, pour out the sulphite and rinse the cask with several changes of cold water to wash out any excess of sulphite.

The cask must now be "conditioned." Some nondescript but sound wine to which a little citric acid and tannin have been added is introduced into the cask, generally one bottle of wine containing a teaspoonful of citric acid and a large pinch of tannin being used per 5 gallons of capacity. Add this wine to the cask, bung down tightly and roll it around vigorously for half to one hour. During this period, the wood will absorb body, acid, tannin and other substances from the wine which will emerge completely undrinkable. Pour out the spent wine and fill the cask with fermenting must within the next hour. It is preferable to conduct at least one fermentation in the cask before it is used for storage purposes because conditioning is then completed with the minimum risk of the character of the wine therein being modified by the wood absorbing certain constituents. Small casks (less than 9 gallons in capacity) should always serve for an initial period as fermentation vessels for this very reason.

The treatment outlined above is undoubtedly quite engthy and arduous, but it is extremely reliable and well worth the trouble. Moreover, there is no need to repeat it again provided the cask remains sound and is never allowed to stand empty for more than an hour ot two after a wine has been removed. The golden rule here is never to empty a cask without having another wine available for refilling it. In this way, the cask is kept in continuous use and need only be rinsed out with cold water to remove any deposit left by the previous wine before introducing another.

PART II

INTRODUCTION TO PART II

"There is in this city a certain fraternity of chymical operators, who work underground in holes, caverns and dark retirements, to conceal their mysteries from the eyes and observations of mankind.

"These subterraneous philosophers are daily employed in the transmigration of liquors, and, by the power of medical drugs and incantations, raising under the streets of London, the choicest products of the hills and valleys of France.

"They can squeeze Bordeaux out of a sloe, and draw champagne from an apple."

From "The Trial of the Wine-brewers"
by Joseph Addison.

IT was once suggested, albeit humorously, that this quotation might have been inspired by the activities of some of the authors' ancestors. Perhaps there may even be a grain of truth in the idea, for the intentions of this book certainly do not differ very radically from those of the subterraneous philosophers mentioned by Addison. Indeed, just to illustrate the closeness of the affinity, we have included a recipe for squeezing "Bordeaux out of a sloe" and drawing "champagne from an apple." We only hope that our modern techniques will not cause our worthy predecessors to turn in their graves.

The purpose of this book is not the imitation of commercial wines but rather to enable the amateur to produce wines comparable to them in both character and quality. Most commercial wines have a recognised place in a meal (many, of course, can also serve equally as well as purely social drinks), which is due more to their basic character than to their exact bouquet and flavour. It is this essential basic character which we are trying to duplicate here, for if the amateur can achieve this object then his or her wines will be well able to fulfil the same functions at the prototype commercial wine. Naturally, these amateur wines will not usually possess exactly the same bouquet and flavour as their commercial counterparts, but as long as no really fundamental differences can be detected we feel it is a good thing for them to retain some individuality of their own in these respects. After all, it is on just such nuances of bouquet and flavour that the great wines of commerce can be distinguished, and there is no reason why the unique features of amateur wines cannot also be regarded in this light.

Indeed, the reader may very well find that a particular recipe produces a wine of great merit whose quality is confirmed both at wine tastings and by its winning prizes in open competitions. In such cases, it is often worth concentrating on the production of this wine, not to the exclusion of other types but more as a "specialité de la maison." A careful study of the ingredients and techniques employed will then permit the elimination of minor imperfections so that even higher quality can later be achieved. The precedent is set by the greatest vineyards of Europe which devote all their time to the production of just one wine and are continually striving to bring it to perfection. While we must admit the amateur will rarely find it advisable to adopt quite such a restricted outlook, a great deal can nevertheless be said in favour of specialising in one or possibly two types of wine and producing other types as a secondary interest.

In a book of this size, it is obviously impossible to do full justice to more than a limited number of the better known commercial wines. Our aim has therefore been to provide the reader with a comprehensive picture of at least the principal types of aperitifs, table and dessert wines produced commercially. Each chapter begins with a fairly extensive review of the production and characteristics of the wine or wines under consideration. Practical suggestions on how the wine may best be simulated are next discussed, and this section is finally concluded with a few recipes which have been designed to illustrate the principles involved. Only a limited number of recipes have been included, however, since we hope that winemakers reading this book will be stimulated to design their own and regard ours primarily as guides towards achieving this end. In addition, all these recipes are for 5-gallon quantities since we feel that smaller volumes are less conducive to quality. There is nevertheless nothing to prevent the winemaker from scaling them down to as little as 1 gallon, but scaling up to 10 gallons or more is, of course, infinitely preferable.

In conclusion, we hardly need to add that this section of the book has been written with the more experienced winemaker in mind. Readers have been assumed to possess a good knowledge of the basic principles of amateur winemaking discussed in the previous section and to be familiar with such techniques as gravity and acid checking. In connection with the latter, it should be noted that all acidities in the following chapters are expressed as parts per thousand (p.p.t.) of sulphuric acid. The first part of this book may, of course, be used for general reference purposes and will prove especially valuable when sugar/gravity/potential alcohol ables and similar items of essential information are needed.

P. M. DUNCAN

G. W. B. ACTON

The Vineyards of FRANCE

Chapter XXII

WHITE TABLE WINES

THIS chapter is primarily designed to introduce the amateur winemaker to some of the techniques and skills required for the successful imitation of commercial wines. With comparatively little modification of basic winemaking procedures, the amateur can and should produce white table wines at least as good as and often better than the cheaper commercial wines of this type. Thus, by beginning with white table wines, the winemaker will gain both the confidence and experience which is necessary to tackle other more difficult types of wine.

The commercial production of white table wine is an extremely simple process. The freshly picked grapes are first crushed and pressed, the juice normally being separated immediately from the pulp. The juice is then allowed to ferment in concrete or wooden vats or in oak casks until all or nearly all the sugar has been converted into alcohol. After fermentation has ceased, the new wine is racked off its lees into large oak casks to mature. Periodic rackings are carried out at about three-monthly intervals during the year or so the wine spends in cask. By this time, the wine should be brilliantly clear, but if stubborn hazes are present fining may prove necessary and is carried out some 6–12 months after the first racking. Finally, the wine is bottled and allowed to mature in bottle for another few months or years. In general, however, white table wines do not require long maturing and the majority reach their best within five years of the vintage. A year in cask and another year or two in bottle is normally ample and only a few of the better wines will continue to improve in bottle for more than about five years.

The most important areas producing white wines are Burgundy, Graves in Bordeaux, the Loire Valley, Alsace and the valleys of the Rhine, Mosel and their tributaries in Germany. Although Spain is currently the largest exporter of wines to Britain, most of the wines are cheaper types (sound but unpretentious) designed to cater for the lower price ranges of the market and do not merit any closer attention here. Other regions of France, e.g. Jura, Jurançon, Gaillac, the Rhône valley as well as such countries as Italy and Switzerland also produce pleasant white wines, but with the exception of Italy the quantity exported is relatively small. In addition, the five most famous areas mentioned above will give the winemaker a fairly representative picture of white table wines and provide an adequate variety of types to simulate.

BURGUNDY

Although Burgundy is perhaps better known for its magnificent red wines, it is only because much more red than white Burgundy is produced. The quality of the white wine is nevertheless such that the demand far exceeds the supply and its cost is correspondingly high. Indeed, many connoisseurs consider white Burgundy to be the best wine of its kind in the world and few can truthfully dispute this view.

The best white Burgundies come from the same region as the best red wines of the region and are produced in a northern district called the Côte d'Or. The latter comprises a long narrow ridge of hills which begins just south of Dijon and continues almost due south for another 35 miles. The Côte d'Or is itself further sub-divided into the northern Côte de Nuits and the southern Côte de Beaune, but the former is almost exclusively devoted to the production of red wines. The Côte de Beaune does not produce quite such good red wines as the Côte de Nuits, but its superb white wines more than compensate for this deficiency. The best white wine of Burgundy comes from Montrachet in the Côte de Beaune, while the white wines of Meursault (and Aloxe-Corton) also have no mean reputation.

Further south than the Côte d'Or lie the districts of the Côte Chalonnaise and the Mâconnais. In the former are the communes of Buxy, Rully and Montagny all of which are famed for their white wines. The Mâconnais is less well endowed, but the villages of Pouilly and Fuissé which jointly produce the white Burgundy called Pouilly-Fuissé are perhaps the best known.

Some eighty miles north-west of the Côte d'Or but still included in the Burgundy vineyards lies the district of Chablis in the département of Yonne. Chablis itself is a small and undistinguished town built on a limestone plateau, but its greenish-yellow wines are renowned for their delicate flinty flavour. Like all other great white Burgundies, however, the demand for Chablis far exceeds the supply so that genuine Chablis is an expensive wine.

The soil and climate of Burgundy are fully discussed in the following chapter on red table wines and so need not be considered here except for Chablis. The latter is situated on a limestone plateau so that the soil is chalky and the flints it contains are thought to be responsible for some of the unique flavour of the wine. Climatically, the northern location of Chablis gives it a slight disadvantage over the rest of Burgundy. Both late Spring and early Autumn frosts are not uncommon and at times occur in the same year with disastrous effects on the quality of the wine. Indeed, there are occasions when no wine or hardly any has been produced in Chablis because of adverse weather conditions, 1945 being a notable example when hail devastated the vineyards.

The only important variety of grape grown in Burgundy for white wine production is the Chardonnay or Pinot Blanc. Like the Pinot Noir, this vine is not noted for the quantity but for the quality of its grapes as the excellence of its wines clearly shows. The vintage usually commences around mid-September to mid-October, but the exact date is determined by the weather conditions and the ripeness of the grapes.

Vinification is carried out more or less exactly in the manner previously described. The new wine is matured in cask for 1–2 years and then given another short period of bottle ageing. Like most white table wines, however, white burgundy matures fairly rapidly and will normally reach its best some 3–5 years after the vintage.

A feature of white burgundies is their dryness. Little or no unfermented sugar normally remains in these wines although in exceptionally good years enough may be left to blunt their dry edge, e.g. the 1959 wines are very slightly sweet for this reason. White burgundies are also characterised by their relatively full body and, for a table wine, a high alcoholic strength (11% to 13% alcohol by volume). Their crisp and fresh but nevertheless delicate flavour is accentuated by a fairly high acidity which commonly lies in the range 3.7–4.5 p.p.t. A good average acidity for these wines is about 4.0 p.p.t., but because a significant proportion of malic acid is present a strong acid flavour rarely obtrudes on the palate. The bouquet is full and fragrant and the colour is a pale yellow which often exhibits a greenish tint. Chablis is especially well-known for its pale greenish-yellow colour

There can be little doubt that white burgundies deserve their high place among the great white table wines of the world. Their great delicacy and finesse is coupled with a robust and invigorating character and the appeal of this combination is hard to resist. They are wines which are meant to be drunk young at an age of 3–5 years, for after about five years their freshness of flavour and bouquet usually begin to decline and the wine then loses much of its appeal.

GRAVES

In this country, Graves is commonly understood to mean white wine from the Graves region of Bordeaux. This idea is only partly correct, however, for this district actually produces just about as much red as white wine! The misconception that Graves is a white wine probably arose because relatively little red Graves is exported. The reason is that the quality of the white wine is on the whole rather higher than that of the red, although some notable exceptions admittedly do exist. Indeed, Château Haut-Brion in Graves produces such excellent claret that it is ranked as an equal with the three best châteaux in the Médoc! White Graves is therefore very common in Britain whereas red Graves is a comparative rarity.

Graves is situated in the western part of Bordeaux between the Garonne River (Gironde Estuary) and the Atlantic Ocean. Most of the district is relatively level and low-lying and it is notable for being one of the few flat regions of Europe which succeeds in consistently producing good quality though rarely great wines. The principal soil found here is, as the name Graves implies, an alluvial gravel well suited to the production of fine white wines. The climate is warm and sunny but the heat of the summer is moderated by the nearby Atlantic Ocean which also provides the area with ample rain.

The main grape varieties grown in Graves are the Semillon, Sauvignon Blanc and Muscadelle. Semillon vineyards predominate, but a considerable acreage is also devoted to Sauvignon Blanc vines, for the wine of Graves is primarily made from a blend of these two cépages. Muscadelle grapes are much less common. Their function is more to assist in the "marriage" of the Semillon and Sauvignon Blanc, and for this purpose only about 5% of Muscadelle grapes is required. The faint Muscat undertone sometimes detected in the bouquet and flavour of Graves wines is thus due to the inclusion of Muscadelle grapes.

The warmer climate of Bordeaux usually permits the vintage to begin earlier there than in Burgundy. Picking normally begins around mid-September, but again the exact date depends upon weather conditions and the ripeness of the grapes. Vinification follows the pattern already described, and the new wine is matured in cask for a year or so. Many Graves then require only another 1–2 years in bottle to reach their best. Some of the top quality Graves do require longer maturing, however, and may spend slightly longer in wood and require ageing for several years in bottle before full maturity is attained.

Although Graves is often said to be a dry wine, such a generalisation does not do it full justice. Most of the better Graves are certainly drier than their lesser counterparts, but in comparison with white Burgundy a certain sweetness is almost invariably apparent. Strangely enough, the converse is true for the red wines of the two areas, for Claret is undoubtedly drier than red Burgundy. White Graves may in fact range from fairly dry almost to medium sweet, but the term medium dry probably describes the majority fairly accurately.

The wines of Graves are light to medium in body and alcohol, the latter usually lying in the range 10% to 12% by volume. Their acidity is significantly lower than that of white Burgundy and is normally around 3.3 to 4.0 p.p.t.

A good average figure here is about 3.5 p.p.t. The colour of Graves is fairly light yellow but it is darker than and lacks the greenish tints often present in white Burgundies. The bouquet is again full and fragrant, reflecting the rich perfume of the grapes from which it is produced.

Although most of the Graves sold in Britain cannot be classed as great wine, some of the vineyards do produce excellent wines comparable in their own right to the better wines of other districts. On the whole, however, Graves may be regarded as a sound unpretentious table wine which is best consumed while still fairly young when its pleasantly perfumed bouquet and clean flavour are still fresh. Delicacy, finesse and depth of character should only be sought in the best wines of the district.

LOIRE

The pleasant white wines of the Loire are still comparatively unknown in Britain, but nowadays the district seems to be attracting more attention. Possibly the increasing popularity of continental holidays has played some part in awakening this interest as a result of visitors to the region requesting Loire wines on their return home. Whatever the reason, it cannot be disputed that this trend is very welcome and illustrates the growing appreciation of wine in Britain.

The Loire is the longest river in France and vineyards are planted along much of its length. The region itself lies some 150 miles north of Bordeaux and runs roughly from around Nevers in the east to Nantes on the Atlantic seaboard. The most important wine districts lie to the west of Orleans, however, and three main areas are recognised. Near the river mouth is Nantes, the home of Muscadet wines, and further upstream to the east the province of Anjou will be found. Beyond Anjou is the Coteaux du Touraine, the last of the three principal districts, but vineyards will still be encountered many miles further up-river and along such tributaries as the Cher. Red, rosé and some excellent sparkling wines are also produced in these Loire districts, the sparkling wines of Vouvray and Saumur or the Rosé d'Anjou being quite well-known in this country.

The soil here is rich and fertile and can support many other crops as well as vines. Around Nantes a mixture of pebbles and clay predominates, but further east in Anjou the soil gives way to a shelly sand known as feluns. The topography is, on the whole, that of a river valley surrounded by low rolling hills.

The climate in the Loire is none too well suited to viticulture. Its northerly location makes for unpredictable weather and cool wet summers are not uncommon so that the grapes may fail to ripen fully. In such years, the wines are poor and lack bouquet and character. Late Spring frosts are also a problem so that it is wise to pay heed to the vintage years when purchasing Loire wines.

The grapes grown here for white wine production are related to the famous cépages of other regions. The Muscadet is grown around Nantes and gives its name to the wine, while further east in Anjou and Touraine the Pinot Blanc reigns supreme. Some of the smaller vineyards in the eastern extremity of the Loire also grow Semillon grapes.

The vintage takes place around the end of September or in October, but like everywhere else its date depends upon the vagaries of the weather and the ripeness of the grapes. Vinification follows the normal procedure and the new wine is aged in cask for about a year although in some areas, notably around Vouvray in Touraine, the wine is bottled in the Spring immediately following the vintage. Most Loire wines will then reach their best after another year or so in bottle. Full maturity is thus usually attained some 3–5 years after the vintage although a few wines can last for several decades without deterioration. Such wines are rare, however, and it is doubtful whether much improvement occurs after the first five years or so in bottle.

The white Loire wines are on the whole light, dry to medium-dry wines with a full and fragrant bouquet, and a pleasant fruity flavour is often apparent if the wine has been bottled young after only a few months in cask. Their alcohol content is normally around 10% to 12% by volume but can at times attain as much as 13% by volume. In the local cafés, however, wine containing as little as 8% alcohol is sold and the customer in fact orders wine according to

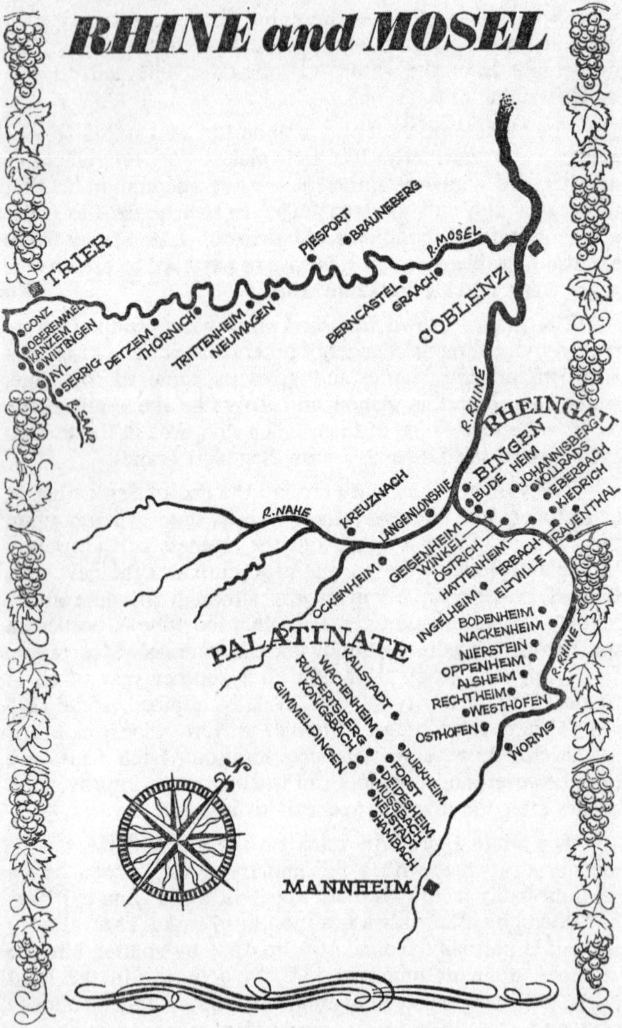
RHINE and MOSEL
TRIER
CONZ
OBEREMMEL
KANZEM
WILTINGEN
AYL
SERRIG
R. SAAR
DETZEM
THORNICH
TRITTENHEIM
NEUMAGEN
PIESPORT
BRAUNEBERG
BERNCASTEL
GRAACH
R. MOSEL
COBLENZ
R. RHINE
RHEINGAU
BINGEN
BUDE HEIM
JOHANNISBERG
VOLLRADS
EBERBACH
KIEDRICH
RAUENTHAL
KREUZNACH
LANGENLONSHIE
R. NAHE
GEISENHEIM
WINKEL
ÖSTRICH
HATTENHEIM
ERBACH
ELTVILLE
OCKENHEIM
INGELHEIM
BODENHEIM
NACKENHEIM
NIERSTEIN
OPPENHEIM
ALSHEIM
RECHTHEIM
WESTHOFEN
OSTHOFEN
WORMS
R. RHINE
PALATINATE
KALLSTADT
WACHENHEIM
RUPPERTSBERG
KONIGSBACH
GIMMELDINGEN
DURKHEIM
FORST
DEIDESHEIM
MUSSBACH
NEUSTADT
HAMBACH
MANNHEIM
N

alcoholic strength (8%, 9% or 10% as desired). As might be expected from the northerly location of the vineyards, the acid content of the wine is fairly high, around 3.5 to 4.5 p.p.t., but the presence of considerable amounts of malic acid helps to prevent too strong an acid flavour. A good average acidity for these wines is about 4.0 p.p.t. Loire wines are thus crisper and more refreshing than Graves and in many respects are intermediate between the latter and white Burgundies. These characteristics make an appealing combination which will undoubtedly do much to promote the rising popularity of the Loire wines, especially as their cost is quite reasonable!

ALSACE AND GERMANY

The Rhine and Mosel valleys are rightly renowned throughout the world for their scenic beauty as well as for their magnificent white wines. Although generally speaking these wines are considered to be exclusively German in origin, it must be remembered that the French province of Alsace also lies on the Rhine. Its wines are therefore equally as entitled to the name of Rhine wines as are those of Germany. Furthermore, because they are much more akin to the latter in character and other respects than to other French wines, it is logical to consider Alsatian and German Rhine wines together.

The wines of Alsace and Germany are predominantly white, but a significant quantity of red wine collectively known as spätburgunder is also produced. The amount of red wine made here is in fact rather larger than is generally realised, but due to its relatively mediocre quality very little is exported. The climate is not really suitable for red wine production because the vineyards of the Rhine and Mosel lie further north than any others of note in Europe. Even the most northerly fringes of Champagne extend only to the latitude of the southern extremities of the Rhine wine districts. More heat than these northern regions receive is required to produce great red wines, but this is more than offset by the quality of the white wines made here.

The coolness of the climate nevertheless does mean that every beneficial factor must be exploited to its fullest if the grapes are to ripen fully. Most of the important regions are fortunate in that low surrounding hills afford the vines considerable protection from the wind. The vineyards are also planted on the steep sides of deep river valleys which further help to shelter the grapes and prevent storm damage. In addition, the meandering of the rivers, especially the Mosel, allows many vineyards to have a southern or western exposure which permits the ripening grapes to derive the maximum benefit from what sun is available. Stones placed beneath the vines reflect heat on the grapes and the nature of the soil is often such that it retains the heat of the sun far into the night, thus preventing too drastic a temperature drop during the hours of darkness. The success of the vintage nevertheless depends ultimately upon the weather. Late Spring or early Autumn frosts or a cold wet Summer can prove disastrous (and all too often do) in these northern latitudes.

The Rhine valley and its environs are divided into a number of districts. In the south lies the French province of Alsace, and across the river on the west bank is the Palatinate or Rheinpfalz which is the most southerly of the German regions. Lower down the Rhine, but now on the south as well as the west bank because the river makes a sharp turn to the west at Mainz, is found the area known as the Rheinhesse. Opposite the latter across the river is the Rheingau which is the most northerly of the German Rhine wine districts. The valleys of the Nahe and the Mosel, both tributaries of the Rhine, complete the list of important wine-producing regions.

Although Alsace is now part of France, it has had a turbulent history and has belonged to France and Germany alternately several times during the past century. It was finally acquired by France in 1918 after the First World War. During the preceding German occupation the vineyards had been planted for quantity rather than quality, but under French rule better vines have been introduced so that nowadays the quality of Alsatian wines has much improved

Most of the vineyards of Alsace are located in river valleys which afford some protection from the vagaries of the weather. The soils here are highly variable and sands, gravels, alluvial soils or weathered igneous rocks can all be found. The climate is surprisingly dry and the winters rather long and cold, but on the whole it is quite favourable to viticulture.

The principal grape varieties grown here are the Sylvaner, Riesling, Traminer and Pinot, but the Gewurtztraminer is also planted fairly extensively. The vintage is usually fairly late and starts around the end of September, but picking continues throughout October, each vineyard being gone over several times during the period.

Vinification of the grapes follows the normal procedure but the new wine is customarily bottled within six months of the vintage. Alsatian wines are generally drunk young at an age of only a few years since most are past their best after five years. These wines are light, fresh and crisp with a full and flowery bouquet. Their alcohol content is usually fairly low around 9% to 12% by volume and their acidity moderately high in the region of 4.0 to 4.5 p.p.t. Some of the better wines may retain a trace of sweetness and be fuller in body than the rest, and those produced from Gewurtztraminer grapes tend to show these characteristics.

The German wine district known variously as the Palatinate, Rheinpfalz or simply Pfalz is located on the west bank of the Rhine at the Alsatian border with France. Unlike the other more northerly German regions, most of the Palatinate vineyards are planted on the high ground of the Haardt Plateau, but the nearby Haardt mountains serve to protect them from east winds. The Palatinate is the largest and most southerly of the German wine districts.

The soils here are again fairly variable with sands, gravels, loess, alluvial deposits, clays and weathered basalt predominating in different areas. The climate is hotter and more dependable than further north so that the grapes tend to ripen more fully. Winters are usually fairly mild and rainfall adequate. The principal grape grown in the Palatinate is the Sylvaner, but Riesling vineyards are also fairly common. The latter are said to produce the best wines. The vintage commences towards the end of September, but because the vineyards require going over several times it continues well into October.

Vinification again follows the usual pattern and the new wine is bottled after spending some 3 to 12 months in cask. Like Alsatian wines, those of the Palatinate are best drunk fairly young as they tend to lose their appeal rather rapidly. Most of these wines are fairly strong in alcohol (around 12% by volume) and range from medium-dry to sweet. They are consequently medium to full-bodied and some may only adequately be described as luscious in flavour. Their acidity is moderately high (around 4.0 to 4.5 p.p.t.) which confers a pleasant freshness further accentuated by a powerful, fragrant bouquet. Despite these attributes, however, few Palatinate wines can lay any claim to greatness because they lack the necessary depth of character.

The Rheinhesse region extends along the west or south bank from Worms in the south to Bingen in the north-west, although most of the better vineyards with the exception of Bingen itself lie between Worms and Mainz. The vineyards are planted on the steep sides of the river valley and on the slopes of the surrounding hills which offer considerable protection from winds and storms.

The soil here is noted for its fertility. In some places deposits of loess predominate, in others a red sandy soil may be found while around Nierstein the vines are planted in a rich red loam. The climate is rather variable, however, and there is a tendency for the summers to be cool so that some difficulty may be experienced in ripening the grapes fully.

The principal Rheinhesse grape is again the Sylvaner, but Riesling and Sylvaner-Riesling hybrids are also planted fairly extensively. The vintage is normally delayed to allow the grapes to ripen as fully as possible. It commences around the end of September and continues throughout October.

Vinification is carried out by the standard method and the new wine bottled within about 12 months of the vintage. Rheinhesse wines mature fairly rapidly and reach their best within about five years, but many of the better wines will continue to improve slightly in bottle for about a decade or more before falling into senility. In character, these wines vary from medium to fairly full-bodied and usually retain a small amount of unfermented sugar which takes the edge off their dryness. Some, indeed, are quite sweet and can serve as dessert wines. Their alcoholic strength is moderate, around 11% to 12% by volume, and a pleasant freshness of flavour is conferred by a relatively high acidity (4.0 to 5.0 p.p.t.). The bouquet is strong and perfumed and often possesses a distinct flowery fragrance. These wines have greater depth of character than those of the Palatinate and may reach very high standards, notably the wines of Nierstein and Oppenheim.

The Rheingau is the most northerly of the German Rhine wine districts and is located on the north bank of the Rhine between Rüdesheim and Mainz. Like the Rheinhesse across the river, the vineyards are planted on the steep slopes of the valley and the surrounding hills where the vines are sheltered from bad weather conditions. The total area devoted to wine production is relatively small compared with other districts.

The soils here are rocky with a slaty or siliceous basis, but here and there patches of gravel are found. The climate is surprisingly mild for such a northern latitude but still none too suitable for viticulture. Every effort must be made to obtain the maximum benefit from what sun is available if the grapes are to ripen fully, but if the summer is cold and wet, as well it may be, only a few favoured vineyards will be able to produce good wine.

The principal grape grown in the Rheingau is the Riesling which is planted in more than 75% of the vineyards. Since the Rheingau is considered to produce the best wines of Germany, it follows that the Riesling grape is supreme for quality. Its yields are lower than the Sylvaner favoured in the Rheinhesse and Palatinate, but this lack of quantity is more than compensated for by the superb quality of its wines. The vintage is once again delayed as long as possible to allow the grapes to ripen fully and it is late September or early October before harvesting begins.

Vinification follows the usual pattern and the new wine is bottled within about 12 months of the vintage. Rheingau wines are often mature after about five years in bottle, but many will last longer and 25 years is not exceptional for a good wine. Little real improvement takes place after 5–10 years, but the wine will continue to mellow slightly over longer periods. The most notable characteristic of these wines is their extremely powerful and fragrant bouquet which is reputed to stay on the palate for hours. A slight amount of unfermented sugar remains in many of the wines (some, indeed, can be quite sweet), and they are medium to full in body with a fairly high alcoholic strength around 11% to 12% by volume. The acidity is quite high and generally exceeds that of Rheinhesse wines although again 4.0 to 5.0 p.p.t. is an average range. The best wines of the district are superb with a finesse and depth of character matched by few other white wines in the world except possibly Sauternes and white Burgundy.

The Mosel is a tributary of the Rhine which enters the latter at Coblenz. This river valley is also famed for its wines, so much so that German wines are usually referred to as Hocks and Moselles. The former is, of course, a collective name for all German Rhine wines and it is interesting to note that Moselle wines are sufficiently highly regarded to be segregated in this way. The Mosel runs approximately north-east from its source to where it joins the Rhine, but it meanders so much in its course that many of the vineyards on its banks can have a south or west exposure. The principal wine-producing area lies between Trier and Coblenz, but considerable wine is also produced on its tributaries, the Ruwer and the Saar. The latter wines are rarely of commercial importance, however, and little is exported except in unusually good years such as 1959. The Mosel wines produced above Trier are also of little interest.

The vineyards of the Mosel are planted on the precipitous slopes of the river valleys. The soil is principally a slate which will support few other plants besides vines, although dwarf oaks were once cultivated here for tannin manufacture. The climate is rather cool and barely permits viticulture in some parts, especially on the Ruwer and Saar, but the persistence of the growers is amply rewarded by the quality of the wine.

The principal grape grown here is again the Riesling. The vintage is once more in late September and October. Vinification is carried out in the normal manner and the new wine is bottled some 6–12 months after the vintage. The wine will then be ready for drinking within a few years although some can be in bottle for decades without degenerating.

Mosel wines are noted for their fresh, crisp flavour. Most are light and dry but some unfermented sugar is commonly encountered in the better wines. The alcohol content is generally low (around 10% to 11% by volume) and the acidity high (4.5–6.0 p.p.t.). Some Mosel wines have in fact been found to contain as much as 8.0 p.p.t. acid although such wines are rarely exported. The bouquet is full, fragrant and flowery and for a light wine the depth of character is often surprising.

The Nahe is another tributary of the Rhine which enters the latter at Bingen. It runs roughly parallel to but east of the Mosel. Nahe wines are not too well-known abroad at the moment but are pleasant white wines intermediate in many characteristics between Hocks and Mosels.

One of the most notable features of all German wines is their high acidity. The ranges quoted in this chapter are normally encountered only in the better wines and considerably more acid is often present in the ordinary wines of the districts. It is therefore hardly surprising that many Hocks and Mosels have a crisp acid flavour, and some local wines may be so tart as to be almost undrinkable. Fortunately, a high proportion of malic acid is present so that the wine tends to taste milder than its titratable acidity would at first suggest. In addition, the retention of a little unfermented sugar in the wine helps to mask some of the acid. It is therefore extremely important to remember that malic acid is a prominent factor in German wine quality and moreover plays no mean part in determining their character. Were the malic acid in these wines replaced by tartaric acid, there is little doubt that they would be completely unpalatable due to an excessively acid flavour.

A second point of note is the care which is taken over the wine at every stage in its production. Each cask is often kept and treated separately so that every vineyard may produce several qualities of the same wine. That of the same vintage is not equalised or homogenised by blending the contents of the various casks as usually is the case elsewhere. Considerable scientific control is exercised during fermentation and maturing and a final polishing filtration (out of contact with the air) through a medium which will even remove yeast cells is often carried out under careful supervision.

Selection of the grapes is also practised more extensively in Germany than in other countries. Many of the grapes are picked normally, but some are deliberately left on the vine to ripen more fully and are thus harvested later than the rest. Some of these grapes may be attacked by the beneficial mould *Botrytis Cinerea* which is here called the Edelfäule, but in France it is known as La Pourriture Noble. (The effects of this mould are fully discussed in the chapter on Sauternes and so will not be dealt with here.) Wines produced from late-gathered grapes, whether or not they have been attacked by the Edelfäule, are known as *spätlese* wines. This term is, of course, no guarantee of quality but merely signifies that the grapes have been left on the vine longer than usual.

A further refinement is to select bunches of grapes which are riper than the rest. Such bunches may or may not be late-gathered and wines made from these grapes are termed *auslese* wines. Taking the process a stage further, *beerenauslese* wines are produced from selected berries. The culmination is *trockenbeerenauslese* wines which are produced from specially selected berries which have almost raisinfied on the vine. The latter two types of wine are naturally very expensive due to the amount of labour and care needed for their production and because exceptionally good climatic conditions are required before any wine of this nature can be made at all. A trockenbeerenauslese will often cost more than £10 a bottle for this reason.

PRODUCTION OF WHITE TABLE WINES

The amateur winemaker should not experience undue difficulty in producing good quality white table wines provided a few important basic ideas are always kept in mind. To begin with, the type of white wine required must be decided before starting the preparation of the must. In addition to providing the winemaker with a goal at which to aim, this information will also permit the blend of ingredients most in keeping with the character of the wine to be selected with the minimum of trouble. Such important factors as the acidity of the must can also be settled at the time it is prepared when any adjustments which may be required will exert their optimum beneficial influence.

Almost all fruits and vegetables which do not yield a deeply-coloured juice or extract are suitable for white table wine production, but a blend of at least two such ingredients is generally necessary to achieve a balanced must. Many fruit juices require some dilution with water either to reduce their acidity to a more palatable level or to prevent too strong a fruity flavour being apparent in the wine. Some fruit juices can be used without dilution, however, peach juice being a notable example, and as a general rule as little dilution as possible commensurate with the character of the wine should be practised. The addition of too much water can all too easily result in a wine which lacks body.

Pulp fermentation of fruits is best avoided whenever possible because this procedure tends to extract substances which coarsen the flavour of a wine. White table wines should be rather delicately flavoured and smooth on the palate so that even a background harshness detracts from their quality. Boiling fruits in water is undesirable for the same reason. The only really satisfactory procedure is to press out the juice either by hand where this is feasible or with the aid of a fruit press or electric juicer. For example, peaches are easily stoned, the halves placed in a linen bag and the juice pressed out by hand. Apples and rhubarb on the other hand require some type of mechanical press. At any rate, the juice of most common fruits can be extracted by pressing in one way or another and better results will normally be achieved if the fruit juice alone can be employed, since most of the undesirable constituents of the fruit will then be rejected with the spent pulp.

Once the fruit juice has been extracted, it should be sulphited with 100 p.p.m. sulphite and left to settle in a suitable sealed container for 24 hours. A certain amount of the fine pulp particles which are inevitably present will by then have settled to the bottom of the container. The clear juice should be racked off this deposit and the latter transferred to a suitable small container to settle further for another 24 hours. The clear juice obtained in this latter manner may be fermented separately from the bulk and used for topping up purposes. The volume, gravity and acidity of the bulk of the fruit juice should be checked as soon as it is racked off its pulp deposit. The amount of natural sugar and acid contributed to the must from this source can then be evaluated.

Vegetables normally require a different treatment. Many vegetables can be cut up and pressed directly, especially by means of an electric juicer, but this procedure is often rather unsatisfactory. Certain vegetables contain constituents which coarsen the flavour and bouquet of a wine. Fortunately, some of these substances are volatile in steam and can thus be at least partly removed by boiling the vegetable in water for a short time (10–30 minutes is normally sufficient). The extracted pulp may then be strained off and pressed and the juice left to cool and settle in a suitable sealed container for 24 hours. It should then be racked off the pulp deposit and treated exactly as described for fruit juices. One point to note here is that this treatment denatures the natural pectin-destroying enzymes present in the ingredients. It is therefore essential to rectify this deficiency by adding one ounce of pectozyme (or similar preparation) per 10 gallons of must, otherwise the wine may subsequently prove difficult to clear. A few fruits, notably bananas, are also most conveniently extracted by boiling in water, and such ingredients should be dealt with exactly as described for vegetables.

Although some fruits can be used on their own for white wine production, a better-balanced wine is normally obtained if a blend of ingredients is selected. Vegetables should never be employed alone but make excellent basic ingredients in conjunction with fruits, especially for the sweeter types of white wines. The inclusion of half to one pound of bananas (without skins) per gallon will help to improve the body of the wine and is much superior to grain for this purpose since the latter tends to introduce too strong a flavour of its own.

The actual choice of ingredients and the amounts to use for a given type of wine can only really be decided on the basis of past experience, but the recipes at the end of this chapter will serve as a guide to what should be sought. The important point to remember is that the character of the must should be in keeping with that of the prototype commercial wine. For example, there would be no sense in preparing a heavy, full-bodied must if a Mosel-type wine was desired since the latter is a light very delicate wine.

Once the basic blend of ingredients has been selected, consideration must be given to the finer characteristics of the must. Many basic blends tend to produce wines which are lacking to some extent in vinous quality and depth of character. This fault can easily be remedied by including ½ to 1 lb. of raisins or ½ to 1 pint white grape concentrate per gallon of must. Indeed, grape concentrate is widely held to be better for this purpose than for any other, and there can be no doubt that even as little as ½ pint per gallon can vastly improve the quality of any wine, but particularly that of a white wine.

One feature of the utmost importance for any white wine is bouquet. Few ingredients other than flowers can supply the necessary strength and fragrance of bouquet which is absolutely essential if a white table wine is to have any real appeal. Lack of bouquet is in fact a major defect encountered in many amateur white wines at present and most winemakers would do well to pay closer attention to this matter. Fortunately, the problem of improving the bouquet of a wine is very easily solved. All that is necessary is the inclusion of flowers in the must, and if fresh flowers are not available the dried variety will prove almost equally satisfactory. Elderflowers (half to three-quarters of a pint) and yellow or pink rose petals (quarter to three-quarters of a pint) are probably the best to use, but hawthorn flowers (two pints), gorse flowers (two pints) and several others can also be employed. The quantities in parentheses are the amounts recommended per gallon of must. For dried flowers, one packet per gallon will normally suffice.

Although many books advise boiling flowers in water to extract their flavour and bouquet, this procedure should never be adopted. Many of the aromatic constituents of the flower are volatile and are thus easily lost so that boiling will dissipate a large proportion of these substances. The bouquet of the wine will then be unnecessarily deprived of much of its strength and fragrance. A short period of pulp fermentation (2–4 days) is a far superior method of dealing with flowers. Indeed, in order to avoid or minimise the loss of some of the more volatile floral constituents, it is often better not to add the flowers to the must until the initial violent primary fermentation has moderated to some extent. In this way, the danger of losing much of the fragrance by its entrainment in the large volumes of carbon dioxide evolved during this initial period is considerably reduced.

The final feature of the must which requires close attention is its acid content. The value for which the winemaker should aim depends primarily upon the type of wine required. Graves are best made fairly low in acid (around 3.0 to 3.5 p.p.t.), while white Burgundies and Loire wines need to contain slightly more (3.7 to 4.3 p.p.t.). Alsatian and German wines are the most acid types of all (4.0 to 6.0 p.p.t.), but it is advisable not to exceed about 5.0 p.p.t. even in these wines. In this connection, the winemaker should note very carefully that about one-third to one-half of the acid in the must should be malic acid if its acidity lies in the range of 3.5 to 4.5 p.p.t. and that at least one-half of the acid should be malic acid if the acid content of the must exceeds 4.5 p.p.t. Failure to include malic acid will inevitably result in an excessively tart or sharp flavour since neither citric nor tartaric acids make satisfactory substitutes.

The preparation of a white table wine must is thus normally quite straightforward. The fruit is pressed and the juice treated as described earlier. Any vegetables or bananas are also extracted with boiling water and processed as previously recommended. The various fruit juices and vegetable extracts are then blended. The grape concentrate is next added together with the yeast nutrients. Finally, sufficient water and sugar or honey to bring the must up to its final volume and appropriate initial gravity is added. Either sugar or honey can be employed (or a blend of the two). The initial gravity of the must naturally depends upon what alcoholic strength is required, but because table wines are being produced it will normally lie between 75 and 100.

There is therefore no need to add the sugar in small increments so that the total amount may be introduced prior to fermentation. A strong sugar or honey syrup is the most convenient means of adding the sugar since it then mixes readily with the rest of the must and does not require vigorous stirring to effect complete solution.

Once this stage is reached, the acidity of the must should be checked and adjusted if necessary. No acid testing need be carried out until this point, but it is useful to check the acid and sugar contents of fruit juices as recommended earlier to gain some insight into what can be expected from various fruits (and vegetables). The yeast may then be introduced as an actively fermenting starter, the type of yeast chosen naturally being in keeping with the type of wine being produced. After about seven days the flowers should be added, pulp fermented for 2–4 days and finally strained off.

The fermentation may be allowed to go to completion if a completely dry wine is desired, e.g. white Burgundy, but when the winemaker wishes a small amount of unfermented sugar to remain in the wine it must be racked early at a gravity of 0 to 10. The actual gravity at which to rack depends upon the degree of sweetness required. After this racking, the wine should be treated with 50 p.p.m. sulphite. Fermentation will probably be renewed within a few days but will proceed more slowly and a second racking followed by the addition of 100 p.p.m. sulphite should be carried out at a gravity of −5 to 5. The final degree of sweetness desired will again decide the gravity at which to rack.

Most wines will not referment after this racking, but even if they do the rate of fermentation will be very slow. Since controlled autolysis of the yeast often improves the bouquet and flavour of white wines quite considerably, the wine should not be racked again for three months. Thereafter it may be racked at intervals of three months and, if necessary, stubborn hazes removed by fining at an age of 6 to 12 months.

In conclusion, a few words may be said about the maturing of white table wines. A short period of cask maturing (6–12 months) is very beneficial to most white wines, but care must be taken not to permit too much oxygen to reach the wine. For this reason, a 16-gallon cask is the minimum size in which white table wines can be matured for longer than about six months. The maximum period in a 9-gallon cask is about 3–6 months, while most white table wines should not spend more than three months in a 4½-gallon cask. Smaller casks should not be used for white wines at all. After maturing in wood for 3–12 months, the wine should be bottled and matured in bottle for at least another 6–12 months. Few will continue to improve in bottle for more than 3–5 years so that longer maturing should not normally be contemplated. Most white wines will in fact reach their best at an age of 2–3 years.

ROSÉ WINES

Rosé wines have become very popular in Britain over the past few years and, because this trend seems likely to continue, it is perhaps advisable to say a few words about these wines at this point. As its name implies, a rosé wine is pink in colour and in this respect occupies an intermediate position between red and white table wines. As far as character is concerned, however, most rosé wines are very similar to white wines and often differ from the latter only in colour. A great deal of what has already been discussed in this chapter is therefore directly applicable to rosé as well as to white table wines.

The commercial production of rosé wines calls for a short period of pulp fermentation, the skins being left in contact with the fermenting must just long enough to allow it to acquire a pink tint. Various shades of pink can, of course, be achieved by varying the length of the pulp fermentation, but in general a day or two is ample for satisfactory colour extraction with most varieties of grapes. Otherwise, the procedure is very closely analogous to that employed in white table wine production.

The amateur can make rosé wines in this way, but it is preferable not to do so as most red fruits give too harsh a wine for this particular purpose. The best method is in fact to proceed exactly as for a white table wine but use red grape concentrate instead of white (1 pint per gallon is ample) or include a small proportion of a red fruit juice such as elderberry or blackcurrant juice (½ to 1 pint per gallon) in the must. Except for adding an ingredient to confer colour, the procedure to follow is exactly as described previously for white table wines. The only point to note is that many rosé wines retain a small proportion of unfermented sugar and so are medium-dry rather than completely dry. Racking should consequently be carried out initially at a gravity of 0 to 5 and later when the gravity has dropped another 5 to 10 points in order to retain a little unfermented sugar in the wine. Slightly longer maturing may also be necessary due to the higher tannin content of rosé wines, but on the whole a few months in cask followed by 2–3 years in bottle should prove adequate.

Recipe 1
LOIRE WHITE WINE

Ingredients:

2½ galls. dandelion petals
10 lb. raisins
2 pints white grape concentrate
4 lb. honey
Tartaric and malic acids as required
Yeast nutrients
Steinberg yeast starter
Water to 5 galls.

Method:

Add 3½ gallons boiling water to the raisins and yeast nutrients and leave to cool. When cool add the yeast starter and ferment on the pulp for two days. After this time add the dandelion petals (free from green calices) and continue the pulp fermentation for another two days. Strain off the pulp and press lightly. Add the grape concentrate and honey and make the volume up to 5 gallons with water.

Check the acidity and increase it to about 4.0 p.p.t. with malic and tartaric acids (equal weights of the two acids should be used). Check the gravity periodically and rack for the first time when the gravity drops to about 2. Add 50 p.p.m. sulphite. If fermentation is renewed later, rack again at a gravity of −5 and add another 100 p.p.m. sulphite. Otherwise the wine need not receive a second racking until a heavy deposit has formed. Thereafter racking should be carried out at intervals of three months until the wine is bottled.

The wine may be matured for a month or so in cask or for 6–12 months in bulk in glass before bottling. It will then continue to improve in bottle for some time but should be fully mature at an age of two to three years.

Recipe 2
WHITE BURGUNDY

Ingredients:

40 lb. peaches
4 pints white grape conc.
3 pints yellow rose petals
4 lb. honey (or 3 lb. sugar)
½ oz. Pectozyme
Yeast nutrients
Burgundy yeast starter
Water to 5 gallons

Method:

Stone the peaches and press out the juice. Sulphite and leave this juice to settle exactly as described in the text. Add the grape concentrate, honey (or sugar), yeast nutrients and yeast starter to the settled juice (after it is racked off its deposit), make up to 5 gallons with water. Stir vigorously to homogenise the must. Check the acidity and adjust it to about 4.0–4.2 p.p.t. Allow to ferment for about a week, then add the rose petals. Ferment on the flowers for 2–3 days then strain off the flowers and top up the volume to 5 gallons with water.

Allow fermentation to proceed to completion before racking. Add 50 p.p.m. sulphite after the first racking and another 50 p.p.m. after the second racking which should be carried out after three months or as soon as a heavy deposit forms, whichever is the sooner. Thereafter rack at intervals of three months until the wine is bottled.

This wine should be matured in the same manner as described in the preceding recipe.

Recipe 3
MOSEL WINE

Ingredients:

30 lb. green gooseberries
4 pints white grape conc.
4 pints elderflowers
5 lb. honey
½ oz. Pectozyme
Yeast nutrients
Bernkastel yeast starter
Water to 5 gallons

Method:

Add 3 gallons boiling water to the gooseberries (preferably topped and tailed), yeast nutrients and honey. When cool, crush the fruit then add the pectozyme and yeast starter. Ferment on the pulp for three–four days then strain off the latter and press lightly. Add the grape concentrate and elderflowers and ferment on the flowers for two–three days. Strain off the flowers and make the volume up to 5 gallons with water. Check the acidity and if necessary adjust it to 4.8 to 5.2 p.p.t. with chalk or malic acid as the case may be. Check the gravity periodically and, because it is advisable to retain some unfermented sugar in the wine, rack at a gravity of 2. Thereafter add 50 p.p.m. sulphite and proceed as directed in the first recipe (for Loire wine). This wine is best matured in bulk in glass for about 6–12 months before bottling. It should then be allowed some one–two years bottle ageing although it may often be drunk with enjoyment after a year (six months in bulk and six months in bottle).

Recipe 4
HOCK

Ingredients:

30 lb. rhubarb
4 pints white grape conc.
2 pints yellow rose petals
2 pints elderflowers
8 lb. honey
½ oz. Pectozyme
Yeast nutrients
Steinberg yeast starter
Water to 5 gallons

Method:

Press the rhubarb, sulphite the juice and leave to settle exactly as described in the text. An alternative though less satisfactory procedure is to crush the rhubarb, strain off the juice and extract the pulp three times with a half to three-quarters of a gallon *cold* water. The settled juice or extract should then be mixed with the honey, yeast nutrients, pectozyme and yeast starter. After a week add the flowers and grape concentrate. Ferment on the flowers for two–three days then strain off the latter and make the volume up to 5 gallons with water.

Check the acidity and adjust it to 4.5–5.0 p.p.t. with chalk or malic acid as the case may be. Thereafter proceed exactly as described in the first recipe except that rack for the first time at a gravity of 5 and for a second time at a gravity of −2.

Maturing should be carried out as suggested in the first recipe.

Recipe 5
GRAVES

Ingredients:

20 lb. parsnips
4 pints orange juice
4 pints white grape conc.
2 pints elderflowers
6 lb. honey
1/6 oz. tannic acid (or grape tannin)
1 oz. Pectozyme
Tartaric acid as required
Malic acid as required
Yeast nutrients
Bordeaux yeast starter
Water to 5 gallons

Method:

Press the juice from sufficient oranges to obtain about 4½–5 pints of juice (the extra is to allow for settling losses) and add 100 p.p.m. sulphite. Wash the parsnips, cut into chunks and boil in 3 gallons water for 10–15 minutes. Strain off the pulp and press lightly. Leave the orange juice and parsnip extract to settle for 24 hours exactly as described in the text.

Blend the orange juice and parsnip extract (after racking them off their deposits) with the grape concentrate, honey, tannic acid and yeast nutrients and make up to 5 gallons with water. Stir thoroughly to homogenise the must. Check the acidity and adjust it to 3.0–3.5 p.p.t. with equal weights of tartaric and malic acids. Add the pectozyme and yeast starter, allow to ferment for about a week then add the elderflowers. Ferment on the flowers for two–three days, then strain off the latter and if necessary top up to 5 gallons with water.

Subsequently proceed as directed in Recipe 1, except that the first racking should be carried out at a gravity of 5–8 and the second at a gravity of about 0. The wine should also be matured as recommended in the first recipe.

Recipe 6
GRAVES

Ingredients:

40 lb. apples (dessert)	**Tartaric acid if required**
4 pints white grape conc.	**Yeast nutrients**
2 pints yellow rose petals	**Bordeaux yeast starter**
5 lb. sugar (or 6 lb. honey)	**Water to 5 gallons**

Method:

Press the apples, add 100 p.p.m. sulphite to the juice, and leave to settle exactly as described in the text. Rack off the clear juice 24 hours later, add the grape concentrate, sugar and yeast nutrients and make up to 5 gallons with water.

Check the acidity and adjust it to 3.0–3.5 p.p.t. with chalk or tartaric acid as the case may be. Add the yeast starter and thereafter proceed as directed in the preceding recipe as regards fermenting and maturing the wine.

An alternative though less satisfactory procedure is to cut the apples into chunks, add the sugar, nutrients and 3 gallons of boiling water and leave to cool. Add the yeast starter, ferment on the pulp for five days (adding the rose petals after three days) then strain off the pulp and press the latter. Add the grape concentrate, make up to 5 gallons with water, check the acidity and thereafter proceed as before.

CHAPTER XXIII

DRY RED TABLE WINES

IT may safely be said that the production of good quality dry red table wines is one of the most exacting trials of skill an amateur winemaker can face. The difficulties involved in the successful production of wines of this type devolve round two facts. In the first place, any fault or imbalance in the overall quality of a dry red wine can at once be detected even by a relatively inexperienced palate. Secondly, minor imperfections in the wine cannot readily be corrected or masked without altering its character to a greater or lesser extent. The hardest problems but at the same time the greatest rewards in amateur winemaking are therefore encountered when the production of dry red table wines is attempted.

Almost all dry red wines are produced commercially in more or less the same fashion with only minor variations on the general theme according to the country or district from which the wine originates. Consequently, it seems logical to describe the process by which these wines are made in general terms first and then discuss some of the more important types of dry red table wines in greater detail later. This approach will also permit the winemaker to compare and contrast such famous wines as claret and burgundy more easily.

Red wines are, of course, produced from red grapes. It may therefore come as a surprise to some winemakers that the juice of red grapes is not normally red in colour but instead has a pale yellow tint. Admittedly, a few vines known as teinturiers do bear red grapes possessing red juice, but in general these grapes are rarely used fo winemaking purposes. The colouring matter of red grapes is in fact usually localised in the skins so that it cannot be extracted simply by pressing. How, then, does a red wine acquire its deep red colour?

In the first place, the colouring matter in the grape skins is not readily soluble in cold grape juice, but it can be extracted by crushing the grapes and heating the resultant mixture of pulp and juice to about 130°F. (55°C.) for some time. Unfortunately, this procedure is generally considered to be injurious to the quality of the wine so that it cannot really be recommended. On the other hand, the colouring matter in grape skins dissolves fairly readily at room temperature even in comparatively dilute solutions of alcohol. Thus, if the grapes are crushed and fermentation is allowed to proceed without removing the pulp, the alcohol formed during this period will extract the colouring matter from the grape skins. This pulp fermentation, as it is called, may then be continued until the must attains the desired depth of colour. Once this stage is reached, the pulp may be strained off and thereafter the fermentation can proceed to completion in the normal manner.

The initial phase in the production of all red wines is therefore a period of pulp fermentation. The duration of this phase varies according to the amount of colouring matter in the grapes, the rate of colour extraction and the depth of colour required in the must. Any length of time between a few days and two weeks or more may consequently be necessary. On the whole, however, it is inadvisable to prolong the period of pulp fermentation unduly otherwise the quality of the wine may suffer due to the over-extraction of constituents other than colouring matter. Clarification may also subsequently prove difficult under these conditions.

The fact that carbon dioxide is evolved during fermentation poses certain unique problems during this stage of red wine production. Its effect is to force the mass of skins, pips and other constituents of the pulp or marc to the surface of the fermenting must where it collects to form a thick compact layer called a "cap." Fermentation proceeds very rapidly in this cap. Thus, because fermentation is an exothermic (heat-producing) process and the insulating properties of the cap prevent a rapid loss of heat to the surroundings, the temperature in the cap can very quickly rise to a point at which the yeast is seriously weakened or even killed. Since the more thermophilic acetifying bacteria can still grow and multiply without difficulty under these onditions, acetification of the must can all too easily occur if the cap is left undisturbed. Moreover, the rate of colour extraction will be slow unless good contact is maintained between the skins and the fermenting must. The cap must therefore be broken up and mixed thoroughly with the fermenting must at regular intervals for both these reasons.

In the commercial field, where large vessels holding several thousand gallons are commonly employed, the cap may be two or three feet thick. In such cases, its insulating properties frequently prevent a sufficiently rapid loss to the surroundings of the excess heat produced by the fermentation, so that close temperature control and cooling of the must is essential to avoid the danger of a stuck fermentation. Breaking up a cap capable of supporting the weight of a man is rather a problem, but it is nevertheless regularly "punched down" manually with wooden poles or shovels and/or fermenting must is pumped over the top of the cap several times a day.

Once sufficient colour has been extracted from the skins, the marc is strained off and the must transferred to large vats or barrels where the secondary fermentation is allowed to proceed to completion. The new wine is racked off its lees as soon as fermentation has ceased and thereafter at intervals of approximately four months. This periodic racking helps to clear and stabilise the wine and simultaneously provides part of the oxygen essential for its maturing. The wine is then matured in cask for at least a year during which it is usually fined once or twice to assist clarification and to reduce its tannin content. The commonest fining agents used for this purpose include white of egg, fresh ox-blood, isinglass, gelatine and various proprietary materials. Finally, the wine requires a period of bottle ageing before it is ready for consumption.

CLARET

Most winemakers know that claret is red wine from Bordeaux, that region on the Atlantic coast of France around the Gironde estuary and its confluent rivers. Although claret is still one of the most popular red table wines sold in Britain today, its price has risen phenomenally in recent years due

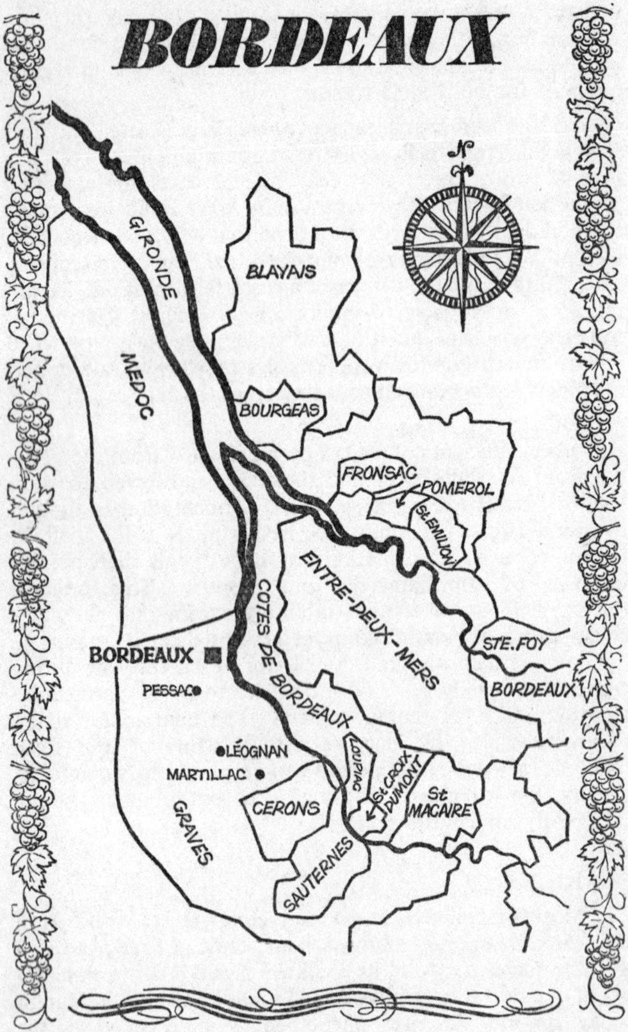
BORDEAUX
GIRONDE
MEDOC
BLAYAIS
BOURGEAS
FRONSAC
POMEROL
St. EMILION
ENTRE-DEUX-MERS
COTES DE BORDEAUX
STE. FOY
BORDEAUX
BORDEAUX
PESSAC
LÉOGNAN
MARTILLAC
GRAVES
CERONS
LOUPIAC
St. CROIX DUMONT
St MACAIRE
SAUTERNES
N

to demand exceeding supply. As a result, the best quality clarets are now unfortunately too expensive for most people to purchase except perhaps on special occasions. British wine lovers must therefore be content with the cheaper, though still good, bourgeois class clarets, at least for the time being.

Several districts of Bordeaux are rightly renowned for their red wines, and such famous names as Graves, Pomerol, St. Emilion and Médoc immediately come to mind when this subject is mentioned. It is nevertheless universally recognised that the bulk of the highest quality clarets originate from the relatively small district in Bordeaux called the Médoc. The latter is a long narrow strip of land bordering the western shore of the Gironde. It is divided into two main parts, the northern Bas-Médoc (or simply Médoc) and the southern Haut-Médoc, but generally speaking only this southern half of the region is famed for the very high quality of its clarets. The truth of this statement may be judged from the fact that three out of the four châteaux classified as producing the very best quality clarets in Bordeaux lie within the boundaries of the Haut-Médoc. These châteaux are Lafite, Latour and Margaux. The remaining member of this "big four," Château Haut-Brion, is located on the outskirts of the city of Bordeaux and thus lies within the Graves region.

The soil in Bordeaux is basically sandy or gravelly and rather poor, but it is difficult to be more precise without describing individual vineyards in detail because a bewildering diversity of different soil profiles and compositions is found throughout the province. Sandy marls, alluvial deposits and decomposed conglomerates are but a few of the variations which may be encountered within even a comparatively limited area. Since the nature of the soil can profoundly influence the quality of the wine, it is clear that the fine quality of the claret produced in certain districts and even in some individual vineyards may be due in no small way to their superior soil. This factor alone would not, of course, be sufficiently important to explain all the differences in quality which are actually observed, but it is nevertheless of considerable significance in this respect.

The climate here is fairly hot as may be expected at a latitude of 44° N. The nearby Atlantic Ocean exerts a strong modifying influence, however, and helps to prevent extremes of heat or cold as well as providing an abundant rainfall. Bordeaux nevertheless does not lack warmth and sunshine so that years in which grapes fail to ripen fully are comparatively rare. Indeed, the balance of sun and rain in this province makes it an admirable area for viticulture, a fact amply supported by the wide range of high quality red and white wines produced there.

Several different varieties of grapes are grown for claret production, but the principal cépage planted for this purpose is the Cabernet Sauvignon. This vine is noted for the very high quality of its small sweet deeply coloured grapes, but in common with many other highly esteemed varieties grown across Europe its yields are relatively poor. Moreover, in order to maintain a high standard of quality, both the height of the vines and the number of vines planted per acre are strictly limited by law. The vintage usually commences about mid-September, but may be earlier or later according to the ripeness of the grapes.

Vinification is carried out more or less exactly as described previously, although it is worth noting that in Bordeaux the stalks are traditionally removed prior to the pulp fermentation. The duration of the latter rarely exceeds 6–7 days and is quite often less since sufficient colouring matter can be extracted from Cabernet Sauvignon grapes in a relatively short time. The secondary fermentation is conducted in large oak casks called barriques which hold about 50 gallons of wine. The new wine is racked off its lees as soon as fermentation is complete and thereafter at intervals of approximately four months. Clarets are usually fined at least once during their first year in cask, egg-whites or fresh ox blood commonly being used for this purpose.

New claret is initially matured in cask for two or three years, and during this period a malo-lactic fermentation frequently occurs. It is difficult to determine whether this bacterial fermentation improves the wine produced in good years when its initial acidity is comparatively low, but in poorer years when the wine is slightly more acid there seems little doubt that a limited malo-lactic fermentation proves beneficial. In any case, the bacteria responsible for its occurrence can always be killed by lightly sulphiting the wine before its acidity decreases to too low a level.

After spending a few years in cask, the wine is bottled in green or amber bottles (which prevent photochemical deterioration). Even at this stage the wine is far from being fully mature, for it will continue to improve in bottle for many more years. Indeed, claret is noted for its longevity and may occasionally require as long as forty or fifty years in bottle before reaching its best. Such cases are exceptional, however, for on the average a good quality claret will require some 2–3 years in cask and 5–15 years in bottle to attain full maturity. The exact periods of maturing in cask and bottle to achieve this object cannot be defined more precisely since such factors as weather and soil conditions have an important bearing in this context. Lesser clarets are often ready for drinking before higher quality clarets for these reasons.

Claret is a refined wine, full of expressive yet subtle qualities. Its longevity and much of its delicacy and finesse can be ascribed to its high tannin content which preserves the wine from deterioration and prevents unduly rapid maturing. In this latter connection, it is commonly found that the more rapidly a wine matures the less likely it is to possess depth and expression, and this view seems particularly applicable to clarets and, indeed, to red wines in general. Thus, a claret high in tannin (and acid) matures more slowly than a similar wine better balanced initially, but in the end the former usually proves to be the superior wine.

Claret is one of the driest red wines produced in France, for it contains virtually no unfermented sugar. It is light to medium-full in body with a fairly low alcohol content around 10%–12% by volume. The average acidity of a claret is 3.8 p.p.t., but the exact figure varies from year to year according to weather conditions and may lie anywhere in the range 3.0–4.5 p.p.t. The more acid clarets produced in cooler years contain a relatively higher proportion of malic acid than is normally encountered and are therefore more subject to malo-lactic fermentations.

BURGUNDY

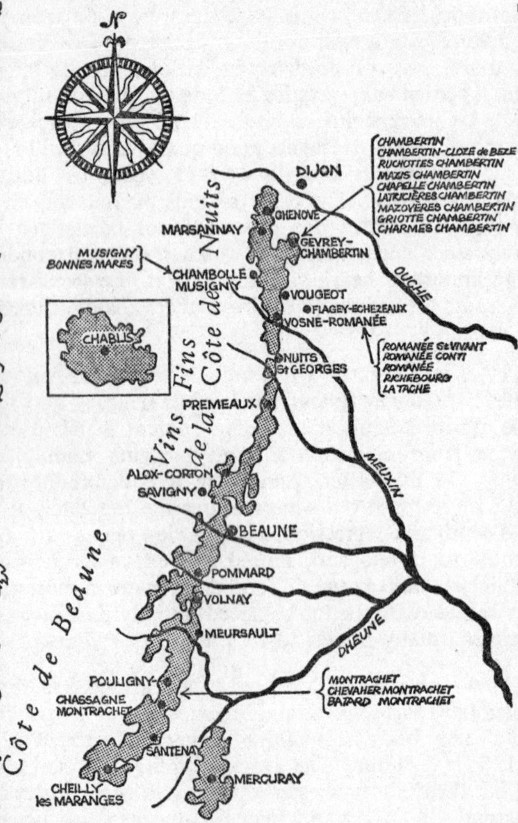
N
DIJON
CHAMBERTIN
CHAMBERTIN-CLOZE de BEZE
RUCHOTTES CHAMBERTIN
MAZIS CHAMBERTIN
CHAPELLE CHAMBERTIN
LATRICIÈRES CHAMBERTIN
MAZOYÈRES CHAMBERTIN
GRIOTTE CHAMBERTIN
CHARMES CHAMBERTIN
CHENOVE
MARSANNAY
GEVREY-CHAMBERTIN
MUSIGNY
BONNES MARES
CHAMBOLLE MUSIGNY
OUCHE
VOUGEOT
FLAGEY-ECHEZEAUX
VOSNE-ROMANÉE
CHABLIS
ROMANÉE St VIVANT
ROMANÉE CONTI
ROMANÉE
RICHEBOURG
LA TACHE
NUITS St GEORGES
Vins Fins de la Côte de Nuits
PREMEAUX
MEUXIN
ALOX-CORTON
SAVIGNY
BEAUNE
Côte de Beaune
POMMARD
VOLNAY
MEURSAULT
DHEUNE
MONTRACHET
CHEVAHER MONTRACHET
BATARD MONTRACHET
POULIGNY-
CHASSAGNE MONTRACHET
SANTENAY
MERCURAY
CHEILLY les MARANGES

BURGUNDY

Red wine from Burgundy also enjoys considerable popularity in Britain. The area in which the wine is produced corresponds quite closely with what was formerly the Duchy of Burgundy. The best red burgundies come from a northern district of the province called the Côte d'Or which comprises a long narrow ridge of hills beginning just south of Dijon and continuing southwards for another 35 miles. The Côte d'Or is itself divided into two sub-districts—the Côte de Nuits to the north and the Côte de Beaune to the south. Still farther to the south lie the important red wine districts of Côte Chalonnaise, Mâconnais and Beaujolais. The latter extends to within a few miles of Lyons, and although it is generally considered to be a district of Burgundy, its wines are so different from other burgundies that some disagreement exists as to whether it should in fact be classified as a burgundy. Some excellent very dry white wines, e.g. Montrachet are also produced in these districts and in Chablis, an isolated northern outpost of Burgundy some 80 miles north-west of the Côte d'Or.

The principal soil type found in the Burgundy vineyards may be described as ferruginous argillaceous gravel, which simply means a mixture of gravel and clay rich in iron. In Beaujolais, on the other hand, the soil is rather different in that it has been formed by weathering of granitic rocks. On the whole, the soils here are very much less variable than in Bordeaux, but their quality is poor so that viticulture is by no means an easy task.

The climate too is less favourable than in Bordeaux. The latitude of the Côte d'Or is about 47° N. and that of Beaujolais in the far south of Burgundy is still only 45° N. The climate of the province is further modified by the nearby Alps which moderate the temperature and promote cooler summers than might otherwise be experienced. Sun and warmth are therefore less abundant in Burgundy so that years in which the grapes fail to ripen fully are not too uncommon.

The most important burgundy grape grown for red wine production is the Pinot Noir. This vine is difficult to cultivate and gives poor yields, but as usual the high quality of its grapes far outweighs these disadvantages. The prolific Gamay vine is planted extensively on the plains around the Côte d'Or, but there it produces an inferior wine fit for sale only as vin ordinaire. For this reason, it is illegal to plant Gamay vines in the better class vineyards of Burgundy, the only notable exceptions to this rule being in Beaujolais where the Gamay reigns supreme. There it produces a very pleasant, light, fruity wine which, for a red wine at any rate, matures quite rapidly. The granitic soil predominant in this region is probably partly responsible for this unexpected and atypical behaviour of the vine. The vintage in Burgundy is usually later than in Bordeaux because the grapes ripen more slowly in the cooler climate, but it commonly takes place between mid-September and mid-October.

Vinification once again follows more or less the same pattern as already described, although it is worth noting that in poorer years when the grapes have failed to ripen fully, chaptalisation, i.e. the addition of sugar (cane-sugar) to the must, may be necessary to ensure that the wine contains sufficient alcohol. Also, in some years, particularly when the vintage has been late, fermentation may be slowed down or even almost terminated by a sudden cold snap. When this occurs, a portion of the must is withdrawn, heated carefully and then returned to the bulk of the must. This procedure certainly permits the temperature of the must to be maintained at a level conducive to continued fermentation, but unless great care is exercised the quality of the wine may suffer. It has also led to allegations that burgundy at times possesses a "cooked" flavour although it is doubtful if there is much truth in this accusation. An early cold spell can nevertheless increase the duration of the pulp fermentation to as long as two weeks instead of the more normal one week, which may in itself lower the quality of the wine for the reasons explained previously.

After the fermentation has proceeded to completion, the new wine is matured in cask for 1–3 years with periodic rackings about every four months. Burgundy requires less bottle ageing than claret due to its lower tannin content, however, so that it usually reaches full maturity some 5–10 years after the vintage. Beaujolais is again an exception since it is normally matured in cask for only about one year and is ready for drinking in most instances within five years of the vintage.

Burgundy is generally a more full-bodied wine than claret, but it must be admitted that exceptions to this rule are relatively common. It is also rarely as dry as a claret and its alcohol content is slightly higher, the usual range being 11%–13% by volume. The average acidity quoted for burgundies is 4.1 p.p.t., but in normal years it may range between 3.5 p.p.t. and 4.8 p.p.t. A significant proportion of malic acid is found in most burgundies, so that malo-lactic fermentations frequently occur during maturing. In this instance, it seems fairly well established that this bacterial action is beneficial to the wine due to the reduction in acidity and mellowing of the wine it promotes.

The appeal of a burgundy is more direct than that of a claret, and for this reason many people at first prefer burgundy to claret. The charms of claret only become apparent once a discerning palate has been cultivated, but then the converse of the above statement tends to hold true. The two wines should nevertheless not be regarded as rivals in the true sense of the word, for each has its place in a meal.

RHONE WINES

The Rhône valley is the only other region of France which produces any significant quantity of top quality red wines. All the best wines from this region come from the Côtes du Rhône which embraces the Rhône valley from Lyons in the north to Avignon in the south. The principal districts producing red wines are, from north to south, Côte Rotie, Crozes, Hermitage, Cornas and Châteauneuf-du-Pape. The Côtes du Rhône is also noted for its white wines and the rosé Tavel.

The soil here varies along the length of the valley. In the north, a continuation of the granite found in Beaujolais predominates and the soils are correspondingly similar. The wines of Hermitage and other northern districts of this region are therefore produced mainly from grapes grown on this type of soil. South of Hermitage the granite is replaced

The RHONE Valley

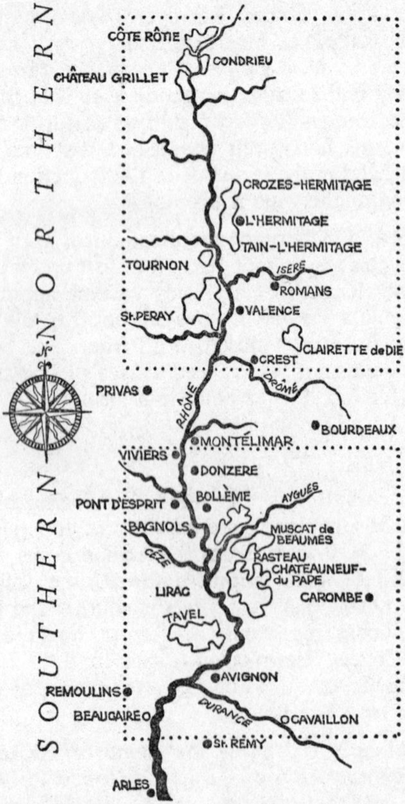

by limestone or alluvial deposits, while still farther to the south, especially around the Tavel vineyards, a siliceous sand comprises the principal soil type.

The climate of the Côtes du Rhône is hot as the name Côte Rotie or "roasted slope" might at once suggest. Indeed, it is rather surprising that such high quality wines as Hermitage and Châteauneuf-du-Pape can be produced in so hot a region, for these vineyards are only a few hundred feet above sea-level so that elevation does not temper the heat to any great extent. Rhône wines are in fact exceptional in this respect, for any other wines of comparable quality grown so far south are almost invariably produced in vineyards located high up on hillsides. Colder winds from the north channelled along the Rhône valley have a slight moderating influence on the temperature, but there is always ample sun and warmth to ripen the grapes so that vintages do not vary greatly.

Numerous different varieties of both red and white grapes are grown here, and in most cases the wines are made from blends of several different cepages. For example, no less than thirteen varieties of grape may be blended to produce Châteauneuf-du-Pape. Some of the more important vines include Syrah, Viognier, Grenache, Rousanne and Marsanne.

Vinification is accomplished in the manner already described. Its only notable feature is that a proportion of white grapes is often included in the red wine must. The new wine is matured in cask for about three years prior to bottling and for another 7–10 years in bottle. Despite the long period of maturing required, however, these wines seem to deteriorate rather rapidly after reaching their best and definite signs of senility are often detectable after about 15 years in bottle.

Rhône wines are much more full-bodied than burgundy or claret, and their alcohol content is correspondingly higher. At least 12½% by volume is normally present in a good Rhône wine, and some of the best crus of Châteauneuf-du-Pape contain more than 15% alcohol by volume. The acidity of these wines is low as might be expected with these climatic conditions, and ranges between 3.0 p.p.t and 3.5 p.p.t. in most instances.

PRODUCTION OF DRY RED WINES

Before commencing a discussion on the practical details of red wine production, it will probably be advantageous to consider first what constitutes the important features of these wines. In the first place, as the title of this chapter implies, dry red wines are primarily table wines which are intended for consumption with a meal. Since the principal object of a table wine is to enhance the enjoyment of the meal (and conversely, of course!), it follows that a dry red wine should be neither too strongly flavoured nor too full-bodied for the food which it accompanies. Wines going too much to the opposite extreme are naturally equally as bad. Remembering that a dry red wine usually partners the main course of a meal, it follows that these wines should on the whole be light to medium-full in body and alcohol, well balanced with respect to acid and tannin, adequately matured so that their flavour is mellow and their colour a deep red without the purple tint of youth or the tawny shade of age and should have a fine but not overpowering bouquet. Thus, the lighter clarets may be said to represent one end of the scale and the fuller-bodied strong Rhône wines the opposite.

How, then, can these requirements best be met in practice? The first problem encountered when making red wines of any description is clearly the selection of a basic ingredient which will provide the necessary colour. The choice here is consequently limited almost entirely to fruits, and in this connection elderberries, sloes, bilberries, damsons, cherries, etc. are all ideal. The dried elderberries and bilberries now on the market are also excellent for this purpose, their relatively high cost being at least partly balanced by the fact that 1 lb. of the dried fruit berries is roughly equivalent to 4–5 lb. of the fresh fruit. Soft fruits such as raspberries, loganberries and to a lesser extent blackcurrants are best avoided when producing dry red wines since these ingredients tend to give wines too fruity in flavour for this purpose. Blackberries are also of little use since wines produced from this fruit rapidly become tawny in colour.

Tannin is another important constituent of red wines, and will be discussed in more detail later. For the practical purposes at present under consideration, it will only be necessary to ascertain that the must is supplied with sufficient tannin from the ingredients. Fortunately, all the fruits recommended above for providing colour are also rich in tannin, so that the same ingredient will supply both of these essential constituents. In actual fact, there is more often than not rather too much tannin in fruits which are suitable insofar as colour is concerned, and the problem is to attain the correct depth of colour in the must without introducing too much tannin. Elderberries are particularly difficult to handle in this respect and can produce very harsh dry red wines requiring prolonged cask maturing unless great care is taken.

The amount of fruit required is therefore dependent upon how much colour it can impart, its tannin content and the type of wine required. Fruits high in tannin, e.g. elderberries and sloes, must be used with caution otherwise an unduly harsh wine may be obtained, so that only about 2½–3 lb. per gallon of these fruits should normally be employed. Larger amounts of high tannin fruits can be used with advantage, but only if the winemaker is prepared to mature the wine in cask for several years until the initial harshness has mellowed. More liberal quantities of other suitable fruits, e.g. cherries, may be employed since their tannin content is generally lower, so that up to 4–5 lb. per gallon can be used. The duration of the pulp fermentation should be kept at a minimum commensurate with good colour extraction to avoid extracting too much tannin from the fruit. The pulp should therefore be carefully strained off immediately an adequate depth of colour has been achieved. In the case of elderberries, the juice is often sufficiently deeply coloured to use alone without the need for a pulp fermentation so that 2½–3 pints elderberry juice can be substituted with advantage for 2½–3 lb. of the fruit, thus avoiding the possibility of extracting excessive amounts of tannin from the pulp.

In addition to colour and tannin, it is also necessary to consider the body, balance and vinous quality of the wine. Body and balance can be improved by including 1–2 lb. of a fruit such as peaches, greengages, plums, etc., but bananas should be avoided unless a full-bodied wine after the style of Rhône wines is desired. Vinous quality can be achieved by the addition of ½–1½ lb. raisins or ½–1 pint grape concentrate (preferably red) per gallon. The inclusion of up to ¼ pint elderflowers per gallon may also be suggested as a means of improving bouquet, but the use of this ingredient is more a matter of personal preference since it is not essential for bouquet development.

Winemakers intending to design their own recipes on the basis of these remarks should be guided by the "model" recipes given at the end of this chapter. It is clear that a balance must be struck between the relative and absolute amounts of each ingredient employed according to the body and character of the wine required. In the case of dry red wines, considerable experience is necessary to judge the optimum quantities of each ingredient for a given type of wine if high quality is to be achieved. Moreover, winemakers should also note that the differences in acidity, alcoholic strength, body and so on of the commercial wines described previously are too small to permit the designing of recipes which will invariably give a wine closely resembling a specific commercial type. The probability of success is certainly increased if the acidity, body and general character of the must are in keeping with those of the prototype commercial wine, but the final outcome is still by no means assured, e.g. a wine intended as a claret may in fact finally resemble a burgundy. Nevertheless, the winemaker can usually be sure of producing an eminently drinkable dry red wine under these conditions, even if it does not turn out quite as was intended, provided the general principles described below are followed.

The ingredients of the must should first be chopped, crushed or stoned (when possible), and any elderberry juice, grape concentrate, yeast nutrients, etc., included in the recipe blended in with the pulp. Sufficient cold or boiling water to cover the pulp with about an inch of water should then be added. Cold water is preferable when dealing with red wine musts, but under these conditions it is advisable to sulphite the must with 50–100 p.p.m. sulphite (1–2 Campden tablets per gallon). An actively fermenting yeast starter may be introduced as soon as the must has cooled to 80°F. if boiling water was employed or after 24 hours if sulphiting was practised. The appropriate yeast for the desired type of wine should be chosen, although the Grey Owl Pommard yeast (strictly a burgundy strain) is excellent for all dry red wines.

The pulp fermentation is best conducted in a plastic pail or similar container which is sufficiently large to allow a clear space of two inches or more above the cap. A protective blanket of carbon dioxide will then form above the must and help to prevent the development of aerobic spoilage organisms. Insects should, of course, be rigorously excluded by means of a tightly fitting lid or a cloth covering the mouth of the container. The pulp fermentation should be continued until sufficient colour has been extracted from the marc. During this time, it is essential to break up the cap at least twice daily to facilitate colour extraction and to minimise the risk of acetification.

The pulp should be carefully strained off as soon as the must achieves a satisfactory depth of colour. This stage is usually reached within 1–5 days according to the amount of colour available in the ingredients and the rate of fermentation. The residual pulp may be leached with water or pressed lightly, but care is then necessary to prevent the introduction of too much pulp debris into the must by this operation. Experienced winemakers can leave the must to settle overnight, after straining off the pulp, and rack it off its deposit the next day to overcome this problem, but this procedure can cause fermentation to stick and should not therefore be attempted by beginners.

The amount of sugar supplied by the ingredients should next be estimated. For this purpose, 1 lb. of raisins is roughly equivalent to ½ lb. sugar and 1 pint of grape concentrate to 1 lb. sugar, but it is more difficult to estimate the figure for other ingredients since their sugar content can vary widely. On the whole, however, the winemaker will not err too greatly by assuming that 10 lb. of fruit is approximately equivalent to 1 lb. sugar. Since the final alcohol content of a dry red wine should be about 10%–12½% by volume, which corresponds to an initial gravity of 70–100, the total sugar requirements of the must will be 1¾–2¼ lb. per gallon. The amount of sugar which has still to be added to the must can thus be calculated by subtracting the weight of sugar supplied by the ingredients from the total weight of sugar required. This quantity of sugar should be made into a strong syrup and added to the must together with sufficient water to dilute it to its final volume after pulp fermentation is complete and the pulp has been strained off.

The acidity of the must should next be adjusted to 3.3–4.7 p.p.t. according to the type of wine required. For general red wines not based on any specific commercial prototype, an acidity of 3.5–4.0 p.p.t. is advisable. These acidity adjustments should preferably be carried out with a mixture containing equal weights of malic and tartaric acids, although a mixture comprising equal weights of citric, malic and tartaric acids may also be employed. It is certainly most inadvisable to omit malic acid, despite its relatively high cost, since this acid can be an important quality factor, especially for red wines whose acidity exceeds about 4.0 p.p.t.

Fermentation should then be allowed to proceed to completion and the wine racked. Thereafter regular racking at intervals of 3–4 months will be necessary, although it is worth noting that the second racking may be required two months or less after the first if a heavy deposit forms. About 50 p.p.m. sulphite (1 campden tablet per gallon) may be added after each racking unless a malo-lactic fermentation is desired. Sulphiting should be delayed under these circumstances until the winemaker judges that this bacterial activity has accomplished its object. A monthly acidity check is advisable during this period to ensure that the acidity of the wine does not decrease to too low a level through the conversion of the dibasic malic acid into the monobasic lactic acid.

Fining may be necessary to effect complete clarification of the wine (or to reduce its tannin content), and for this purpose either egg-whites or a good proprietary fining agent may be used. The value of fining as a means of reducing the tannin content of a wine will be discussed in more detail later, but at present it is worth noting that if a red wine is still very harsh in flavour after spending a year in cask, fining to reduce its tannin content is advisable.

MATURING

A great many amateur winemakers hold the view that their wines mature rapidly and are ready to drink after a few months. Admittedly, this idea is often more or less true for the light-bodied white wines such as elderflower which are commonly produced. On the other hand, fuller-bodied white wines and sweet red wines which can also be consumed with enjoyment within a year of their production are rarely fully mature at this early age and would benefit considerably by a longer period of maturing. In most instances, then, winemakers who drink their wines young do not reap the full benefit of their work.

Dry red wines are rarely pleasant in their youth, however, so that many winemakers accustomed to enjoying young white or sweet red wines are very disappointed when their dry red wines are undrinkable at the same age. The truth of the matter is that these wines may very well turn out to be excellent a few years later. It is therefore extremely important not to pass judgment on a dry red wine too soon since its potentialities may only begin to show after a year.

The reason why all red wines (dry and sweet) can withstand long maturing without deterioration is due largely to their high tannin content. Acid also has a similar but less pronounced effect. Red wines contain on the average about 0.2% tannin, while the figure for white wines is usually below 0.05%. This difference arises because tannin as well as colouring matter is extracted from the marc during the pulp fermentation stage in red wine production. At first, the harsh astringent taste of tannin tends to dominate the flavour of a red wine, but as time passes a certain amount of tannin is lost as a result of oxidation, combination with aldehydes and proteins and other reactions. Fining, as already mentioned, also reduces the tannin content of a red wine because the fining agent, which is usually a protein, forms an insoluble complex with the tannin and consequently precipitates some of the latter. Moreover, the initial harshness normally apparent in any young wine irrespective of its tannin content also becomes less prominent as the wine ages. Hence, this effect together with the reduction in the tannin content and other changes which occur during maturing all serve to improve the flavour of the wine to an almost unbelievable extent. The bouquet too develops much of its delicacy and finesse as the wine matures.

The improvement of a dry red wine during storage is normally a slow process, however, and as already stated the reason why many winemakers so often fail to produce good quality wines of this type is simply because too short a period of maturing is allowed. This problem is less significant in the case of sweet red wines because their sugar content effectively masks much of their initial harshness, but these wines will benefit equally as much as their dry counterparts from longer maturing. A sweet elderberry wine may be enjoyable within a year of its production, but it will be incomparably better some years later. It must also be emphasised that dry red wines are not immortal, for eventually they do reach a peak of perfection beyond which a slow deterioration gradually occurs. The point to note is that full maturity is not attained in a few months but in a few years, and a dry red wine may still be very immature when a white wine of the same age is well past its best.

Winemakers should also bear in mind that dry red wines, more so than any other type, cannot be adequately matured in glass. The chances of producing good quality dry red table wines are in fact rather poor unless cask maturing is contemplated. It is therefore inadvisable to make less than 4½ gallons of a dry red wine at any one time since casks with a smaller capacity permit the entry of too much oxygen and prevent satisfactory maturing of wines other than sherry or madeira due to over-rapid oxidation.

It may be concluded from the preceding remarks that even a fairly light-bodied dry red wine should be matured in cask for at least a year, and that fuller-bodied wines of this type may require up to three years in cask before being ready for bottling. The decision to bottle the wine can only be made with certainty by tasting it regularly during its period in the cask to assess how well it is developing, and a certain amount of experience is necessary before the exact time to bottle the wine can be judged with confidence. The wine must then be bottled in dark bottles (amber or green) to prevent loss of colour and deterioration by photochemical action. A final period of bottle ageing will then be required to bring the wine to its peak of perfection, and at least 12 months but preferably a minimum of 18 months should be allowed for this purpose. Indeed, many dry red wines continue to improve for many years in bottle, and after the initial 12–18 months in bottle their progress may be assessed by tasting one bottle every four months.

Finally, the winemaker must bear in mind that considerable losses due to evaporation are sustained when wine is aged in small casks for a period of several years. Since both water and alcohol are lost but not dissolved solids, such as acids and sugar, the ideal topping up liquid would obviously be vodka diluted with water (1 part vodka, 3 parts water) which would merely replace what has been lost. The present high cost of spirits makes this suggestion rather unrealistic, however, so that an alternative topping up medium must be sought. A low-acid fairly light-bodied dry wine containing about 13%–15% alcohol and roughly 2.5 p.p.t. acid makes a reasonably good substitute provided it has little flavour or character of its own. A dry wine based on white grape concentrate or rhubarb fulfils this purpose very well, but any other dry wine can be used as long as it does not influence the character of the maturing wine. It is in fact a good idea to prepare a gallon of wine solely for topping-up purposes. Such a wine may be stored in glass, heavily sulphited for safe keeping (100 p.p.m. sulphite or 2 campden tablets per gallon every four months), and added directly to an ullaged cask as and when required.

Recipe 1

DRY RED TABLE WINE

Ingredients:

12 lb. elderberries
10 lb. raisins
2 pints red grape conc.
Burgundy or Beaujolais yeast starter
Yeast nutrients
2 lb. sugar
Water to 5 gallons

Method:

Crush the elderberries and strain off the juice. Extract the pulp with ¾ of a gallon of hot water, stir for five minutes, then strain off the pulp. Repeat this treatment twice more, then discard the pulp. Add another 1 gallon of water to the elderberry juice and extracts together with the yeast nutrients and raisins. When cool add the yeast starter. Ferment on the pulp for four–five days then strain off the pulp and press lightly. Add the grape concentrate, sugar and sufficient water to make the volume up to 5 gallons. Stir vigorously to homogenise the must. Check the acidity and adjust it to about 3.8 to 4.0 p.p.t. with chalk or acid mixture A (see Part I) as the case may be.

Fermentation should be allowed to proceed to completion and the wine racked, matured and so on as directed in the text.

Recipe 2

DRY RED TABLE WINE

Ingredients:

30 lb. apples
15 lb. elderberries
4 pints red grape conc.
4 lb. honey
Yeast nutrient
Burgundy yeast starter
Water to 5 gallons

Method:

Press the apples, add 100 p.p.m. sulphite to the juice and leave to settle exactly as described in the white table wine chapter. Crush the elderberries and strain off the juice. Extract the pulp with ½ gallon hot water, stir for five minutes, then strain off the pulp. Repeat this treatment twice more using ½ gallon hot water each time, then discard the pulp. Blend the apple and elderberry juices and extracts, add the yeast nutrients, grape concentrate, honey and yeast starter and make up to 5 gallons with water. Stir thoroughly to ensure a homogenous must. Check the acidity and adjust it to 4.0–4.2 p.p.t.

Thereafter proceed exactly as directed in the preceding recipe.

Recipe 3

DRY RED TABLE WINE

Ingredients:

12 lb. sloes
5 lb. raisins
4 pints red grape conc.
3 lb. honey
Yeast nutrients
Bordeaux yeast starter
Water to 5 gallons
½ oz. Pectozyme

Method:

Pour 4 gallons boiling water over the raisins, honey and crushed (preferably stoned) sloes. When cool, add the pectozyme, yeast nutrients and yeast starter. Ferment on the pulp for two–three days or until a satisfactory depth of colour is achieved then strain off the pulp and press lightly. Add the grape concentrate and dilute to 5 gallons with water. Check the acidity and adjust it to about 3.8 p.p.t.

Thereafter proceed as directed in the first recipe.

Recipe 4

DRY RED TABLE WINE

Ingredients:

15 lb. elderberries
5 lb. raisins
3 lb. bananas
4 pints red grape conc.
2 lb. honey (or 1½ lb. sugar)
Yeast nutrients
Rhône yeast starter
Water to 5 gallons

Method:

Crush the elderberries and strain off the juice. Cut the bananas into slices (discarding the skins) and boil in 1 gallon water for ½ hour. Strain the hot liquor over the elderberry pulp, stir for five minutes then strain off the pulp.

Repeat the treatment of the elderberry pulp twice more with ¾ gallon boiling water each time. Add the raisins, honey and nutrients to the hot liquor. When cool add the yeast starter. Ferment on the pulp for three–four days then strain off the pulp and press lightly. Add the grape concentrate and dilute the must to 5 gallons with water. Check the acidity and adjust it to about 3.3 p.p.t.

Thereafter proceed as directed in the first recipe.

Chapter XXIV

SAUTERNES-TYPE WINES

SAUTERNES is a sweet white wine produced in the Bordeaux region of France. This deep golden yellow wine with its luscious full-bodied flavour and magnificent, almost overpowering, bouquet is considered by many connoisseurs to be the best of its type in the world, and it certainly cannot be denied that a well-chilled Sauternes makes an ideal partner for the dessert course of a meal. The French often drink Sauternes with fish, but elsewhere it is generally considered to be too rich and sweet a wine for this course, particularly if dry red wines follow later in the meal.

The aristocrat of Sauternes is Château d'Yquem, a grand premier cru which costs £2 or more per bottle. Less superb, though nevertheless good quality Sauternes can be bought for 60p and upwards per bottle, but it will become clear later that good Sauternes can never be a cheap wine simply because it is so costly to produce. Spanish Sauternes at about 30p per bottle is very inferior to the genuine French product, although when judged solely on its merits as a wine it is very good value for the money, at least insofar as commercial wines are concerned.

The Sauternes district is situated on the west bank of the river Garonne adjacent to the important Graves region and to the lesser-known minor district of Cerons, and covers an area of some 40 square miles. Five communes or parishes lie within its boundaries, viz. Sauternes, Barsac, Bommes, Fargues and Preignac, but of these only Sauternes and Barsac are universally famous. The climate is very similar to that in Graves and the soils in both regions also share many features in common since throughout Sauternes the soil is principally a gravel underlain by clay. In Barsac, however, the predominant soil is a mixture of limestone and clay beneath which lie beds of limestone, and as a result the wines of this parish differ slightly from those produced in other parts of Sauternes.

The principal grape grown here is the Semillon, a variety noted for its powerful aroma, but the richly perfumed Sauvignon-Blanc is also planted extensively and vineyards of the muscat grape Muscadelle are not altogether uncommon. All these grapes are, of course, white varities. The wine is generally produced from a mixture of Semillon and Sauvignon-Blanc grapes (usually in the ratio of about 2 : 1), but up to 5% Muscadelle grapes are also often included.

Perhaps the most striking and unusual feature in the production of Sauternes is the practice of deliberately exposing the grapes on the vine to the attack of a mould called Botrytis Cinerea which in France is more commonly known as "la pourriture noble" (the noble rot). The growth of this fungus is also encouraged in Hungary and in parts of Germany (where it is called Edelfäule). In these regions its appearance is welcomed, for should Botrytis fail to infect the grapes there, then an inferior wine is generally produced. On the other hand, in Burgundy and certain other wine producing areas (and on other fruit crops) Botrytis is regarded as a serious spoilage organism which can cause a great deal of damage.

What, then, are the reasons why Botrytis Cinerea is so welcome in Sauternes and certain other regions yet elsewhere its presence is greeted with dismay? First of all, it must be pointed out that this fungus will only begin to grow on the grapes under warm humid conditions, but for it to prove beneficial a period of dry sunny weather is needed immediately after the grapes have been attacked. If the weather remains dry and sunny when Botrytis normally first makes its appearance, little or no mould growth occurs, whereas if the desired warm humid weather lasts too long the grapes will be completely spoiled since their skins then split open and allow spoilage organisms to gain entry. Normally, micro-organisms other than Botrytis cannot become established because the skins of the grapes remain whole, for unlike most other moulds Botrytis Cinerea secretes a special enzyme which enables the fungal hyphae to penetrate the undamaged skins of the grapes without causing the berries to disintegrate. It is clear, however, that the successful cultivation of la pourriture noble is an extremely risky business dependent very largely upon suitable weather conditions.

The principal effect of Botrytis Cinerea is to concentrate the sugar content of the juice within the grapes, for the mould abstracts a great deal of water from the berries during its growth. Grapes normally contain 15%–25% sugar, but during a period of infection by Botrytis their sugar content will increase to about 40% and at times to as much as 60%. The mould does in fact utilise some of the sugar in the grapes for its own development, but this loss is quite minor in comparison with the amount of water which is simultaneously removed. A small amount of very sweet juice is thus obtained so that quantity is sacrificed for quality in Sauternes. It is also worth noting at this point that the attachment of the skin to the pulp of the grape is loosened as a result of the shrinkage in the size of the berries which takes place as water is lost. Pressing is thus facilitated.

Apart from showing a greatly enhanced sugar content, grapes infected by Botrytis (often called botrytised grapes) also exhibit a number of other unique features. To begin with, the acid balance and titratable acidity of the juice is altered because the mould absorbs tartaric acid rather than malic acid. Consequently, roughly equal quantities of these two acids are present in the must obtained after pressing the grapes. Moreover, because only a relatively small amount of the acid is lost in this way, the acidity of the juice increases due to the more rapid removal of water by the mould in the same way as its sugar content does. As a result, the average acidity of a Sauternes is 5.2 p.p.t., but due to the large proportion of malic acid and the high sugar content of the finished wine this high acidity does not make it unpalatable in any way.

Another unusual characteristic of botrytised grapes is the presence of about 1% glycerol (glycerine), a substance not normally found in grapes although it is encountered in wines as an important by-product of fermentation. The glycerol content of Sauternes is therefore rather higher than that of wines produced from sound grapes and is usually in the region of 2%–3%. Although the importance of glycerol as a quality factor for Sauternes has not been closely investigated, it seems likely that the abnormally large amounts of glycerol present in these wines have some influence on their flavour and general quality.

The mould also promotes the formation of complex compounds called dextrans (not to be confused with dextrins which are partially degraded starch molecules). Since dextrans can act as protective colloids and stabilise hazes in much the same manner as pectins, Sauternes are often difficult wines to clear and frequently require careful fining. Comparatively large amounts of the enzyme o-polyphenoloxidase are also found in botrytised grapes. This enzyme catalyses a series of oxidation reactions which terminate in the formation of brown products whose colour spoils the appearance of the wine. This enzymic browning or oxidasic casse can be prevented by sulphiting the wine regularly, the sulphite in this case acting in the capacity of an anti-oxidant. Other changes in the composition of grapes infected by Botrytis Cinerea can also be detected, e.g. the juice often contains more gluconic acid and glucuronic acid than usual, but these differences are of minor importance although it is perhaps worth noting that the presence of traces of an antibiotic has recently been reported.

It is therefore clear that the effects of la pourriture noble on the composition of the grapes which it attacks are very far-reaching so that wine produced from botrytised grapes has a unique quality and character of its own. Under suitable weather conditions Botrytis does not spoil the flavour of the wine but rather enhances it. Moreover, the mould also seems to contribute a great deal to the bouquet of the wine since Sauternes produced in poor years when the grapes have only been lightly attacked lacks its customary power and fragrance of bouquet.

The vintage in Sauternes normally takes place in late September or early October, but it is deliberately delayed for as long as possible in order to allow la pourriture noble ample time to complete its work. At this stage, the grapes have a grey withered and unattractive appearance and seem to be covered with a grey dust which in actual fact consists of millions of minute mould spores. Since it is impossible to separate the grapes from the stalks if the complete bunch has been attacked, the bunches are pressed whole immediately after they are picked. In Germany, where the bunches are often incompletely covered by the Edelfäule, discrete groups of berries or even individual grapes which are more heavily infected than their neighbours may be selected for the production of the special Auslese and Beerenauslese wines. In Sauternes, however, such practices are usually necessary only in poor years. The normal procedure is to go over the vineyards several times picking only those bunches which are ready for harvesting on each occasion.

After pressing, the heavy sweet must is heavily sulphited to combat further mould growth, left to settle overnight and racked off its deposit the next day. Settling prior to fermentation is a device which assists the subsequent clarification of a wine by permitting the early removal of much suspended matter from the must, an especially valuable technique here in view of the natural tendency of Sauternes to clear only with difficulty. Fermentation and racking are then carried out in accordance with normal winemaking techniques, the only notable feature being regular sulphiting after each racking to help stabilise the wine and prevent enzymic browning. It is matured in cask for up to four years and requires another few years in bottle to reach maturity.

Fermentation is conducted with the yeast indigenous to the region. Sauternes yeast is rather a peculiar strain of the wine yeast Saccharomyces Ellipsoideus, however, for unlike most strains which ferment glucose more rapidly than fructose, the converse is true of Sauternes yeast. As a result, this yeast ferments more slowly than other strains of Saccharomyces Ellipsoideus, but in view of the fact that a long slow fermentation is an aid to quality this property of Sauternes yeast is probably an asset.

The principal problem in producing a wine after the style of Sauternes is to prepare a must similar in character to the must obtained from botrytised grapes. The successful production of wines of this type therefore depends primarily on the skill with which the ingredients are selected and blended and the must is prepared to meet the basic requirements of body, acidity, colour and so on. Since Sauternes is a very full-bodied, deep golden-yellow wine, it follows that one to two pounds of bananas per gallon form an essential basic ingredient for reasons of body and colour. The inclusion of 1 pint of white grape concentrate or 1½–2 lb. sultanas per gallon is also advisable to give the wine vinous quality. Other ingredients such as yellow plums, greengages, apricots, peaches, ripe gooseberries, parsnips, etc., can then be blended with these basic ingredients so that a total of about 6–10 lb. fruit per gallon is used. Surprisingly enough, the substitution of about half a gallon of young oak leaves for one pound of fruit will help to improve the wine, since for some obscure reason this ingredient seems to lend itself particularly well to the production of a Sauternes-type wine. The extremely powerful and fragrant bouquet of Sauternes can only be adequately matched by including flowers in the recipe and elderflowers (½ pint), mayblossom (2 pints), gorseflower (2 pints) or yellow rose petals (½ pint) are best for this purpose; the quantities in parentheses refer to a gallon of must. Dried flowers make a good substitute if fresh flowers are not readily available. The addition of ⅛ oz. of succinic acid per gallon in place of an equal weight of tartaric acid will also help to improve bouquet.

The acidity of the must should be adjusted to 4.5–5.25 p.p.t. preferably with a mixture containing equal weights of tartaric and malic acids. The fact that botrytised grapes contain about 1% glycerol has already been mentioned so that the addition of 45 mls. (1½ fluid ozs.) glycerol per gallon is recommended. Since a further 1%–2% glycerol will be produced during fermentation, the correct glycerol content of about 2%–3% for Sauternes will thus be achieved. It is also advisable to add about 1/12th oz. tannin per gallon of must to assist clarification and prevent insipidity since most of the ingredients listed above are deficient in tannin (if oak leaves are used, tannin need not be added since this ingredient is relatively rich in tannin).

The average alcoholic strength of Sauternes is about 14% by volume, but this figure varies from year to year and may be as low as 12½% or as high as 17%. The winemaker should aim to get 13%–15% alcohol, however, and little difficulty should be experienced in attaining this figure. The initial gravity of the must may be adjusted directed to 100–115, but alternatively the fermentation may be started at a lower gravity (say 60–80), and the technique of feeding the yeast with small doses of sugar syrup adopted. This latter procedure will, of course, enable the winemaker to produce stronger wines.

Once fermentation has ceased, the wine should be racked off its deposit and sulphited at the rate of 2 Campden tablets (or the equivalent amount of sulphite solution) per gallon, and if necessary its gravity adjusted to 10–25 with sugar syrup or better still with white grape concentrate. Thereafter regular racking and sulphiting (1 Campden tablet or equivalent per gallon) should be carried out to stabilise and clarify the wine and to prevent the development of a malolactic fermentation.

Maturing will undoubtedly prove a problem for many winemakers since in France Sauternes spend 2–4 years in a cask before bottling, and continue to improve in bottle for many more years. Unfortunately, this splendid improvement in Sauternes-type wines can only be successfully brought about by maturing in large cooperage. The small casks (3–9 gallons) commonly used by the amateur winemaker permit the entry of too much oxygen for this purpose, with the result that the fine flavour of the wine can be ruined. A 16-gallon cask (or larger) would suffice, but for smaller quantities of wine it is best to mature in wood for a few months only (say three months, and certainly not longer than six months) and then continue the maturing in glass containers. A racking every 3–4 months (without undue splashing) will then provide the wine with sufficient oxygen for maturing purposes. The wine will continue to improve under these conditions for several years. If maturing in large casks is contemplated, it is advisable to allow the wine at least two years in wood and several more years in bottle for its development.

In conclusion, it may be suggested that the production of Sauternes-type wines from botrytised fruit is worth investigating. Botrytis Cinerea is a common spoilage organism found growing on fruit, particularly gooseberries, in this country and it seems reasonable to assume that such fruit would form an excellent basis for the production of Sauternes. The acidity, sugar content and balance of the must would almost certainly require careful adjustment, and the inclusion of grape concentrate (and possibly a small quantity of bananas) would be advisable, but on the whole the use of botrytised gooseberries as a basic ingredient should enhance the quality of the wine. This idea has not so far been put into practice, however, but an experienced winemaker who grows his own fruit may care to conduct some experiments along these lines. A recipe for a wine produced from botrytised gooseberries has been included at the end of this chapter for this reason.

Recipe 1

SAUTERNES

Ingredients:

40 lb. peaches	**½ oz. Pectozyme**
10 lb. bananas	**Malic acid as required**
4 pts. white grape conc.	**Tartaric acid as required**
3 pts. yellow rose petals	**Yeast nutrients**
225 mls (8 fl. ozs.) Glycerol	**Sauternes yeast starter**
Sugar or honey as required	**Water to 5 gallons**

Method:

Peel the bananas (discarding the skins) and cut into slices. Boil the slices in 1 gallon water for ½ hour then strain off the pulp carefully. Stone the peaches and press the fruit. Sulphite the juice, add the pectozyme and leave to settle overnight together with the banana extract exactly as described in the white table wine chapter. Next day, rack the juice and extract and blend them together with the grape concentrate, glycerol, yeast nutrients, yeast starter and sufficient sugar or honey and water to give 5 gallons of must of gravity approx. 110. Check the acidity and adjust it to 4.5 to 5.25 p.p.t. with equal weights of malic and tartaric acids. After fermentation has been proceeding for about 7 days, add the rose petals. Ferment on the pulp for 3–4 days then strain off the pulp. The yeast should then be fed with ¼ lb. doses of sugar per gallon every time the gravity drops to 5 or less until fermentation finally ceases. Thereafter, the wine should be treated exactly as described in the text.

Recipe 2
SAUTERNES

Ingredients:

20 lb. parsnips
10 lb. bananas
4 pts. white grape conc.
3 pts. elderflowers
225 mls. (8 fl. ozs.) Glycerol
Sugar or honey as required
Malic acid as required
Tartaric acid as required
1 oz. Pectozyme
Yeast nutrients
Sauternes yeast starter
Water to 5 gallons

Method:

Peel the bananas (discarding the skins) and cut into slices. Boil the slices in 1 gallon water for ½ hour then strain off the pulp carefully. Wash the parsnips and cut into chunks. Boil the latter in 2½ gallons water for 10–15 minutes then strain off the pulp and press lightly. Combine the banana and parsnip extracts and leave to settle exactly as described in the white table wine chapter. Next day, rack off the clear liquor and add the grape concentrate, glycerol, pectozyme, yeast nutrients, yeast starter and sufficient sugar or honey and water to give 5 gallons of must of gravity approx. 110.

Thereafter check acidity and so on exactly as described in the preceding recipe.

Experimental Recipe
SAUTERNES

Ingredients:

8 lb. botrytised gooseberries
1 lb. bananas
1 pt. white grape conc.
Honey as required
Tartaric acid as required
½ oz. Pectozyme
Yeast nutrients
Sauternes yeast starter
Water to 1 gallon

Method:

Peel the bananas (discarding the skins) and cut into slices. Boil the slices in 2 pts. water for ½ hour then strain the hot liquor carefully over the crushed gooseberries. Add 100 p.p.m. sulphite. After 24 hours add the pectozyme, yeast nutrients, sufficient water to cover the fruit (if necessary) and the yeast starter. Ferment on the pulp for 2–3 days then strain off the latter and press lightly. Add the grape concentrate, 1 lb. honey and sufficient water to dilute the must to 7½ pints. Check the acidity and adjust it to 5.0–5.2 p.p.t. with tartaric acid. Thereafter feed the yeast with honey (¼ lb. per gallon) every time the gravity drops to 5 or less until fermentation ceases and subsequently proceed as directed in the text.

Note:—This recipe is only for a one-gallon quantity since it is usually advisable to restrict the volume of experimental wines to this relatively small amount. As far as is known at the time of writing, this recipe has not yet been attempted, since in the past good gardeners would in all probability have destroyed botrytised gooseberries as infected fruit.

PW12

CHAMPAGNE

CHAMPAGNE

1. Montagne de Reims
2. Vallée de la Marne
3. La Côte des Blancs
4. Vallée de la Marne et Aisne

CHAPTER XXV

SPARKLING WINES

CHAMPAGNE is the famous white sparkling wine of France which the general consensus of opinion credits as being the invention of a certain Dom Perignon, the cellar master of the Benedictine Abbey of Hautvillers near Rheims during the late 17th and early 18th centuries. The champagne producing district is situated in the north-east of France rather less than 100 miles east of Paris, and is centred around the towns of Rheims and Epernay. The area which is entitled to call its wines "champagne" is very strictly delimited by law and is itself sub-divided into three distinct regions—Montagne de Rheims, Vallée de la Marne and Côte des Blancs—each of which also has its limits closely defined by law. The Côte des Blancs, as the name implies, is so called because mainly white grapes are grown there.

The Champagne region lies further to the north than any other important wine-producing district in France. The climate here is therefore comparatively cool with an average annual temperature of about 50°F., i.e. close to the lower temperature limit for successful viticulture. On the whole, the winter is usually mild and is followed by a rather unpredictable spring in which late frosts are not too uncommon. The summer is fairly hot and the cycle of seasons is generally completed by a fine comparatively cool autumn. Rainfall is also abundant.

The soil here is basically a permeable chalk which is covered and mixed with argillaceous (clay) deposits so that the vineyard soils are often marls very rich in chalk. The light colour of the soil reflects sunlight on the grapes and thus helps ripening, but its poor quality makes it suitable for the growing of few crops other than vines. Drainage is, of course, no problem since the permeable nature of the chalk subsoil does not permit superfluous surface water to accumulate.

The topography of the Champagne region is similar in many ways to that of the English downs, although it is perhaps rather less undulating than the latter. The vines are planted on the slopes of the low hills above the general level of the surrounding plain and usually face towards the south or south-west in order to allow the ripening grapes to receive the maximum amount of sunshine. The elevation of the vineyards, though seldom more than a few hundred feet above that of the immediate neighbourhood, also serves to protect the vines to some extent from the spring frosts common in the valleys.

Although champagne is essentially a white wine, it is nevertheless produced primarily from red grapes (which, of course, do not normally have red juice). The principal grape variety planted here is the famous Burgundy cépage, the Pinot Noir. Another Burgundy grape, the Pinot Blanc or Chardonnay, a white variety, is also grown, but on the average about twice as much Pinot Noir as Pinot Blanc is planted. The vintage takes place between mid-September and mid-October, and nowadays the decision to begin the harvest is often based upon determinations of the acidity and sugar content of the grape juice. During the picking, all unsound and unripe grapes are carefully cut out because such fruit would taint the delicate flavour of the wine were it not removed.

The freshly picked grapes are then transported to large shallow hydraulic presses. The construction of these presses is extremely important, for in the case of red grapes it is essential to separate the colourless juice from the pulp as soon as possible lest any trace of colour from the skins contaminate the must. Pressing is therefore carried out very rapidly and the shallow presses not only facilitate rapid pressing but also ensure that the expressed juice can escape easily and quickly from the pulp.

The amount of juice which can be extracted per ton of grapes and converted into Champagne is also strictly limited by law. The normal load per press is 4,000 kg. (about 4 tons) and from this weight of grapes only 2,600 litres (about 600 gallons) of juice can be used for Champagne production. Thirteen 200-litre casks are therefore obtained per 4,000 kg.

of grapes. The first ten casks are known as the vin de cuvée and go for the production of the finest wines, while the remaining three are called the tailles and are used to make lesser quality sparkling wines. Any other juice obtained from the grapes constitutes the rebêche, which is converted into still wine for sale as vin ordinaire.

The must is fermented at a temperature of 64°F. to 68°F., and after the first violent primary fermentation has abated a few weeks later the new wine is racked off its lees. A slow secondary fermentation subsequently occurs and continues for another two or three months, at the end of which the wine is dry. Clarification is then hastened by opening all the doors and windows of the cellars, and the resultant drop in temperature not only causes settling of the yeasts and other suspended matter but also serves to precipitate excess cream of tartar. The wine is again racked off its lees and at this stage acid and/or tannin, more commonly the latter, may be added.

In the spring, all the casks of new wine from the same vineyard are thoroughly blended in large vats specially constructed for this purpose, so that a homogenous wine from each vineyard is obtained. After a brief resting period in cask, the highly-skilled task of blending the wines from different vineyards begins under the supervision of a panel of experienced tasters. These wines are blended together in such a way that the bouquet and flavour of the wine are as nearly as possible identical with that of previous blends, and some older high-quality wines from earlier vintages specially reserved for blending purposes may be included to improve the overall quality of the new blend. The difficulty of this task may be appreciated from the fact that the tasters must succeed in producing a blend of wines whose final quality remains uniformly high from year to year *before* the second stage of bottle fermentation described below is even begun. In other words, the tasters must not only assess the present quality of the blend but they must also judge what its quality will be several years hence and after another fermentation in bottle, during which time the character of the wine will alter considerably.

The final blend of wines selected by the tasters is called the cuvée and the actual physical operation of blending these wines, which is carried out in enormous specially designed vats, may take several days to complete since mixing must be continued until an absolutely homogenous wine is obtained. At this stage, the cuvée is dry, or nearly so, with an alcohol content of about 11% by volume, and an acidity around 5 parts per thousand (expressed in terms of sulphuric acid), i.e. rather higher than that of similar still white wines. Moreover, it is not yet a sparkling wine for the gas which is responsible for the sparkle has still to be generated by inducing another controlled fermentation to occur in bottle.

Fining is also often necessary to ensure a brilliantly clear wine and usually isinglass is employed for this purpose, although in stubborn cases more drastic treatment with gelatine and tannin may be required.

The sugar content of the cuvée is first carefully checked so that allowance can be made for any residual sugar in the wine when calculating how much sugar must be added to produce the desired pressure of carbon dioxide in the bottle. Since about 0.4% sugar in the wine will give a pressure of 1 atmosphere (about 14 lb. per sq. in.) on complete fermentation, and the usual gas pressure in Champagne is about 5–6 atmospheres (70 to 90 p.s.i.), it follows that approximately 24 grams of sugar per litre (just under 4 oz. per gallon) must be present in the wine prior to its fermentation in bottle to achieve this result. The required amount of sugar is added to the wine in the form of a strong syrup prepared by dissolving pure cane sugar in old sound wine, and at the same time a special cultured yeast which is insensitive to carbon dioxide and forms a compact granular deposit is introduced. The sugar syrup and yeast culture may either be blended in with the cuvée or added in carefully regulated doses to the individual bottles when the wine is bottled, but the latter procedure is now rarely employed.

The cuvée is bottled in thick strong green bottles which will simultaneously withstand the internal pressures subsequently developed and protect the wine from photochemical deterioration during maturing. These bottles were formerly sealed temporarily with a cork which was held in place by means of a special adjustable metal clamp called an agrafe, but nowadays crown caps are becoming more popular for this purpose, mainly for reasons of cheapness and convenience. The bottles are then stored horizontally in racks in the cellars (underground caves in the chalk) at a temperature of 50°F., and under these conditions a slow but steady fermentation in bottle takes place.

At least three months generally elapses before this bottle fermentation is complete, and during this time the yeast converts the sugar added to the cuvée into alcohol and carbon dioxide. The latter is, of course, unable to escape so that a pressure of gas gradually builds up in the bottle until the supply of sugar in the wine becomes exhausted. Simultaneously, a small deposit of yeast is formed. The French wine laws stipulate that all Champagnes must be matured for at least one year on this yeast deposit (for vintage Champagnes the period is three years), but in practice the shippers find it more advantageous to do so for some time beyond this legal minimum. During this period, yeast autolysis occurs and decomposition products from the autolysing cells, notably amino acids, are released into the wine with beneficial effects on its bouquet and flavour. Most normal wines would, of course, be spoiled by such prolonged contact with an autolysing yeast deposit, but the special properties for which the yeast is cultured and the abnormal conditions under which autolysis occurs ensure that the converse is true in Champagne production. In the passing, it may be noted that sherry is another type of wine which benefits by prolonged contact with autolysing yeast, but here again a special yeast is used and a rather unusual system of maturing is practised.

Once the wine has been matured for some years in bottle on its yeast sediment, the latter must be removed for the sake of both quality and appearance. The bottles are therefore placed neck downwards at an angle of about 45° in the oval holes of special racks called pupitres so that the yeast deposit will settle on the cork. The holes in the pupitres are so carved that a bottle is held steady at almost any angle of inclination. To facilitate settling the bottles undergo a unique shaking operation to which the name remuage has been given. Each day a highly-skilled operator known as the remueur takes the bottle by its base, gives it a sharp twist to the left and then a sharp twist to the right (or vice versa) and finally drops the bottle back into position one-eighth of a turn round from its former location. Remueurs work with both hands, and in one day an experienced man can work through the staggering total of 30,000 bottles! During the remuage, the bottles are also raised towards the vertical by an almost imperceptible amount each day until at the end of two or three months of this treatment the bottles are all completely vertical or sur les pointes, and all the sediment is resting firmly on the cork. Some considerable skill is required to persuade both the fine and coarse particles in the sediment to settle together on the cork as a single compact layer, but the remueurs succeed in achieving this object with deceptive ease. Although bottle breakage is nowadays a relatively infrequent occurrence, a small proportion of bottles are unable to withstand the internal pressure for one reason or another so that the remueur wears a special face shield and gloves for protection from flying glass.

After the yeast has been shaken down on the cork, the next problem is to remove the sediment without releasing the gas pressure within the bottle. This stage in Champagne production is called dégorgement. The bottle is first cooled to reduce its internal pressure to a manageable level. A highly-skilled worker known as a dégorgeur then carefully removes the agrafe or crown cap with the neck of the bottle pointing downwards at an angle into an empty barrel or box so that the cork flies out and a small amount of wine which contains the sediment is ejected. A split second later, the dégorgeur places his thumb over the mouth of the bottle to prevent further loss of wine or pressure and returns the bottle to an upright position. Any yeast still adhering within the mouth of the bottle is carefully wiped off with a finger and finally the dégorgeur sniffs the wine to check its soundness before inserting a temporary cork. Within recent years, however, the task of dégorgement has been simplified to some extent by freezing the wine in the neck of the bottle for about an inch above the cork so that the sediment is enclosed within a plug of ice. When the agrafe or crown cap is removed, this plug of ice is ejected so that the sediment is removed quickly and cleanly with no risk of its floating back into the wine should the dégorgeur make a mistake.

At this point, the Champagne is dry and the bottles are slightly ullaged because a small amount of wine is inevitably lost with the yeast sediment ejected during dégorgement. The wine is therefore sweetened and the ullage in the bottles made good by the addition of a special mixture of cane sugar, old wine and brandy called liqueur d'expédition. The amount of the latter added to each bottle is termed the dosage and the sweetness of the dosage is determined by the type of Champagne which is being produced. Thus, brut or nature Champagnes are dry or nearly so and receive little or no sugar in the dosage, extra-sec Champagnes are slightly sweet and receive a small amount of sugar while sec and demi-sec Champagnes are medium-sweet and sweet respectively and dosed more liberally with sugar. The dosage is nowadays added by a special machine which then corks the bottles with special thick corks held in place by wire ties. Finally, the Champagne is matured with the bottles in a horizontal position (to keep the corks moist) for at least six months prior to shipment so that the wine has a chance to recover from these operations.

Champagne is sold both as a vintage and a non-vintage wine, but the former is only produced in outstanding years and even then just a small proportion of the best wine is reserved for this purpose, the remainder being required to maintain the quality of the non-vintage Champagnes. Although vintage Champagne is, of course, the product of a single year, it is nevertheless still a blended wine, but in this case the cuvée is prepared by blending the wines produced in different vineyards solely in the year of its origin and no older "blending wines" are included in its formulation. Small amounts of pink Champagne are also produced, but it is more a novelty wine which is of minor commercial importance. Blanc de blancs Champagne is made solely from white grapes.

Although Champagne is the only important French wine district which produces more sparkling than still wine, sparkling wines are also made in most other regions of France and indeed in most other countries of the world where the wine industry has its roots. In France, however, it is illegal to call a wine Champagne unless it has been produced within the delimited region of that name, and all wines produced outside these boundaries must be called Vin Mousseux. This description must therefore be applied to the pleasant sparkling wines produced in the districts of Vouvray and Saumur on the Loire and to the sparkling red, rosé and white wines from Rully, Beaune and Savigny in Burgundy. German sparkling wine is known as Sekt or Schaumwein and is often produced from the same grapes as Champagne, although large amounts of sparkling Hock, Mosel, and fruit wines are also made. The sweet Asti Spumante of Italy made from muscat grapes is also a well-known wine of this type.

It is clear from the preceding description of Champagne production that a great deal of care and attention by highly-skilled and hence highly-paid labour is required before the wine is ready for shipment. As a result, Champagne whose sparkle is introduced by bottle fermentation must inevitably be an expensive wine, and its sales are thus limited to some extent for this reason.

An alternative method for producing sparkling wine which is known as the tank or Charmat process was therefore developed in an effort to produce a cheaper wine of this type. Nowadays, a great deal of sparkling wine is made by tank fermentation for economic reasons and the well-known Asti Spumante of Italy is a good example of the high quality which can be achieved by this method. The principal advantage of the Charmat process is that the stages of remuage and dégorgement are eliminated, thus effecting a considerable reduction in labour costs. The cuvée is prepared exactly as described earlier and the amount of cane sugar required to produce the desired pressure of carbon dioxide is next added. The wine is then transferred to a closed enamelled stainless steel tank fitted with safety valves and inoculated with actively fermenting starter of special cultured yeast.

Fermentation proceeds comparatively rapidly under these conditions and is generally complete within two or three weeks, although its duration does vary to some extent according to the temperature. In the original Charmat process a temperature of 75°F. was recommended, but later studies have shown that better quality wines are obtained if fermentation is conducted at about 50°F. to 55°F. The gas pressure generated during this time usually reaches 5 to 6 atmospheres, but the amount of sugar added to the cuvée is less critical when the Charmat process is employed than for bottle fermentation, since in the former case excess pressure can be released by means of the safety valves fitted to the tank.

Once fermentation has ceased, the wine is cooled to about 36°F. to facilitate clarification and as soon as the bulk of the yeast has settled the clear wine is transferred to another tank. Excess tartrates are then removed by chilling the wine to a temperature just above its freezing point (about 25°F.) for some days. Finally, the wine is filtered under an isobarometric pressure of nitrogen to remove suspended yeast cells and tartrate crystals and bottled by special machines which both apply the corks and wire them in place. The dosage is usually added to the tank and mixed thoroughly with the wine just prior to filtering and bottling.

Sparkling wine produced by the Charmat process also differs from that produced by bottle fermentation in the length of the time which it spends in contact with the yeast sediment formed during fermentation. A thick deposit of yeast settles to the bottom of the tank in the Charmat process, but due to its depth strongly reducing conditions which could easily prove detrimental to the quality of the wine are established, e.g. hydrogen sulphide may be produced by the reduction of sulphur-containing compounds, notably sulphite. The wine must therefore be racked off its yeast sediment without delay to avoid spoilage of this nature. Since Champagne owes much of its unique bouquet and flavour to prolonged contact between the wine and an autolysing yeast deposit, however, tank-fermented sparkling wines normally lack some of the finesse of Champagne simply because this stage of maturing must of necessity be omitted. Admittedly, recent studies have indicated that the amino acid content of tank-fermented wine can be markedly increased by agitating the wine for a short time immediately after fermentation has ceased by means of high-speed stirring equipment installed in the tank, but even with the improvement in quality resulting from this treatment, the wine still falls short of the bottle-matured product.

A method of producing sparkling wines which combines the best aspects of both the Charmat process and bottle fermentation and maturing was developed in Germany and is known as the transfer system. Fermentation and maturing take place in bottles, but to avoid the costly and difficult stages of remuage and dégorgement the bottles are chilled to about 32°F. and their contents emptied into a stainless steel tank pressurised with nitrogen. A special piece of equipment permits the bottles to be emptied into the tank with a minimum loss of wine or pressure. Clarification and bottling are then carried out exactly as described for the Charmat process. It is interesting to note that the transfer system enables wines of different ages and character to be blended after bottle fermentation and maturing is complete, i.e. at a very late stage in the production of the wine when blending could not be practised if the normal finishing stages of remuage and dégorgement were followed.

It is also possible to produce sparkling wines by carbonation, i.e. by artificially impregnating still wines with carbon dioxide. The best wines of this type would appear to result when the wine is slowly carbonated in bulk at a temperature near its freezing point (about 25°F.), and better gas retention is achieved by de-aerating the wine under a slight vacuum prior to its impregnation with carbon dioxide. Bottling must be carried out at low temperatures to minimise frothing. Carbonation can also be carried out with equipment of the type used for soda water production but this procedure is less satisfactory than that already described. It is also worth noting that carbonated wines tend to throw a deposit on storage.

Many commercial wines are found to be slightly sparkling because of malo-lactic fermentation caused by certain types of lactic acid bacteria which convert malic acid into lactic acid and carbon dioxide. Such wines do not sparkle to the same extent as Champagne, but their "prickly" taste and the appearance of small gas bubbles clinging to the sides of the glass both confirm the presence of small amounts of carbon dioxide. The term "petillant" or "spritzig" is used to describe wines of this type. Some of the more acid table wines of Italy, Portugal, Switzerland, Germany and France quite commonly have a slight sparkle as a result of malo-lactic fermentation in bottle and in certain cases, e.g. the Vinho Verde and Matéus Rosé of Portugal, the wine is expected to possess this quality as an integral part of its character.

It is interesting to compare the sparkle of wines produced by bottle fermentation, the Charmat process and carbonation. Carbonated wines quickly lose their sparklein a glass while tank-fermented wines do not effervesce for as long as bottle-fermented wines, although the former are considerably superior to carbonated wines in this respect. The explanation most commonly advanced to explain these differences is that when the carbon dioxide responsible for the sparkle is generated by fermentation in bottle, it becomes chemically combined with the alcohol to form the unstable compound ethyl pyrocarbonate. When the bottle is opened, the gas is released comparatively slowly because this ethyl pyrocarbonate does not all decompose into carbon dioxide and alcohol immediately. Its rate of decomposition therefore governs the rate at which gas is released. Similar remarks apply to tank-fermented wines except that under the conditions of the Charmat process less ethyl pyrocarbonate is formed, so that a higher proportion of the gas is lost soon after the bottle is opened. In the case of carbonated wines, however, the gas is merely dissolved for no significant amounts of ethyl pyrocarbonate are formed by impregnating a still wine with carbon dioxide. No chemical forces therefore operate to control the rate at which gas comes out of solution with the result that carbonated wines effervesce vigorously at first but quickly lose their sparkle.

Champagne is probably the most widely-imitated wine in the world. It is rarely possible to produce a sparkling wine indistinguishable from Champagne in other wine districts because the conditions under which the grapes are grown and the wine is fermented and matured differ from region to region, and these variations are reflected in the character of the wine. Many sparkling wines other than Champagne nevertheless reach a high standard of quality so that amateur winemakers should not find undue difficulty in making pleasant sparkling wines provided sufficient care and attention is given to their production. Indeed, the fact that sparkling fruit wines are made commercially in Germany may encourage the winemaker to attempt their production.

What, then, are the principal characteristics of Champagne and sparkling wines in general? To begin with, the bouquet and flavour must be very well-balanced, for the slightest imperfection in a sparkling wine is at once obvious. The wine itself should be neither too light nor too heavy in body but medium-bodied in harmony with the alcohol content which is usually about 10% to 12% by volume. The acidity of sparkling wines is normally rather higher than that of most still white wines, and a fair proportion of malic acid is present in Champagne because in the cool climate of this northern region of France the grapes tend to contain rather less sugar and more acid (especially malic acid) than grapes grown farther to the south. An acid content of at least 4.0 p.p.t. (expressed in terms of sulphuric acid) is therefore required and the presence of a certain amount of malic acid in the wine is advisable. Champagne itself is generally a very pale yellow in colour, but other sparkling wines are often more deeply coloured so that no limitations need be imposed in this respect.

Since amateur winemakers would obviously be unable to produce sparkling wines by the Charmat process, it follows that the carbon dioxide responsible for the sparkle must be generated by bottle fermentation. Little difficulty is likely to be encountered in inducing a fermentation in bottle and the danger of bottle breakage should be slight provided suitable bottles are employed and too great a pressure is not generated. The latter is, of course, determined by the amount of sugar present in the wine just prior to bottling and is therefore readily controlled by the winemaker. Unfortunately, the stages of remuage and dégorgement cannot be avoided unless the sediment is left in the bottles, but with practice the winemaker should be able to accomplish these tasks with a reasonable degree of success, particularly if the directions given later are followed.

Although almost any ingredients can be used for the production of sparkling wines, a few fruits seem to be particularly well-suited for this purpose, e.g. green gooseberries, apples (Bramley Seedlings or cider or crab varieties), pears (cooking or perry varieties). Honey and white grape concentrate are also eminently suitable. The inclusion of flowers to improve bouquet will further help to improve the quality of the wine. It is generally advisable to blend these ingredients unless cider apples or perry pears are available, and the inclusion of half to one pound of sultanas or one pint of white grape concentrate per gallon of must is equally necessary to provide body and vinous quality. Several different blends of the same ingredients should be made so that a range of wines similar but slightly different in character is available for the preparation of the cuvée, and some recipes are given at the end of this chapter for guidance. It is important to note that only the best fruit should be used for sparkling wine production, and all unsound or otherwise unsuitable fruit should be discarded since its inclusion would spoil the delicate flavour of the wine.

A short period of pulp fermentation will usually be necessary when dealing with sultanas and gooseberries, but in the case of apple it is preferable to press out the juice. Unfortunately, many winemakers do not possess equipment which is capable of extracting the juice from apples so that pulp fermentation is again generally required for this fruit. A juice fermentation is essential with pears otherwise a poor quality wine is obtained.

The duration of the pulp fermentation should not exceed 3–4 days or else the wine may prove difficult to clear and its flavour is apt to be coarse. The must may be lightly sulphited prior to inoculating with the yeast starter and should, of course, be stirred at least twice daily during the pulp fermentation to disintegrate the cap.

In view of the fact that pulp fermentation is generally required, it is difficult to estimate how much sugar will be provided by the ingredients, but normally it will be sufficiently accurate to add 1½ lb. of sugar per gallon if the recipe does not include grape concentrate and 1 lb. of sugar per gallon if 1 pint of grape concentrate per gallon is employed, unless an ingredient particularly rich in sugar is used. All the sugar may be added during the preparation of the must. It is advantageous to use honey instead of sugar for the preparation of some of the wines which will constitute the cuvée, and in this connection 2 lb. of honey may be taken as roughly equivalent to 1½ lb. sugar. A mildly flavoured honey should be chosen and it should be sterilised by boiling with water or, preferably, by sulphiting before being added to the must.

Fermentation should be conducted with a Champagne yeast preferably at a temperature of 65° to 70°F. and after 3–4 days the pulp should be completely strained off. The must should then be diluted to its final volume with water and its acidity adjusted to about 4.0 to 4.5 p.p.t. with a mixture containing equal weights of tartaric and malic acids. Once fermentation ceases, the wine should be racked off its lees and stored in cool surroundings (50°–55°F.). Subsequent rackings should be carried out every two months but the wine should preferably not be sulphited after racking in case bottle fermentation is later retarded by residual sulphite. If the new wine is still hazy some 6–9 months after the first racking, it will require fining and a reliable proprietary fining agent should be used for this purpose. At this stage, the wine should be brilliantly clear, dry and stable.

The cuvée can then be prepared by blending a number of wines in such a way that a well-balanced bouquet and flavour are achieved. The inclusion of a little banana and elder-flower wines, especially the latter, in the cuvée to give body and bouquet respectively is often worthwhile and these wines may be regarded in much the same light as the blending wines held in reserve by the Champagne shippers for the same purpose. Such wines should, of course, not increase the alcohol content of the cuvée above 10%–11% by volume for the reasons mentioned earlier. Proficiency at blending only comes with experience, however, so that the winemaker may at first find some difficulty in deciding which blend is best.

Once the cuvée has been prepared, its sugar content should be checked by means of a Clinitest kit (sold by Boots for 50p). No more than 1% sugar (and preferably less) should be detected by this test, otherwise the cuvée must be blended with dry wine until a sugar content of 1% or less is reached. The sugar content of the cuvée should next be adjusted to about 1½% by means of a strong solution of sugar syrup (gravity 150 syrup prepared by dissolving 1 lb. of sugar in 1½ pints of water is suitable). The amount of sugar which must be added to the cuvée obviously depends upon its initial sugar content as determined by the clinitest kit, but for convenience the approximate weight of sugar and volume of gravity 150 syrup required per gallon for wines of different initial sugar contents is given in the accompanying table.

Sugar content of cuvée (%)	*Weight of sugar required in ozs./gall.*	*Vol. of gravity* 150 *syrup required in fluid oz. per gall.*
0.0	2½	6
0.25	2	5
0.5	1½	4
0.75	1¼	3
1.0	¾	2
1.25	½	1

It will be noted that the weight of sugar recommended is only about half of that used in commercial practice so that a gas pressure of only about 3½ atmospheres (50 lb. per sq. in.) will be achieved. This lower gas pressure means that bottle breakage is unlikely to occur and that dégorgement will prove less tricky and dangerous. Amateur winemakers are strongly advised not to exceed a pressure of 3–4 atmospheres at the most for these reasons.

After mixing the requisite amount of sugar syrup thoroughly with the cuvée, a little yeast nutrient and actively fermenting Champagne yeast culture should be added. The wine should then be bottled in Champagne bottles or similar containers to within no more than one and a half inches of the top and the corks wired into place. Screw top bottles can be used for this purpose but prove rather inconvenient if dégorgement is intended. If the sediment is going to be left in the bottle, however, screw top beer or cider bottles are ideal. The bottles should then be stored horizontally (to keep the corks moist) preferably at a temperature of about 50°F to allow fermentation to proceed. Bottle fermentation should be complete within two or three months, and the wine should then be left undisturbed for at least nine months, but preferably for *at least* a year. With screw-top bottles, the bottles can be stored upright so that a firm deposit of yeast will settle at the bottom. Much of the wine can thus be poured out without disturbing the sediment when the bottle is opened.

Once the wine has matured for at least 9 months on the yeast sediment, the difficult task of removing the latter must be tackled unless the winemaker is content to leave it in the bottle. Remuage should not prove too difficult although the winemaker will obviously not be able to coax the yeast to settle on the cork with the same ease as a professional remueur. Nevertheless, with daily twisting and shaking a firm deposit of yeast will eventually form on the cork to leave a brilliantly clear wine above. The use of a Champagne yeast which settles as a heavy granular deposit is virtually essential otherwise remuage is likely to be difficult, and for the same reason brilliantly clear wines must be used to prepare the cuvée.

Most winemakers will find that dégorgement is the most tricky operation in sparkling wine production, and to avoid undue loss of wine at this stage inexperienced winemakers would do well to practise for a time with small bottles of soda water which are cheap and expendable. Only after the technique of dégorgement has been mastered with a soda water bottle is it advisable to begin dealing with bottles of sparkling wine. The bottles should be stood upside down in a bucket of ice for at least half an hour to reduce their internal pressure and then the necks (for about one inch above the cork) placed in a container filled with a freezing mixture such as ice and calcium chloride, ice and salt or dry ice (solid carbon dioxide) and methylated spirits. A plug of ice will quickly form in the neck of the bottle and enclose the sediment so that the latter will be ejected cleanly when the cork is removed.

Holding the bottle in the left hand pointing downwards at an angle into a box or similar empty container, the winemaker should then carefully ease out the cork. Immediately the plug of ice has been ejected, the winemaker should place his thumb over the mouth of the bottle to prevent further loss of wine or pressure and return the bottle to an upright position. The dosage of sugar syrup and brandy is then added carefully by pouring it down the neck of the bottle and finally a new cork is inserted and wired into place. It is also worth noting that the whole bottle of wine may be chilled to just above its freezing point before attempting the dégorgement. Some winemakers find this procedure simplifies matters, although the sediment must sometimes be scraped out of the bottle since insufficient pressure to eject the yeast may then remain. The winemaker should therefore choose whichever procedure is more convenient. The newly clarified sparkling wine should be stored horizontally for another few months before drinking to allow it to recover from hese operations.

Since much of the character of a sparkling wine is determined by the dosage of liqueur d'expédition which is added immediately after dégorgement, winemakers should give some thought to this aspect of their production. A suitable liqueur d'expédition can be made by mixing equal volumes of brandy and gravity 300 sugar syrup (prepared by dissolving 2lb. of sugar in 1 pint of water), one fluid ounce of which per bottle will give a medium-sweet wine. The proportions of sugar syrup and brandy in this mixture can, of course, be altered as desired to give a drier or sweeter sparkling wine according to the personal preference of the winemaker.

Many winemakers are unwilling to attempt the production of sparkling wines because of the risk of bottle breakage and because it is admittedly not an easy task to remove the yeast sediment after bottle fermentation and maturing are complete. The latter problem can be overcome simply by leaving the yeast sediment in the bottle, but this solution is psychologically rather unsatisfactory and the appearance of the wine is, of course, spoiled should the sediment be disturbed when the bottle is opened. Alternative procedures by which sparkling wines can be made without involving remuage and dégorgement are therefore of great interest to the amateur winemaker.

Perhaps the most obvious alternative method of producing sparkling wines is the carbonation of still wine, and articles have appeared in "The Amateur Winemaker" magazine describing a relatively simple and safe procedure by which carbonation can be accomplished without elaborate equipment. In view of the fact that commercial carbonated wines are rarely noted for their quality, however, it would not be appropriate to advise amateur winemakers to produce sparkling wine in this manner. A detailed discussion on the practical aspects of carbonating still wines has thus been omitted for this reason.

The malo-lactic fermentation can also be utilised for producing sparkling wines, but in all fairness it should be pointed out that this procedure gives less reliable results than bottle fermentation by yeast and that a maximum gas pressure of only about 1 atmosphere (15 lb. per sq. in.) can be achieved. The success of this method depends upon the ability of certain species of lactic acid bacteria to convert malic acid into lactic acid and carbon dioxide and on the fact that little or no sediment is formed during this bacterial fermentation. The reaction promoted by these bacteria can be summarised in the following chemical equation from which it can be calculated that 134 grams of malic acid should yield 90 grams of lactic acid and 44 grams of carbon dioxide. Moreover, because lactic acid is a monobasic acid whereas malic acid is a dibasic acid, the acidity of the wine will decrease as the reaction proceeds, until eventually the acidity will only be one half of its former value when all the malic acid has been converted into lactic acid.

$$\begin{array}{lcl} CH_2\,COOH & & CH_3 \\ | & \text{lactic acid} & | \\ CHOH & \xrightarrow{\hspace{3em}} & CHOH + CO_2 \\ | & \text{bacteria} & | \\ COOH & & COOH \\ & & \\ \text{Malic} & & \text{Lactic} + \text{Carbon} \\ \text{acid} & & \text{acid} \quad\quad \text{dioxide} \end{array}$$

What, then, are the conditions under which a malo-lactic ferment takes place? To begin with, no sulphite should be used at any time during the production of the wine since the bacteria responsible are very sensitive to sulphite. The alcohol content of the wine should also be low (less than 11% by volume) and the *pH above* 3.0, otherwise bacterial growth may not occur. Finally, a good supply of malic acid and warm surroundings are essential. The addition of small amounts of nutrients is also advisable.

Since the gas pressure generated by a malo-lactic ferment depends upon how much malic acid is present in the wine, the must should preferably be prepared from ingredients naturally low in acid, e.g. white grape concentrate, honey, so that larger amounts of malic acid can be added, and only a small proportion of the acid in the wine consists of other acids. The acidity of the must should be adjusted to about 5 p.p.t. with malic acid and fermentation and clarification should be carried out exactly as described previously. It is important to have a dry wine for this purpose, however, for the lactic acid bacteria will attack sugar as well as malic acid, and if sugar is present by-products harmful to the flavour of the wine will be formed. A cuvée may be prepared by blending several different wines of this type but no sugar should be added prior to bottling. Instead its acidity should be adjusted to about 8 p.p.t. with malic acid.

The wine may then be bottled in Champagne bottles and the corks wired into place (or in screw-top bottles) and stood in warm surroundings at about 65°F. in the hope that lactic acid bacteria will become active. The chances of success are considerable greater if a small amount of a wine already undergoing a malo-lactic fermentation is added to the cuvée just prior to bottling, but even then the bacteria are so unpredictable that a few bottles will still fail to become sparkling. Provided conditions suitable for the growth of the bacteria are maintained, however, a good proportion of the bottles will become sparkling within about two years, and if all the malic acid has been converted into lactic acid the wine should possess gas pressure of about 1 atmosphere and an acidity of about 4–5 p.p.t., while little or no deposit should be formed in the bottle.

NOTES ON SPARKLING WINE RECIPES

All the recipes in this chapter are for 1-gallon quantities since no more than a few gallons of wine are likely to be prepared for bottling at any one time and several different wines will be blended to form the cuvée. There is nevertheless no reason why a recipe should not be scaled up should this prove desirable. Although most of the following recipes will normally produce well-balanced wines which could be converted directly into a sparkling wine without further ado, it is generally advisable to prepare a cuvée by blending several such wines. In addition, should more body and/or bouquet be required, some banana and/or flower wine may be included in the cuvée provided the alcohol content of the latter is not increased unduly in this way. Other "blending wines" may also be employed to add character to the cuvée subject to the same conditions.

Pink sparkling wines can be produced by including the appropriate amount of red wine in the cuvée. Red sparkling wines can be made by preparing the cuvée mainly from red wines, but unless the latter are extremely high in quality it is advisable to sweeten the wine rather more than usual when adding the dosage otherwise its flavour may prove rather harsh.

Recipe No. 1

SPARKLING WINE

Ingredients:

6 lb. green gooseberries	**¼ oz. Pectozyme**
1 pt. white grape conc.	**Yeast nutrients**
¾ pt. elderflowers	**Champagne yeast starter**
1½ lb. honey	**Water to 1 gallon**

Method:

Top and tail the gooseberries, add the honey and add 5 pints of boiling water. When cool crush the gooseberries and add the pectozyme, yeast nutrients, elderflowers and yeast starter. Ferment on the pulp for 3–4 days, then strain off the latter and press lightly. Add the grape concentrate and make the quantity up to 1 gallon with water. Check the acidity and adjust it to 4.0 to 4.5 p.p.t. (if the acidity is higher than this figure, no alteration need be made but the wine must then be used as a high acid wine in the preparation of the cuvée).

Fermentation should then be allowed to proceed to completion and thereafter the procedure recommended in the text should be followed.

Recipe No. 2

SPARKLING WINE

Ingredients:

8 lb. apples	¼ oz. Pectozyme
1 pt. white grape conc.	Yeast nutrients
½ pt. yellow rose petals	Champagne yeast starter
1½ lb. honey	Water to 1 gallon

Method:

The same procedure may be used here as in the preceding recipe.

An alternative and superior method is as follows. Press the apples and sulphite and settle the juice exactly as described in the white table wine chapter. Rack the clear juice off its deposit and add the honey, yeast nutrients and yeast starter. Make the volume up to 1 gallon with water. Check the acidity and adjust it to 4.0 to 4.5 p.p.t. Add the rose petals and ferment on the flowers for three days. Strain off the flowers and allow fermentation to proceed to completion. Thereafter continue as recommended in the text.

NOTE:

The weight of apples can advantageously be increased to 12 lb. if the alternative procedure described above is followed. In addition, up to 6 lb. of pears may be employed instead of an equal weight of apples under these conditions. The two juices may then be blended and settled together should the winemaker wish to do so.

Recipe No. 3

SPARKLING WINE

Ingredients:

2 pts. sweet orange juice	Yeast nutrients
1 pt. white grape conc.	Champagne yeast starter
2 pts. hawthorn flowers	Water to 1 gallon
1 lb. honey (or ¾ lb. sugar)	

Method:

Extract the juice from sufficient oranges to obtain about 2½ pints of juice, sulphite and settle it exactly as described in the white table wine chapter. Blend 2 pints of the clear orange juice with the grape concentrate and add the honey (or sugar), yeast nutrients and yeast starter. Dilute to 1 gallon with water. Check the acidity and adjust it to 4.0 to 4.5 p.p.t. using only malic acid.

Allow to ferment for about a week before adding the hawthorn flowers, then ferment on the flowers for three days. Strain off the flowers and let the fermentation proceed to completion.

Thereafter proceed as directed in the text.

Recipe No. 4

SPARKLING WINE

Ingredients:

4 lb. apricots
1 lb. sultanas
½ pt. yellow rose petals
1½ lb. sugar
¼ oz. Pectozyme
Yeast nutrients
Champagne yeast starter
Water to 1 gallon

Method:

Stone the apricots, mix in the chopped sultanas and add 6 pints of cold water and 50 p.p.m. sulphite. Add the yeast nutrients, Pectozyme, yeast starter and rose petals. Ferment on the pulp for three days then strain off the pulp and press lightly. Add the sugar and adjust the volume to 1 gallon with water. Check the acidity and adjust it to 4.0 to 4.5 p.p.t. Let the fermentation proceed to completion.

Thereafter continue as directed in the text.

Recipe No. 5

SPARKLING WINE

Ingredients:

4 lb. rhubarb
1 pt. white grape conc.
¾ pt. elderflowers
1½ lb. honey (or 1 lb. sugar)
Yeast nutrients
Champagne yeast starter
Water to 1 gallon

Method:

Press the rhubarb, sulphite and settle the juice exactly as described in the white wine chapter. Alternatively, crush the rhubarb, strain off the juice and extract the pulp with 1 pint of *cold* water. Strain off the extract, and repeat the treatment twice more using 1 pint of cold water each time. Reject the spent pulp. Combine the extracts and sulphite and settle as above. Add to the clear juice or extract the grape concentrate, honey (or sugar), yeast nutrients and yeast starter. Dilute to 1 gallon with water. Check the acidity and adjust it to 4.0 to 4.5 p.p.t. Add the elderflowers, ferment on the flowers for three days, then strain off.

Ferment to completion, then proceed as directed in the text.

NOTE:

Chalk treatment should not be attempted here since either of the above extraction procedures will minimise the amount of oxalic acid entering the must. Hot water extractions of rhubarb should be avoided for this reason. In any case, since this wine will later be blended to form the cuvée, its oxalic acid content is of minor importance.

Recipe No. 6
SPARKLING WINE

Ingredients:

6 lb. peaches
1 pt. white grape conc.
½ pt. yellow rose petals
½ pt. elderflowers
1 lb. honey
Yeast nutrients
Champagne yeast starter
Water to 1 gallon

Method:

Stone the peaches and press out the juice. Sulphite the latter and leave it to settle exactly as described in the white table wine chapter. Blend the clear juice with the grape concentrate, honey, yeast nutrients and yeast starter. Dilute to 1 gallon with water. Check the acidity and adjust it to 4.0 to 4.5 p.p.t. Allow to ferment for about a week, then add the rose petals and elderflowers. Ferment on the flowers for three days then strain off.

Ferment to completion and thereafter proceed as directed in the text.

NOTE:

The elderflowers may be replaced by 2 pints of gorse flowers.

The SHERRY District
TREBUJENA
RIO GUADALQUIVIR
SANLUCAR de BARRAMEDA
SPAIN
TORREBREBA
MIRAFLORES
MACHARNUDO
CARRASCAL
CHIPIONA
AÑINA
MADRONALES
TEHIGO
BALBAINA
LOS TERCIOS
JEREZ de la FRONTERA
ROTA
PUERTO de SANTA MARIA
RIO GUADALETE
ATLANTIC OCEAN
CADIZ
PUERTO REAL
SAN FERNANDO
CHICLANA de la FRONTERA
ARENA AREAS
ALBARIZA AREAS
N

Chapter XXVI

SHERRY-TYPE WINES

SHERRY is essentially a fortified white wine produced in a delimited area around the Andalusian town of Jerez de la Frontera, which lies some ten miles inland between Seville and Cadiz. The vineyards are enclosed in an area shaped rather like a triangle, the three sides of which are each approximately twenty miles in length with their boundaries roughly marked by the towns of Cadiz, Seville and Jerez. The total area of land permitted by law to grow grapes for sherry production is therefore rather less than 100 square miles in extent. The climate here is hot and arid, especially during much of the growing season, with maximum summer temperatures well over 100°F. so that during the dry summer months irrigation is essential for successful viticulture. As a result, the grapes are sweet and high in sugar, but rather low in acid, a feature whose significance will become clear later.

A great deal of the soil in this district is a mixture of clay and limestone to which the name barros has been given, but in many places a dazzling white earth called albariza which owes its colour to its high gypsum content is also found. Grapes grown on this latter soil are considered to produce the finest wines, but this gain in quality is partly offset by a loss in quantity since the albariza does not give such high yields as the barros. Near the coast around Sanlucar the soils are sandy in character and known as arenas.

The principal grape grown here is the Palomino, a small thick-skinned variety noted more for its resistance to disease and for its quality than for yield. Another cépage called Pedro Ximenes is also fairly extensively cultivated, but these grapes seem to be reserved more for the production of a very sweet type of wine or for crude forms of grape concentrate which are used for sweetening and colouring purposes. A few other types of vine may occasionally be encountered, e.g. Mantuo de Pilas, Albillo and so on, but these grapes are of relatively minor importance.

The vintage normally commences about mid-September, but because the grapes are not picked until they are fully ripe, the vineyards are usually worked over several times during this period. The grapes are transported by mule-cart or lorry to the casas de lagares, or crushing sheds, where the bunches are laid out on esparto grass mats in the adjacent almijar or open courtyard to dry in the sun. The juice thus becomes more concentrated and the sugar content of the must is higher than if the grapes had been pressed immediately after picking. The period of insolation may vary from less than 24 hours to three days or occasionally more in the case of Palomino grapes according to the type of sherry for which they are intended. Pedro Ximenes grapes, in contrast, are usually left to dry for about a fortnight until they have more or less raisinified so that a very heavy sweet must is subsequently obtained. During this time, the grapes may be covered at night to prevent the deposition of dew, but this protection is by no means universally afforded.

Although modern continuous presses (mainly German Wilmes presses) now seem to be fairly widely used in Spain, until recently most of the grapes used in sherry production were trodden in shallow wooden vats called lagares by men wearing special cowhide boots studded with nails. This method of extraction has the advantage of breaking fewer pips and extracting less tannin from the skins than all but the most recent types of presses. This object is very desirable in sherry production since sherries should not contain more than about 0.01% tannin, otherwise their flavour is apt to be coarse and their quality therefore suffers. After treading, the crushed grapes are pressed in the lagar by means of a centrally mounted, manually operated screw, but normally only the free-run juice from the treading and the juice from the first pressing go to make sherry, that from the subsequent pressings being used for the production of lower quality wines intended for local consumption, or for distillation.

Prior to the actual pressing of the crushed grapes the pulp is first plastered with yeso, a rather impure form of anhydrous calcium sulphate prepared by baking gypsum mined from the large natural deposits found locally, at an elevated temperature for some hours. The practice of adding gypsum to the must is frowned upon in other parts of Europe, and although Spanish sherry producers often do not openly advocate plastering it nevertheless seems to be an essential if covert feature of sherry production. The main reason for plastering the must with gypsum is simply to increase its acidity, or rather to decrease its pH (to minimise the risk of bacterial spoilage which occurs more readily if the pH of the wine is high). It will be recollected that mention has already been made of the high sugar content but low acidity and therefore unusually high pH of Palomino grape juice.

The following chemical equations illustrate how the gypsum interacts with cream of tartar (which is a normal constituent of grape juice and always present in grape musts) to form finally tartaric acid, insoluble calcium tartrate and potassium sulphate. This latter substance is soluble and remains in the must so that Spanish sherries almost invariably contain more sulphate than most other wines. An analysis for this anion will therefore immediately show whether plastering has been practised or not.

$$KH(C_4H_4O_6) + CaSO_4 \longrightarrow Ca(C_4H_4O_6) + KHSO_4$$

Cream of Tartar	Gypsum	Calcium Tartrate	Potassium Bisulphate

$$KH(C_4H_4O_6) + KHSO_4 \longrightarrow H_2(C_4H_4O_6) + K_2SO_4$$

Cream of Tartar	Potassium Bisulphate	Tartaric Acid	Potassium Sulphate

i.e.—

$$2KH(C_4H_4O_6) + CaSO_4 \rightarrow Ca(C_4H_4O_6) + H_2(C_4H_4O_6) + K_2SO_4$$

Cream of Tartar	Gypsum	Calcium Tartrate	Tartaric Acid	Potassium Sulphate

Although only a small proportion of the total amount of gypsum employed actually reacts in the above manner due to its low solubility in water or grape juice, the PH of the must nevertheless shows quite a marked decrease. The weight of gypsum used for this purpose seems to vary to some extent, but it would appear that approximately $\frac{1}{2}$-1oz. gypsum per gallon of must is a fairly average figure.

Suggestions have been made from time to time that other methods than plastering with gypsum could be used to reduce the pH of the must. For example, calcium phosphate $CaHPO_4$ could be employed since this substance would react with the cream of tartar already in the must to form tartaric acid in an analagous fashion to gypsum. Moreover, potassium phosphate would be produced instead of potassium sulphate. Thus, not only would the sulphate content of the wine remain at a normal level, but the liberated phosphate would also function as a yeast nutrient and promote a sounder fermentation. This refinement has been tried in other parts of Europe, but little practical information on its success or otherwise seems to be available for evaluation. Alternatively, the acidity of the must could be increased, and its pH thus decreased, simply by the addition of tartaric acid. These ideas have not been accepted in Spain, mainly for reasons of expense—after all, gypsum is plentiful there and costs next to nothing. It is also worth remembering that the effects of a high sulphate content on the quality of the sherry are largely unknown, and may therefore be of some importance. Nevertheless, amateur winemakers would probably find it extremely interesting to compare the effects of gypsum, calcium phosphate and tartaric acid as agents for decreasing the pH of sherry musts.

The juice from the presses is usually lightly sulphited before being transferred to large casks called butts, each of which holds about 600 litres (about 130 gallons). These butts are placed in ground-level stores known as bodegas where the fermentation is conducted. At first, fermentation is very rapid but it soon slows down and may not be complete for ten weeks or so. The new wine is usually racked for the first time towards the end of December, but racking may be delayed until January if fermentation continues rather longer than usual.

Contrary to normal practice, the butts are not completely filled with wine after racking, but instead a large air space amounting to about one-sixth of the volume of the cask is left above the new wine. At this point, the wine is usually fortified to about 15% alcohol to prevent, or at least minimise, the risk of acetification, but in some cases fortification to about 18% alcohol is carried out for reasons which will soon become clear.

Some six weeks or so after the first racking, although at times the delay may be as long as a year, a film of yeast may begin to grow on the surface of the wine, initially as white isolated patches or islands which gradually increase in size and coalesce until eventually the wine becomes completely covered with a creamy skin or flor of yeast. As time passes, this flor gradually darkens and becomes brownish rather than creamy in colour, while at the same time it thickens and assumes a wrinkled appearance. It may also periodically sink and later reform, depending upon the temperature and the season of the year.

The nature of this flor puzzled wine experts for many years, but recently it has been definitely established that the flor yeasts consist of cells identical with those responsible for the main fermentation. The reasons for the formation of a surface film of yeast are believed to be closely linked with its avid desire for oxygen. The Spanish sherry yeasts are in reality a series of closely related strains of the wine yeast Saccharomyces Ellipsoideus, but their film-forming ability is so unusual and unique that Spanish and Californian wine technologists have classified them as separate sub-species under the collective name of Saccharomyces Beticus. At the time of writing, the number of different strains of S. Beticus so far identified is somewhere in the region of 170, and all have been isolated from sherry flors!

Apart from posing this interesting taxonomic problem, the flor yeast also plays a most important part in the production of dry sherries. The yeast itself can tolerate a higher concentration of alcohol than most other strains of S. Ellipsoideus. As well as producing alcohol from any residual sugar which may be present in the new wine, however, it also acts upon the alcohol, glycerol, tartaric acid and certain nitrogenous matter already present in the wine to form aldehydes and other complex substances which are responsible for much of the unique pungent bouquet and flavour of sherry. A considerable reduction in the glycerol and tartaric acid content of the wine is therefore observed after a period of maturing under a flor, e.g. as much as one-third of the tartaric acid may be metabolised by the yeast. The flor absorbs much of the oxygen required for its growth from the air space above the wine, but so greedy is it for oxygen that even the small amounts of this gas entering and dissolving in the wine through the wood of the cask are immediately abstracted by the yeast. Consequently, sherries matured under a flor do not become dark and oxidised but remain pale in colour, the conditions in the bulk of the wine being very strongly reducing due to the influence of the flor.

All new sherries do not grow a flor, and even nowadays in Spain the formation of a flor seems to be very much a matter of chance although fortification to 18% alcohol will certainly prevent its appearance should this be desired. If a film yeast fails to grow, oxidising conditions soon become established in the wine which then darkens as it matures and once again a marked increase in aldehydes is observed. It would appear that the paler colours and smooth flavours typical of dry sherries are best achieved when the aldehydes in the sherry are formed by the action of the flor yeast, whereas the darker colours and less delicate flavours of sweet sherries are most easily obtained if the aldehydes are produced by slow oxidation rather than by flor action. Indeed, new wines intended for the production of sweet sherries are fortified to 18% alcohol immediately after the first racking to prevent flor growth for this very reason.

The formation of a sherry flor is rarely observed in this country, partly because these film yeasts are difficult to reacclimatise since the conditions under which a flor can be induced to grow are very exacting and difficult to establish. Nevertheless, it is occasionally possible to produce discrete floating islands of yeast. Despite the fact that a complete flor may fail to form, such is the power of the yeast that even this partial flor will exert a very noticeable effect on the wine. Unfortunately, most attempts to grow a flor on wines in this country meet with failure for one reason or another with the result that many winemakers unjustifiably consider it impossible to obtain even a partial flor.

What, then, are the conditions that favour the formation of a sherry flor? First of all, an abundant supply of oxygen is essential for the growth and continued well-being of the flor yeast, so that the container should not be more than five-sixths filled with wine after the first racking. In addition, it should be sealed with a cotton-wool plug instead of a fermentation lock to allow unrestricted entry of air without permitting moulds or bacteria access to the wine. The must may be lightly sulphited prior to its inoculation with the yeast starter. Sulphite should not be added after the first racking nor at any later date as its bactericidal action and anti-oxidant properties could seriously interfere with the growth of the flor and the development of the typical sherry character in the wine. Only one racking should be carried out at or near the end of fermentation to remove the bulk of the dead yeast cells and accumulated pulp debris. Thereafter the wine should not be racked again until it is bottled, since autolysis of the yeast simultaneously adds to the flavour of the wine and provides nutrients for any flor which may develop. Finally, because a flor will not develop satisfactorily if at all on a wine containing too much or too little alcohol, the initial gravity of the must should be adjusted to 110–120 to ensure a suitable alcoholic strength. In view of the fact that acetification can more easily occur in wines whose alcohol content is lower than about 14½% by volume, especially when a large air space is left in the container, wines upon which it is hoped a flor will grow should contain at least this amount of alcohol. This alcoholic strength will normally be achieved quite easily by natural fermentation, but occasionally slight fortification with spirit may be necessary. Extremes of heat or cold must, of course, be avoided and a temperature of 60°F.–65°F. (15°C.–18°C.) should be maintained during flor growth.

Although a flor normally makes its first appearance soon after the first racking, or at least within a year of this time, the quality and characteristics of a new sherry are slow to appear so that three years are allowed to elapse before any decision is made regarding its classification. Flor formation may be prevented by fortifying the wine to 18% alcohol after the first racking, as is the custom if the shipper is mainly interested in the production of sweet sherries which are not matured under a flor. Even then, however, a reliable assessment of the quality of the wine can only be made after a year or two have elapsed. The new sherries (often at this stage called añada wines) are tasted during this initial period of maturing to assess their progress, but the final verdict is deferred for two or three years until the wine is settled in its behaviour.

Towards the end of this period, the maturing embryonic sherries are classified as palmas, cortados and rayas, and although other sub-classes are also recognised they are less important and may therefore be ignored. Palmas are wines which have grown a flor and will eventually become the best pale dry fino or amontillado sherries. Cortados on the other hand are fuller-bodied wines which have failed to grow a flor, usually because they are fortified to 18% alcohol after the first racking. These wines form the basis of the dark sweet oloroso, brown, cream and similar sherries. Rayas may simply be sherries which are unduly slow to mature and thus may eventually develop into palmas or cortados, but on the whole rayas are poorer quality coarser wines than the other two types. There are several important sub-classes of rayas, e.g. una, dos and tres rayas, the better of which are often used for blending with cortados for the production of the cheaper sweet sherries. On the other hand, some of the poorer rayas may ultimately turn out to be fit only for distillation.

After the initial probationary period of about three years, the palmas and cortados are racked off the sediment which has accumulated during this period and transferred to other butts situated in what is called a criadera (literally translated as nursery) where the final phase of maturing and blending takes place. These butts are again only about five-sixths filled with wine to allow oxygen free access either directly to the wine or to any flor which may be present. Moulds or bacteria are excluded by lightly plugging the bung-holes with corks or cotton wool. Once the new sherry reaches the criadera, it slowly passes down through a system of butts called a solera in such a way that it becomes intimately mixed with many different older wines as it matures. Although palmas and cortados are handled separately in soleras of their own in the criadera, the same procedure is followed in both cases. All sherries are therefore blended wines so that vintage sherries simply do not exist.

A solera consists of a series of butts arranged in tiers or scales set one above the other, but both the number of butts in each tier and the number of tiers may vary within wide limits according to the size of the criadera and the type of sherry being produced. The lowest or final row of butts which contain the oldest wine is called the solera while the intermediate stages above the solera are known as criaderas. Strictly speaking, the entire system should be known as a criadera-solera instead of simply a solera as is the case nowadays.

When a solera is tapped, wine is withdrawn from all the butts in the lowest tier, the ullage is made up with wine from the butts in the next higher scale and so on until new palma or cortado wine as the case may be is added to the butts in the topmost tier. This procedure is less straightforward than it would first appear to be, however, for wine is not merely transferred from one butt to another in a lower scale. Instead, a portion of the wine from each butt in any given tier is divided equally between all the butts in the next lower tier. For example, if stage I contains the oldest wine and stage V the youngest, when stage I is tapped the ullage is made up by distributing an equal portion of the wine taken from each single butt in stage II amongst all the butts in stage I and so on until stage V is replenished with new palmas or cortados. The wine is transferred from butt to butt by pouring it through a funnel which is perforated in such a way that the wine enters the butt horizontally and mixes with the wine already present without disturbing the sediment or any flor on the surface of the wine.

Since palmas mature better at slightly lower temperatures than cortados, the lower scales of what appear to be a single solera may contain palmas and the upper scales where the temperature is a little higher may contain cortado wine. In such cases, the adjacent soleras are usually constructed in the same way. The top two or three tiers of several adjacent soleras will together form an oloroso (cortado) solera, while the lower tiers of these same soleras will together constitute a fino (palma) solera. These composite soleras are operated exactly as described above although the two types of sherry are, of course, handled quite independently of each other.

One of the principal advantages of the solera system of maturing lies in the degree and efficiency of blending which is achieved. As a new wine progresses through the solera, not only does it mature but it also becomes intimately blended with a great many other still older wines. The sherry emerging from the solera is therefore an extremely complex blend of wines whose average age is usually seven or eight years. Moreover, this wine contains a certain amount of every wine which has entered the solera since its foundation, although the proportion of any given wine in the blend will diminish as its age increases. The solera system also automatically ensures that the quality of the sherry remains uniformly high from year to year, a factor very much in its favour since many sherries are sold under proprietary brand names which are expected to maintain a constant quality at all times. On the debit side, however, soleras are expensive to operate because only about 10% of the wine in the butts can be withdrawn annually without upsetting the balance of the system and because a significant amount of wine—up to 4% per annum—may be lost by evaporation and/or leakage from the butts.

The wine withdrawn from the butts of the solera is not yet a finished sherry, for it still requires a considerable amount of skilled attention before being ready for shipment to its destination. To begin with, the wine is rarely clear when it emerges from the solera so that as a rule it must be fined at this stage, usually with egg-whites and/or Spanish clay (a highly absorptive clay closely resembling Bentonite). The clear wine is then racked off the deposit and any remaining insoluble particles are removed by a polishing filtration. Next, the colour and sweetness of the wine must be adjusted to suit popular demand, for many sherries are too pale in colour and all sherries are dry up to this stage in their production. The colour of the wine can be darkened by the addition of arrope, a viscous dark caramelised form of grape concentrate prepared by evaporating the must obtained from insolated Pedro Ximenes grapes in open vessels. Alternatively, vino de color, a strong wine produced by adding arrope to fresh must or new wine and fermenting to dryness may be used. Arrope also helps to sweeten a wine as well as to deepen its colour and is therefore used more in the production of sweet sherries where its dual role is an advantage, although too much arrope will give the wine a noticeable flavour of caramel. Sherries are also sweetened by means of sweet Pedro Ximenes wine which has been prepared by fortifying the must during fermentation long before all the sugar has been converted to alcohol by the yeast so that a strong wine rich in sugar is obtained. Finally, the sherry is fortified to 16%–20% alcohol with high proof brandy distilled from rejected rayas, the comparatively high degree of rectification preventing the spirit from imparting too much flavour of its own to the wine. Branded sherries may also receive a final blending at Jerez to ensure that their quality remains absolutely uniform.

It is also worth noting that even nowadays the precipitation of cream of tartar from sherries bottled in this country still constitutes a difficult problem. An undesirable deposit of hard glassy needles of this substance may quite often be encountered in bottles of sherry which have been kept for a few months. The formation of these deposits is mainly due to the fact that the temperature in Britain is normally much lower than in Spain. As the solubility of cream of tartar decreases with temperature, it slowly crystallises out of the sherry in the colder climate of this country. Moreover, since cream of tartar becomes less soluble as the alcohol content of the wine increases, the final fortification which the wine receives in Jerez before shipment serves to aggravate this problem. The installation of refrigeration units either in Spain or in the bottling plants in this country enables this excess cream of tartar to be removed rapidly by chilling the sherry to a temperature just above its freezing point for some days, however, so that this problem will possibly not arise a few years from now.

In conclusion, a description of the various types of sherry which are currently available in this country may be of interest. Finos are pale, dry sherries, matured under a flor, containing little or no sugar and 16%–18% alcohol which are best drunk chilled as aperitifs. Manzanillas are very similar to finos in most respects except that their flavour is rather more bitter; these wines are produced in the coastal regions around Sanlucar, where the sea air is reputed to influence the flavour of the wine. Amontillados are, or should be, old finos slightly darker in colour, slightly sweeter and a little more alcoholic than true finos. Olorosos are usually sweet, rather dark dessert wines containing about 20% alcohol, but at least one dry oloroso sherry is sold in this country although it is really more a novelty wine. Amorosos are very similar to olorosos except that their colour is rather lighter and their sugar content slightly higher. Brown sherries and East India sherries are darker and sweeter than olorosos but very similar in other respects, while Cream, Milk, Gold and other sherries are special types of amorosos or olorosos sold under brand names.

Most amateur winemakers will probably have realised by now that it is by no means easy to produce good quality imitation sherries, and that finos and amontillados are more difficult to simulate than olorosos and other sweet sherries. Careful blending of selected fruits and vegetables is required to produce a balanced must, suitable in character for this purpose, and the use of ingredients which would not permit the unrestricted development of the typical sherry bouquet and flavour during maturing must be avoided at all costs. Suitable ingredients include apples (varieties low in acid), peaches, greengages, yellow plums, bananas, white grapes, vine prunings, white grape concentrate, raisins, parsnips, sugar beet and so on. Ingredients which are high in acid (especially citric acid), strongly flavoured, highly scented or deeply coloured do not lend themselves well to sherry production and should not therefore be used, e.g. citrus fruits, green gooseberries, grain, flowers, elderberries, sloes, damsons.

Although a blend of at least two and probably more ingredients will be required, it is clearly impossible to do more than outline the general principles which should be followed since each type of sherry poses its own unique problems in this respect. As a general rule, however, fino sherries are best made from lighter-bodied delicate musts, while oloroso sherries need fuller-bodied more robust musts: the inclusion of bananas in oloroso musts is usually advisable for this reason. It is therefore essential for the winemaker to decide which type of sherry is desired, so that the blend of ingredients best suited for this purpose can be designed. The recipes quoted at the end of this chapter will provide some guidance in this connection, but on the whole wine-makers should be prepared to experiment and design their own blends of ingredients.

Once the must has been prepared, its acidity should be checked and adjusted to about 3.5 p.p.t. (in terms of sulphuric acid) by chalk treatment or the addition of acid as the case may be. The best acid to use for this purpose is tartaric acid. If plastering with gypsum is intended, however, the acidity of the must should be adjusted to about 3.0 p.p.t. in the appropriate manner and then half an ounce of cream of the appropriate manner and then roughly ½–1 oz. cream of tartar per gallon should be added. The reason for this advice is simply that few ingredients other than grapes contain significant amounts of cream of tartar. Because the success of plastering depends upon the interaction between the added gypsum and the cream of tartar already in the must, sufficient of this latter substance must be present to allow these chemical reactions to proceed. Since cream of tartar is soluble in water only with difficulty, it can only be dissolved completely by stirring the must vigorously for some time, but care should be taken to ensure that all the cream of tartar does go into solution.

The sulphate content of commercial sherries is about ten times higher than that of most other commercial wines as a result of plastering the must with gypsum. The effects of this high sulphate content both on the overall quality of the sherry and on the growth of a flor nevertheless appear to be largely unknown, and thus could easily be quite far-reaching. In view of this lack of knowledge, it would seem advisable to plaster all sherry musts with gypsum, particularly if flor growth is desired. It is certainly the authors' experience that better flors and hence better sherries are produced if this procedure is adopted. The amount of gypsum required is about ½–1 ounce per gallon, and this quantity should be stirred into the must after its acidity has been adjusted as described above.

It goes without saying that an adequate supply of yeast nutrients should be added to the must prior to fermentation to promote the development of a large healthy yeast colony and hence a sound fermentation, particularly if a high alcohol yield is the objective. Pulp fermentation in the appropriate cases will also help to increase the body of oloroso wines, but is best avoided in the case of fino musts otherwise a certain coarseness may be detectable in the flavour of the wine. The duration of pulp fermentation should nevertheless be kept reasonably short otherwise the wine may acquire an unpleasant flavour due to pulp disintegration products.

As already mentioned, the initial gravity of the must should not exceed 110 to 120 if flor growth is to occur. In such cases, the must should immediately be adjusted to its final volume with water and sugar syrup in such a way that its initial gravity lies within the above range, preferably about 115. An actively fermenting sherry yeast starter can then be introduced and the must fermented to dryness with no further interference beyond an occasional gravity determination with the hydrometer to check the progress of the fermentation. In the case of musts intended for oloroso sherries which are not matured under a flor, a slightly different procedure should be followed. The must should be adjusted to rather less than its final volume (say to 3½ gallons instead of 4½ gallons) to leave space for further additions of sugar syrup. Its initial gravity should at the same time be adjusted to 80–100. An actively fermenting yeast starter should then be introduced and the technique of feeding the yeast with small doses of sugar syrup should be adopted (¼ pint sugar syrup per gallon should be added every time the hydrometer shows a gravity reading below 5). The final dose of sugar syrup should be added while a gravity decrease of 1 to 2 per day is still occurring so that the wine ultimately finishes dry. By this time, of course, its volume should have increased to near that originally intended, e.g. from 3½ gallons to close on 4½ gallons. An alcohol content of 16% to 17% can easily be achieved in this way by natural fermentation so that subsequently little or no fortification will be necessary, an important consideration in view of the high cost of fortifying spirit.

About a week after fermentation has ceased, the wine should be racked off the sediment of dead yeast cells and pulp debris which has accumulated during fermentation. Although an air space need not be left above the wine while it is in an active state of fermentation, after the first racking the container should only be filled to about five-sixths of its capacity and plugged with a wad of cotton wool so that air has free access to the wine but bacteria are denied entry. The wine should then be left to mature undisturbed and no further racking should be attempted until it is bottled unless the solera system of maturing is practised.

The wine should preferably be allowed to mature in cask rather than in glass containers since the impermeable nature of the latter restricts the supply of air to the wine. The superiority of wood over glass is, of course, well known, but probably becomes even more marked in the case of sherries which require considerably more oxygen for their development than most other types of wine. Moreover, because sherries are notoriously slow wines to mature, a period of at least 1½ to 2 years and probably longer in cask will almost certainly be necessary before bottling is even contemplated. Shorter periods of maturing are likely to lead to rather coarse wines which lack delicacy and finesse.

It is not at all necessary to establish a solera for maturing the wine since the principal object of this system is to ensure a standard high quality product. In any case, most amateur winemakers would find it impossible to do so simply from space considerations. Nevertheless, a few enthusiasts may wish to found a small solera of their own and this is by no means as difficult as it first appears provided sufficient space is available. It is worth noting that an oloroso solera and not a fino solera should be set up, however, for the chances of growing and maintaining the flor essential for the successful maturing of fino sherries are normally poor even at the best of times in Britain. The minimum size of cask suitable for this purpose is 4½ gallons, and the solera itself should comprise 12 such casks arranged in four scales each consisting of three casks. Each cask should contain no more than 4 gallons of wine and the bungs should be plugged tightly with cotton wool. It is preferable though certainly not essential to found the solera with 12 casks of wine which are not at all of the same age, and these casks should be arranged in such a way that the oldest wines form the lowest scale and the youngest wines the topmost scale.

Once the solera has been set up, 1 gallon of wine should be withdrawn from each cask in the lower scale and the ullage made up with wine from the next higher scale (scale II). An equal portion (here one-third of a gallon) of the wine withdrawn from each cask in scale II is then added to every cask in the lowest scale. This process should then be repeated with scale II and so on until the topmost scale is reached and here the ullage should be made good with the wine previously withdrawn from the casks in the lowest scale. By repeating this procedure every three months for two to three years the wines used to found the solera should become thoroughly blended and well matured. The solera can then be tapped by withdrawing three-quarters of a gallon of wine (or less) from all the casks in the lower scale and the ullage made up from the higher scale in the usual way. The topmost scale should then be replenished with new wine which should preferably be at least six months old (a 4½ gallon cask of wine may be prepared for this purpose some six months before the solera is due for tapping). Under no circumstances should the solera be tapped more frequently than once every six months, and the maximum amount of wine which can be withdrawn from each cask at one time is ½–¾ of a gallon, otherwise the balance of the solera is likely to become upset.

After maturing or withdrawal from the solera the sherry should first be inspected for clarity, fined with a good proprietary fining agent, e.g. Serena wine finings if any haze is observed, and racked immediately the deposit has settled. At this stage, the sherry should be dry or nearly so and oloroso sherries can be sweetened to gravity 10–20 with sugar syrup, white grape concentrate or a type of arrope prepared by boiling raisins for an hour in water and evaporating the carefully strained extract to a thick dark syrup. Care should be taken to remove all pulp particles from this raisin extract prior to evaporation, otherwise an objectionable sediment will later be found in the wine. Fino sherries may be sweetened slightly to modify undue dryness, but only white grape concentrate should be used for this purpose. The colour of the sherry may be darkened to any desired extent by means of caramel, but the raisin extract described above will serve the dual rôle of a sweetening and colouring agent for oloroso sherries and is therefore more suitable than caramel.

In conclusion, fortification of the wine is not essential if its alcohol content is about 17%. This figure is not too difficult to achieve by natural fermentation in the case of oloroso sherries, if the yeast is carefully fed with sugar syrup but finos will contain slightly less alcohol if attemp were made to induce flor growth. Since fortification is extremely expensive, however, only the most promising wines shonld be fortified, and a neutral spirit such as 140 proof vodka should be chosen for this purpose. Finos may be fortified to 16%–18% alcohol in this way while the alcohol couteut of olorosos should be increased to about 19%–20%. The fortified wine should then be bottled and stored for about six months before consumption to allow the spirit to marry with the wine

Recipe 1

FINO SHERRY

Ingredients:

16 lb. dessert apples	**½ oz. Pectozyme**
6 lb. bananas	**7 lb. sugar**
4 pts. white grape conc.	**Yeast nutrients**
2½ ozs. cream of tartar	**Sherry yeast starter**
5 ozs. gypsum	**Water to 5 gallons**

Method:

Peel the bananas and cut into slices. Boil only the slices (no skins) in 1½ gallons water for ½ hour then strain off the liquor carefully. Transfer this banana extract to a suitable sealed container and leave to cool and settle for 24 hours. Press the apples, add 100 p.p.m. sulphite to the juice and also leave to settle for 24 hours. Next rack the banana extract and apple juice off their deposits (the latter may be combined, left to settle further for 24 hours and used for making top-up wine). Combine the apple and banana juices, add the grape concentrate, sugar, yeast nutrients, cream of tartar and sufficient water to make the volume up to 5 gallons. Stir vigorously until the sugar, nutrients and cream of tartar have completely dissolved. The gravity at this stage should be 110–120. Add the gypsum and stir to disperse it thoroughly throughout the must. Finally, add the pectozyme and yeast starter.

Allow the fermentation to proceed to completion and after all the yeast activity ceases let the wine settle for one week before racking. Rack the wine at this point, being careful not to suck over any pulp debris otherwise a second racking about two weeks later will be necessary. A second racking is also advisable should a very thick sediment form a few weeks after the first racking, but otherwise the wine should not be racked more than once. The bung-hole of the cask should now be plugged with cotton wool, so that air has free access to the wine but dust, insects and bacteria are excluded. The cask should not be more than five-sixths full at this stage.

The wine should now be left undisturbed and a flor may form within the ensuing few months. In this case the wine should not be touched for another 2–3 years or longer so that the flor can do its work. Even if a flor fails to develop, the wine should still be left undisturbed for 2–3 years although it will then acquire more of an oloroso than a fino character. When the wine is bottled, it should not be sweetened unless a flor has failed to form. In the latter case, some grape concentrate and/or raisin extract may be added for sweetening and colouring purposes.

The addition of sufficient alcohol to increase the strength of the wine to about 18% alcohol by volume is also recommended for better quality wines. A fino sherry should be ready to drink within a year of bottling and so too will an oloroso although the latter will continue to improve in bottle for a few years.

This wine can, of course, be blended and matured in a solera should space permit its foundation. In the absence of a solera, it can still be blended with other similar wines at the discretion of the winemaker.

Recipe 2

FINO SHERRY

Ingredients:

25 lb. peaches	**½ oz. Pectozyme**
5 lb. bananas	**7 lb. sugar**
4 pts. white grape conc.	**Yeast nutrients**
2½ ozs. cream of tartar	**Sherry yeast starter**
5 ozs. gympsum	**Water to 5 gallons**

Method:

The procedure which should be followed here is exactly as described in the preceding recipe. This wine will be slightly more full-bodied, however, and can advantageously be converted into an amontillado sherry after maturing. Should the latter be the case, the wine should be matured for not less than three years in cask prior to bottling and a small amount of grape concentrate added when it is bottled to blunt its dry edge. If a flor fails to form, of course, it should again be treated as an oloroso sherry.

Recipe 3
OLOROSO SHERRY

Ingredients:

15 lb. greengages or yellow plums
10 lb. bananas
5 lb. figs
5 lb. raisins
2 pts. white grape conc.
½ oz. Pectozyme
Tartaric acid as required
Sugar as required
Yeast nutrients
Sherry yeast starter
Water to 5 gallons

Method:

Peel the bananas (rejecting the skins) and cut into slices. Boil the slices in 1½ gallons water for ½ hour and then strain the hot liquor carefully over the raisins, figs and stoned greengages or plums. Add another 1½ gallons cold water together with the yeast nutrients. When cool add the pectozyme and yeast starter. Ferment on the pulp for 3–4 days then strain off the latter and press lightly. Add 5 lb. sugar and the grape concentrate and make the volume up to about 4½ gallons with water.

Check the acidity and if necessary adjust it to about 3.5 p.p.t. with tartaric acid. Measure the gravity periodically and add ¼ pint sugar syrup per gallon whenever the gravity drops to 5 or less until the rate of gravity decrease is 1–2 per day. Once this stage is reached, no more sugar syrup should be added and the wine should be left to ferment to dryness.

Racking and maturing should then be carried out as described in the preceding recipes. In this case, however, no flor should develop and the wine should darken in colour as it matures. After spending at least 2–3 years and preferably more in cask, it may be sweetened and fortified according to the personal taste of the winemaker. The wine will then continue to improve slightly in bottle for a few more years, but it may be drunk within a year of bottling.

Recipe 4

OLOROSO SHERRY

Ingredients:

20 lb. parsnips	**Tartaric acid as required**
5 lb. bananas	**Sugar as required**
5 lb. raisins	**Yeast nutrients**
4 pts. white grape conc.	**Sherry yeast starter**
½ oz. Pectozyme	**Water to 5 gallons**

Method:

Scrub the parsnips and cut into chunks. Peel the bananas (rejecting the skins) and cut into slices. Boil the parsnips and bananas together or separately in 3 gallons water for ½ hour then strain the hot liquor carefully over the raisins and yeast nutrients. When cool add the pectozyme and yeast starter. From this point proceed exactly as directed in the preceding recipe.

PORTUGAL
MONCÃO
VIANA DO CASTELO
BRAGA
AMARANTE
PENAFIEL
DOURO
Oporto
LAFÕES
PINHEL
AGUEDA
DÃO
BAIRRADA
ALCOBACA
CARTAXO
ALMEIRIM
ALENQUER
TORRES VEDRAS
BUCELAS
COLARES
CARCAVELOS
SETÚBAL
Lisbon
LAGOA
N

CHAPTER XXVII

PORT-TYPE WINES

PORT is essentially a sweet red fortified wine produced in a closely delimited region of the Upper Douro Valley in Northern Portugal. The name Port is derived from Oporto, a city at the mouth of the River Douro from which the wine is shipped to its final destination. In Britain it is illegal to label and sell a wine as Port unless it has been produced in Portugal. This regulation was introduced by the Anglo-Portuguese Commercial Treaty Act (Article 6) passed in 1914 and more clearly defined in 1916. All other wines after the style of Port must be clearly labelled as such with the words "Port Type," and furthermore the latter word in this title must be printed in letters as large as the former. The law is therefore very specific on this subject. It is of interest to note that with the exception of Madeira, also a Portuguese wine, the same protection is not afforded to other types of wine. Recent legislation forbidding the labelling of Spanish sparkling wines as Spanish Champagne may, however, open the way to a more enlightened legal position in this connection.

The familiar red Port is not the only type exported from Portugal, for nowadays significant amounts of both dry and sweet white Port are also being produced, and these wines seem to be gaining in popularity. A well-chilled dry white Port certainly makes a very pleasant aperitif, although at times it may prove rather too heavy and full-bodied for this purpose. The quantity of white Port currently produced is small in comparison with the volume of red Port, however so that this chapter will be limited to a detailed discussion on the latter.

The Upper Douro Valley is an extremely steep rocky district where viticulture is only made possible by terracing the precipitous slopes. Cutting the terraces is in itself a major task, for beneath the rather scanty covering of soil lie adamantine schistose or granitic rocks. A schist is a rock similar to slate, and in the Upper Douro the bedrock is usually a hard schist overlying granite, although outcrops of the latter are also found in a few places. The soil here has mainly been derived from the weathering of the underlying schists and is consequently very flaky, but this texture is advantageous in that it helps to counteract the excess of clay which is also encountered. In general, however, the soil is rather thin and poor and contains a high proportion of potassium (over 10%) but little lime, nitrogen or organic matter. The sparseness of the soil and the hardness of the bedrock may be judged from the fact that often the vines can only be planted with the aid of dynamite.

It is worth noting that these schistose soils contain small amounts of manganese and titanium and that the better wines are said to come from vines planted in soils relatively rich in these elements. Although the effects of these trace elements on the quality of the wine seem to be largely unknown, it is nevertheless a well-established belief that Port owes much of its character to the soil of the Douro. Since Port-type wines produced in other parts of the world rarely, if ever, attain the standard of good Ports from Portugal, this contention may very well be true.

The grapes grown here are, of course, mainly red varieties, and most growers plant several different types of vine in order to produce a balanced wine. The principal cépages include the Touriga which is similar to the Cabernet of Bordeaux, the Tinta Francisca which resembles the Pinot Noir of Burgundy, the deeply-coloured Souzao, the noble Mourisco, and so on. The vintage normally takes place in late September or early October and the grapes are transported from the vineyards by ox cart or lorry to the Quintas where the pressing and fermentation are conducted.

Although a few Quintas are now equipped with mechanical devices which crush the grapes between revolving metal rollers, innovations of this type are still comparatively rare in Portugal and the grapes are therefore crushed by the time-honoured method of treading. The freshly-picked grapes are tipped into shallow stone lagares which are usually constructed of granite quarried locally and measure about

18′ × 15′ × 3′. These lagares lack the centrally mounted screw found in their Spanish counterparts and are made of stone instead of wood, but apart from these constructional differences their purpose is similar in both countries. Once the lagar has been filled with grapes, the barefoot treaders (cf. Spanish treaders) begin their arduous work which continues until the grapes have been thoroughly crushed.

The mass of skins, stalks, pips and juice is then left to ferment spontaneously. Fermentation is allowed to proceed for 2–4 days during which colour is extracted from the skins and about half the sugar in the must is converted into alcohol. The cap which forms during fermentation is, of course, periodically broken up to facilitate colour extraction and to minimise the risk of acetification, while regular gravity determinations are carried out to check the progress of the fermentation. As soon as the must is judged to contain sufficient colour and alcohol, the pulp or marc is strained off and the fermenting must is run into the fortifying vats which already contain sufficient brandy to raise the alcohol content of the must to about 18% to 20% by volume (about 100 litres of brandy per 115 gallons of must). The brandy used for this purpose is comparatively low-proof spirit distilled locally and thus adds some flavour of its own to the wine. The distinctive aroma of fusel oil is often more pronounced in Port than in other fortified wines for this reason.

All yeast activity is terminated within a very short time as a result of this fortification so that the wine may contain up to 10% residual unfermented sugar. The new fortified wine is then left in the fortifying vats for some months to clarify before it is racked off its lees in the spring into large narrow-ended 115-gallon oak casks called pipes ready for transportation to the shippers' lodges in Oporto. Formerly, most new Port was shipped down the Douro to Oporto in small picturesque sailing ships called barcos rebelos, but unfortunately rail transport is now proving more popular mainly for economic reasons. Once the pipes of new Port from the Quintas reach Oporto, they are transported to the lodges by ox cart or lorry and there a further small dose of brandy is usually added. The wine is then left to mature undisturbed except for periodic rackings every few months to promote its final clarification and to provide the oxygen necessary for its development. Persistent hazes are removed by fining, usually with gelatine but occasionally with egg-whites, and some tannin may also be added to replace that lost as a result of fining.

Perhaps the most important function of the lodges is blending, for most Port, like sherry, is sold under proprietary brand names which are expected to maintain a constant high quality from year to year. Since the wine purchased by the shippers will vary quite widely in character according to the grower and year of its origin, it is clear that some form of blending must be practised to achieve this uniformity. Sherry producers overcome this problem very neatly by maturing their wines in soleras as already described in a previous chapter, but no parallel system of this nature is found in Portugal. The arduous and highly-skilled task of blending is therefore performed by the lodge taster under whose direction different types of Port are blended together in such a way that each shipment leaving the lodge is identical with its predecessors. Thus, old wines are refreshed with younger wines, hard or harsh wines are matched with soft or smooth wines, small amounts of very old pungent wines reserved solely for blending purposes are used to add character and so on until the taster is satisfied that a satisfactory blend of wines has been achieved.

There are four main types of Port and all are to a greater or lesser extent blended wines. These four types are vintage, crusted, ruby and tawny Ports, and the principal characteristics of these wines are discussed in detail in the following paragraphs.

Vintage Port is a deep ruby red full-bodied wine with an extremely fine bouquet and flavour, although it does vary to some extent in both colour and character according to the vintage and the shipper. As the name implies, vintage Port is the product of a single year, but nevertheless it is still a blended wine made by judiciously blending the wines produced from different grapes and in different vineyards in the year of its origin. The reason for blending vintage Ports is, of course, simply to balance out any minor imperfections which the individual wines may possess, thus ensuring a very high quality product.

Rather surprisingly, the declaration of the vintage is entirely a matter for the individual shippers so that in very good years most shippers will declare a vintage, whereas in less outstanding years only a few will do so. In spite of the confusion which this system sometimes causes, it is the only really sensible procedure since the climate and hence the quality of the grapes and the wine can vary quite widely from vineyard to vineyard. Thus, in some years most shippers may be able to purchase vintage quality wines because conditions on the Douro were generally good, while in other years locally good weather may enable just a few select shippers to declare a vintage.

Only a small proportion (less than 10%) of the very best wine of any year is reserved for the production of vintage Port since the remainder is required to maintain the high quality of the less expensive and therefore more popular non-vintage branded Ports. After blending, the new vintage Port is matured in cask for two years (rarely longer except in the case of late-bottled vintage Ports which spend up to seven years in cask and therefore come to maturity much more quickly). The wine is then shipped in bulk to its destination where it is bottled after a brief resting period of a few months and placed in a dark cool cellar to mature. The bottles used for this purpose are very dark brown (or green) in colour to protect the wine from exposure to light during storage and their inside surfaces are often artificially roughened for reasons which will become clear shortly. Extra long high-quality corks are used to seal the bottles to minimise the risk of wine spoilage due to cork failure during the long years of maturing which lie ahead.

The upper side of each bottle is marked by a splash of whitewash or a label (or at times both) to show the position in which the bottle must be replaced should rebinning be necessary, e.g. in a purchaser's cellar. All vintage Ports deposit what is called a crust, a fine reddish-brown sediment of oxidised colouring matter and tannin, as they mature, and it is important to return the bottle to its original position once it has been moved to avoid unduly disturbing this crust. The inside surfaces of the bottles are therefore roughened to facilitate the deposition of a firm compact crust which will remain intact provided the bottle is carefully handled.

Vintage Port will improve comparatively rapidly in bottle for 7 to 10 years and thereafter more slowly for perhaps as long as another 30 or 40 years. Sooner or later, however, it will reach its peak of perfection beyond which a slow deterioration will gradually begin until eventually the wine will fall into senility and become flat and lifeless. It follows that a vintage Port should never be drunk until it is at least 10 years old, and that all except the lightest vintages will be equally as good, if not better, another 10 or even 20 years later.

Crusted Port, sometimes also called vintage character Port, is very similar to vintage Port and may in fact be the product of a single year in which the quality of the wine was not sufficiently high to declare a vintage but nevertheless extremely good. More often, however, crusted Port is a blend of wines produced in different years as well as from different grapes and in different vineyards. Some of these wines must obviously have been in cask longer than the two years normally permitted for a vintage Port, but the overall age of the blend is such that much of the vintage character of the wines is retained. It is shipped and bottled early in the same manner as vintage Port and like the latter throws a crust during storage. In general, then, crusted and vintage Ports are very similar wines in almost all respects except that the quality of a crusted Port tends to be very slightly lower. Nevertheless, at times the differences between the two types are negligible, since to avoid declaring a vintage in two successive outstanding years many Port shippers prefer to bottle the second year's wine simply as crusted Port.

Most Port is not used for the production of vintage or crusted Port, but instead it is carefully blended and matured for many years in cask for sale under proprietary brand names. New or young Ports are usually described as red Ports although in fact they are purplish rather than red in colour. Port may be shipped in bulk to its destination, bottled and sold as Full Port after spending only three or four years in cask and while it still retains this purple tint, but it is still somewhat young and fruity and lacks sophistication at this early stage in its development. Once the wine has spent seven or eight years in cask, however, its colour has altered to a deep ruby red and at this point it may be blended with other similar wines. It is then shipped and bottled as ruby Port. This longer period of maturing in cask produces a pleasant vinous yet still slightly fruity Port which is ready for immediate consumption. Although ruby Port will continue to improve slightly in bottle for up to about five years and may even throw a slight crust, in comparison with crusted or vintage Ports it has a very limited bottle life. Prolonged storage of ruby Port therefore serves no useful purpose and should not be contemplated.

If Port is left in cask for about 15 years or more its colour becomes brownish rather than red, and it is then described as tawny Port. The colour of a tawny Port becomes increasingly lighter with age so that on this basis it may be described as medium tawny or pale tawny. Very old pale tawny Ports are prized in Portugal inmuch the same way as vintage Ports are in this country. The quality of tawny Port depends very much upon skilful blending, for refreshment with younger more vigorous wines and replacement of alcohol lost by evaporation with old aromatic brandy are necessary from time to time to prevent the wine maturing too rapidly and becoming stale. Blending with other similar wines must also be practised to produce a well-balanced wine.

Once a tawny Port is shipped in bulk to its destination and bottled, it is ready for immediate consumption since no improvement will occur after the wine is bottled—the long period of maturing in cask ensures that nothing will be gained by further maturing in bottle. It is also worth mentioning here that some tawny Ports are made simply by blending white and red Ports. Although this practice is perfectly legitimate, the wines produced in this manner will lack the finesse and depth of character of true old tawny Ports.

From this discussion, it is clear that the two most notable features of Port production are firstly the early fortification which arrests the fermentation abruptly to give a very sweet full-bodied rather fruity wine, and secondly the long period of maturing in cask and/or bottle required to bring out the latent quality of the wine. Although most of the cost involved in fortification can be avoided as described later, little can be done about reducing the period of maturing needed to develop a satisfactory Port character. Admittedly, the wine will mature more rapidly in the 4½ to 9-gallon casks commonly employed by amateur winemakers than in the 115-gallon pipes used in Portugal, but 18 months in cask should still be regarded as the minimum period of maturing which would be acceptable and several years would be more realistic. Obviously, the wine could be drunk with enjoyment at an earlier age, but it would then lack Port character and may thus prove disappointing. Some years of bottle ageing are also advantageous though less important than cask maturing unless the wine is bottled young after the style of a vintage Port.

Since most amateur winemakers would find it prohibitively expensive to fortify to about 20% alcohol long before all the sugar in the must had been metabolised by the yeast, it follows that most of the alcohol in the wine must be produced by natural fermentation. Little difficulty should be experienced in achieving about 16% to 17% alcohol in this manner provided the yeast is adequately supplied with nutrients and the technique of feeding the yeast with small doses of sugar syrup is adopted. Fermentation should be conducted in reasonably warm surroundings (65°F. to 75°F.). In fact, it is advisable to maintain the temperature at about 75°F. when fermentation is nearing completion so that the yeast has every chance to produce the maximum possible yield of alcohol. In the latter connection, winemakers should note that a madeira yeast may sometimes be employed instead of a Port yeast since both produce wines similar in character but the former tends to have a slightly higher alcohol tolerance.

The new wine must contain at least 16% to 17% alcohol for a satisfactory Port character to develop, and if necessary it should be fortified to this alcoholic strength with brandy or 140 proof vodka immediately after fermentation has ceased. Fortification to about 20% alcohol is not absolutely essential although the wine will usually show a greater improvement during storage if its alcohol content is around this figure. The high cost of distilled spirits generally makes fortification to 20% alcohol far too expensive a proposition, however, so that only those wines which show a great deal of promise after spending about a year in cask are normally worth fortifying to this extent. It is then advisable to use a strong neutral spirit such as 140 proof vodka for this purpose, and a half-pint of this spirit will increase the alcohol content of a gallon of wine by roughly 3½%, e.g. from 16% to approximately 19½% alcohol.

During storage, the wine should be racked about once every three or four months to promote clarification and to provide the oxygen required for its development. If the wine is still hazy some six to nine months after fermentation has ceased it should be fined, preferably with egg whites (1 per 10 gallons) or a good proprietary fining agent. Gelatine should not be used for this purpose except by experienced winemakers since this fining agent needs careful handling. Racking at six-monthly intervals should suffice once the wine is about 12 months old.

The first essential when making Port style wines is obviously to begin with a deep red full-bodied must. Sloes, damsons, blackberries, deep red plums, cherries, red grape concentrate and, in particular, elderberries and bilberries are excellent basic ingredients. Blackberries are especially suited to the production of tawny Ports since wines made principally from this fruit rapidly become tawny in colour during storage. The inclusion of 1–2 lb. of bananas per gallon is essential to give the wine sufficient body while raspberries, loganberries or blackcurrants are useful minor ingredients for adding a background fruity flavour. About half a pint of elderflowers or a packet of the dried flowers per gallon is also very much a worthwhile addition since the bouquet of the wine benefits remarkably from this ingredient.

The acidity of the must should preferably be within the range 3.0 to 3.5 p.p.t. (in terms of sulphuric acid) since Port is produced commercially from well-ripened grapes which are high in sugar but low in acid. In most cases, a period of pulp fermentation will be necessary to achieve a satisfactory depth of colour, but in the case of ingredients which are rich in tannin, e.g. elderberries, sloes, the duration of the pulp fermentation should be kept at a minimum to avoid extracting too much tannin from the fruit, otherwise an unduly harsh wine may be obtained.

Fermentation with a Port (or madeira) yeast should be started using about 1 lb. of sugar per gallon of must as well as the natural sugar from the ingredients. Further small doses of sugar syrup should then be added at intervals as indicated by the hydrometer (¼ pint of sugar syrup per gallon whenever the gravity drops below 5) until the yeast reaches its maximum alcohol tolerance and fermentation ceases. The new wine should then be racked, sweetened with honey, grape concentrate or sugar syrup and fortified if necessary or if desired and left to clear with periodic rackings every three or four months. Finally, the wine should be matured in cask as already described for at least 18 months but preferably for several years. Bottling may be contemplated at any time after the wine has spent 18 months in cask but then a long period of bottle ageing will almost certainly be necessary. It is probably best to mature the wine in cask until it is almost fully mature before bottling is attempted. The wine is then ready for immediate consumption but will still improve slightly in bottle for a limited time.

Recipe No. 1

RED PORT

Ingredients:

30 lb. bilberries (or 8 lb. dried)
8 lb. bananas
5 lb. raisins
4 pints red grape conc.
2 pints elderflowers
½ oz. Pectozyme
Sugar or honey as required
Yeast nutrients
Port or Madeira yeast starter
Water to 5 gallons

Method:

Peel the bananas (rejecting the skins) and cut into slices. Boil the latter for ½ hour in 1 gallon water, then strain the hot liquor carefully over the crushed bilberries and raisins. Add another 1½ gallons cold water and the yeast nutrients. When cool add the pectozyme and yeast starter. Ferment on the pulp for 3–5 days (until a satisfactory depth of colour is achieved) then strain off the pulp and press lightly. Add the elderflowers and grape concentrate and ferment on the flowers for 2–3 days. Strain off the flowers and make up the volume to about 4½ gallons with water (if necessary).

Check the acidity and adjust it to 3.5–3.8 p.p.t. (the dilution experienced later will reduce this figure to the desired range of 3.0–3.5 p.p.t.). Measure the gravity periodically and add ¼ lb. sugar or honey (as strong syrup) per gallon whenever a gravity of 5 or less is recorded. Continue feeding the yeast with sugar or honey in this manner until fermentation finally ceases. Rack the new wine at this stage and add 100 p.p.m. sulphite. Rack again as soon as a heavy deposit forms. After this second racking adjust the final gravity of the wine to 10–25, preferably with honey syrup, according to personal taste. Add another 50 p.p.m. sulphite. Thereafter rack every 3–4 months until the wine is brilliantly clear. Subsequently, a racking every six months should suffice.

This wine should be matured in cask for some 2–3 years and in bottle for another few years. Alternatively it may be bottled young at an age of about one year and then allowed to mature in bottle for at least five years.

Fortification may be carried out after the second racking should the winemaker consider the expense worthwhile. In view of the high cost of alcohol, however, fortification should normally be considered only when the quality of the wine promises to be exceptionally good. The alcohol content of the wine may then be increased to 19%–20% by volume, preferably with a strong spirit such as 140 proof vodka.

Recipe No. 2

TAWNY PORT

Ingredients:

30 lb. blackberries
6 lb. bananas
6 lb. raisins
4 pts. red grape conc.
2 pts. elderflowers
½ oz. Pectozyme
Sugar or honey as required
Yeast nutrients
Port or Madeira yeast starter
Water to 5 gallons

Method:

The procedure which should be followed here is exactly as described in the preceding recipe and need not therefore be repeated. This wine should, however, be matured somewhat differently. Although the red colour of the new wine should become tawny relatively rapidly, maturing in cask for some 3–5 years will probably be necessary before a true pale tawny colour is achieved. (Some refreshment with a smaller proportion of younger wine may be advisable during this period). The wine should then be ready for drinking a year or so after bottling.

Recipe No. 3

RED PORT

Ingredients:

50 lb. peaches
25 lb. elderberries
4 pts. red grape conc.
2 pts. rose petals
Sugar or honey as required
Yeast nutrients
Port or Madeira yeast

Method:

Stone the peaches and press out the juice. Strain the latter carefully to remove pulp particles, add 100 p.p.m. sulphite and leave to settle for 24 hours in suitable sealed containers. At the end of this time rack off the clear juice (see note below) and add it to the crushed elderberries together with the yeast nutrients. Add the yeast starter and ferment on the pulp for 1–2 days (until an adequate depth of colour is achieved). Strain off the pulp and press lightly. Add the rose petals and grape concentrate and ferment on the flowers for 2–3 days. Strain off the flowers.

Thereafter check acid, etc., exactly as described in the first recipe. This wine should be matured in the same way as the preceding red port although in this case early bottling after one year in cask is not advisable. Its high tannin content makes 2–3 years in cask essential prior to bottling.

NOTE:

The deposits formed when the peach juice settles may be combined (after the clear juice has been racked off) and left to settle further in a suitable small container. The clear juice obtained in this way may then be fermented separately and used for blending or topping-up purposes.

Recipe No. 4
RED PORT

Ingredients:

40 lb. dessert apples
25 lb. elderberries
4 pts. red grape conc.
6 lb. blackcurrants
Port or Madeira yeast starter
2 pts. rose petals or elder-flowers
Sugar or honey as required
Yeast nutrients

Method:

The procedure which should be followed here is exactly as described in the preceding recipe. The juice must be extracted from the apples since the addition of water to the sliced apples followed by pulp fermentation will result in a poorer quality wine. The blackcurrants should be blended with the elderberries and the two fruits then treated together.

Maturing for 2–3 years in cask is again necessary due to the high tannin content of the wine. Early bottling after one year is thus inadvisable for this reason.

CHAPTER XXVIII

MADEIRA-TYPE WINES

MADEIRA is a tawny fortified wine produced on the island of the same name which is a Portuguese possession situated in the Atlantic Ocean some 500 miles off the coast of Morocco at a latitude just south of Casablanca. Since the island is a Portuguese colony, its wines are protected in Britain by the same regulations which govern the sale of port. It is therefore illegal to sell a wine as madeira unless it is actually a product of that island. Any other wines which resemble madeira must consequently be labelled "Madeira Type" (cf. imitation ports), but it is a noteworthy fact that few imitation madeiras are produced commercially.

Although Madeira cannot nowadays be regarded as a serious rival of port or sherry, at least insofar as sales are concerned, it was at one time an extremely popular wine in this country. In the past, middle-class families were accustomed to partaking of a mid-morning piece of cake accompanied by a glass of madeira wine, and the frequent mention of this delightful custom in the literature of previous eras is a notable tribute to the popularity of the wine. Unfortunately, a series of disasters befell the Madeira vineyards during the latter half of the 19th century, so that for some years only limited supplies of the wine were available. At more or less the same time, tea, then a novel beverage, became considerably cheaper because its transportation costs were markedly reduced by the introduction of the fast tea clippers. The net result was that tea replaced Madeira as a mid-morning drink and now only the term "Madeira cake" remains as a reminder of the older custom.

The climate of Madeira is temperate and has often been described as idyllic. It is certainly rare to find days without a few hours of sunshine and the weather remains fine and warm throughout the year. The comparatively low rainfall, especially on the lower slopes, is an excellent tourist attraction, but it does mean that during the drier summer months irrigation is necessary for successful viticulture, and to ensure a fair distribution the growers may be required to receive their allotment of water at almost any hour of the day or night. Madeira has a rugged, rocky, and in places a precipitous topography, for a central ridge of fairly high mountains virtually bisects its length. The steep slopes must therefore be terraced to hold the vines. The island is basically volcanic in origin and its rich soil has been derived from the weathering of thick beds of tuff (rock formed by the consolidation of volcanic ash deposits). Under these almost ideal conditions, it is hardly surprising to find that the land supports a riot of wild plant growth as well as vines, sugar cane, bananas and other crops.

The vines in most wine-producing regions of the world are kept short and well pruned back or trained along horizontal wires so that the grapes develop fairly close to the ground where ripening is assisted by the heat reflected and retained by the soil. Indeed, stones are often piled beneath the vines in order to promote the effects of the soil in this connection, particularly in northern regions. In Madeira, however, there is no need to conserve and focus the heat of the sun in this manner, for the climate is sufficiently warm to ripen the grapes fully in all but exceptional years. The vines are therefore trained to grow over tall wooden trellises some five or six feet high called pergolas so that the grapes develop well above the ground. This arrangement has been said to resemble a miniature hop garden. At vintage time the grapes are usually picked from within the pergola. In order to make the maximum use of the soil, a second crop which ripens earlier than the grapes, e.g. sweet potatoes, is commonly planted beneath and between the vines.

The grapes grown here are principally white varieties, the most important cépages being Sercial, Bual, Verdelho and Malvasia, but a red grape called Negra Mole is also planted in places. The wine from this latter grape was formerly exported under the name of Tinta, but nowadays it is reserved almost solely for blending purposes. It is interesting to note that the Sercial and Verdelho vines are close relatives of the German Riesling and the Spanish Pedro

Ximenez respectively, but the wines produced from the Madeira vines bear little resemblance to those produced from their European ancestors. The different climates and soils in which the vines grow and the vastly different methods by which the wines of Madeira are produced are all potent factors in this respect. The best quality grapes come mostly from the lower-yielding southern districts of the island or from the heights where the Sercial grape is cultivated. A proportion of very sweet grapes grown on the sandy soil of the neighbouring island of Porto Santo is also used for madeira production.

The vintage usually begins towards the middle of August with the picking of the grapes on Porto Santo. Many of these grapes are destined for table use, but some are pressed and the must transported to Madeira by small boats. On Madeira itself the harvest begins late in August with the picking of the Bual and Verdelho grapes but continues until October when the Sercial grapes are ripe. Malvasia grapes are also picked late, for they are left to raisinify on the vine so that a very sweet heavy must is obtained on pressing.

Until recently, the freshly-picked grapes were transported on the backs of carriers to small shallow wooden lagares fitted with a centrally mounted screw which are very similar in appearance and function to their counterparts in Spain. The grapes were then trodden in the lagar and the pulp pressed by binding it in place with thick rope and applying pressure by screwing down a massive stone weight. Nowadays, however, much of the pressing is carried out with the aid of modern automatic presses which save a great deal of time and labour. At this stage, the must may be plastered with gypsum in order to decrease its pH and discourage bacterial spoilage, but plastering does not appear to be so important in madeira production as it is in sherry production, for the practice seems less common in Madeira. The amount of gypsum used is normally equivalent to about $\frac{1}{2}$—1 oz. per gallon of must.

After pressing, the must is transported in goatskins on the backs of carriers and/or by lorry to the shippers' lodges in Funchal, the capital of the island, where the fermentation is conducted. It is at this point that the differences in the production of the various types of madeira first become apparent. Musts intended for the production of the lighter and drier wines (Sercial and Verdelho) are allowed to ferment with little interference except for occasional small additions of brandy which seems to moderate the fermentation should it become unduly vigorous. A long slow fermentation lasting for at least ten weeks, during which the yeast converts most of the sugar into alcohol, is desirable in the case of these wines since these conditions are particularly conducive to quality. On the other hand, musts intended for the heavier and sweeter wines (Bual and Malmsey) are fortified with brandy at the outset so that fermentation is partially inhibited and terminates before all the sugar has been metabolised by the yeast, thus ensuring that a strong sweet full-bodied wine is obtained.

After fermentation has ceased, all types of madeira receive another small dose of brandy which simultaneously increases their alcohol content and promotes more rapid clarification. Some weeks later, the clear wine is racked off its lees and then subjected to what can only be described as the peculiar and unique estufagem system of maturing. Briefly, this system entails heating the wine for some months at a temperature of 90°F. to 140°F. and appears to owe its origin to the old belief that a long sea voyage in the tropics, e.g. to the East Indies and back, was beneficial to the wine. In actual fact, the improvement in quality resulting from such a voyage was due to the heating received by the wine during its storage in the ship's hold rather than to the motion of the ship or the journey itself. Once this fact was realised, the shippers began to mature their wines in specially heated rooms called estufas instead of sending them on a long sea voyage, and it would appear that this procedure had found fairly general acceptance by the early 19th century. It is interesting to note that a drastic heat treatment of this nature would ruin most other types of wine, yet here it is responsible for much of the characteristic bouquet and flavour of madeira and is therefore an integral and indispensable phase in the production of these wines.

At first, most of the estufas were constructed of glass and the butts of wine were heated by the sun, the estufa acting more or less as a greenhouse does in colder climates. Temperature control was difficult under these conditions, e.g. the estufa cooled down during the night, so that many shippers installed artificial means of heating in an effort to maintain a reasonably even temperature. In addition, however, losses by leakage or evaporation from the butts were high and on occasion as much as 10% to 15% of the wine could be lost in this way. These problems have nowadays been largely overcome by pumping the wine into large glass-lined concrete tanks holding 10,000 gallons or more of wine. The impervious nature of this material prevents loss by evaporation and close temperature control can readily be achieved by means of heat exchangers. Some idea of the temperature control exercised in a modern estufa of this type can be gained from the fact that the temperature of the wine is increased by no more than 5°F. per 24 hours until the wine reaches the desired temperature. After the heating process is complete, the wine is then cooled at an equally slow rate.

The baking temperature and the time which the wine spends at this temperature vary according to the quality of the wine, for better quality is achieved if the wine is heated for a longer period at a lower temperature. Thus, the best wines are heated for about a year at 90°F. to 100°F. and slightly lower quality wines spend about six months at 110°F. What may be termed "popular" quality wines are baked for roughly 4½ months at 120°F. while the cheapest madeiras are only heated for about three months at 130°F. or even 140°F.

The effects of this baking process are very far-reaching. The wine darkens considerably in colour and acquires a distinct and unique bouquet and flavour which is difficult to define precisely and is due to the caramelisation of some of the residual unfermented sugar in the wine. The estufagem system of maturing also appears to confer longevity on the wine, for madeiras never seem to fall into senility and will outlive any other type of wine, although the reasons for this behaviour are only poorly understood. Indeed, it is reputed that Sir Winston Churchill drank a bottle of 1792 madeira on a visit to the island some years ago and at that time the wine was in the same excellent condition as Sir Winston himself.

The wine emerging from the estufa may be too dark in colour and its flavour may be slightly marred by what is called an "estufa" flavour. These faults are rectified by careful treatment with animal and vegetable charcoal respectively. Hazes are also usually present due to the precipitation of proteins and other substances which are unstable towards heat so that fining is necessary to effect complete clarification. The fining agents most commonly used for this purpose are Spanish earth (a highly absorptive clay), ox-blood or casein, although good quality wines are often fined with egg white. (Isinglass may be employed if hazes reappear later). Some alcohol may also be added at this stage to replace evaporation losses.

The law requires that the wine must be matured for 13 months after its period in the estufa so that it will be about 1½ to 2 years old before shipping can even be considered, but most shippers mature their wines for some years beyond this legal minimum. Maturing takes place in casks made from American oak. A small proportion of this wine may go for the production of vintage madeira when it will be blended with other wines of the same type produced in the year of its origin in order to balance out any minor imperfections and give a wine of the highest possible quality. A great deal of high quality madeira is matured by the solera system already described in the previous chapter on sherry, but in addition blending may also be carried out in a more conventional manner under the supervision of a taster (cf. port). The important point to note is that different madeiras of the same type are carefully blended in order to achieve the optimum quality, and special blending wines reserved solely for this purpose, e.g. Tinta from the Negra Mole grape, are often included because their presence enhances the character and quality of the blend.

Most madeira is shipped in bulk to its destination where it is bottled after a brief resting period of a few months. The shipping casks, unlike those used for maturing, are generally constructed from Portuguese oak. These casks were formerly propelled to the ships by swimmers, but nowadays boats are used and the custom of "swimming the wine out" has virtually been abandoned. A certain proportion of the wines is exported in bottles, however, and these bottles are usually encased in attractive wicker baskets which are made locally in the Comacho district north-east of Funchal.

The winemaker will have gathered by this time that several different types of madeira are produced, but so far only a vague description of these wines has been given. To begin with, madeira is or should be named after the grape from which it is made so that four principal types of wine are recognised, viz. Sercial, Verdelho, Bual and Malmsey (Malvasia). Sercial is the driest type of madeira, amber in colour and with a pleasant clean almost nutty flavour which makes it ideally suited as an aperitif wine. Verdelho is golden-coloured, rather sweeter than Sercial but with an aromatic bouquet and flavour which is appealing either as an aperitif wine or as a table wine. Bual is a full-bodied medium sweet tawny dessert wine whose flavour develops more in bottle than any other type of madeira and which has often been praised for its elegance and fragrance. The last of the four is Malmsey, a very full-bodied, sweet, deep tawny dessert wine which may well be substituted for port at the end of a meal.

What, then, are the basic principles which should be followed by the winemaker contemplating the production of madeira-style wines? One outstanding characteristic of a madeira is its full body and the dessert wines are certainly heavier in this respect than the drier wines. It is therefore essential to include at least 1–2 lb. bananas per gallon to obtain a wine with sufficient body, while 1–1½ lb. raisins or sultanas or ½–1 pt. white grape concentrate per gallon will help to provide vinous quality. Many other ingredients can be used in conjunction with the bananas and raisins or grape concentrate, but blackberries, yellow plums, greengages, peaches, parsnips and sugar beet are particularly well suited for this purpose. With the exception of the bananas, pulp fermentation is often though not always desirable in the case of fruits in order to extract as much body and flavour as possible, and about 2–4 days of pulp fermentation will usually be required according to the ripeness of the fruit and the rate of fermentation. To avoid pectin hazes and clarification difficulties, however, it is advisable to add about 1 oz. Pectozyme per 10 gallons prior to pulp fermentation.

After a period of pulp fermentation, the pulp should be carefully strained off and the acidity of the must adjusted to about 3.0–3.5 p.p.t. by means of a mixture containing equal weights of tartaric and malic acids or with tartaric acid alone. Plastering with gypsum at the rate of ½–1 oz. per gallon of must may be carried out exactly as described in the previous chapter on sherry (including the cream of tartar addition advised there), but in this case it is doubtful if plastering has any far-reaching effects on the quality of the wine.

Since all madeiras are fortified wines, most winemakers will prefer to avoid or at least cut down the cost of fortification by producing as much alcohol as possible by natural fermentation. Fortunately, madeira yeast has a very high alcohol tolerance and will normally produce 16%–18% alcohol without much difficulty provided it is given an adequate supply of nutrients and the technique of feeding the yeast with small doses of sugar syrup at intervals indicated by the hydrometer is followed. When making the drier types of madeira, the final dose of sugar should be added while a gravity decrease of 1–2 per day is still occurring so that the specific gravity of the wine finishes below 1.000. In the case of wines after the style of Bual or Malmsey for which a final gravity of 5–15 is required, however, further doses of sugar syrup can be added whenever the gravity of the must decreases to 5 or less until fermentation finally ceases. It is preferable to conduct the fermentation at a temperature of 65°F.–70°F., and if possible the temperature should be raised to 75°F.–80°F. when the fermentation is nearing completion to ensure that the yeast reaches its maximum alcohol tolerance and to stabilise the wine.

Once fermentation has ceased, the wine should be racked off its lees and at this stage sufficient alcohol to increase the alcoholic strength of the wine by about 1% may be added (just under 3 fluid ounces of 140 proof vodka per gallon). This fortification will promote a more rapid clarification and will prove beneficial to the quality of the wine, but it is by no means essential and in view of the high cost of fortifying spirit most winemakers will probably not care to do so. The wine, whether fortified or not, should then be stored for a few months to allow clarification to proceed and racked at least once more before it is heated in an estufa. The effect of heating on a wine which is not clear and stabilised, and in which yeast cells still exist in considerable quantities, is to produce a "bread" flavour in the finished wine.

The importance of the estufagem system of maturing for developing the typical caramelised bouquet and flavour of a madeira has already been stressed, so that it is essential for winemakers intending to produce wines of this type to set up an estufa of some description. For example, a shelf above a hot-water boiler or above a free-standing stove, an airing cupboard or, outside, a heated greenhouse may be suitable if a temperature of above 90°F. can be maintained. A fairly large temperature variation is permissible, but obviously the more closely the temperature is controlled the more reliable and reproducible will be the results, so that a lagged cupboard fitted with a thermostatic control would be ideal for this purpose.

The wine is best heated in a glass container, for prolonged heating tends to make casks leak and losses by evaporation and/or leakage would be high under these conditions. The container should not be completely filled since there will be some expansion of the wine as its temperature rises. Moreover, any yeast still suspended in the wine will cause a vigorous fermentation for the first few hours until it is killed by the heat so that a bored cork or bung plugged with cotton wool must be used initially to allow the carbon dioxide generated in this way to escape. The jar can later be topped up with warm wine and closed with a solid rubber bung to minimise evaporation losses. The wine should be racked every 3–4 months during its period in the estufa to remove any deposits which may have formed, but a racking may also be necessary about a month after heating has commenced if a large sediment forms within this time.

Although the period of heat treatment is an essential feature of madeira production, it is nevertheless not entirely above criticism. Thus, it is frequently responsible for the development of a slight but persistent off-flavour commonly known as estufa flavour, especially in wines where a fairly high baking temperature has been employed. The winemaker is therefore well advised to remove this off-flavour by treating the wine emerging from the estufa with charcoal. Most grades of activated charcoal seem to be suitable for this purpose (vegetable charcoal is probably the best), but whatever type is selected should preferably be in the form of a fairly fine powder so that a large surface area is exposed to the wine. About ½–1 oz. charcoal per gallon should be thoroughly mixed with the wine which is then left to settle and racked as soon as a firm deposit forms. Should the charcoal fail to settle out within a few days, it may be filtered off or alternatively the wine may be fined with a reliable proprietary fining agent. The latter procedure is probably preferable, especially as the wine may be slightly hazy and thus require further clarification in any case. Any residual hazes should, of course, be removed by fining whether the charcoal settles out or not, but wherever possible the bulk of the charcoal should first be removed by racking.

The wine should finally be matured for at least another year, preferably in cask, to smooth off any rough edges and to allow the typical madeira bouquet and flavour developed in the estufa to stabilise. Indeed, a period of up to five years in cask and several more years in bottle would strictly be necessary to bring out the full latent quality of the wine, but few amateur winemakers are likely to have the patience or will-power to put this suggestion into practice.

Recipe No. 1

SERCIAL OR VERDELHO

Ingredients:

25 lb. peaches
5 lb. bananas
4 pts. white grape conc.
Sugar as required
Tartaric acid as required
Yeast nutrients
Madeira yeast starter
½ oz. Pectozyme
Water to 5 gallons

Method:

Peel the bananas (rejecting the skins) and cut into slices. Boil the slices in 1 gallon water for ½ hour then strain off the pulp carefully. Stone the peaches and press out the juice. Sulphite the latter with 100 p.p.m. sulphite. Leave the peach juice and banana extract to settle for 24 hours exactly as described in the white table wine chapter. Blend the settled extract and juice (after racking them off their deposits), add the grape concentrate, yeast nutrients, yeast starter and sufficient sugar and water to give about 4½ gallons of must of gravity 90. Check the acidity and adjust it to 3.8–4.0 p.p.t. with tartaric acid (subsequent dilution with sugar syrup will reduce this figure to within 3.0–3.5 p.p.t.).

Thereafter conduct the fermentation as recommended in the text, adding small doses of sugar (¼ lb. per gallon) every time the gravity drops below 5. Sugar additions should be stopped while the gravity is still dropping at the rate of 1–2 points per day to ensure that a dry wine is obtained. Racking, estufa treatment and maturing should be carried out as directed in the text.

As an alternative but less satisfactory procedure the stoned peaches may be pulp fermented for three days, but this should be avoided if at all possible.

Recipe No. 2

SERCIAL OR VERDELHO

Ingredients:

30 lb. ripe gooseberries	**Tartaric acid as required**
5 lb. bananas	**½ oz. Pectozyme**
4 pts. white grape conc.	**Yeast nutrients**
Sugar or honey as required	**Madeira yeast starter**
	Water to 5 gallons

Method:

Peel the bananas (rejecting the skins) and cut into slices. Boil the slices in 1 gallon water for ½ hour then strain the hot liquor carefully over the crushed gooseberries (preferably topped and tailed). Add 2 lb. sugar or honey and another 1 gallon cold water. Stir well and when cool add the nutrients, pectozyme and yeast starter. Ferment on the pulp for 3–4 days then strain off the pulp and press lightly. Add the grape concentrate, 2 lb. sugar (or honey) and sufficient water to bring the volume up to about 4½ gallons. Check the acidity and adjust it to 3.8–4.0 p.p.t. with tartaric acid.

Thereafter proceed exactly as directed in the preceding recipe. Either sugar or honey, but preferably the latter, can be used for feeding the yeast during the fermentation.

Recipe No. 3

BUAL OR MALMSEY

Ingredients:

20 lb. blackberries
20 lb. greengages or yellow plums
10 lb. bananas
4 pts. white grape conc.
Sugar or honey as required
½ oz. Pectozyme
Tartaric acid as required
Yeast nutrients
Madeira yeast starter
Water to 5 gallons

Method:

Peel the bananas (rejecting the skins) and cut into slices. Boil the slices in 1 gallon water for ½ hour then strain the hot liquor carefully over the stoned greengages or plums and crushed blackberries. Add 2 lb. sugar or honey, the yeast nutrients and another 1 gallon cold water. When cool add the pectozyme and yeast starter. Ferment on the pulp for 3–4 days then strain off the pulp and press lightly. Add the grape concentrate, 2 lb. sugar or honey and sufficient water to bring the volume up to about 4½ gallons. Check the acidity and adjust it to 3.8–4.0 p.p.t. with tartaric acid (or chalk).

Thereafter proceed as instructed in the text, adding ¼ lb. sugar or honey per gallon every time the gravity drops to 5 or below, until fermentation finally ceases. The final gravity should be around 5–25 according to personal preference. Racking, estufa treatment and maturing should be carried out as recommended in the text.

Recipe No. 4

BUAL OR MALMSEY

Ingredients:

20 lb. parsnips or sugar beet
10 lb. bananas
5 lb. figs
5 lb. raisins
4 pts. white grape conc.
Sugar or honey as required
Tartaric acid as required
Malic acid as required
½ oz. Pectozyme
Yeast nutrients
Madeira yeast starter
Water to 5 gallons

Method:

Peel the bananas (rejecting the skins) and cut into slices. Boil the slices in water for ½ hour then strain the hot liquor over the chopped figs and raisins. Wash and chop the parsnips into chunks. Boil the chunks in 2 gallons water for 10–15 minutes then strain off the hot liquor over the figs and raisins. Press the residual parsnip pulp lightly. Add the yeast nutrients and ½ oz. each of citric acid and tartaric acids. When cool add the pectozyme and yeast starter and thereafter proceed exactly as described in the preceding recipe. An acidity check will be necessary here since that added initially will be insufficient in itself. Equal parts of malic and tartaric acid should be used to increase the acidity in this instance. Thereafter proceed as directed in the preceding recipe.

INDEX TO TABLES

Table		*Page*
I	Temperature Correction Factors, for Use with Hydrometer Readings taken at Different Temperatures	55
II	Gravity Tables, for the Interpretation of Hydrometer Data	57
III	Initial Gravity/Alcohol Factor Tables, for Calculating Alcoholic Strength from Hydrometer Data	68
IV	Principal Acid Present in Some Common Fruits	85
V	Typical Acid and Sugar Content of Some Common Fruit Juices	87
VI	Corresponding Acidities, in Parts per Thousand, of Various Acids	88
VII	Weights of Various Acids and Acid Mixtures, in Ounces per Gallon, Required to Provide a given Acidity	96
VIII	Formulae, Molecular Weights and Dissociation Constants of Three Common Plant Acids	108
IX	Typical Analyses of Domestic Water Supplies	118
X	Recommended Procedure for Handling Some Common Ingredients	157
XI	Relation between Percentage Alcohol by Volume and British Proof Spirit	242
XII	List of Components Required to Construct a Rack and Cloth Press	280
XIII	Amount of Sugar or Sugar Syrup Required for Sparkling Wines	367

INDEX TO ILLUSTRATIONS

	Illustration	*Page*
I	Equipment for Boiling	10
II	Earthenware Containers	12
III	Glass Containers	14
IV	Plastic Containers for Pulp Fermentation	15
V	Plastic Containers for Juice Fermentation or Bulk Storage	16
VI	Oak Half Cask and Fruit Pulper	17
VII	Cask and Supporting Framework	19
VIII	Cloths and Nylon Sieve for Straining	22
IX	Funnels for Filtration or Transfer	23
X	Vacuum Filtration Assembly	24
XI	Various Types of Fermentation Lock	26
XII	Screw Fruit Press	28
XIII	Rack and Cloth Fruit Press	29
XIV	Fruit Crusher and Electric Juice Extractor	30
XV	The Vinometer	32
XVI	Various Types of Closures	33
XVII	Corking Equipment	35
XVIII	More Corking Equipment	36
XIX	How to Wire Corks	38
XX	Bottle Brush	40
XXI	The Hydrometer and How to Read It	54
XXII	Yeast Cells under the Microscope	125
XXIII	Chart Showing the Principal Chemical Reactions of Alcoholic Fermentation	163
XXIV	Equipment for Racking Wine	179
XXV	A Continuous Wine Filter	201
XXVI	The Pearson Square	249
XXVII	Plans for Constructing a Rack and Cloth Press	274
XXVIII	Map of the Major Wine Producing Regions of France	288
XXIX	Map of the Rhine and Mosel Regions	296
XXX	Map of the Bordeaux Region	320
XXXI	Map of the Burgundy Region	324
XXXII	Map of the Rhône Valley Region	328
XXXIII	Map of the Champagne Region	352
XXXIV	Map of the Sherry Region	376
XXXV	Map of the Port Region and Other Portuguese Wine Districts	396

INDEX TO RECIPES

	Type of Recipe	*Page*
	General Selection	263
II	For White Table Wines	311
III	For Dry Red Table Wines	337
IV	For Sauternes-Type Wines	348
V	For Sparkling Wines	372
VI	For Sherry-Type Wines	393
VII	For Port-Type Wines	408
VIII	For Madeira-Type Wines	422

INDEX TO PARTS I AND II

A

Acetaldehyde **165**, 167, **196**, 203, **208**
Acetals 204, 222
Acetate, Ethyl **254**
Acetic Acid 161, 167, 203, **254**
Acetification 11, 18, 41, 43, **253**, 318, 333, 380, 401
Acetifying Bacteria 18, 43, 48, 81, 150, **253**, 318
Acetobacter **253**
Acid ..... See under Specific Acid Required
Acid Content ..... See under Acidity References
Acids, Mixtures of **94**, 99, 231, 334
Acids, Plant **84**
Acids, Stock Solutions of 21, **95**
Acids, Strong 84, 106
Acids, Weak 84, 106, 110
Acidity 71, **83**, 139, 156, 166, 209, 216, 234, 308, 334, 364, 370, 389, 407
Acidity, and Acid Taste 91, 94, 110
Acidity, and Maturing 209, 222, 323, 335
Acidity, and pH 92, **106**, 110
Acidity, Determination of **89**, 116, 123, 156
Acidity, of Commercial Wines See under Specific Commercial Wine
Acidity, of Fruits **84**, 93, 97, 146
Acidity, of Musts **91**, **156**, 231
Acidity, of Rhubarb 84, 97, **99**
Acidity, Reduction of 71, 83, **97**, 156
Acidity, Titratable ..... See under Acidity References
Acidity, Tolerance of Yeast to 97, 111, 136
Acid Taste, and Acidity 91, 94, 110
Acid Taste, and pH 92, 110
Albariza Soils 377
Albuminous Proteins **191**
Alcohol 33, 161, 172, 175, 181, 203, 209, 216, 234, **239**, 254, 257, 383
Alcohol, Amyl 166
Alcohol, Colour Extraction by **149**, 223
Alcohol, Determination of 33, 65, 240
Alcohol, Ethyl ..... See under Alcohol References
Alcohol, in Commercial Wines See under Specific Commercial Wine
Alcohol, Methyl 167, 247
Alcohol, Potential **63**, 165, 172
Alcohol, Tolerance of Yeast to 61, **127**, 139, **172**, 181, 243, 408, 420
Alcohol, Yield from Fermentation **59**, **63**, **164**, 171, 234, 255
Alcohols, Higher 166, 203, 241
Alcohol, Strength ..... See under Alcohol References
Aldehydes 114, 204, 335, 381
Alsace **297**
Amino-acids 141, 167, 357

Ammonium Phosphate 136, **141**, 167
Amyl Alcohol 166
Amylozyme 100 .... **190**
Aneurin Hydrochloride 141
Anjou **294**
Aperitifs, from Oranges 228
Apples 84, 113, 143, 190, 278, 305, 364, 388
Arabinose 74
Arena Soils 377
Argols 94
Armagnac 244
Asbestos Pulp 23, **194**, 200
Astringency .... See under Tannin References
Auslese Wines **304**, 345
Australian Honey 80
Autolysis 101, 128, 130, 133, **177**, 180, 309, **357**, 361, **383**

B

Bacteria 25, 27, 41, 48 93, 96, 111, 126, 132, 137, 205, 245, 383, 391
Bacteria, Acetifying 18, 43, 48, 81, 150, **253**, 318
Bacteria, Lactic Acid 48, 100, 245, **257**, **370**
Baker's Yeast **129**, 171
Balances, for Weighing 21, 95
Balling 56
Bananas 11, 44, 85, 93, 115, 180, 186
Bananas, for Body 220, **227**, 331, 346, 407, 419
Bananas, Preparation of 44, **148**, 306
Barrels .... See under Casks
Barros Soils 377
Barsac **341**
Baumé 56
Beaujolais 210, **325**
Beerenauslese Wines **304**, 345
Beet Sugar 74
Bentonite **193**, 386
BHC 318 .... **50**
Bingen 303
Bins, for Bottle Storage 40
Bitterness .... See under Tourne Disease
Blackcurrants 219, 227, 330, 407
Blending Ingredients 115, 154, **215**, 263, 305, 388
Blending Wines 100, 176, **232**, 259, 355, 359, 386, 402, 418
Blood 191, 319, 418
Bloom on Fruits 42, 123
Body 19, 98, 145, 166, 216, **218**, 234, 283, 331
Body, Bananas for **220**, 227, 331, 346, 407, 419
Body, Blending Ingredients for **218**
Body, Grain for **220**
Body, of Commercial Wines See under Specific Commercial Wine
Bordeaux 69, **292**, **319**, 341
Boring Corks **37**

Botrytis Cinerea 166, 304, **342**
Bottle Brushes 39, 47
Bottle Fermentation **356**, 370
Bottle Sickness **196**, **208**
Bottle Storage Bins 40
Bottles 14, 34, 207, 356, 403
Bottles, Maturing in 34, 40, 204, **207**, 236, 310, 336, 347, 357, 361, 408, 422
Bouquet 79, 98, 167, 189, 203, **220**, 234, 248, 292, 336
Bouquet, Blending Ingredients for **220**
Bouquet, Flowers for 153, **222**, 307, 332, 346, 364, 407
Bouquet, of Commercial Wines See under Specific Commercial Wine
Brandy 239, **243**, 248, 393, 401, 406, 416
Brewer's Yeast **131**
Brix 56
Buchner Funnels 24, 195
Budding **124**
Buffer Solutions **110**
Bulk Storage 114, 182, **205**
Bungs **34**, 421
Burette 89
Burgundy, Red **325**, 360
Burgundy, White 218, 221, **290**, 360
By-products of Fermentation 78, 85, **165**, 204, 222, 343

C

Calcium Salts 98, 120, 139, 184, **379**
Campden Tablets **45**, 48, 181, 208, 337
Candida Albicans 123
Candida Mycoderma **256**
Candy Sugar 75
Cane Sugar 71, 74, 356
Cap of Pulp 150, 256, 318, 365
Caps, Crown 38, 356
Capsules **37**
Carbohydrates See under Sugar References
Carbonation **362**, 369
Carboys, Glass 13, 43, 47
Casein **193**, 418
Casks **16**, **281**
Casks, Care of **19**, 43, **281**
Casks, Half 17
Casks, Maturing in 17, 114, **205**, 236, 309, **336**, 347, 391, 405, 408, 422
Casks, Oxidation in **205**, 310, 336, 347
Casks, Sizes of **18**, 205
Casse, Metallic **260**
Casse, Oxidative 50, **260**, 344
Chablis **291**, 325
Chalk, Reducing Acidity with **98**, 389
Champagne 236, 246, **297**, **353**, 399

Chaptalisation 74
Charmat Process for Sparkling Wines **360**
Châteauneuf-du-Pape 327
Citric Acid 46, 84, **93**, 99, 107, 135, 161, 222, 260, 283, 308, 334, 388
Claret 209, 293, **319**
Clarification 25, 79, 130, 157, **182**, 206, 236, 355, 407, 418, 420, 422
Clarification, and Pectin 44, 148, **184**, 419
Clarification, and Sulphite 49, 183
Clarification, and Tannin 113, 346
Clarification, by Refrigeration 94, 100, 141, 183, 361, 387
Classification of Sugars **72**
Classification of Wines 68, **214**
Cleaning Casks 18, **281**
Cleaning Equipment 12, 14, 22, **42**, 47, 50
Climate in Commercial Wine Regions See under Specific Commercial Wine
Clinitest, for Sugar Determination 65, 69, **82**, 366
Closures, Plastic 12
Cloths, for Pressing **275**
Cloths, for Straining **22**
Cognac 244
Colanders **21**
Collagenous Proteins **192**
Colloids 50, 183
Colloids, Protective **184**, 190, 344
Colour Extraction from Red Fruits 113, **148**, 310, **318**, 331, **401**
Concentrate, Grape ..... See under Grape Concentrate
Conditioning Casks 18, **281**
Concentrates **245**
Containers **12**, 149, 253
Containers, Earthenware **13**, 260
Containers, Glass **13**, 145, 206, 347, 421
Containers, Glazing of **11**, **13**, 260
Containers, Oak **16**, **205**, **281**
Containers, Plastic..... **15**, 47, 149
Containers, Stoneware ..... See under Containers, Earthenware
Continuous Filters..... 23, 195, **199**
Cork Borers 37
Corks **34**, 359, 403
Corking Equipment 36
Coteuax du Touraine **294**
Côte Chalonnaise **290**, **325**
Côte de Beaune **290**, **325**
Côte de Nuits **290**, **325**
Côte d'Or **290**, **325**
Côte Rôtie **327**
Côtes du Rhône **327**
Cradle, for Casks 20
Cream of Tartar **93**, 100, 140, 183, 355, 361, **379**, 387, 389, 420
Criadera **384**

Crown Caps 38. 356
Crushers **31**
Crust, in Port **403**
Cultures, Yeast **134**
Cylinders, Measuring **21**

D

Dégorgement **246**, **358**, **368**
Demerara Sugar 74
Designing Recipes **229**, 263
Detergents, Sterilising 50
Determination of Acidity **89**, 116, 123, 156
Determination of Alcohol 33, **65**, 240
Determination of pH **108**
Determination of Sugar **65**, **69**, **81**, 356, **366**
Determination of Tannin 116
Dextrans 344
Dextrins 72, 344
Dextrose 77
Dihydroxyacetone **165**
Dilution, Effects of **58**, **64**, 71, 97, 140, 149, 156, 182, 219, 305
Dilution, to Reduce Acidity **71**, **83**, **97**, 156, 219
Disaccharides 72, 76, 189
Disorders of Wine **253**
Dissociation Constant 106
Distillation of Spirits **243**, 246
Dosage **359**, **368**
Drosophila Melanogaster **42**
Dry Wine, Definition of **69**, **82**

E

Earthenware Containers **13**, 260
Eau-de-Vie **243**
Ebullioscope 68, 240
Edelfäule ..... See under Botrytis Cinerea
Egg White 115, 187, **191**, 319, 334, 386, 402
Elderberries 110, 113, 151, 191, 330, 336, 388, 407
Elderflowers, for Bouquet **224**, 307, 332, 346, 407
Enzymes 73, 76, **162**, **171**, 173, 177, **187**, 342
Enzymes, Oxidative 50, 145, **260**, 344
Enzymes, Pectin-destroying 44, 148, **186**, 230, 306
Enzymes, Starch-destroying **190**
Enzymes, Zymase Complex **162**
Equipment ..... See under Specific Item Required
Equipment, Cleaning of 12, 14, 22, **42**, 47, 50
Equipment, for Racking 39, 170
Equipment, Metal Warning **10**, 253, 268

Equipment, Sterilisation of **43, 47**, 50, 278, 282
Esterification **203, 207**, 222
Esters 79, **153, 204**, 207, 222, 245, 254
Estufa **416, 421**
Ethanol **239**
Ethyl Acetate **254**
Ethyl Pyrocarbonate 363
Exhibiting 83, 214
Extracting Colour from Red Fruits 113, **148**, 310, **318**, 331, 401
Extractors, Juice **29**, 145, 305

F

Fehling's Solution 81
Feluns Soil 295
Fermentation 59, 73, 83, 98, 111, 123, 139, 157, **161**, 236, 246, 283
Fermentation, Alcohol Yield from **59, 63, 164**, 171, 234, 251, 406
Fermentation, and Phosphates **140**, 164
Fermentation, and Racking **178, 181**
Fermentation, and Temperature 134, 166, 169, **173**, 256, **318**, 326
355, 357, 360, 420
Fermentation, By-products of 78, 85, **165**, 204, 222, 343
Fermentation, in Bottles **356**, 370
Fermentation, Juice 27, 113, **145**
Fermentation, Locks 9, **25**, 34, 50, **127**, 197, 254
Fermentation, Malo-Lactic **100**, 167, 322, 334, 347, 362, **370**
Fermentation of Commercial Wines. See under Specific Commercial Wine
Fermentation, Phases of 154, 157, **167**, 308
Fermentation, Pulp 21, 27, 45, 59, 99, 113, 145, **148**, 180, 217
232, 307, **310, 318**, 333, 365, **401**, 419
Fermentation, Sticking 62, 76, 126, 134, 139, 172, **175**, 181,
255, 333
Film Yeasts 253, **256**
Filter Papers 194
Filters and Funnels **22**, 194
Filters, Continuous 23, 195, **199**
Filters, Rapid 194
Filters, Vacuum 23, **195**
Filtration 98, 185, 190, **194, 199**, 208, 304, 361, 386, 422
Filtration, Oxidation during **196**, 204
Filtration, Vacuum 23, **195**
Filtration, with Asbestos Pulp 23, **194**
Fining and Fining Agents..... 114, 183, 185, **190**, 196, 208, 309,
319, 334, 356, 386, 391, 402
Fining, and Tannin 114, **191**
First Racking 49, 98, 137, **179**, 390
Fish Gelatine .... See under Isinglass
Flasks, Conical 89
Flavour, Blending Ingredients for **226**
Flies, Fruit or Vinegar 42, 50, 254
Flogger, for Corks 36

Flor, Sherry 257, **381**, 388
Flowers, for Bouquet 153, **222**, 307, 332, 346, 364, 407
Flowers, Preparation of **153**, 223, 307
Flowers of Wine **256**
Fortification 61, 166, 210, 227, **243**, 380, 387, 401, 406, 416, 420
Fortification, Spirit Requirements for **248**
Freezing Mixtures **368**
Fructose 72, **76**, 345
Fruit Flies 42, 50, 254
Fruit Juices 30, 71, 113, 117, 135, 140, **145**, 278, 305, 331
Fruits, Acidity of **84**, 93, 97, 146
Fruits, Bloom on 42, 123
Fruits, Preparation of **145**, **151**
Fruits, Pressing of 27, 113, **145**, **276**, 305, 343, 354, 365, 415
Fruits, Red .... See under Red Fruits
Fruits, Tannin in 113, 151
Fungi 25, 27, 41, 49, 93, 96, 111, 116, 123, 126, 132, 137, 152, 166, 245, **342**, 383
Funnels, Buchner 24, 195
Funnels and Filters **22**, 194, 385
Fusel Oil 141, **166**, 204, 247, 401

G

Galactose 73
Gardening 144
Gases, in Water 117
Gay-Lussac..... .... **161**, 240
Gay-Lussac Equation 63, **161**, 164
Gelatine **192**, 319, 356, 420
Gelatine, Fish .... See under Isinglass
German Wines 74, 91, 133, 181, 209, 219, 221, **297**, 360
Glass Containers **13**, 145, 206, 347, 421
Glass, Maturing in **206**, **336**, 391
Glazing of Containers 11, **13**, 260
Glucose 72, 76, 126, 345
Glycerine .... See under Glycerol
Glycerol 35, 48, 100, 115, 163, **165**, **343**, 381
Glycogen 126, 165
Gooseberries 86, 151, 278, 346, **348**, 364, 388
Grain 43, 84, 93, 123, 144, 151, 190, 221, 388
Grain, for Body **220**
Grain, Preparation of **152**
Grape Concentrate, for Vinous Quality **229**, 307, 332, 346 365, 419
Grapes and Grape Juice 74, 84, 92, 131, 139, 144, 148, 166, **216**, 221
Grapes for Commercial Wines. See under Specific Commercial Wine
Grape Tannin **115**
Graves .... 69, 219 ,**292**, 321, 341

Gravity **56**, 146, 234
Gravity and Alcohol 59, **65**, 68
Gravity, Specific .... See under Specific Gravity
Gypsum **379, 389**, 415, 420

H

Half Casks 17
Hardness of Water **120**, 140
Hazes .... See under Clarification References
Heat, Colour Extraction by **149**
Heat ,Sterilisation by **43**, 135
Herbs, for Flavour 226, 228
Hermitage **327**
Hexoses **72**
Higher Alcohols 166, 203, 245
Hock .... See under German Wines
Honey **43, 75, 79**, 123, 155, 231, 308, 364
Hydrogen Ion Concentration 92, **105**, 110
Hydrogen Ions 76, 92, 105
Hydrometer 32, **53**, 58, 81, 123, 155, 165, 172, 240, 390, 408, 420
Hydrometer, Uses of **58**, 155, 175, 217, 240, 390

I

Illustrations .... See Separate Index
Indicator Papers, Narrow Range 92, **108**
Ingredients, Blending of 115, 154, **215**, 263, 305, 388
Ingredients, Pectin in **186**, 230
Ingredients, Preparation of **143**, 151, 254
Ingredients, Sterilisation of **44**, 47, 254
Inversion of Sugar 77
Invertase **76**
Invert Sugar 75, **78**
Iodine, for Starch Testing..... .... **190**
Ion Exchange Resins 103, 121
Ions, Hydrogen 76, 92, 105
Isinglass **191**, 319, 356, 418
Isomerism 73, 166

J

Juice Extractors **29**, 145, 305
Juice Fermentation 27, 113, **145**
Juices, Fruit .... See under Fruit Juices

K

Keeping Records **146**
Kitchen Scales 21
Kloeckera Apiculata **129**

L

Labels 39
Lactic Acid 85, 100, 167, 258, 370
Lactic Acid Bacteria 48, 100, 245, **257**, 370
Lactose 73
Laevulose 77
Lag Phase of Fermentation **167**, 174
Lead Glazed Containers 11, **13**, 260
Lead Poisoning 10, **13**, 260
Lemons 84, 93
Light, Spoilage by 13, 14, **204**, 323, 336, 356, 403
Liqueur d'Expédition 246, **359**, **369**
Litmus Papers 108
Locks, Fermentation 9, **25**, 34, 50, **127**, 197, 254
Loire Wines **294**, 360
Longevity of Wines **209**, **335**

M

Mâconnais **290**, **325**
Madeira 61, 210, 227, 244, 246, 399, **413**
Magnesium Salts 120, 136, **140**
Malic Acid 84, **94**, 99, 100, 107, 222, **303**, 308, 334, 346, 364, 366, **370**, 420
Malo-Lactic Fermentation **100**, 167, 322, 334, 347, 362, **370**
Maltose 72, 76, 81, 189
Mannitol 101, 258
Mannose 73
Marc Brandy 244
Marmite 136, **141**
Mashing ..... See under Soaking
Maturing **94**, **157**, **189**, **203**, **209**, 217, 247, 259, 335
Maturing, and Acidity 209, 222, 323, 325
Maturing, and Oxidation **203**, **335**
Maturing, and Tannin 114, **209**, 323, 335
Maturing, and Temperature **204**, 385, 416
Maturing, in Bottle 34, 40, 204, **207**, 236, 310, 336, 347, 357, 408, 422
Maturing, in Bulk 114, 182, 205
Maturing, in Cask 17, 114, **205**, 236, 309, **336**, 347, 357, 408, 422
Maturing, in Glass **206**, **336**, 391
Maturing, of Commercial Wines See under Specific Commercial Wine
Measures and Measuring Cylinders **21**
Media, for Yeast Starters **135**
Médoc 292, 321
Meso-Inositol 139
Metabisulphite, Sodium and Potassium **45**
Metallic Casse **260**
Metals, Contamination by **10**, 253, 260
Methyl Alcohol 167, 247

Meursault 290
Mineral Salts in Water 120, 140
Mixtures, Freezing 368
Mixtures of Acids 94, 99, 231, 334
Montrachet 290, 325
Monosaccharides 72, 76
Mosel(le) Wines ..... See under German Wines
Moulds ..... See under Fungi
Muscatel Wines 244, 246
Musts, Acidity of 91, 156, 231
Musts, Preparation of 143
Musts, Preparation from Ingredients. See under Specific Ingredient
Musts, Sterilisation of 44, 47, 254, 305, 332
Musts, Sugar for or in 53, 58, 64, 71, 136, 146, 154, 175, 231, 333, 343
Mycoderma Aceti 253
Mycoderma Vini 256

N

Nahe Wines 303
Nantes 294
Narrow Range Indicator Papers 92, 108
Natural Sugar in Musts 53, 58, 66, 71, 146, 154, 231
Natural Yeasts ..... See under Wild Yeasts
Neutral Spirits 244, 248
Nierstein Wines 301
Noble Rot ..... See under Botrytis Cinerea
Nutrients, Yeast 101, 135, 139, 155, 167, 172, 180, 263, 332, 367, 370

O

Oak Containers 16, 205, 281
Oil, Fusel 141, 166, 204, 247, 401
Oiliness 258
Oligosaccharides 72
Oppenheim Wines 301
Oranges, for Aperitifs 228
Osmotic Pressure 175
Oxalic Acid 85, 99
Ox Blood 191
Oxidation 18, 145, 207, 260, 335, 382
Oxidation, and Sulphite 50, 145, 197
Oxidation, during Filtration 196, 204
Oxidation, during Maturing 203, 335
Oxidation, in Casks ..... 205, 310 ,336, 347
Oxidation/Reduction Reactions 165, 207
Oxidative Casse 50, 260. 344
Oxidative Enzymes 50. 145, 260, 344

P

Palatinate Wines 299
Papers, Filter 194
Papers, Litmus 108
Papers, Narrow Range Indicator 92, 108
Parsnips 148, 183, 186, 279, 346, 388, 419
Peaches 79, 230, 279, 305, 331, 346, 388, 419
Pears 86, 230, 260, 364
Pearson Square 249
Pectin 44, 59, 110, 148, 151, 167, 183, 230, 344, 419
Pectin, and Clarification 44, 148, 184, 419
Pectin, in Ingredients 186, 230
Pectin, Solubility of 44, 148, 187
Pectin, Test for 185
Pectin-destroying Enzymes 44, 148, 186, 230, 306
Pectinol, Pectozyme, Pektolase 44, 148, 186, 189, 230, 306, 419
Pentoses 74, 82
Pfalz Wines..... 299
pH 77, 92, 105, 370, 379, 415
ph, and Acidity 92, 106, 110
pH, and Acid Taste 92, 110
pH, and Spoilage 111, 379
pH, Determination of 108
pH-Meter 92, 109
Phenolphthalein 89
Phosphates 139, 140, 164, 167, 380
Pipette 89
Plant Acids 84
Plasmolysis 175
Plastering 379, 389, 415, 420
Plastic Containers 15, 47, 149
Plastic Closures 12
Poisoning, by Lead 10, 13, 260
Polish Spirit ..... See under Vodka
Polysaccharides 72, 126, 184
Pomerol 321
Port 61, 210, 219, 227, 236, 244, 246, 399, 418
Potassium Metabisulphite 45
Potassium Salts 100, 136, 140
Potential Alcohol 63, 165, 172
Pouilly-Fuissé 290
Pourriture Noble ..... See under Botrytis Cinerea
Preliminary First Racking 49, 180
Preparation of Bananas 44, 148, 306
Preparation of Flowers 153, 223, 307
Preparation of Fruits 145, 151
Preparation of Grain 152
Preparation of Ingredients 143, 254
Preparation of Must 143
Preparation of Red Fruits 149, 331
Preparation of Rhubarb 99
Preparation of Vegetables 44, 147, 306

Presses **27**, 145, **273**
Pressing Fruits 27, 113, **145**, **276**, 305, 343, 354, 365, 415
Pressure, in Sparkling Wines **356**, **367**, 370
Pressure, Osmotic 175
Primary Fermentation 154, 157, **169**, 308
Proof Spirit..... **240**
Protective Colloids **184**, 190, 344
Proteins 110, 113, 141, 162, 187, 189, 335, 418
Proteins, Albuminous **191**
Proteins, Collagenous **192**
Pulp, Asbestos 23, **194**, 200
Pulp Fermentation 21, 27, 45, 59, 99, 113, 145, **148**, 180, 217, 232, 307, **310**, **318**, **333**, 365, **401**, 419

R

Rack and Cloth Press 28, **273**
Racking 101, 130, 146, 157, **177**, 206, 236, 334, 366, 390, 406, 421
Racking, and Fermentation **178**, **181**
Racking, and Sulphite **49**, **181**, 183
Racking, Equipment for 39, 178
Racking, Optimum Times for 49, 98, 137, **179**
Rain Water 120
Raisins, for Vinous Quality **229**, 307, 332, 346, 365, 419
Rapid Filters 194
Raspberries..... 43, 97, 227, 330, 407
Recipes 83, 123, 128, 144, 221, 226, **262**, **311**, **337**, **372**, **393**, **408**, **423**
Recipes, Designing of **229**, 263
Recipes, " No-Yeast " 123, 128
Records, Keeping of **146**
Red Burgundy **325**, 360
Red Fruits, Colour Extraction from 113, **148**, 310, **318**, 331, 401
Red Fruits, Preparation of **149**, **331**
Red Table Wines 148, 206, 209, 218, 226, 234, 297, **317**, **330**
Reduction 165, 203, 361
Refining of Sugar 74
Refrigeration, for Clarification 94, 100, 141, 183, 361, 387
Remuage **357**, **368**
Resins, IonExchange 103, 121
rH 208
Rhamnose 73
Rheinhesse Wines **300**
Rheingau Wines **301**
Rheinpfalz Wines **299**
Rhine Wines ..... See under German Wines
Rhône Wines 218, **327**
Ropiness **258**
Rose Petals, for Bouquet **225**, 307, 346
Rosé Wines..... 223, 234, 294, **310**, 360
Rüdesheim Wines 301

S

Saccharomyces Apiculatus 129
Saccharomyces Beticus **381**
Saccharomyces Carlsbergensis 131
Saccharomyces Cerevisiae **129**
Saccharomyces Ellipsoideus **131**, 345, 381
Sanbri Corkers **36**
Sauternes 133, 206, 209, 221, **341**
Scales, Kitchen 21
Second Racking 137, **181**
Secondary Fermentation **171**
Settling Fruit Juices **145**, 278, 305, 345
Sherry **61, 133, 206, 210, 219, 227, 236, 244, 246, 377,** 402, 418
Sherry Flor 257, **381**, 389
Showing ..... See under Exhibiting
Sickness, Bottle **196, 208**
Sieves, for Straining 22
Soaking Ingredients **151**
Soda, Washing 120, 282
Sodium Carbonate 120, 282
Sodium Hydroxide Solution **89**
Sodium Metabisulphite **45**
Softening Water **120**
Soil, in Commercial Wine Regions. See under Specific Commercial Wine
Solera **384, 391**, 402, 418
Sparkling Wines 38, 91, 100, 145, 294, **353**
Sparkling Wines, Charmat Process for **360**
Sparkling Wines, Pressure in **356, 367**, 370
Sparkling Wines, Transfer Process for 362
Spätburgunder 297
Spätlese Wines **304**
Specific Gravity 53
Specific Gravity, and Sugar **56**
Specific Gravity, and Temperature **55**
Spirit, Neutral 244, 248
Spirit, Polish ..... See under Vodka
Spirit, Proof **240**
Spirits, Distillation of **243**, 246
Spirits, Fortification with **248**
Spoilage 10, 20, 41, **42**, 101, 128, 135, 150, 168, 176, 245, **253**, 278, 281, 333, 361, 371, **415**
Spoilage, and pH 111, 373
Spoilage, and Sulphite 49, 101, **250**
Spoilage, by Light 13, 14, **204**, 323, 336, 356, 408
Spoilage, in Pulp Caps 150, 256, 310
Stability of Sulphite Solutions 45
Starch **72**, 126, 185, **190**
Starch-Destroying Enzymes **199**
Starch, Test for **196**
Starters, Yeast 49, 97, 98, **134**, 142, 168, 174, 309, 390

Steeping .... See under Soaking
St. Emilion **321**
Sterilisation, by Heat **43**, 135
Sterilisation, by Sulphite **47**, 134
Sterilisation, of Equipment **43, 47**, 50, 278, 282
Sterilisation, of Musts **44, 47**, 254, 305, 332
Sterilising Detergents 50
Sticking Fermentation 62, 76, 126, 134, 139, 172, **175**, 181, 255, 333
Stock Solutions of Acids 21, 95
Stock Solutions of Sulphite 21, **45**, 134, 282
Stock Solutions of Tannin 21, **116**
Stoneware Containers. ..... See under Earthenware Containers
Stoppers 34
Storage. .... See under Maturing References
Storage Bins for Bottles 40
Strainers **21**, 253
Straining Cloths **22**
Strong Acids 84, 106
Succinic Acid 85, **167**, 222, 346
Sucrose. .... See under Sugar References
Sugar 33, 61, **71**, 110, 126, 139, 155, 162, 167, 172, 229, 258, 263
Sugar, and (Specific) Gravity **56**
Sugar, Determination of 65, 69, **81**, 356, **366**
Sugar, Feeding Yeast with **61**, 155, 347, 390, 406, 420
Sugar, for Musts **58, 64**, 71, 136, 146, 154, 175, 231, 333, 343, 365
Sugar, from Cane and Beet 71, 74, 359
Sugar, Inversion of **77**
Sugar, Invert 75, 78
Sugar, Natural in Musts **53, 58**, 66, 71, 146, 154, 231
Sugar, Refining of 74
Sugar Syrup 62, **75** 97, 137, 180, 309, 347, 356, **366**, 390, 406, 420
Sugar, Types of **74**
Sugar, Volume Occupied by 54, **76**, 154
Sugars, Classification of **72**
Sugars, Fermentable 73, 76
Sulphates 121, 136, **140, 379**, 389
Sulphite 34, **45**, 81, 101, 135, **150**, 166, 208, 236, **255**, 282, 305, 334, 337, 361, 370
Sulphite, and Clarification 49, 183
Sulphite, and Oxidation 50, 145, **197**
Sulphite, and Racking **49, 181**, 183
Sulphite, and Spoilage 49, 101, **255**
Sulphite, and Sterilisation **47**, 134
Sulphite, Antioxidant Properties of **50, 145**, 197, 260, 344, 383
Sulphite, Stock Solutions of 21, **45**, 134, 282
Sulphite, Tolerance of Yeast to 48, 168
Sulphite Solutions, Stability of **46**
Sulphur Dioxide. .... See under Sulphite References
Sultanas. .... See under Raisins
Sweetening, with Non-fermentable Sugars 73

T

Tables .... See Separate Index
Table Wines, Red 148, 206, 209, 218, 226, 234, 297, **317**, **330**
Table Wines, White 145, 206, 218, 226, 230, 234, **289**, **304**
Tablets, Campden 45, 48, 181, 208, 337
Tank Process for Sparkling Wines **360**
Tannic Acid **115**
Tannin 19, 110, **113**, 151, 156, 166, 209, 216, 234, 281, 302, 330, 378, 407
Tannin, and Clarification 113, 346
Tannin, and Fining 114, **191**
Tannin, and Maturing 114, **209**, 323, 335
Tannin, Determination of 116
Tannin, Grape **115**
Tannin, in Fruits 113, 151
Tannin, in Tea 115
Tannin, Stock Solutions of 21, **116**
Taps, for Casks 20
Tartar, Cream of **93**, 100, 140, 183, **355**, 361, **379**, 387, 389, 420
Tartaric Acid 46, 84, **93**, 100, 107, 136, **191**, 303, 308, 334, 346, 379, 381, 420
Tavel Wines **327**
Tea, Tannin in 115
Teinturier Grapes 317
Temperature, and Fermentation 134, 166, 169, **173**, 256, **318**, 326, 355, 357, 360, 420
Temperature, and Maturing **204**, 385, **416**
Temperature, and (Specific) Gravity **55**
Thermometers **39**
Thiamine Hydrochloride 141
Ties, Wire 38, 359
Titratable Acidity .... See under Acidity References
Topping-up..... .... 146, **182**, 337
Tourne Disease **258**
Transfer Process for Sparkling Wines **362**
Trockenbeerenauslese Wines **304**
Tubing, for Racking 39, 178
Twaddell 56

U

Urea **141**

V

Vacuum Filtration 23, 195
Vegetables 11, 43, 93, 115, 144, 183, 186, 215, 221, 279, 388
Vegetables, Preparation of 44, 147, 306
Vinegar .... See under Acetification
Vinegar Bacteria .... See under Acetifying Bacteria

Vinegar Flies .... See under Fruit Flies
Vinometer 33, 240
Vinosity .... See under Vinous Quality References
Vinous Quality, Blending Ingredients for 229
Vinous Quality, Grape Concentrate for **229**, 307, 332, 346, 365, 419
Vinous Quality, Raisins for **229**, 307, 332, 346, 365, 419
Vitamin B 136, **141**
Vitamins 139
Vodka 245, **248**, 337, 406, 420
Vouvray Wines **294**, 360

W

Washing Soda 120, 282
Water **117**
Water, and Wine Quality **121**
Water, Gases in 117
Water, Hardness of **120**, 140
Water, Mineral Salts in **120**, 140
Water, Rain 120
Water, Softening of **120**
Weak Acids 84, 106, 110
White Burgundy 218, 221, **290**, 360
White of Egg 115, 187, **191**, 319, 334, 386, 402
White Table Wines 145, 206, 218, 226, 230, 234, **289**, 304
Wild Yeast 42, 48, 81, 123, **128**, 135, 152, 171
Wine .... See under more Specific Reference
Wine, Definition of Dry 69, 82
Wine, Flowers of **256**
Wine Vinegar 254
Wine Yeasts **131**, 156, 172, 231
Wines, Blending of .... See under Blending Wines
Wines, Classification of 68, **214**
Wines, Commercial .... See under Specific Commercial Wine
Wines, Disorders of 253
Wire Ties 38, 359

Y

Yeast 49, 61, 78, 123, 161, 177, 246, 263, 318, 356, 366, 406
Yeast, Autolysis of .... See under Autolysis
Yeast, Baker's **129** 171
Yeast, Brewer's **131**
Yeast Cultures **134**
Yeast, Feeding with Sugar **61**, 155, 347, 390, 406, 420
Yeast Nutrients 101, 135, **139**, **155**, 167, 172, 180, 263, 332, 367, 370
Yeast, Reproduction of 124
Yeast Starter Media **135**
Yeast Starters 49 97, 98, **134**. 142, 168, 174, 309, 390

Yeast, Tolerance to Acidity 97, 111, 136
Yeast, Tolerance to Alcohol 61, **127**, 139, **172**, 181, 243, 408, 420
Yeast, Tolerance to Sulphite 48, 168
Yeasts, Film 253, **256**
Yeasts, Wild 42, 48, 81, 123, **128**, 132, 152, 171
Yeasts, Wine **131**, 156, 172, 231
Yeso 378

Z

Zymase Complex of Enzymes **162**